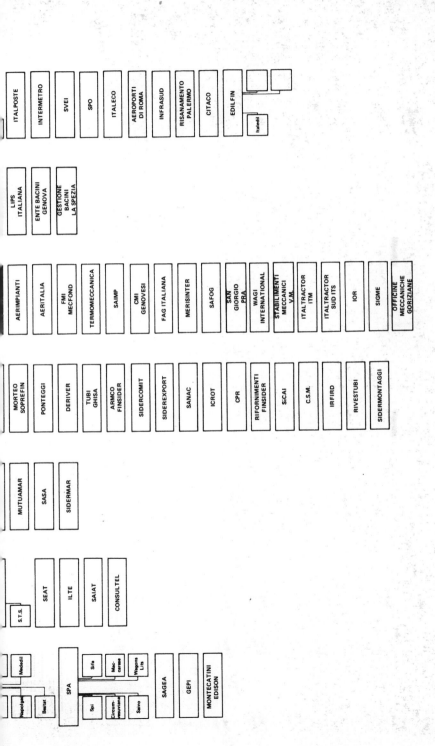

*Government Controlled
Enterprises*

Government Controlled Enterprises

International Strategic and Policy Decisions

Renato Mazzolini
Graduate School of Business,
Columbia University

A Wiley–Interscience Publication

JOHN WILEY & SONS
Chichester · New York · Brisbane · Toronto

Library of Congress Cataloging in Publication Data:

Mazzolini, Renato, 1950–
     Government controlled enterprises.

     'A Wiley–Interscience publication.'
     Bibliography: p.
     Includes index.
     1. Government business enterprises–European
Economic Community countries.   2. Corporation, Foreign
–European Economic Community countries–Management.
3. International business enterprises–Management.
I. Title.
HD4140.5.M39   354'.4'092   78–10961

ISBN 0 471 99727 7

Typeset by Preface Ltd., Salisbury, Wilts.
and printed by Unwin Brothers Ltd.,
The Gresham Press, Old Woking, Surrey

'To my mother and father'

*A quoi bon multiplier les nationalisations, si c'était pour
ne rien changer à la structure du pouvoir économique ni
aux principes de la gestion des entreprises?*

VALERY GISCARD D'ESTAING

Contents

Foreword

'Company strategy' now is in the centre of the stage. Because strategy encapsulates the way a company elects to deal with its environment, all the current external turbulence –economic, social, political, technological –creates pressure on strategy formulation and reformulation.

This attention to strategy is born out of necessity. Companies must adapt to new and often conflicting demands placed upon them if they are to survive. Not-for-profit as well as profit-seeking enterprises face changes in social expectations, in sources of income, in international competition, in governmental support and regulation, and in a host of other external and internal factors.

Practical response—real-life action—has preceded theoretical concepts of how to deal with this new set of operating forces. And within the academic world normative prescriptions for managers on how to analyse and cope are now ahead of scholarly research. Now we are scrambling to catch up—to build a scholarly base. We need not only more perceptive and comprehensive descriptions of the strategic behaviour of companies—with an evaluation of what works well and why. Even more urgently, we need better conceptual frameworks and research methodologies which enable us to get at the heart of strategy formulation.

In the present book, Mazzolini makes distinctive contributions on both of these frontiers. He presents an original and penetrating description of a prickly strategy issue –multinational expansion by companies owned by national governments. *And* he develops a way of diagnosing strategic behaviour which, in addition to unlocking insights on the above issue, holds great promise for numerous other strategy studies.

TRIPLE APPROACH TO STRATEGY DECISIONS

Even though the vital role of corporate strategy is widely recognized, our present understanding of how a company's basic direction takes form is rudimentary. We have many more ideas of the way the process should be performed than systematic studies of how in fact it is done.

The central issue is: How can we explain—and predict—the strategy decisions which in fact are made? For any company, who charts its course and why is that particular direction selected? Mazzolini describes and then copiously illustrates three complementary approaches:

'Traditional' view

Here the company is treated as a single, coherent unit. The presumption is that it acts in a rational manner, selecting its strategy logically to maximize its objectives. Like a person, each company is considered to have its own motives and viewpoints; it is purposeful and seeks internal consistency among its subobjectives and policies.

A great strength of this approach is that concepts from microeconomics and operations research are directly applicable. Actually, in our dynamic, uncertain world achieving such a degree of rationality may be difficult. Nevertheless, as a path to understanding corporate choices, the traditional approach assumes that each company acts like a rational individual. Following this premise, strategy can be explained in terms of the most logical choice available to the company under the prevailing conditions and selected objectives.

Organizational process

The traditional approach to strategy formulation is both simplistic and idealistic. Devising strategy is much too complex and fraught with unknown factors to be neatly rational. And social organizations such as companies rarely achieve a unity of perception, communication, and values. Instead, division of labour, specialized sensors, uncertainty absorption, risk aversion, and parochial values prevail.

In this more realistic organizational world strategy is strongly conditioned by established patterns of behaviour. The need for change, the alternatives considered, the estimates of outcomes, the significance attached to predicted results, the way a strategy statement will be interpreted and implemented—all depend to a large degree on existing organizational structure and the prevailing momentum in each subunit.

So, the second approach argues that we must analyse this social structure—or bureaucracy—if we wish to understand and predict a company's choice of strategy.

Organizational politics

Both the traditional and organizational process approaches neglect the role of individuals in strategy formulation. Yet we know that the path a company takes can be sharply influenced by strong personalities.

The organizational politics approach identifies key individuals, analyses their personal objectives and their power, and relates these to strategic change. The analysis is complicated by the fact that these individuals interact over a period of time. When their objectives differ, they bargain and compromise. Moreover, typically they have a variety of interests and sources of power, so trades and coalitions are common.

Unless these political realities are recognized we cannot fully explain many strategic moves.

Mazzolini proposes, and his evidence strongly supports, the need for all three approaches. No one approach alone provides an adequate explanation of what transpires when a major, unstructured problem arises.

Clearly, this triple approach to company strategy draws heavily on Graham Allison's study of the Cuban missile crisis.*However, in both his reformulation of the theory and in his field work Mazzolini makes major additional contributions.

(1) He shifts the focus from national governments to business enterprises. This entails identification of different sets of likely external and internal influences on strategic choice.

(2) More important, he adds provision for the substantial difference between meeting a major crisis – such as the missile threat – and formulating a company strategy. In the former situation the immediate problem is known, the need for action is widely accepted, and urgency encourages short cuts and authoritative decisions. In formulating company strategy Mazzolini points out that typically just establishing need for change is a major task; the sources of opportunities and threats are open for debate; lower urgency for action often permits procrastination, and this extended time-period prolongs and perhaps enlarges debate and manoeuvring by interested parties; and, for all these reasons the strategy is likely to be formulated in a sequential, evolutionary manner over a period of years. All three approaches listed above must be amplified to embrace this prolonged, multifaceted process.

(3) For the organizational politics approach – which has only fuzzy antecedents – Mazzolini clarifies and expands the analytical framework.

What Allison did so well for the study of governmental response of crises situations, Mazzolini has developed for business strategy and policy. We now have a powerful way to explore and explain corporate strategic action.

IMPACT OF GOVERNMENT OWNERSHIP ON COMPANY STRATEGY

The second major contribution of this book is a pioneering study of the way government ownership of business corporations affects their strategic behaviour. The specific focus is on multinational expansion.

The issue itself is particularly significant in Europe because of two trends – first, investment by national governments in companies engaged in regular commerce is increasing, and second, many companies must adjust to the European Common Market by expanding the number of countries in which they conduct substantial operations. Clearly, if government ownership hinders foreign expansion – as often seems to be the case – then those companies will be slowed down in their response to the Common Market concept.

Through over three hundred interviews, Mazzolini has assembled an amazing array of information on this substantive issue. And by using the triple

Essence of Decision, Little, Brown and Co., Boston, 1971.

approach sketched above he emerges with a penetrating and persuasive analysis. The specific findings for various types of situations will be found in the text. The more general observation is that all three approaches are needed to fully understand why the government controlled corporations behave as they do.

The field study supporting the concrete analysis was comprehensive. Using an interviewing technique developed in his previous work,* Mazzolini was able to obtain private information and opinions from many people about many government controlled enterprises. The breadth of the sample precludes a case-by-case report. Instead, the book gives us a topical summary of many situations. It is a *tour de force* which only a multilingual cosmopolitan such as Mazzolini could complete.

Mazzolini himself cautions that his study lacks the tight definitions and controlled observations espoused by our scientific colleagues, and he suggests that a basis is now laid for more quantitative analysis. True enough. But in the present state of the art – and of the world – our greatest need is for creative, dynamic, ambitious studies such as the work before us.

WILLIAM H. NEWMAN

Samuel Bronfman Professor
of Democratic Business Enterprise,
Graduate School of Business,
Columbia University

*European Transnational Concentrations: Top Management's Perspective on the Obstacles to Corporate Unions within the EEC, McGraw-Hill Book Company, London, 1974.

Preface

This book analyses how European government controlled enterprises (GCEs) make strategic and policy decisions, with a special focus on their international operations. It purports to explain why such companies do or do not have activities abroad (principally foreign direct investments) and if they do, what if anything is distinctive about such activities and why. The data for this research come essentially from (304) interviews with leading executives, government officials, union leaders . . . throughout the nine EEC countries.

This study rests on a theoretical foundation: three conceptual approaches for the analysis of organizations' strategic and policy behaviour. Each approach is a lens uncovering different aspects of companies' decisions and actions. The traditional way of thinking about organizations is juxtaposed to two different views. This framework is not limited to the international activities of GCEs. Beyond this study, it should have relevance for strategic and policy decisions in general.

Our goal is not to formulate a model of corporate behaviour and then test hypotheses empirically (though the concluding chapter will argue this is a logical next step). Rather, it is to develop a framework which is a systematic way of observing what happens in organizations in view of understanding and predicting their actions. Then to apply this framework and look at GCEs from the various angles called for by this framework: each approach leads us to ask certain questions and to focus on particular phenomena. In this process the merits as well as faults of our different approaches emerge in a concrete context.

The primary audience of this book is intended to be academically oriented – scholars concerned with the way GCEs function, international business students as well as students of organizations with a special preoccupation for strategic and policy decision-making. Further, this book hopefully is also pertinent for certain practitioners – both those interested in GCEs *per se* and those wishing to achieve a better understanding of large organizations' behaviour in general. Among these are managers – those in GCEs and those in competing private sector companies trying to forecast the behaviour of GCEs; also government people as well as those in a position to influence government policy.

Those interested in organizational decision-making as such will focus primarily on the theoretical chapters (II, V and VIII as well as parts of I and XI). Still, we feel the chapters on the actual behaviour of GCEs should receive the reader's attention not only because they are an instructive application of the theory, but also because they inevitably prolong and add to the conceptual argument itself. Those interested in GCEs *per se* will focus primarily on the chapters dealing with companies' decisions and actions in practice (III, IV, VI, VII, IX and X, as well as parts of I and XI). Still, they should be forewarned that skipping the theoretical treatments will not leave them with a confident account of what really happens: while they may find certain more formal considerations and references to the literature somewhat abstract, the essence of the conceptual chapters appears critical for comprehensively following the various accounts of companies' actual behaviour.

Acknowledgements

I would like to acknowledge my indebtedness to my colleagues at the Columbia Business School who have provided me with invaluable criticisms during the various stages of this project, from its inception in 1974 to its completion in 1978 – in particular Professors William Newman, Melvin Anshen, Neil Chamberlain, Eli Ginzberg, Nathaniel Leff, Ian MacMillan, Paul McNulty, John O'Shaughnessy, Giulio Pontecorvo, Stefan Robock, Leonard Sayles, Gordon Shillinglaw, Noel Tichy, Michael Tushman, and Kirby Warren. Outside Columbia, a number of persons have also been willing to read early drafts of this book and make extremely helpful comments – first and foremost Professors Joseph Bower (Harvard University), Derek Channon (Manchester Business School), Claude Faucheux (CESA), Dominique Héau (INSEAD-CEDEP), Henry Mintzberg (McGill University), Gail Oxley (Stanford University), George Steiner and Richard Rumelt (UCLA), John Stopford (London Business School), and Raymond Vernon (Harvard University).

In 1975–1976 I spent a year as visiting professor at INSEAD-CEDEP in Fontainebleau. This was a most stimulating and enjoyable period during which I did the bulk of the field work for this study. I thank my colleagues as well as the Administration for the flexibility they showed in scheduling my classes so that I could have time enough for my research.

This study is part of the Columbia University project on non-US multinational corporations directed by Professor Stefan Robock under a grant from the Ford Foundation. I wish to express my gratitude to the Foundation for its financial support. Thanks are also due to Institut Massimo Mazzolini, which provided complementary support.

The success of this study has been dependent upon the help and cooperation of scores of leading persons in business and government. To them I offer my warmest thanks. The 123 companies and organizations that contributed to this study are listed in the following pages. Yet, I would like to pay particular tribute to: Raymond Barre, Prime Minister of France; Herman Abs, Chairman of Deutsche Bank; Jacques Attali, Chief Economist of the French Socialist Party; Rocco Basilico, President of Fincantieri; Hans Birnbaum, President of Salzgitter; François Bloch-Lainé, President of Crédit Lyonnais; Vincenzo Cazzaniga, Vice Chairman of Montedison; Angelo Costa, President of Confindustria; Herbert Culmann, President and Chief Executive of Lufthansa; Giordano Dell'Amore, Rettore of Università Bocconi; Albert Dondelinger, President of Banque Internationale à Luxembourg; Pierre Dreyfus, President of Renault; Derek Ezra, President of The National Coal xx

Board; Eric Faulkner, Chairman of Lloyds Bank; Renaud Gillet, President of Rhône-Poulenc; Silvio Golzio, President of Credito Italiano; Anthony Griffin, Chairman of British Shipbuilders; Ermanno Guani, President of Alfa Romeo; Pierre Guillaumat, President of Société Nationale Elf-Aquitaine; Knut Hagrup, President of SAS; Kenneth Keith, Chairman of Rolls-Royce 1971; Heinz Kemper, Chairman of Veba; David Kennedy, President and Chief Executive of Aer Lingus; Luciano Lama, Secretary General of CGIL; Maurice Lauré, President of Société Générale; Hubert Lögters, President of Deminex; Patrick Lynch, Chairman of Aer Lingus; Ajmone Marsan, Direttore Centrale of IRI; David Nicolson, Chairman of the British Airways Board; Gilbert Pérol, Directeur Général of Air France; Georges Plescoff, President of Assurances Générales de France; Pasquale Saraceno, Chief Economist of IRI; Gaetano Stammati, President of Banca Commerciale Italiana; A. F. Tuke, Chairman of Barclays Bank; Robert Vandeputte, Governor of Banque Nationale de Belgique; Bruno Velani, President of Alitalia.

Finally, I owe a major debt to my mother: throughout this study she has served as a most competent and indefatigable research assistant.

List of the 123 Organizations Interviewed

BELGIUM

Banque Nationale de Belgique
CEEP – Centre Européen de l'Entreprise Publique
EEC
Kredietbank
Petrofina
Sabena
Société Belge d'Investissement Internationale

DENMARK

Danmarks Nationalbank
Den Danske Landmandsbank
Den Kongelige Grønlandske Handel
Kongeriget Danmarks Hypotekbank
SAS

FRANCE

Air France
Assurances Générales de France
Avions Marcel Dassault
Banque de France
Banque de Suez et de l'union des Mines
BNP
CFP – Compagnie Française des Pétroles
CGE
Charbonnages de France
CII – Compagnie Internationale pour l'Informatique
Commissariat Général du Plan
Crédit Lyonnais
EMC – Entreprise Minière et Chimique
Force Ouvrière

HAVAS
IDI – Institut de Développement Industriel
Institut d'Études Bancaires et Financières
Ministère de l'Économie et des Finances
Ministere de l'Industrie
Parti Socialiste
Renault
Rhône Poulenc
Saint-Gobain-Pont-à-Mousson
SNECMA
SNIAS
Société Générale
Société Nationale Elf Aquitaine
Vallourec

GERMANY

ARAL
Bayerische Braunkohlen Industrie
BDI – Bundesverband der deutschen Industrie
Der Bundesminister der Finanzen
Der Bundesminister für Wirtschaft
Commerzbank
Deminex
Deutsche Bank
Deutsche Schachtbau und Tiefbohr
Energie Versorgung Schwaben
Gelsenberg
IVG – Industrieverwaltungsgesellschaft
Lufthansa
Papierfabrik Weissenstein
Rheinische Braunkohlenwerke
RWE – Rheinisch-Westfalisches Elektrizitätswerk
Salzgitter
Stadtwerke Wolfsburg
VAW – Vereinigte Aluminium-Werke
VEBA
VIAG - Vereinigte Industrie-Unternehmungen
VKU- Verband Kommunaler Unternehmen
Volkswagenwerk

GREAT BRITAIN

BAB – British Airways Board
Bank of England
Barclays Bank
BP
British Aerospace
British Leyland
British National Oil Corporation
British Shipbuilders
British Steel Corporation
British Sugar Corporation
Lloyds Bank
National Coal Board
National Enterprise Board
Rolls-Royce (1971) Ltd.
Shiprepairers and Shipbuilders Independent Association
Trades Union Congress
Treasury Chambers

HOLLAND

DSM
Estel-Hoesch-Hoogovens
KLM
Ministerie van Economische Zaken
Royal-Dutch/Shell

IRELAND

Aer Lingus
Comhlucht Siuicre Eireann Teoranta
Confederation of Irish Industry
Coras Trachtala
Industrial Credit Company
Industry Development Authority
Irish Congress of Trade Unions
Irish Shipping
Ministry of the Public Service

ITALY

Aeritalia
Alfa Romeo
Alitalia
Arthur Andersen
Banca Commerciale Italiana
Banca d'Italia
Banca Nazionale del Lavoro
Banco di Roma
CGIL
CISDCE – Centro Internazionale di Studi e Documentazioni sulle Comunità
        Europee
CNEN
Confindustria
Credito Italiano
EFIM
EGAM
ENI
Fincantieri
Finmeccanica
Finsider
GEPI
IMI
IRI
Istituto Nazionale per il Commercio Estero
Leyland Innocenti
Ministero delle Partecipazioni Statali
Montedison

LUXEMBOURG

ARBED
Banque Générale du Luxembourg
Banque Internationale à Luxembourg

CHAPTER I

Introduction

This chapter is divided into four sections. In the first we define the research focus – the analysis of government controlled enterprises' behaviour. In the second we present the conceptual framework we use to explain these organizations' decisions and actions. In the third we provide some background on the particular companies we are interested in. And in the fourth we say a few words about the research methodology.

A. THE RESEARCH FOCUS

The empirical objective of this study is to explain the multinational strategic and policy behaviour of European government controlled enterprises. The best way to be specific is to define three fundamental terms of this sentence.

(1) By 'government controlled enterprises' (hereinafter GCEs) we mean companies for which ultimate formal authority rests in the hands of the state. This power corresponds to that of stockholders in private sector companies. To have such authority, the government must own a company's equity or at least a substantial part thereof. Strictly speaking, this should mean an absolute majority – more than 50 per cent. Still, in many cases a strong relative majority is *de facto* sufficient, particularly when the rest of the capital is widely dispersed.

Certain companies are not directly controlled by the government but by other enterprises which are themselves owned by the state. When enough of the equity belongs to the controlling or holding enterprise, these companies will also be considered GCEs.

By state or government we mean the national or federal government; we can, however, also mean local governments. Indeed, certain regional governments control companies of considerable importance (notably certain *Länder* in Germany).

GCEs are often referred to as public companies or publicly owned companies while private or privately owned companies are private sector companies. GCEs are also sometimes called state-sponsored bodies (mostly in Ireland), or national companies (mostly in France), or companies with state participation (mostly in Italy).

Moreover, we are interested in certain GCEs only. An important distinction must be made: there are GCEs which are public monopolies and GCEs which are to compete in a free market with other companies.

1

The former are at the service of the collectivity. Their purpose is to serve the public interest by providing more attractive or cheaper goods or services than would allegedly be available if supplied by private sector companies operating under free market conditions. Good examples are public utilities – postal and telephone services. The majority of such industries are subsidized and are normally in a monopoly position in that they serve the totality (or the vast majority) of the collectivity's needs either in terms of the entire country or in terms of a given region. In France, these companies are sometimes termed *à fortes contraintes*: they are highly regulated and their field of activity is typically defined quite specifically (their latitude for foreign activities in particular is normally quite restricted). These companies fall *outside* the scope of this study.

The latter *a priori* have no particular mission of serving the collectivity one way or the other. They are a *faibles contraintes*: they are to be under minimal special regulations and are to operate as normal commercial undertakings, producing and selling goods and services demanded by the market, in competition with private sector firms. It is *these* companies which we are concerned with in this book. Section (C) below will describe more precisely what enterprises are involved here.

Finally, we should specify that by European GCEs we refer to companies belonging to one of the EEC member countries (for multinational companies, those whose home country is an EEC nation).

(2) By 'strategic and policy behaviour' we mean specific kinds of decisions: strategic decisions refer to the determination of the basic long-term purpose of an enterprise and the adoption of courses of action consistent with this purpose; they define the fundamental mission of a firm in terms of goods or services to produce and markets to serve. Policy decisions refer to the basic *modus operandi* of a firm; they define the ground-rules by which an organization functions, the way key resources are raised and allocated.

According to Newman and Logan, a company's strategy normally should indicate:

(a) *Services* to be provided. What products or intangible services will the company sell to what group of customers?

(b) *Resource conversion technology* to produce these services. What will the company make and by what processes, and what will it buy from what sources – so as to obtain a relative advantage in supply?

(c) Kinds of *synergy* to be exploited. Will the combination of selected thrusts provide extra, mutually reinforcing benefits?

(d) *Timing and sequence* of major steps. What moves will be made early, and what can be deferred?

(e) *Targets* to be met. What are the criteria for success, and what levels of achievement are expected?[1]

Examples of strategic decisions include a major investment in the development, production and marketing of a particular kind of product; the decision to integrate vertically; a commitment to diversify in a particular product area; the decision to go into multinational manufacturing. By contrast: 'A policy is a standing plan; it is used over and over again to guide specific actions . . . Every company needs policy covering many aspects of its operations in order to simplify decision-making and to give predictability and consistency to actions taken at different times by different people'.[2] Newman and Logan identify four major areas for the analysis of corporate policy:

(a) Marketing policy (product line, customers, pricing and marketing mix)
(b) Production and purchasing policy
(c) Personnel policy
(d) Financial policy.[3]

While these four areas constitute the set of the commonest key issues, others can also be critical. For example, in high technology sectors, the R & D policy is essential and in acquisition-minded organizations, policy concerning takeovers is important.[4] And in the case of international operations, important policy issues include relations with the local employees, government officials, foreign suppliers and competitors.

Strategy and policy are clearly interrelated: 'A carefully selected policy sharpens the meaning of the strategy and guides specific decisions in a direction that supports the strategy. In a sense, no strategy has really been thought through until its implications for policy . . . have been explored'.[5] While policy tends to flow from strategy, policy variables also affect strategy: issues affecting the workings of a company have a bearing on the courses of action which are actually pursued.[6] Thus, constraints on the international *modus operandi* of a company have an impact on what foreign investments are made in the first place.

(3) By 'multinational' (hereinafter MN) behaviour we refer to two notions.

First, we refer to the decisions and actions of a multinational corporation (hereinafter MNC) as well as those decisions and actions which lead a company to *become* an MNC. By MNC we mean an enterprise the value added of which is produced in a substantial proportion outside of the parent company's home country – a firm having foreign direct investments important enough to critically affect the health and performance level of the total enterprise.[7] Such investments are firstly production operations. They can also be major assembly operations. And where the industry characteristics are such that the selling activities represent a major part of the company's value-added, major foreign-marketing subsidiaries may be sufficient for a firm to qualify as an MNC. Further, foreign mining or drilling activities for primary sector industries and major branches or offices for tertiary sector industries can also give its MN character to a company. Moreover, such investments can be undertaken in a number of ways: foreign subsidiaries set up *ex novo* or takeovers of existing local concerns; and a firm can 'go it alone' or engage in a joint venture either with a local partner or with a partner from its own or from another country.

To repeat, our focus is on the behaviour of MNCs *and* on the decisions and actions of firms resulting in their becoming MNCs, that is, foreign direct investment decisions, including the first foreign direct investments.

Second, by MN behaviour we refer to certain activities occurring on a transnational level regardless of whether the firms involved are MNCs. These are essentially *major* cross-frontier co-operative agreements – outright mergers of long-term, far-reaching joint ventures (for example, in high technology industries where several companies are vitally dependent on a few projects undertaken with foreign enterprises).

While a number of studies are available on GCEs (to which we will refer and draw upon),[8] particularly since the creation of CEEP (Centre Européen de l'Entreprise Publique),[9] little has been done in connection with these companies' attitude *vis-à-vis* MN activities. Moreover, this book hopefully makes a distinctive contribution in view of its conceptual framework: our analysis should be more insightful than the existing classical accounts; it should uncover aspects of and reasons for corporate behaviour which the more conventional investigations are unable to capture. The next section should begin to clarify this.

B. THE CONCEPTUAL FRAMEWORK

Our analysis of GCEs' behaviour is based on an explicit theoretical framework – three approaches or lenses uncovering particular aspects and providing particular explanations of strategic and policy behaviour. This section introduces this framework.

1. The traditional approach

Most people trying to understand corporate decisions and actions more or less explicitly follow a common path: confronted with a puzzling pattern of behaviour they proceed to look for objectives which make these actions appear as reasonable choices. For example, if a GCE does not appear to exploit clearly attractive foreign investment opportunities, investing instead in less-developed regions of its country, this view is most likely to lead one to a conclusion along the following lines: the company is acting consistently with the government's policy of fostering the development of these regions. Further, when attempting to predict corporate behaviour, people try to decide what is the best thing for the company to do given certain postulated objectives.

In so doing, one assumes that the firm is a unitary agent – a single undivided entity of which all the actions are coherent. Further, one assumes rationality – that the firm acts consistently to maximize its objectives.

2. The organizational process approach

This view challenges the assumptions of the traditional approach. In particular, it sees an organization not as a unitary agent but as a complex conglomerate of semi-independent suborganizations. The workings of such a conglomerate are dependent on set processes – standard routines which critically condition what an organization can and cannot do. To understand and predict an organization's behaviour, one must uncover these processes.

The fact that an organization functions via standardized procedures means that what an organization does today is vitally dependent on what it did yesterday. Even when some exogenous force (such as a high-ranking executive) succeeds to cause it to pursue a new path, it will do so in a fashion which is familiar to it – borrowing steps from other paths it followed in the past. Thus, if we ask why a GCE does not go abroad, investing instead in national depressed regions, explanation will be sought less in terms of objectives calling for domestic investments as in the history of corporate activities: if the firm has always been investing in depressed regions in the past, its internal processes will be geared to such investments and it should be no surprise that it tends to go on investing there.

3. The organizational politics approach

This view conceives of decisons as resultants of bargaining games between key individuals. For any given issue a number of influential persons are involved with varying degrees of authority and with more or less competing concerns. To understand the actions of an organization, one must grasp the stands each person takes, his relative power as well as the interfaces between the various persons.

The focus is on the internal politics – conflicts, bargains, compromises – which take place between those who have a say in corporate decisions. Such individuals are in different positions, which causes them to have different perceptions of the issue under consideration and different stakes in terms of what they have to gain or lose from one outcome or the other. In fact, their interest in the outcome of an issue is not limited to what they have to gain or lose in terms of the issue itself. Rather, the outcome of an issue may affect them in other games: to explain the stands individuals take with regard to issues, one must understand the broader games they play – overall concerns they have both in terms of their professional responsibilities and aims and in terms of their personal aspirations. Most of the time various individuals end up having different views. Pulling and hauling thus ensues. And it is the result of this pulling and hauling which determines organizational action. This approach then suggests that explanation of a GCE staying home to invest in depressed areas should be sought in the attitude various influential players take on the issue and the interfaces between them: if a GCE pursues a certain pattern of action, it means that certain key persons for whom such actions mean help in solving 'their problem' were successful in imposing their views; or it means that such a pattern of action was the most desirable compromise upon which players were able to agree.

Each approach points to different phenomena and offers different reasons for corporate action. Each lens leaves certain questions unanswered and leaves the analyst with certain puzzles in his mind. Still, our argument in the concluding chapter is that – at least for the most part – the three approaches are reconcilable. Indeed, they are in many ways complementary.

Over and beyond the study of GCEs, this framework aims at furthering knowledge in the field of business policy. While most of the thinking of the business policy type is of a traditional approach kind, focusing on postulated objectives to explain corporate behaviour, the process approach's emphasis on standard routines sheds a new light on companies' strategic decisions and actions. And in any enterprise there are a number of key individuals who critically affect the firm's behaviour; the organizational politics approach is instrumental in uncovering the games which take place between these individuals, the result of which causes a company to take one direction rather than another.

In recent years, a number of articles have appeared discussing business policy as a field for academic study in which to develop theory and research.[10] Though different in emphasis, these writings appear to have a common theme: the importance of the issues addressed by the field (the decisions giving an organization its basic direction and form) contrasts with the scarcity of scholarly literature dealing with such issues.

> The most familiar category of policy literature is normative in character, presenting prescriptions and heuristics about policy design and execution. It describes and recommends tested 'good practice'. This normative literature falls into two classes. The first presents observations and insights of individuals who have held or have been close to those who have held responsibility for managing a total enterprise . . . The second class presents more systematic concepts and tools generally focused on the management tasks and problems of planning the long-range future of the organization.[11]

This is no place to engage in an in-depth discussion and analysis of this literature, particularly since others have done so before us.[12] We should simply note the critical weakness of this literature: it can generally be faulted for prescribing principles where the validity has not been clearly verified. This literature tends to lack a solid empirical base. As two major critics have noted: one 'must be cautious in accepting [the findings] or statements which may represent as much personal belief and prejudice of principle as distillation of reality'.[13] Indeed, most of the existing literature can be faulted on the grounds of its 'simplicity, dogmatic character and absence of attempts to verify those parts of the theory that could be researched'.[14] As noted by one author: 'By prescribing the procedure to be used, without reference to procedure actually used, it exposes itself to [criticisms]: terminology which may be undefinable in terms of management practice, no tests or relevance of its proposals, a tendency to take for granted assumptions that remain to be verified (most notably, that grand integrated planning works and is always appropriate)'.[15] Further, Galbraith writes: 'Few subjects of earnest inquiry have been more unproductive than study of the modern large corporation. The reasons are clear. A vivid image of what should exist acts as a surrogate for reality. Pursuit of the image then prevents pursuit of the reality'.[16] And Mintzberg states: 'There has been a tendency to prescribe prematurely in Management Policy – to tell how it should be done without studying how it is done and why'.[17]

Contrasted to the normative approach, an empirical approach has been suggested, 'concerned with researching and describing policy making as it exists in reality'.[18] Arguing that 'prescription becomes useful only when it is grounded in sophisticated description',[19] Mintzberg in particular makes a strong argument for the field of business policy to focus primarily on identifying and understanding what happens in practice: 'To a considerable extent prescription should be left to the well-informed practitioner. Perhaps the manager and staff specialist can best develop new approaches to policy-making, since they are the ones faced with the specific issues in specific organizations . . . The main role of the teacher of Management Policy becomes that of providing the best of descriptive theory to the practitioner'.[20] In particular, Mintzberg suggests attention to the following questions:

What is the job of the manager?
How do organizations function and structure themselves?
How do their power relationships develop and their goals form?
By what processes do they make important strategic decisions?
How are their strategies formed?[21]

Needless to say, we endorse this argument: our aim in this study is not to develop normative conclusions about what companies should or should not do or to argue about the desirability and efficiency of the public sector. (Hopefully, this book will also help the reader make judgements of his own on such questions.) Our aim in this study is to understand why companies behave as they do – to describe what causes them to undertake certain actions rather than others.

While an increasing number of writers call for an empirical approach, few have in fact done so: as yet, there have been few serious attempts to model the way strategic and policy decisions are made and to verify empirically the validity of such theory.[22] This book should then constitute an innovation.

Having said this, our framework builds on existing literature. Each of our three approaches draws on various pieces which provide a useful base for our own formulation; these will be discussed in the chapters (II, V and VIII) devoted to our three approaches. Here we should simply discuss the debt our *overall* conceptual framework owes to previous work.

To anybody familiar with it, the influence on this book of Graham Allison's *Essence of Decision* is obvious.[23] Allison's aim is to explain the Cuban missile crisis of October 1962 – why Russian missiles were put on Cuba, why the US responded with a naval blockade, why the Soviet Union finally withdrew the missiles. To address these questions, Allison develops three models of analysis. These constitute a theoretical breakthrough: his framework now appears essential to the understanding of decisions and actions of governments in crisis situations. Allison's framework has clearly served as a starting-point for our own formulation and our three approaches obviously take his three models as a basis. Yet, the resemblance is in fact more apparent than real.

The fundamental distinctiveness of our framework relative to Allison's stems from the different types of decisions considered. First, Allison looks at government behaviour while our focus is on corporate behaviour. As will become clear as we go along, the issues involved as well as the setting in which they are considered make the nature of the decisions quite different.

Further, *Essence of Decision* is concerned with decisions in crises; we are not. A crisis is characterized by the obviousness of the decision need, in other words, the fact that there is little question that something must be done. Issues spring to the deciders' minds automatically, so to speak: they are provoked by events which are glaring enough for the analyst not to have to worry about how they arise in the first place. In strategy and policy decisions, on the contrary, there is often little or no specific pressure to take a particular action. If a conscious effort is not made to analyse, say, market or competitive conditions as well as the firm's own resources, the desirability of changing the existing course and way of doing things may well remain long unrecognized. Therefore, one must begin with the analysis of the realization of the decision need. As we will see, the actual behaviour of an organization is critically affected by this phase: the vantage point from which issues are addressed determines the actions which are taken – including often non-action.

Also, there is a sense of urgency in crises. The decisions Allison deals with have to be taken in an unexpected and fast manner. And they concern specific short-term actions – actions to be implemented immediately and generally extending over a relatively brief period of time. On the other hand, strategic and policy decisions have a long-term character. They generally are not taken under the same time pressure. They concern not a limited set of actions but the overall mission or course taken by the total enterprise. Thus, under any one of our three approaches, we will see that the structure of the decision process is different. For example, in the context of an oganizational politics approach, for strategic and policy decisions individuals play for an extended period of time. While in a crisis the need for a decision to be taken rapidly forces individuals to move quickly, leaving relatively little room for complex tactics, in strategy and policy decisions individuals bargain not only with their direct opponents but with a number of persons who have few *a priori* reasons to be concerned by the issue; it is a complex net of cabals and coalitions which cause them to become involved and to grant their support to certain individuals in exchange for reciprocal favours in other issues unrelated to the current one but closer to their own hearts. Therefore, the politics of such decisions are more complex than those of crises decisions.

Beyond Allison, our framework draws on the literature on organizational decision-making with a descriptive and empirical emphasis.[24] Typical of this type of work is the so-called 'behavioral school'.[25] Yet, while providing a valuable starting point, this literature is not directly applicable to our own interests. Again, the reason stems from the different nature of decisions concerned. The literature focuses on operating decisions – those concerned with 'the efficiency of the firm's resource conversion process, or, in more conventional language, to maximize profitability of current operations. The major decision areas and product lines, scheduling of operations, monitoring of performance, and applying control actions'.[26] Such decisions are clearly far from strategy and policy decisions. As argued time and again by many, the basic difference is that operating decisions are repetitive in character while strategic and policy decisions are not. The former are made at regular intervals and tend to follow pre-established routines. By contrast, the latter are virtually *ex hypothesis* different each time. Besides, they are not self-regenerative: while operating decisions *have to* be made lest the firm's activity is paralysed, a company can well go on for an extended period of time without changing its basic scope or *modus operandi*.[27]

In light of this fundamental difference in the nature of decisions, some students have argued that, for the most part, this literature is irrelevant for strategy and policy questions.[28] While others have taken an opposite position, arguing that this work can provide a valuable foundation for a descriptive view of business policy,[29] few in practice have attempted to develop a theory of strategy and policy decisions proceeding from a careful analysis of the insights contained in this literature.[30] For us, whereas it does not offer any satisfactory formulation for our concerns, this literature does provide a foundation for our framework's empirical and explanatory focus.

We should not end this section without mentioning our awareness of the limitations of this framework: this formulation is clearly an initial step and more work is needed. There is room for refinement in each one of our three approaches. And the three views can be related to each other more effectively – points of friction smoothed and areas of complementarity clarified. Chapter XI will deal with this.

C. GCEs: A FEW POINTS OF INTRODUCTION

State ownership in industry is a familiar phenomenon. And several pieces are available dealing with the size, scope, basic characteristics and history as well as with pending proposals for the extension of the public sector.[31] Accordingly, we will not waste the reader's time with still another description of government-controlled enterprises.* Our aim here is merely to be more precise with regard to the GCEs we are interested in in this study.

1. What are the main types of GCEs?

To repeat, we are interested in those GCEs which are *à faibles contraintes* – which are in the competitive sector of the economy. For our purposes, it is most convenient to classify GCEs in four main categories.

a. Nationalized firms

For a variety of reasons which we will survey below, a particular enterprise may be appropriated by the state. A bill is prepared by the government which, if approved by Parliament, becomes a law calling for the enterprise to come under collective ownership.

The companies which are thus taken over have a statute of their own. Generally, they are not, legally speaking, stock corporations and normally have no common shares. They are, by their very nature, the property of the state. An example is Renault.

b. Special status GCEs

A number of companies also have a particular legal form of their own, yet are not nationalized enterprises. Rather, they have been created *ex novo* by the state and have had such status from their inception. A case in point is ELF-ERAP.

There can be a mixture of these two categories. Thus, a number of private firms can be taken over by the state and merged into a new company. For example, SNIAS is the product of a succession of mergers between companies formerly belonging to the private sector which had been nationalized.

c. Stock corporations

The state often owns shares in regular joint-stock companies. In certain cases the state holds 100 per cent of the equity while in others it holds less – either a majority holding or less than 50 per cent. Further, the shares can be held by the state directly or by other GCEs which themselves can be of any one of the four categories discussed here. As we will see, there are certain GCEs whose exclusive purpose is to hold shares of regular stock corporations on account of the government. Indeed, most Italian GCEs are regular stock corporations controlled by the government via such state holding companies.

*Moreover, we assume the reader is familiar with the basic structure of European economic and political systems as well as with the broad trends in the socioeconomic environments of the different countries.

When the government owns less than 100 per cent of the shares, the rest of the stock is usually in private sector ownership. Yet, there are cases where a company's shares are partly held by the government or another GCE, and partly by another GCE. In some instances, the equity is owned partly by the government *per se*, partly by another GCE and partly by the private sector. GCEs in which the private sector has a share of the equity are referred to as mixed enterprises.

GCEs in this category can be borne with government participation in their equity; or the government can buy shares at some point in the firm's life. And not infrequently does the state's participation in these companies change – including a decrease in the government's holding.

d. State holding companies

The best example of such companies are the Italian *Enti di partecipazione statale* or *Enti di gestione* – notably IRI, ENI, EFIM, GEPI, EGAM. Their mission is to own shares in a variety of companies and monitor the state's interests in these undertakings.

To illustrate, consider IRI which as a group is the second largest in Europe.[32] The organization chart (see the end papers of this book) gives an idea of this conglomerate comprising over 150 companies, each having subsidiaries of its own in the greatest variety of sectors. The group has a three-tier structure: the parent holding – IRI; subsidiary financial holding companies (*finanziare* or *holdings di settore*) which control the operating companies of the group by sector (for example, Finsider groups together all the IRI enterprises in the metallurgical industries); the operating companies which are the actual working or producing enterprises (for example, Italsider, Dalamine or Breda Siderurgica in the case of Finsider). While the parent company is 100 per cent owned by the state, the subsidiary financial holding companies can issue equity shares to the public although the parent holding company retains majority control. The operating companies also issue shares to the public; here this can go beyond 50 per cent, the *finanziaria* relinquishing formal majority control.

Other countries have taken IRI as an example (Spain with INI, for example). In particular, the 1967 Rapport Nora in France recommended the creation of a state holding group on the Italian model.[33] Yet, what was actually done – the Institut de Développement Industriel (IDI) – has actually little to do with IRI: it is basically a financial institution sponsoring new ventures, which primarily takes equity participations in and assists the development of emerging enterprises. In the EEC, it is only in the UK where steps have really been taken in this direction with the 1975 creation of The National Enterprise Board.

The fields of activity of GCEs are quite varied. There are GCEs in primary sectors of the economy – oil, steel, coal, gas, etc. There are GCEs in secondary sectors. A partial list includes: automobiles, aircraft construction, computers, chemicals, pharmaceuticals, shipyards, electronics, machine tools, food industries, and there are GCEs in tertiary sectors: banks, insurance companies, transportation companies (shipping or airlines, for example) and even in fields such as advertising. Finally, we find highly diversified companies such as the multisectorial groups. These can be diversified in related industries or they can be outright conglomerates which might be involved in almost any sector of the economy.

2. How did GCEs come into being?

Dealing thoroughly with this question would mean doing another study on organizational decision-making comparable to the present one. Therefore, our present discussion is necessarily skimpy. (In fact, it is essentially a 'traditional approach' discussion with all the limitations this entails – as this book will argue.) Given our aim here is merely to provide some background, we will simply sketch in some of the broader reasons lying behind the existence of GCEs. There are four broad kinds of causes for the government to create or take over a company.

a. To control certain key sectors

These are sectors which are considered vital for the development of the national economy. Consistent with a certain *étatist* or *dirigiste* tradition, certain governments may feel that controlling the 'commanding heights of the economy' (the expression used by the British Labour Party) will enable them to monitor the development of the national economy more effectively. Rather than relying on free market forces or even on indicative planning (in the sense of the French type of planning) to achieve certain results via private industry, certain governments may opt for direct control over those industries they see as keys to the implementation of their economic policies.

Further, certain sectors are felt to be 'too important to be left in the hands of the private sector', as a French government official said. Because of the perceived importance of these sectors for the country's economy as well as for national security motives, the government may decide to directly control the means of production in these sectors. This may result in the takeover of a company or the *ex novo* creation of an enterprise.

b. To fill gaps left open by the private sector

A government may invest in a field in which it feels there should be an active national industry and which private firms have not developed adequately. This is the case notably when the necessary capital outlays are too big and the expected returns of investments in a given sector are not high enough to attract private investors. This is the main reason for many governments' presence in the airline business. This is also the case when expected returns appear to be too risky and/or too distant into the future. Thus, without government backup, most European countries would not have a valid computer industry. Another instance is the French government's initiative to create the above-mentioned IDI – the institute which is to palliate the general reluctance of private investors to accept the uncertainties involved in new ventures.

Further, the government also steps in to fill certain gaps less in terms of fields of endeavour as such, as in terms of geographical areas: as we will see, many European countries have backward regions; the government may cause GCEs to develop in such areas to contribute to their industrialization. For example, Salzgitter AG was created essentially in view of fostering the development of the Salzgitter area.

It is often enough for the government to take a participation in the equity of a company. In these cases, the government's investment not only means reduced capital outlays for private investors but is also generally considered an assurance for private investors: they see the government's involvement as a commitment to the company's development and they feel it will not let the company down should additional financing be necessary; thus, in a way, private stockholders' investment is safer.

c. Rescue operations

The government may step in to avoid the closing down or at least the contraction of an ailing company. Three main cases are relevant.

First, when considerable employment is involved. Given the highly sensitive nature of the issue of layoffs, it is very difficult for a government to allow major shutdowns where many jobs are at stake.

Second, when a company is considered essential, say, for national independence. Thus, high technology firms are rarely let down, particularly if they produce goods of strategic importance for the country – arms, for example.

Third, when a company's failure would entail negative effects in the public and/or for certain other parts of the economy. Thus, the feeling prevails in many countries (for example, Italy) that banks should not be allowed to go bankrupt lest, in particular, the public's confidence would be undermined.

The government can proceed with an outright takeover buying 100 per cent of the equity. Several Italian firms have thus been acquired by an *Ente di gestione* while others, elsewhere, have actually been nationalized. Or the government can buy parts of the company only, leaving the rest in the private sector. Thus, Rolls-Royce was broken up in 1971, the car sector remaining in private hands while the aerospace sector became a public enterprise.

Another alternative still is for the government to co-operate with the private sector in the rescue operation. While in most cases, both inject new capital into the company, there typically is an agreement whereby the government promises to provide special help to the company (via subsidies, for instance); and/or whereby certain parts which are particularly sick are spun off and put under complete government sponsorship. This method can be attractive for the government because, relative to a 100 per cent takeover, it reduces the capital outlays and avoids overly extending the public sector – an often important

14

consideration, particularly from a political standpoint. And this can also be attractive for the private investors because they are often able to safeguard most of their interests and prerogatives as stockholders, while benefiting from governmental assistance for their company and ridding it of its sickest units. An example is Montedison – as explained by the then executive vice-chairman Vincenzo Cazzaniga:

> In the early 70s the company was facing the gravest difficulties . . . A syndicate was formed which took a controlling interest in the company. This syndicate was composed of private and public investors – the latter having the majority. The public capital was, in fact, not underwritten by the government directly, but by ENI and IRI. Thus, new human and financial resources were injected in the company which, together with the spin-off of various hopeless branches of the group (taken up in particular by GEPI), enabled us to take a new start.

d. Dogmatic motives

Such arguments are primarily advocated by leftist politicians. Thus, it is often argued that companies whose field of activity is close to a public service should be the property of the state. For instance, exhortations are uttered at frequent intervals that pharmaceutical companies should be nationalized: given there is a system of state social security or even a state medical system, there is allegedly no reason to leave pharmaceutical producers in private hands. Further, companies which are dependent on public funds should, in the eyes of many, be taken over by the state. For example, the French Left advocates the nationalization of Dassault because it feels the company lives on public money: its R & D is heavily dependent on state financing and most of its sales go to the state.[34] The argument is that it is not right to allow private capitalists to make profits on public funds and that, since the company depends on such funds, the benefits of such investments should accrue to the collectivity.

Moreover, companies can be nationalized in order to dismantle the allegedly excessive power of the capitalistic groups which own them. Thus, in the mid-1930s the French Socialist Party (which came into power with the Communist Party in May 1936) aimed at a vast programme of nationalizations to break the so-called *mur d'argent* (the 'wall of money'): the companies in question were seen as unduly interfering with government affairs, precluding social progress. (In fact, once in power, the *Front Populaire* proceeded with relatively few nationalizations – the Bank of France, military equipment industries and the railroads. It is only in 1945–46 that an extensive nationalization programme took place.)[35]

Historical events have caused nationalizations for purely punitive reasons. A case in point is Renault's nationalization after the Second World War: Louis

Renault was accused of having collaborated with the Germans during France's occupation.

D. A WORD ON METHODOLOGY

While for our traditional view of GCEs official and public statements or documents and existing studies are helpful, our organizational process and politics views rely principally on field interviews. As noted by Richard Neustadt, the father of the organizational politics approach: 'If I were forced to choose between the documents on the one hand, and late, limited, partial interviews with some of the principal participants on the other, I would be forced to discard the documents'.[36] And talking about the problems of data collection of this approach, Graham Allison notes:

> Documents do not capture this kind of information. What the documents do preserve tends to obscure, as much as to enlighten. Thus, the source of such information must be the participants themselves. But, *ex hypothesis*, each participant knows one small piece of the story ... What is required is access ... to a large number of the participants ... such access is uncommon. But without this information, how can the analyst proceed?[37]

The problems we deal with in this book cannot be captured readily. Issues are numerous and varied; they come up in different circumstances and therefore take a multiplicity of facets – different kinds of GCEs in different countries and in different contexts are confronted with different factors affecting their behaviour. Further, each one of our approaches points to different kinds of questions. Such diversity commands a broad data base, compounded by the nature of the issues involved. Variables are often fuzzy and elusive, controversial and charged with passion, as well as touchy. This means there is often room for bias in people's responses: subjective and partial perceptions of frequently evasive or debatable phenomena may introduce involuntary distortions; the sensitive and emotional character of many questions introduces also the risk of more deliberate bias. This calls for focusing on phenomena from several points of view, cross-checking one source with another.

This study therefore rests on a high number of interviews (304) in 123 organizations throughout the nine EEC countries (these organizations are listed on page xxi). The interviews took place over the 1974–78 period. They included the major GCEs in the competitive sector of the economy. In countries such as France where there was a clear chance that the public sector might be extended, we included also companies which were under threat of being nationalized.[38] And in some cases, we also interviewed private companies which for some reason had particular familiarity with GCEs: close competitors (for example, in an oligopolistic market), suppliers or customers, or partners (for example, in the case of joint ventures). Given the nature of the decisions we focused upon, our primary interlocutors were members of top management. Besides, we interviewed a number of individuals who are not directly in a decision-making position as far as strategic and policy decisions are concerned, but who are in a position not only to have an indirect bearing on what decisions are in fact taken, but also to observe the doings of the actual deciders (for example, staff people).

Further, our interviews included government people. First, politicians: Cabinet members and members of Parliament involved in questions concerning GCEs (for example, in monitoring their behaviour or in positions of responsibility calling for particular actions by GCEs). And opposition leaders (often quite insightful about government people's behaviour). The assistants of politicians were also very helpful. Second, civil servants: senior officials of key ministries, leaders of relevant state organizations (such as the central bank), of departments or agencies (such as a regional development agency or a planning bureau).

Finally, we interviewed outside organizations which had a stake in the behaviour of GCEs; the best instance is trade union representatives.

The interviews were designed to ascertain how key decisions are made for GCEs: concerning the question of going MN or not, concerning the means and modalities of foreign expansion, concerning companies' *modus operandi*. The interviews took the form of extensive open-ended discussions. The questions we asked naturally varied as a function of interviewees' position and of the situation in which the relevant organizations were. Further, each of our approaches called for different questions. This will be clear as we go along.

As mentioned before, much of the data for this study are of a touchy character. To secure them, we often had to rely on a certain rapport with our interviewees who agreed to discuss certain subjects under the understanding that they would not be identified with the information. Accordingly, the source of information or the author of a quote will often remain anonymous.

As for our conceptual framework, we should acknowledge some reservations we have about the substantive side of this book. As suggested in the Preface, our goal is not to test a model. Rather, our goal is to develop a way of looking at corporate behaviour and then to apply this in the context of GCEs. Therefore, this study does not have the rigour found in actual tests of hypotheses. Further, given the complexity, diversity and elusiveness of many of the variables we are to deal with, our account is probably not totally devoid of oversimplifications or of misrepresentations of certain nuances. Again, Chapter XI will return to this.

The rest of this book is an alternation of theoretical treatments and practical analyses: a chapter presenting a conceptual approach is followed by two chapters dealing with actual GCE behaviour using that approach. At the end of each conceptual chapter, we will indicate what that particular approach suggests we focus upon to analyse GCEs' MN decisions and actions. At the end of each practical analysis we will summarize what that view suggests concerning GCEs' behaviour. Further, we will see that each view leaves us with a number of puzzles – inexplicable actions or anomalies in corporate behaviour which that view is unable to account for. We will take these up subsequently in the context of a different view.

NOTES

1. William Newman and James Logan, *Strategy, Policy, and Central Management*, South West, Cincinnati, 1976, p. 64.
2. William Newman and James Logan, *Strategy, Policy, and Central Management*, p. 87.
3. William Newman and James Logan, *Strategy, Policy, and Central Management*, p. 88.
4. In all fairness to Newman and Logan, these kinds of issues are indeed dealt with in their book (*Strategy, Policy, and Central Management*, Chapters V and VIII).
5. William Newman and James Logan, *Strategy, Policy, and Central Management*, p. 87.
6. Among others, Bower makes this point. See: Joseph Bower, *Managing the Resource Allocation Process; A Study of Corporate Planning and Investment.* Division of Research, Graduate School of Business Administration, Harvard University, Boston 1970.
7. For a discussion on definitions of MNCs see: Yair Aharoni, 'On the Definition of a Multinational Corporation' in A. Kapoor and P. Grub (editors), *The Multinational Enterprise in Transition*, Darwin, Princeton, NJ, 1972.
8. In particular, in Chapters III and IV.
9. The European Centre for Public Enterprises (CEEP) in Brussels.
10. See: Melvin Anshen and William Guth, 'Strategies for Research in Policy Formulation', *The Journal of Business*, Vol. 46, No. 4, October 1973, pp. 499–511. William Guth, 'Toward a Social System Theory of Corporate Strategy', *The Journal of Business of the University of Chicago,* Vol. 49, No. 3, July 1976, pp. 374–389. Henry Mintzberg, 'Policy as a Field of Management Theory', *The Academy of Management Review*, Vol. 2, No. 1, January 1977, pp. 88–103.
11. Melvin Anshen and William Guth, 'Strategies for Research in Policy Formulation', p. 501.
12. See for example: Henry Mintzberg, 'Strategy-Making in Three Modes', *California Management Review*, Vol. 16, Winter 1973, pp. 44–53.
13. Melvin Anshen and William Guth, 'Strategies for Research in Policy Formulation', p. 501.
14. Henry Mintzberg, 'Policy as a Field of Management Theory', p. 89.
15. Henry Mintzberg, 'Policy as a Field of Management Theory', p. 91.
16. J. K. Galbraith, *The New Industrial State*, Houghton Mifflin, Boston, 1967, p. 72.
17. Henry Mintzberg, 'Policy as a Field of Management Theory', p. 91.
18. Henry Mintzberg, 'Policy as a Field of Management Theory', p. 91.
19. Henry Mintzberg, 'Policy as a Field of Management Theory', p. 91.
20. Henry Mintzberg, 'Policy as a Field of Management Theory', pp. 91–92.
21. Henry Mintzberg, 'Policy as a Field of Management Theory', p. 91.
22. Examples include: Joseph Bower, *Managing the Resource Allocation Process.* Henry Mintzberg, Duru Raisinghani and André Théorêt, 'The Structure of "Unstructured" Decision Processes', *Administrative Science Quarterly*, Vol. 21, June 1976, pp. 246–275; Yair Aharoni, *The Foreign Investment Decision Process,*

18

Division of Research, Graduate School of Business Administration, Harvard University, Boston, 1966.
23. Graham Allison, *Essence of Decision – Explaining the Cuban Missile Crisis*, Little, Brown and Co., Boston, 1971.
24. See the discussion in Chapters V and VIII – particularly the Appendix of Chapter V.
25. For example: Richard Cyert and James March, *A Behavioral Theory of the Firm*, Prentice-Hall, Englewood Cliffs, NJ, 1963.
26. Igor Ansoff, *Corporate Strategy*, McGraw-Hill, New York, 1965, p. 5.
27. See: Igor Ansoff, *Corporate Strategy*.
28. See: Igor Ansoff, *Corporate Strategy*.
29. See: William Guth, 'Toward a Social System Theory of Corporate Strategy'.
30. Exceptions include: Eugene Carter, 'The Behavioral Theory of the Firm and Top-Level Corporate Decisions', *Administrative Science Quarterly*, 1971, pp. 413–428; and generally, the work by Henry Mintzberg.
31. See: Stuart Holland (editor), *The State as Entrepreneur*, Weidenfeld and Nicolson, London, 1972; Lloyd Musolf, *Mixed Enterprise*, Lexington Books, Lexington, Mass., 1972; David Coombes, *State Enterprise. Business or Politics?* George Allen and Unwin, London, 1971; 'Le Bilan des Nationalisations en France et les Intentions de M. Mitterrand', *Le Monde*, 10 May 1974; 'La Liste des Nationalisations Proposées par le Parti Communiste', *Le Monde*, 25–26 September 1977; CEEP, *The Evolution of the Public Enterprises in the Community of the Nine*, Brussels, 1973; CEEP, *L'Impact Economique Actuel des Entreprises Publiques dans la Communauté Européenne*, Brussels, 1975; CEEP, *Les Problèmes Actuels Posés aux Entreprises Publiques dans les Communautés Européennes*, Brussels, 1975; CEEP, *L'Entreprise Publique dans la Communauté Economique Européenne*, Brussels, 1978.
32. See: *Annuario del Gruppo IRI*, Edindustria, Rome, 1976.
33. Groupe de Travail du Comité Interministériel des Entreprises Publiques, 'Rapport sur les Entreprises Publiques', La Documentation Française, Paris, 1967.
34. See: *Programme de Gouvernement du Parti Socialiste et Programme Commun de la Gauche*, Flammarion, Paris, 1972, pp. 71–72.
35. 'Le Bilan des Nationalisations en France et les Intentions de M. Mitterrand'.
36. Quoted in Graham Allison, *Essence of Decision*, p. 181.
37. Graham Allison, *Essence of Decision*, p. 181.
38. See: *Programme de Gouvernement du Parti Socialiste et Programme Commun de la Gauche*, pp. 295–296.

CHAPTER II

The Traditional Approach

When attempting to explain a particular action or pattern of behaviour of a company, how does one proceed? Typically, the academic, businessman or layman instinctively puts himself 'in the company's shoes'; he personifies the company, more or less subconsciously assimilating it to an intelligent individual, and he asks: 'If I were the company, what reasons could push me to act in this way?' Corporate behaviour is taken to be understood when this question is answered – when plausible motives can be put forth which make this behaviour appear as a set of intelligent choices.

In the first section we will present this traditional way of thinking about organizational behaviour in general terms. In the second, we will discuss specific formulations of a traditional type which have relevance for this study. In the third section we turn to the essence of GCEs' purpose – what are their fundamental 'existential' aims (for example, maximize profits, maximize national socioeconomic returns at the macro level, etc.). These aims lay the grounds for developing corporate objectives – actual operational targets forming the basis for strategic and policy decisions. How this takes place is dicussed in the fourth section. In the last section we discuss how specifically we are to analyse GCEs' MN behaviour.

I. THE GENERAL ARGUMENT

'A business firm [is] a *purposive* organization whose behaviour is directed toward identifiable end purposes or objectives'.[1] Most of the traditional economic and managerial writings look at the behaviour of the firm as intelligent, goal-directed activity. A firm is viewed as having objectives and its actions are assumed to be designed to reach those objectives in the best possible way. Behind this kind of thinking there is a more or less implicit model in which a company is viewed as making decisions as rational choices in view of its goals. Two characteristics of such a model are important.

First, the focus is on the firm. When thinking of a particular company's behaviour, analysts talk of *its* motivations, *its* point of view, *its* policies, *its* actions. The assumption is that the company is a monolithic agent and that it is this agent which is the decider and the actor. The attributes of homogeneity or oneness are tacitly given to the firm. It is assumed that there is one corporate pattern of behaviour which is directed by one overall plan and that the company in its entirety is committed to this plan; it is also assumed that all corporate resources are centrally coordinated and mobilized in a consistent fashion throughout the organization to implement the plan as efficiently as possible. This approach is thus concerned with the global behaviour of the company which is viewed as a unitary entity.

Second, the firm is assumed to have a purpose, in other words aims which are distinct guides to action. Further, the assumption is that the company behaves rationally, that it pursues the most efficient course of action; this means the course whose expected consequences are preferred in terms of the company's aims to the other courses' expected consequences. Indeed, people usually think of a company as a purposive, calculating and consistent entity – an entity with goals and with a central logical 'mind' which decides what moves to make in order to achieve these goals. The foundation of such an approach is 'the assumption of rational behaviour – not just of intelligent behaviour but of behaviour motivated by a conscious calculation of advantages, a calculation that in turn is based on an explicit and internally consistent value system'.[2]

Here, to explain means finding logical reasons for a particular phenomenon. When the objectives are taken to be known, what must be explained is an action which is assumed to reflect a purpose or intention and to be a calculated solution to a problem. The point of an explanation of a company's behaviour is to show how the behaviour could have been logically chosen given the company's objectives. The analyst has explained a particular course of action when he has shown how the details of the action are reasonable choices in view of the company's predicament at the particular point in time when the action was decided upon.

> Analysts . . . package the activities of various officials [of an organization] as actions chosen by a unified actor, strongly analogous to an individual human being. An action is explained by reference to the aims of the unitary . . . actor. The explanation permits the reader to understand why the event occurred by redoing the calculation and thereby discovering how, in the given context with certain objectives, the actor came to choose the action in question.[3]

When the objectives are unknown, explanation consists in reconstructing these objectives from the facts, that is, presenting an argument for an aim that permits interpretation of the particular corporate behaviour as a value-maximizing choice. Analysts invoke patterns of inference in which, if an organization behaves in a particular way, it *must* have a particular aim; *must* since the behaviour in question only makes sense in view of that very aim; if the organization had another aim, that behaviour would simply not be rational.

In this approach, the inference pattern is as follows: 'If an [organization] performed a particular action, that [organization] must have had ends towards which the action constituted a maximizing means . . . The puzzle is solved by finding the purposive pattern within which the occurrence can be located as a value-maximizing means'.[4] Furthermore, predictions about what a company will do are generated by calculating the rational thing to do in a certain situation given the company's aims. The analyst attempts to decide what is the most value-maximizing choice about what to do in view of the company's purpose, its resources and the environment it faces.

II. SPECIFIC FORMULATIONS

This conception is the foundation of most classical treatments of organizations' behaviour. It underlies political scientists' thinking about governments' behaviour,[5] and the thinking of students of business enterprises. In particular, it is the foundation of classical economic theory. In the theory of the firm, the actor is the firm *per se* – a unitary agent which is assumed to behave as one monolithic unit. For the firm, rational behaviour consists of producing at a level where profits are maximized, that is, where marginal costs equal marginal revenue. This approach also underlies game theory. In von Neumann and Morgenstern's theory, a 'pure' strategy is an action or a course of action of a firm, and a 'grand' strategy is a decision rule for the firm to select a 'pure' strategy given a particular situation.[6] Statistical decision theory equally rests on this approach. 'The rational decision problem is reduced to a simple matter of selecting among a set of given alternatives, each of which has a given set of consequences: the agent selects the alternative whose consequences are preferred in terms of the agent's utility function which ranks each set of consequences in order of preference'.[7] This conception also underlies the writings of classical management scholars. And more specifically, the traditional work on corporate strategy or business policy rests on this approach. Prime examples are the writings of Christensen *et al.*, [8] Ansoff,[9] Cannon,[10] Guth,[11] Katz,[12] Newman and Logan[13] or Uyterhoeven *et al.*[14] A bit more detail on the traditional view of strategy and policy is in order.

A. Corporate strategy and policy

Most of the writings in the policy and strategy field are normative in character. Yet, building directly on such thinking, a descriptive framework can readily be derived to explain corporate behaviour.

In the traditional perspective, three sets of variables come to bear on strategy and policy. First, environmental variables determine the opportunities and threats the firm confronts. Second, corporate resources determine the firm's strengths and weaknesses. The two combined define what is feasible, that is, what alternatives for action a company has. Finally, personal and 'ethical' values determine what is desired, in other words, they dictate what alternative is chosen and, where necessary, amendments to the chosen alternative. Strategic decisions are seen as flowing from the interplay of these three sets of elements: a postulated rational analysis of the environment, resources and values is seen as the determinant of a plan of action shaping corporate behaviour. (The Appendix to this chapter discusses this framework in further detail.)

In this type of framework we clearly find the conception of the firm as a unitary and rational agent. The focus is on the firm as one actor; this approach is designed to develop a strategy and policy for the total enterprise, that is, a homogeneous course of action for the firm conceived as a well-co-ordinated whole.

The closest one gets to the human element in the strategy formulation process is with the treatment of values. At first sight, it may appear that this approach does provide for key individuals playing a role in the formulation process. Yet, this is not so: the framework does not provide for the analysis of individuals' biases and preferences as such, in other words, analysis of the values of the various key men *per se*. Rather, it discounts any internal machinations within the firm – between suborganizations or individuals in the organization – and focuses on the results, so to speak, of whatever machinations might take place. It assumes that somehow agreement is reached within the firm about what values to pursue; the notion of values, therefore, is a collective one. It refers in fact not to biases or preferences of individuals but to the aggregate biases or preferences of the organization. That these values are the product of the conjugation of individual persons' values or the way such a conjugation might occur, is of little concern to the analyst. To repeat, the analyst focuses on the end product – values as choices of the organization as a whole. For example, when one says that because of a personal preference a firm chooses to pursue the goal of technological leadership, one really does not concern oneself about which individual is in fact responsible for such a choice. What is important is that the *firm* – as the only relevant deciding and acting agent – is seen as accepting this choice as its own (as taking the value as its own) and tailoring its behaviour accordingly.

The strategic and policy plan of action is designed to maximize the firm's goals. These goals are usually a combination of 'economic' aims – for example, maximize long-term returns on equity subject to the 'rules of the game' (legal constraints) – and 'other' aims which are the product of inside values or of influential third parties (ecologists, for example). What is critical is that, while different forces are recognized to be relevant in the determination of goals, the assumption is made that these forces are combined and result in one integrated set of goals. It is assumed that there is one central corporate mind that takes the various forces into account and comes up with one neat statement on the corporate purpose. The plan is then the most rational way to reach the goals. Once the plan is formulated, the company as a whole is assumed to work consistently and coherently toward the optimal implementation of the plan.

B. International business

Equally germane to this study, most theories purporting to explain why companies go multinational assume a rational choice model. A company is assumed to have an aim and MN expansion is seen as the best means of reaching this aim. In some of these theories the imputed aim of the firm is quite simple. Thus, direct investment theory suggests that a company will invest in those countries where the marginal productivity of capital is highest.[15] Here then the only assumption about the company's aim is that it wants the highest possible rate of return on its investments. In other theories, more complex objectives and strategies are invoked. Thus, Vernon's product cycle model more or less explicitly builds on a learning process:[16] production is increasingly transferred abroad as the production process matures. It is therefore assumed that the company has a strategy of going abroad with the more standardized of its products. Once more, what is important is that the focus is on the objectives, strategies and policies of the *company* – the company as a rational and unitary entity. And the more comprehensive formulations such as the Fayerweather framework to be discussed below also assume this model.[17]

III. THE EXISTENTIAL OBJECTIVES OF GCEs

What is the focus of a traditional analyst attempting to understand GCEs' behaviour and MN decisions in particular? This analyst will assume that GCEs are homogeneous and rational organizations and that their behaviour is determined by a set of choices they make in view of reaching their objectives optimally. His basic focus will thus be upon their objectives. It is by reference to these objectives that he will be able to account for their decisions.

In this section we discuss these objectives. We refer to them as 'existential objectives' – a company's purpose in the most basic sense. As we will see, for GCEs this amounts to the question, are GCEs in business to maximize profits or is their fundamental aim rather to help their governments implement their socioeconomic policies? Thus, existential objectives refer to the essence of GCEs' *raison d'être*. Existential objectives should be contrasted to corporate objectives. The latter are operational in character; they are the first step in a strategic and policy plan; they are specific guides to action such as sales and profit targets as well as more qualitative aims (for example, 'maintain technological leadership').[18] Corporate objectives flow from existential objectives. Existential objectives refer to the primary generative force of an enterprise.

As pointed out in Chapter I, our concern is with GCEs that are *à faibles contraintes* which are to operate according to private sector criteria. Does this mean that such GCEs strive for maximum profits or, in economists' words, is their objective to maximize long-run owners' wealth? It should be recognized at the outset that rarely does a firm – government-controlled or private – literally maximize profits alone. Beyond obvious legal requirements constraining profit maximization, the more recent literature has argued that other aims are important in shaping corporate behaviour. For example, Drucker has proposed survival as the main goal of the firm.[19] Baumol has suggested that firms in fact pursue a profit-constrained maximization of growth objective.[20] Abrams speaks of the firm's responsibility to 'maintain an equitable and working balance among the claims of the various directly interested groups –

stockholders, employees, customers, and the public at large'.[21] Moreover, social or 'moral' demands on companies are increasing: firms are under mounting pressure to behave in a way which does not just maximize their own selfish economic interest but also satisfies society's wellbeing and development needs. As a leading French chief executive writes, industry is increasingly expected 'to bring "economic growth" into balance with the human need for a constantly better "quality of life".'[22] And an Italian private sector executive said: 'In this country, if you talk about profits they spit in your eye!'

It is true that profit-maximization as such cannot be taken as the exclusive purpose of the firm. Indeed, 'stability' or 'continuity' are important concerns to a company. And companies are certainly under pressure to sober their appetite for economic returns and take some of the new social demands into account. Still, in our view, profit should be considered a private enterprise's fundamental reason for being in business. We agree with Ansoff: the privately owned firm has 'economic' as well as 'social' or non-economic objectives, though the former (e.g. maximize long-term returns on resources employed) are the central purpose of the firm and 'exert the primary influence on the firm's behaviour' while the latter 'exert a secondary modifying and constraining influence'.[23] Conceptually, notwithstanding other preoccupations which distort and somewhat confine the pursuit of maximum returns, this pursuit can be considered as the primary 'existential objective' of private enterprises. In the context of strategy formulation, profit must be regarded as the fundamental *raison d'être* of the private firm: once exogenous and endogenous constraints or intervening variables are taken into account, it is still the underlying end to be pursued.

Does the same hold true for GCEs? The economist says that the purpose of a company is to maximize the present value of shareholders' wealth. This is fine when privately owned companies are considered, where the owners' goal in investing in a company is to receive the highest possible returns. The 'expected returns' from the investment are then financial. But for GCEs this may or may not be the case. The owner is the 'national collectivity' represented by the government. The returns the collectivity expects may not necessarily be only financial. The collectivity may want a GCE to make certain investments which are not particularly lucrative for the company itself but which are desirable for the country. The government may want to use GCEs to implement its socioeconomic planning and thus ask such and such a GCE to pursue a course of action which meets its own national planning objectives but which goes against the natural course the company might have followed had it made its strategic and policy decisions independently. Indeed, governments may well require GCEs to behave in a way which is different from what the enterprises would do were they to respond solely to free market forces. The more a GCE is under pressure to abide by such requirements the less emphasis can it give to the profit objective.

It thus appears that GCEs have two kinds of existential goals. The first we will call 'profit goal'. When the government has no particular expectations from a GCE in terms of implementing national socioeconomic plans, it behaves like any stockholder and merely expects the highest possible returns from its investment in the company. When the company is left on its own, it responds to market forces and behaves as any firm and seeks to maximize its own economic performance.

The second goal we label 'tool goal'. When the government does have specific expectations about GCEs' behaviour over and beyond the economic performance of the firm *per se*, it will step in and impose certain actions to the firm. The firm then no longer responds to market forces but to specific demands of the government. It no longer just pursues microeconomic results. Rather, it must concern itself with fulfilling the particular expectations required by the state and its purpose is to help implement the government's own plans. The existential aim of the firm is then to be an instrument or tool of the government for the accomplishment of national policies or public interest endeavours.[24]

A. Relative weight of the profit and tool goal

Which GCEs are driven by the profit goal and which by the tool goal? Few GCEs are driven by just one of the goals. Most GCEs are driven by a combination of the two existential goals. Yet, while they normally coexist in every one company, one is usually stronger than the other.

When a GCE is free from encumbrances deriving from government planning demands, it operates as any other commercial undertaking and strives for the best possible microeconomic performance. The lesser the demands of the tool goal, the more weight will the profit goal have. The real question then becomes: when do governments have higher or lower demands? This depends on one hand on what country one considers and on the other on what GCE is involved.

A country with a strong *dirigiste* tradition will tend to intervene more heavily in the decisions of its GCEs. Here the state will usually have a relatively elaborate plan with specific socioeconomic targets. And the likelihood is greater, other things being equal, that the government has relatively high demands on GCEs in terms of actions geared to the implementation of its plan. Besides, the actual political situation of the moment is important. The government may in fact choose not to intervene in GCEs. Thus, a conservative government may want to minimize its involvement in industrial affairs in general and thus leave GCEs on their own. And in certain situations it may not be politically practical to try and force certain decisions upon GCEs. For instance, a weak government may be under criticism for trying to do much in terms of *dirigisme*.

Moreover, the extent to which a country has lasting structural problems increases the propensity of the government to intervene in GCEs with a view to using them to correct such problems. Thus, Italy's chronically underdeveloped South has led the state to develop policies to induce GCEs to invest in the South. And the economic conjuncture is important. If the national currency comes under downward pressure, GCEs will be expected not to speculate against the currency.

Certain GCEs lend themselves to government planning more than others. Some companies are in a sector which is of vital concern to the state while others are of little interest given their field of activity. Also, in some cases a particular sector is important for the government but if GCEs represent a minor factor in that sector, the government will not bother developing a policy for these GCEs which anyway would have but a limited effect in terms of contributing to the attainment of the government's sectorial aims.

B. GCEs and microeconomic performance

The conception of the traditional view is then that when government demands are low, GCEs operate as private enterprises and strive for the best economic results. Yet, when the tool goal is strongest, the concern for financial performance is still very much alive. Earnings are regarded as a measure of success – a criteria of efficiency. More importantly, they are a means to an end: without earnings the company would fail and the tool goal itself would thereby not be attainable.

To be more specific, let us take the extreme case in which a GCE is driven by the tool goal alone: the traditional view considers that even such a company is concerned with earnings maximization. First, such a GCE has the aim of breaking even in order to survive without subsidies. Then, in order to sustain growth, a certain level of cash has to be generated internally.[25] Until that level has been reached, the maximization of earnings is indeed an objective. But this objective in fact remains even once that level has been reached: the actions called for by the tool goal are not conceived as fixed targets but as aims which are themselves to be optimized (for example, the higher the contribution of a GCE to the development of a depressed region, the better); this optimization in turn calls for earnings to be maximized correspondingly. In other words, the more earnings are generated the more will it be possible to pursue the company's goals.

Consequently, even in the extreme case where the tool goal is the exclusive driving force for a GCE, there is a concern for financial performance. At the most, it has a different role: instead of being an end it is a means or necessary condition to reach other aims. Still, we should be reminded that rarely indeed does such an extreme case occur: therefore, *a fortiori* the concern for economic performance is ever present in the traditional view of GCEs. And GCEs' actual behaviour has to balance out the tool and profit goals. It is to how this occurs that we now turn.

IV. FROM EXISTENTIAL GOALS TO CORPORATE OBJECTIVES

While existential goals define the purpose of an enterprise in the most basic sense, they are by nature general. To regulate its behaviour in practice, a company needs more specific direction: given the environment, its resources and its existential objectives, a company follows a set of operational targets representing clear guides to concrete action decisions. These we call corporate objectives.

Existential objectives need to be translated into tangible aims. In the case of the profit goal, this is straightforward, the aim of making money being unambiguous in terms of what the company is striving for. On the other hand, the purpose of serving the government in its policies is not in itself specific enough to serve as a basis for strategic and policy planning. The government needs to specify what exactly it expects under the tool goal (for example, contribute to fighting unemployment, to regional development – and what regions in particular – to a given sector's development). Therefore, the tool goal needs to be qualified in terms of precise governmental guidelines.

The profit goal as such and these guidelines deriving from the tool goal constitute the basis for the development of corporate objectives. Since the two most often call for different courses of action, there is a need for a compromise.

A GCE is viewed as an actor, whose behaviour is determined by a set of choices made in view of reaching certain objectives. Thus the demands of the existential objective must be reconciled to form a set of compatible corporate objectives. Indeed, a GCE's corporate objectives can be thought of as a vector in which the claims for action of the two existential goals are concurrent – a settlement of differences where each goal makes concessions about its expectations for concrete corporate moves. It is this vector which guides the behaviour of the actor rationally – intelligently and consistently.

The traditional approach assumes there is one 'mind' which takes the decisions for a GCE. It does not concern itself with the various streams of opinion which might run against each other before the actual course of action is chosen. In particular, the model is not interested in who specifically in government or in the GCE favours a tool rather than a profit-seeking course of action. It assumes there is one decision-making agent which engulfs the various inclinations of those who have a bearing on the behaviour of the company. This decision-making agent thus encompasses not only the management of the GCE in question but also the government representatives who might have a say in the course of action taken by the company (as well as any other third party such as worker representatives who might be influential in the strategic choices). And it implicitly assumes that ultimately every party involved comes to an agreement on what strategy and policy to adopt – that a compromise is made and that consensus is reached on what aims to pursue. For the analyst any actual clash among differently opining influential people is discounted and the conflict is reduced to a choice a postulated single decider has to make. Given a unitary and rational decider, this choice generates a consistent set of goals which represents in the decider's value system the optimal blend of aims to strive for.

V. SPECIFIC FOCUS ON GCE's MN BEHAVIOUR

To understand a GCE's MN expansion (or absence thereof) we must understand its corporate objectives. And to understand a GCE's vector of corporate objectives we have to analyse the specific actions which the two existential goals call for. While a compromise *has to* be reached between the demands for action of the two existential objectives, it is necessary for purposes of analysis to look at the demands of each of the existential objectives separately.

A. For the tool goal

The traditional approach suggests we analyse what the tool goal calls for in terms of MN expansion, in other words what driving and restraining forces the tool goal exerts *vis-à-vis* MN commitments as well as pressures for GCEs to behave in particular ways on an MN level. This analysis requires the understanding of the various governmental policies and the demands such policies place on GCEs.

As we saw, the tool goal practically automatically leads to specific demands for action: the goal of contributing to the implementation of government policies practically simultaneously entails precise aims for the company to pursue. Therefore, there is no need for much of a framework to see how demands for action evolve; they evolve naturally from government policies. Our focus thus must be on uncovering such policies.

B. For the profit goal

The traditional approach suggests we analyse what the profit goal calls for in terms of actual moves toward MN expansion. These moves are motivated by the same existential goal of privately owned companies. But while the motive is the same, the resulting action can be different. Indeed, two firms with the same goal may have to follow different strategies in order to maximize their goal if they have different characteristics. The behaviour engendered by the profit goal in a GCE is distinctive because of the particular traits of the enterprise. This distinctiveness comes both from the fact that GCEs' resources are in many ways different from those of private companies and from differences in certain environmental conditions confronted by GCEs. GCEs by their very nature have certain special limitations as well as certain advantages *vis-à-vis* private companies which are reflected in their profit-motivated behaviour. These are not consciously planned in view of competing objectives such as the actions called for by the tool goal. Rather, they are almost genetic features induced by GCEs' constitution (a French executive called them 'a trait of their race').

The profit-motivated MN behaviour of GCEs is largely triggered by the same forces which apply for private MNCs. These forces are well documented in the literature.[26]   While we will frequently refer to them, we will go into some detail as to what is distinctive about GCEs.

Whereas there have been several approaches to explaining why a company goes MN, 'probably the most comprehensive framework . . . is that formulated by John Fayerweather around the role of the multinational firm in the transmission of economic resources among nations'.[27] We will use Fayerweather's framework not only because it is indeed a comprehensive theory, but also because it allows the incorporation of other relevant theories.[28]

Fayerweather's framework has three facets. First, he looks at why a company transmits resources internationally, that is, the conditions and reasons which warrant a company's engaging in international business activities. Second, he turns to the positive interactions of an MNC with the host society. This is 'concerned essentially with the determination of a pattern of operations for the multinational firm which will result in the most profitable accommodation with the local national environment'.[29] The third focus is on the conflicts which may occur in the transmission of resources and in the relations with the host country. The emphasis is on the issues of nationalism and national interest. Clearly, of greatest relevance here is the first facet addressing the question of why a company goes MN.

The framework's view of an MNC is that it is an agent for the transfer of resources between countries. The starting point is trade theory which explains international trade in terms of the difference in efficiency with which countries produce various commodities: countries export those products which they can produce most efficiently and import those which they are least efficient in producing relative to other countries. The differences in efficiency result from countries' factor endowment – the availability of various resources used in production. In trade theory these factors of production are labour, capital and natural resources. Fayerweather enlarges the concept of resources to include technological, managerial and entrepreneurial skills. There is an unequal distribution of resources among countries. There are also demand differentials for resources between countries. This unequal distribution of resource supply-demand patterns creates the need for international transactions in order to restore the balance between countries' supply and demand for resources.[30] This need can best be fulfilled by the MNC. 'Differentials in the supply-demand relationships or resources among countries provide the fundamental economic pressures for the movement of resources, and thus the primary logics for the opportunities open to the multinational firm'.[31] Thus, the MNC finds its opportunities in transmitting resources from countries where they are relatively abundant to countries where they are relatively scarce.

These opportunities, however, are distorted by governmental actions, that is, governments step in and alter the opportunities which result from pure market forces. Governmental action can first affect the overall differences between nations by a host of fiscal, monetary and other policies 'which affect the general price level and regulation of exchange rates which affect the overall translation of internal prices into currencies of other nations. The result of a change in either the overall price level or the exchange rate of a nation is to cause a general shift in the apparent relative level of all of its resources'.[32] Second, governments can affect the relationships between nations for individual resources. By various forms of taxation or tariffs as well as subsidies, a country can alter the international price relationships of particular resources. Third, a government can directly intervene in the flow of a given resource by several types of controls (quotas, for example).

This analysis then determines the actual range of opportunities open to the MNC. The company's own characteristics will determine which opportunities are in fact pursued. The crucial characteristics of the company are the resources it can readily control (the most critical ones are its managerial and technical resources, and capital) as well as the basic aims which dictate the course of action to follow. In selecting the opportunities to pursue, the rational company will move in those directions which are most conducive to reaching its corporate goals and most consistent with its distinctive capabilities.

In the following two chapters we take a traditional approach to the MN behaviour of GCEs. This approach assumes rationality and unity. GCEs' behaviour is seen as the product of value-maximizing choices made in view of reaching commonly agreed upon objectives (agreed upon by government and company people in particular). Under this approach, to explain GCEs' MN behaviour calls for analysing what objectives they have and asking how these objectives come to bear on MN behaviour.

In Chapter III we look at behaviour under the profit goal: we analyse the particular environmental conditions faced by GCEs (in Fayerweather's terms, their distinctive opportunities and special government actions when GCEs are involved) and their particular corporate characteristics which cause them to pursue the profit objective in a different way from private MNCs.

In Chapter IV we look at behaviour under the tool goal: we focus on the demands for action of the government which have a bearing on GCEs' MN behaviour – which push them to go abroad or to stay home, or to behave internationally in a special way.

APPENDIX

STRATEGIC AND POLICY BEHAVIOUR: A TRADITIONAL VIEW

The following is a framework to analyse strategic behaviour typical of the classical business policy school of thought.[33]

As indicated in the body of this chapter, the firm's environment determines its opportunities and risks; its resources determine its strengths and weaknesses and values determine preferences as to what is actually done. But let us be more specific.

The environment can be thought of in six major dimensions.

(1) The economic dimension: aggregate economic variables such as GNP or consumer spending affect the opportunities and threats a firm faces. International questions such as exchange rate adjustments also affect the posture of a firm.

(2) The industry dimension: its characteristics and trends are important in determining a firm's opportunities and risks. Critical questions include: what

are the needs or potential needs of buyers? Is the industry fragmented or concentrated? Labour or capital-intensive? What is the degree of vertical integration in the industry? In what stage of its life cycle is it? What are the relevant market segments and their relative growth rates?

(3) The social dimension: this involves demographic variables as well as 'all aspects of the society with its diverse needs and aspirations directly or indirectly bearing on the individual firm'.[34] These include social pressures for things such as pollution control or for greater justice in the remuneration of labour versus capital.

(4) The governmental dimension: when society's needs and aspirations are not satisfied, they often become mandatory. This can either take the form of regulations in a legal sense or of governmental policies. For example, antipollution laws have been passed as industry did not self-restrict pollution enough. Further, politics can change the firm's course. The outbreak of a war can create a threat as well as an opportunity. And the coming into power of a leftist regime can result in nationalizations.

(5) The competitive dimension: competitors' size, the features of their products (price, durability, economy of use, etc.) or their customer service have a major influence on competitive relationships. Beyond the firm-to-firm relationships, one must look at industry-to-industry competition; for example, glass producers looking at the packaging market have to consider potential competition by metal, plastics or paper producers. And even further, competition may take a country-to-country dimension, as in the case of the wine industry or tourism.

(6) The technological dimension: discoveries of science, the impact of related product development and the progress of automation can create tremendous opportunities for new business ventures. At the same time, changing technology can undermine the major basis of an industry's existence.

Turning to corporate resources, one can identify five principal dimensions.

(1) The marketing dimension: the way products or services are received by the market have a crucial bearing on the company's strategic posture. More than the intrinsic or objective characteristics of products or services, the crucial variable is how the market perceives these products or services. Further, the quality of the distribution system and intangibles such as goodwill affect the firm's set of relative strengths and weaknesses.

(2) The production dimension: the size, the operating efficiency, the modernness, the quality of maintenance and the location of the plant and equipment are, together with the labour situation, the crucial variables in determining the firm's production capabilities.

(3) The financial dimension: short-term as well as long-term capital decisions are crucial elements in determining the firm's character.

(4) The R & D dimension: this corresponds to the firm's capabilities to develop technically advanced products, and the market orientation of the R & D department (in other words, do the products it develops correspond to consumer needs?).

(5) The management dimension: the type of people occupying key positions determines what the firm can do. It is noteworthy that one needs different people for different kinds of endeavours and the individual who is an asset for the firm in one particular situation can be a liability in another.

Corporate resources and environmental variables determine what options are open to the firm. Consideration of these two sets of elements enables one to choose what is most effective in an economic sense, in other words, what course is most attractive in view of objective criteria such as the maximization of shareholders' wealth. Yet, strategic decisions reflect also the values of the deciding agent, that is, the biases of the deciders. Two dimensions have to be identified here.

The first are personal values. These refer to deciders' own aspirations or wishes over and beyond the economic performance of the firm. For example, a firm's top management may decide that it wants to achieve R & D leadership and produce the technologically 'best' product on the market even if this entails an opportunity cost in terms of profits. Values need not be 'selfish' or 'private' motives (or geared to benefits accruing to the deciders directly). In the case of this study, for instance, those responsible for a GCE's strategy may decide that the firm should produce a certain product and sell it at a certain price even if this is not profitable, and this in view of complying with the national plan.

The second dimension is an 'ethical' dimension – what ought to be done in view of the public good. Firms are increasingly expected to act in a socially responsible fashion.[35] Examples of the new expectations placed upon business by society include: providing jobs for the hard core of unemployed, contributing to supporting charitable and educational programmes, or voluntary price controls. It is clear that the firm cannot be insensitive to such expectations.

Strategic and policy decisions flow from these three sets of elements. More or less explicitly, such decisions include five elements*:

(1) Corporate objectives: these are the firm's expectations at its highest level and in the longest range sense. The more precise and the more operational in emphasis, the more useful they are. Thus, they can normally contain both a quantitative aspect (for example, ROI, sales volume, or market share) and a qualitative aspect (such as being the technological leader in the field).

(2) The definition of the firm's field of activity: what goods or services to produce and what markets to sell them to. At this point, it is often helpful to define the business in marketing terms saying more about what the customer sees himself buying than what the company believes it is selling, that is, relatively de-emphasizing the physical or objective characteristics of the product and stressing what the product does for the user.

---

*It is clear that this discussion is really more normative than descriptive. Yet, we include it because it appears a useful conceptualization. Even if in practice decisions are not usually made according to such specific plans, the traditional approach conceives of them as being made in this manner at least implicitly. The analyst can reconstruct such a plan *ex post facto* from the actual decisions and actions of the firm.

(3) The competitive posture: it is important to know on what basis a firm competes, why one's products sell better than those of competition. The question is not 'what can the firm do well?' or even 'what can it do best?' The question is 'what can the firm do better than competitors?'

(4) Time-phased action programmes: this is the definition, timing and sequence of major moves and resource allocations which are made concretely (such as, when to launch a new product, when to build a foreign plant, when to consummate a merger).

(5) Determination of policies: policy decisions include choices about distribution, promotion, new product development, manufacturing, financing, human resources, organization, among other decisions.

NOTES

1. H. Igor Ansoff, *Corporate Strategy*, McGraw-Hill, New York, 1965, p. 29.
2. Thomas Schelling, *The Strategy of Conflict*, Harvard University Press, Cambridge, Mass., 1960, p. 232.
3. Graham Allison, *Essence of Decision—Explaining the Cuban Missile Crisis*, Little, Brown and Company, Boston, 1971, p.36.
4. Graham Allison, *Essence of Decision*, p. 33.
5. See: Graham Allison, *Essence of Decision*, Chapter I.
6. J. von Neumann and O. Morgenstern, *Theory of Games and Economic Behavior*, Princeton University Press, Princeton, NJ, 1953.
7. Graham Allison, *Essence of Decision*, p. 29.
8. C. Roland Christensen, Kenneth Andrews, and Joseph Bower, *Business Policy Text and Cases*, Irwin, Homewood, Ill., 1978.
9. H. Igor Ansoff, *Corporate Strategy*.
10. J. Thomas Cannon, *Strategy and Policy*, Harcourt Brace and World, New York, 1968.
11. William D. Guth, 'Formulating Organizational Objectives and Strategy: A Systematic Approach', *Journal of Business Policy*, Fall 1971, pp. 24–31.
12. Robert L. Katz, *Cases and Concepts in Corporate Strategy*, Prentice-Hall, Englewood Cliffs, NJ, 1970.
13. William H. Newman and James P. Logan, *Strategy, Policy and Central Management* (7th edition), South-Western Publishing Co., Cincinnati, 1976.
14. Hugo Uyterhoeven, Robert Ackerman, and John Rosenblum, *Strategy and Organization*, Irwin, Homewood, Ill., 1973.
15. Stefan Robock and Kenneth Simmonds, *International Business and Multinational Enterprises*, Irwin, Homewood, Ill., 1973, p. 19.
16. Raymond Vernon, 'International Investment and International Trade in the Product Cycle', *Quarterly Journal of Economics*, May 1966, pp. 190–207; Vernon, *Sovereignty at Bay*, Basic Books, New York, 1971, pp. 65–112.
17. John Fayerweather, *International Business Management*, McGraw-Hill, New York, 1969.
18. See the Appendix.
19. Peter Drucker, 'Business Objectives and Survival Needs: Notes on a Discipline of Business Enterprise', *The Journal of Business*, Vol. 31, No. 2, pp. 81–90, April 1958.
20. W. J. Baumol, *Business Behavior, Value and Growth*, Macmillan, New York, 1959.
21. Frank Abrams, 'Management Responsibilities in a Complex World', in T. H. Carol,

Business Education for Competence and Responsibility, University of North Carolina Press, Chapel Hill, NC, 1954.

22. Antoine Riboud, 'The Time for the Corporate "Social" Plan', *European Business*, No. 36, Winter 1973, p. 47.
23. H. Igor Ansoff, *Corporate Strategy*, pp. 37–38.
24. For a discussion on government planning, see: John McArthur and Bruce Scott, *Industrial Planning in France*, Division of Research, Graduate School of Business Administration, Harvard University, Boston, 1969; Andrew Shonfield, *Modern Capitalism*, Oxford University Press, London, 1965.
25. Clearly, further debt and equity can also finance growth. But only within limits. As far as debt is concerned, some new equity or retained earnings must be added too as new debt is taken on. Yet, as we will see, GCEs often face problems in raising new equity. Therefore, a high level of retained earnings is indeed important.
26. For a review of this literature, see: Stefan Robock and Kenneth Simmonds, *International Business and Multinational Enterprises*, Chapter II.
27. Stefan Robock and Kenneth Simmonds, *International Business and Multinational Enterprises*, p. 25.
28. John Fayerweather, *International Business Management*.
29. John Fayerweather, *International Business Management*, p. 8.
30. For details, see: Seymour Harris, *International and Interregional Economics*, McGraw-Hill, New York, 1957; Charles Kindleberger, *International Economics*, Irwin, Homewood, Ill., 1963; Peter Kenen, *International Economics*, Prentice-Hall, Englewood Cliffs, NJ, 1967.
31. John Fayerweather, *International Business Management*, p. 49.
32. John Fayerweather, *International Business Management*, p. 25.
33. This discussion draws on: Renato Mazzolini, 'European Corporate Strategies', *Columbia Journal of World Business*, Spring 1975.
34. Victor Z. Brink, *Computers and Management*, Prentice-Hall, Englewood Cliffs, NJ, 1971, p. 128.
35. See: Melvin Anshen (editor), *Managing the Socially Responsible Corporation*, Macmillan, New York, 1974.

CHAPTER III

The Profit Goal

Using the Fayerweather framework presented in Chapter II, we examine the MN behaviour of GCEs as it is triggered by the profit goal. Given this goal, we ask ourselves what is different about what constitutes rational behaviour for GCEs, not because of government interference aimed at pushing them toward the achievement of other objectives but because of the characteristics of the environment they confront or their own corporate characteristics.

I. THE ENVIRONMENT

In the context of Fayerweather's approach, the environment is analysed by two questions:

Are there any distinctive international opportunities faced by GCEs?
Is there anything different in governments' actions which distorts such opportunities when GCEs are involved?

The answer to the first question is of course 'no'. Since the opportunities considered are 'natural' – resulting from pure supply-demand relationships of resources among countries – they are the same for everybody: 'prior to governmental intervention opportunities' refer to the need to correct imbalances in international factor endowments which call for the services of MNCs; whether these MNCs are private or state-controlled is immaterial.

The answer to the second question is in general 'no'. The most significant government interventions are those which alter the relationships between two countries' resources by altering the price of resources in one country relative to the price of resources in the other. The typical case is a devaluation. Since all resources are affected, private and public companies confront the same situation; yet, there are cases in which government action applies to selective resources. In such instance, the actual, real opportunities can be different for GCEs. Three kinds of influences are relevant.

1. *Fiscal measures*

They are primarily represented by tariffs on imports, the result of which is to discourage the inflow of foreign goods and thus protect national goods. Within the EEC, customs union is complete and tariffs banished. But governments impose tariffs around the EEC. The result is that companies are less likely to go MN (at least beyond EEC frontiers). As shown by Vernon, a company's sales abroad are usually first supplied via exports; it is only once a certain market position has been established abroad that foreign production takes place.[1] If a company's products require tariffs to be competitive nationally, it is most likely that they will not be competitive abroad where they do not enjoy a similar protection. The fact that exports are not competitive usually forecloses foreign expansion: given the absence of exports, there is no base to build on for establishing a manufacturing facility overseas. Indeed, when a company is protected at home, it is at home that it has its competitive advantage.

Governments tend in particular to protect mature or declining sectors and high technology/high growth sectors. In the former case, the motivation is that of protecting the market for domestic industries from cheaper foreign competition and thus preserve employment. In the latter, the typical motivation is to give national industry a chance to take off: by protecting domestic demand, national producers are given a market for their goods which would otherwise be supplied by more attractive imports. This hopefully enables them to reach a critical mass and accumulate sufficient experience to become competitive.

It frequently happens that companies in declining sectors are GCEs. 'In many instances such companies would not be around if the government didn't step in,' said an English executive. When the state bails a company out it has a tendency to help it in its operations. Protection *vis-à-vis* foreign competition is a natural tool, similarly in high technology sectors. Thus, a commercial aircraft manufacturer executive said: 'In this industry most big companies are GCEs. There is constant talk of strengthening the European aircraft industry and proposals are frequently formulated towards tightening protection against imports. Should this occur, companies will focus even more on national or European markets and sales to non-European buyers will decrease even further'.

On the other hand, a tariff can also be a disadvantage for national industry: tariffs on essential raw materials are a handicap since they increase the price of these raw materials to national producers. This may lead a company to set up a manufacturing facility abroad where there are no such tariffs. It can happen that a GCE is favoured relative to private companies by a reduction of a tariff on the raw materials it imports. This is another inducement not to seek a foreign manufacturing investment which the tariff might have suggested.

2. *Subsidies*

Here the effect sought is the opposite one. 'The government of a country makes some financial contribution to the supplier of a resource which permits the latter to sell at lower prices and encourages outflow of the resource from the country. The common form is the use of export subsidies which reduce the prices of certain products relative to those of other countries'.[2] While in the case of tariffs a government often has a specific goal of protecting a particular sector, with export subsidies the aim is usually less precise. Help to foreign sales is usually thought of less in terms of contributing to the development of a given sector as in view of macroeconomic goals of a general character (for example, correct a balance of payments deficit). Still, in some cases the government does provide special assistance to a certain sector only: either because it wishes to help the sales in general of a given industry (as in the case of tariffs) or because it wishes to promote the industry's foreign sales in particular, a government can make a special contribution to the exports of the firms involved. Not infrequently GCEs are the target of such contributions – as argued by an Italian interviewee:

> Especially for those GCEs which do not perform well, the government is always tempted to create favourable conditions for their sales; if such companies have a hard time selling abroad in particular and if the government happens to believe that exports are important in that sector, it will sooner or later tend to grant special financial assistance for foreign sales. The best instances are probably found in shipbuilding.

The effects of export subsidies on foreign investments tend on the whole to be negative: if a company can serve a foreign market more cheaply through exports because of subsidies than via manufacturing abroad, it will go via the export route. It is true that the subsidies may lead to more exports which in turn may be conducive to foreign direct investments. But this long-term byproduct is somewhat intangible in nature. Besides, if certain goods need subsidies to be competitive abroad, chances are that if produced abroad and sold without the benefit of the subsidies, they will not be equally competitive. Thus subsidies appear to have a negative short-term effect on the amount of production carried out abroad, and probably a neutral effect in the long run.

3. *Direct intervention in the flow of resources*

The most typical among these controls are quotas restraining the imports of certain products. The effect of quotas is similar to that of tariffs: they limit the competition of foreign goods; this gives a company an advantage at home which in turn tends to limit its MN expansion. Again, intra-EEC quotas are virtually non-existent though there are quotas discriminating against non-EEC products. GCEs do enjoy the benefits of these quotas but so do a host of private companies. A French executive said: 'At the most there is a difference in degree; the state may be especially obliging and willing to put up quotas when public companies are involved; but the difference here is in fact rather minimal'.

Another form of discrimination against imports is 'technical' and 'bureaucratic' barriers to trade: a government may hinder imports of certain goods by requiring that they comply with certain norms; by deliberately devising norms which are different from those applied in the producing country, the government may effectively bar the sale of these products on the national territory. And by making customs red tape particularly cumbersome and slow it can also discourage imports. Again, there have been instances where GCEs have appeared to enjoy more indirect protection from imports than other enterprises. But here too the significance of such policies is on the whole rather negligible.

II. CORPORATE CHARACTERISTICS

'The economic differentials and government actions establish the range of opportunities and limitations within which corporate strategies may be formulated. The selection of actual strategies is dependent upon factors within the corporation itself.'[3] We will discuss four types of fundamental distinctive characteristics which have a bearing on companies' MN behaviour.

A. Goodwill or marketing

Marketing here should be taken broadly as not just characteristics of the product as it is received by the market or the quality of the distribution system, but the overall positioning of the firm *vis-à-vis* its demand function (or potential customers) as well as the public at large.

1. *Domestically*

In many ways GCEs operate in preferential conditions in their home market which results in their having a competitive edge in their national operations. This is often to the detriment of MN expansion.

Such preferential conditions are evident in government procurement. Governments tend to have a buy-national policy and all firms – private or public – benefit from this. Yet in many instances this nationalistic attitude is even greater when GCEs are involved. While this is difficult to actually demonstrate, interviewees argued that when there is a GCE in a given sector, the government buys from that company more eagerly than from private firms. This is illustrated by the computer industry – as a German executive noted:

> In France CII is for all practical purposes a GCE; in the U.K. the government has a minority holding in ICL. In Holland with Phillips and in Germany with Siemens, the industry is totally in private hands. There is little question that where suppliers are GCEs there is a greater inclination for the government to give its preference to such companies; the French government is more anxious to buy national then the British government, which is more anxious than the Dutch or German government. If we had a national government-owned

computer manufacturer we would buy much more German equipment.

The main reason for governments' preferences for GCEs is often that governments themselves push a GCE to develop a given product and then feel they should buy that product to support its development. Thus CII was born in 1968 as a result of governmental will in the context of the so-called 'Plan Calcul' which aimed to give France a certain autonomy in the computer field.[4] To support its development, the government then endeavoured to fulfil as much of its computer needs from CII. True, this happens for certain private companies too. But, as a French executive argued:

> These are more exceptions than the rule. And anyway, even in such cases, the anxiousness of the government is less pronounced than if the company were a GCE. In fact, the government tends to give its preference to private companies only if their products are at least somewhat near in price and performance to competing products offered by foreign producers. But in the case of GCEs, the government is often willing to buy more expensive or less efficient products than those available from abroad.

Moreover, a GCE also faces preferential market conditions in terms of the purchasing policies of other GCEs. 'The government more or less explicitly prompts GCEs to buy from each other so that they can help each other in their respective growth and development', said a French interviewee. In certain instances, a GCE can receive an indemnity from the government for buying from other GCEs. For instance, Air France and British Airways receive a subsidy for flying the Concorde (produced by two GCEs). But such subsidies are usually insufficient to cover the costs (or opportunity costs) stemming from the purchase of domestic equipment. They are given in rather extreme cases and in fact can be given just as well in the case of private companies. Thus BOAC received a subsidy to operate the VC10 produced by BAC (now British Aerospace), then a private company. Most of the time, when GCEs are asked to buy from other GCEs, they receive no particular direct compensation except reciprocity by other GCEs. Italy is a case in point, also because it is here that the public sector is the widest. Steel companies sell to shipyards, car manufacturers, heavy equipment industries – all government-controlled; and public banks have an open door to an almost endless set of GCEs.

It is clear that such conditions provide a readymade market for GCEs at home which in turn is a deterrent to foreign expansion – as explained by an Italian executive: 'Generally, if a GCE can offer products which are equally – or almost – as attractive as those of competition, other GCEs will buy from it. (In fact, this also happens when their products are clearly inferior to those of competition.) Other things being equal, GCEs have their competitive strength at home. Why should they go abroad where they don't have this kind of an edge?'

2. *Abroad*

The image of GCEs in foreign countries is distinctive in several aspects. At the basic level, some interviewees reported a certain discrimination against the products of a public firm in certain countries. In particular, when the customer is a foreign government, conservative in a dogmatic way, there may be a clear preference on its part to avoid buying goods sold by a 'socialistic' enterprise. This form of discrimination, however, is a minor and vanishing factor.

On a broader level, GCEs can face a negative overall attitude in certain host countries. In the past, GCEs reportedly have encountered a certain resistance in countries such as the US where orthodox capitalism prevails as the governing doctrine: 'Local authorities have sometimes worried that the entry of GCEs was an intrusion on the part of a foreign government', said a French interviewee. This has happened especially in the more sensitive sectors such as banking. The same kinds of worries have occasionally been echoed by the local press. Still, this too should not be overemphasized, particularly since experience has shown that such worries were unwarranted.

The question of their image is most serious in the relation of GCEs with foreign business communities.[5] As one executive put it: 'In certain countries where government intervention in industry is still an unknown and dreaded phenomenon, GCEs can encounter preconceptions among local business and financial people who show an initial reluctance to work with these companies'. It is not uncommon to find foreign businessmen feeling that – in the words of a German executive – 'GCEs are not "real" commercial undertakings and are burdened by the traditional inefficiency of government departments'. Because they *a priori* see GCEs as highly bureaucratized, locals often hesitate to engage in cooperative ventures with GCEs. Several GCEs have found this to be a real disadvantage relative to private MNCs.

This is most significant in negotiations for long-term, far-reaching co-operative agreements between GCEs and private firms: 'There is a fundamental mistrust in the private sector of both the administrative capabilities and the achievement motivation of the executives of state-owned companies'.[6] While experience in co-operation agreements between public and private firms typically disproves such concerns, these preoccupations do hinder these agreements precisely because they inhibit the negotiation phase. A good illustration is the agreement between Commerzbank, Banco di Roma and Crédit Lyonnais in which Commerzbank is private while the other two are public.[7] Both GCEs reported that prior to the agreement Commerzbank was preoccupied about entering into such a close link-up with two public partners, and the German bank's management itself admits it had reservations. In the words of the then president of Crédit Lyonnais, François Bloch-Lainé,

> Commerzbank had prejudices about us because we were state-owned and this was a handicap during our negotiations. Yet, these prejudices were limited compared to those of other private banks:

prior to our agreement with Commerzbank, we, Crédit Lyonnais, were much closer to the Deutsche Bank [also a private bank]; we would naturally have been inclined to make an agreement with them, but they themselves had already a close relationship with two private banks – Société Générale de Banque of Belgium and Amsterdam-Rotterdam Bank of Holland – which did not want to get too close to a GCE. It is these two banks' prejudices which stopped Deutsche Bank from entering into a close linkup with us.[8]

Bloch-Lainé concluded: 'Whatever difference there may be in the way private and public companies operate, these differences do not preclude cooperation . . . The problem is not the fact that it is difficult for private and state enterprises to actually work together; the problem is GCEs' image which hinders the development phases of a joint-venture'.

On the other hand, GCEs' image can also be an asset. GCEs tend to have an edge over private companies where the government takes an active part in industrial affairs and where the economic system is such that the quest for profit is tempered in favour of the advancement of collectively desirable ends. This includes socialist nations and LDCs in particular, precisely because LDCs are often inclined towards economic planning and typically have a natural tendency to set explicit industrial priorities. In such countries, GCEs often feel they are more welcome because they are perceived as being naturally more sensitive to governmental expectations and to industrial planning demands. Further, host countries not infrequently feel that GCEs are more concerned with their image than private companies and thus are more careful in engaging into actions disruptive – the local socioeconomic environment. (Among others, ENI cited several examples, particularly in Africa, where they succeeded where private MNCs had failed 'because the credibility in what we would contribute to the host society was higher'.) In the words of a Dutch executive: 'GCEs are seen as having a tradition of social responsibility as well as of banner-bearers of their governments, which implies they have to behave and avoid any embarrassment for their government. Thus, host countries often feel more confident about GCEs than about private MNCs'.

A particular area in which GCEs often have a distinctive goodwill is labour relations. GCEs are seen as being more concerned than private MNCs with workers' interests, especially in their hiring and firing practices. 'A GCE would hopefully not decide overnight to shut down a foreign plant and fire all the employees as certain MNCs do', said an interviewee. Unions more often than not have a preference for GCEs. A good illustration was found in Ireland – a country which still has many underdeveloped areas and a policy of attracting foreign investment as a means of fostering its industrialization. The Irish Congress of Trade Unions feels that 'somehow GCEs are "better" and that foreign investment is more desirable if undertaken by a GCE . . . GCEs could be expected to give higher importance to social factors in determining the location and expansion of their operations'.

In sum, GCEs' image tends to be an asset where the government has a leftist bent with an interventionist tendency in economic affairs, while it tends to be a liability where it has more of a *laissez-faire* attitude.

B. Finance

'The major difference between private companies and GCEs lies in their financial policies; while marketing, production or control are often not too dissimilar from private firms, it is in the finance function that GCEs have their originality.' This quote by a French executive reflects the widely held view that it is in terms of finance that GCEs have their most tangible distinctiveness. But tangible does not necessarily mean critical or determining in terms of MN behaviour. Indeed, the main conclusion of this discussion is that whatever the particularities of GCEs' finances, this dimension is not truly determining as far as MN decisions are concerned. Still, we do need to analyse this dimension in some detail were it only to clarify the prevailing confusion in the area.

It is hard to secure reliable, precise and global data on the financial policies, structures and performance of GCEs throughout the EEC. Existing studies are partial and the financial information from companies is not readily usable because of the different reporting systems used.[9] Yet, using the existing studies and the data from our own field work, we can draw valid conclusions. We will discuss five major sources of external financing; we will then deal with internally generated funds; finally, we will focus on specific international finance aspects.

1. *Equity*

Two distinctions are in order here. First, between GCEs that do and do not have the same legal form as private corporations. The former are primarily stock corporations and the government holds the company's shares and receives dividends as any other stockholder. The latter have a special legal status – for example, the British nationalized industries, the Italian *Enti di gestione* or the French *Régies*. The company belongs to the state by its very bylaws. For instance, in the UK the state owns the 'public dividend capital' of the firm. Here the company pays dividends according to its results and for all practical purposes the 'capital' is, in the words of the Chairman of British Airways, David Nicolson, 'the public equivalent of shares'.

The second distinction is between GCEs which are 100 per cent state-owned and mixed enterprises. In the former case, when a GCE increases its share capital (and if the government wishes to retain 100 per cent control) the new capital must obviously be subscribed by the state. In the latter case, new capital can either be entirely subscribed by the public or, if the government wishes to retain its share of the equity, the new capital can partly be absorbed by the state. In fact, new equity issues sold to the public can amount to partial denationalization. Conservative governments may welcome this (historically, Germany has provided good examples), but the Left usually opposes it.

Beyond regular shares, GCEs can issue preferred or non-voting-right shares. Whereas such shares could clearly offer the advantage of issuing equity (thus avoiding a reduction of the firm's debt capacity) while at the same time avoiding dilution of the state's control, this type of security is not very much in use. In certain countries they do not exist by law. In others, their use is restricted – as noted by Herr Lilienfein, President of Energie Versorgung Schwaben: 'In Germany, for instance, the Law does not permit a company to issue non-voting-preferred shares in excess of an amount equal to half of the company's nominal capital'. Elsewhere this type of security tends not to be very popular with investors.[10]

The Italian-type state-holding company structure provides considerable flexibility in that the parent can issue capital while the sectoral holdings and the operating companies can also issue shares of their own.[11]

GCEs' management argues that it is more difficult for a public company to raise new equity than it is for a private firm: 'The government is a bad shareholder: it is usually unwilling to subscribe to new stock issues', said a British executive. In the words of a banker: 'Particularly in those countries with sophisticated capital markets such as the UK, a healthy private firm whose stockholders are not overly concerned with dilution can go to the market and readily issue new shares. A GCE can't . . . The government is reluctant to put new equity in GCEs because there are many other competing claims on the funds'. It is noteworthy that the government is much less worried by extending generous loans, even if repayment is uncertain – as indicated by a French interviewee: 'Psychologically, it seems that the government cannot accept the idea of having to put new equity into a company, but that it has no problem in granting a loan at very favourable terms or even a *de facto* quasi grant in the form of conditional redemption loans'.

In addition, GCEs often are able to raise less cash for a new equity than a private firm – as explained by President Lilienfein: 'A GCE rarely can receive more cash for a new equity issue purchased by the state than the par value of the securities. No capital surplus is received. Yet, if the issue were sold to the public the cash one could actually raise is much more than the par value – in our case it would at least be 200 per cent of the par value'.

Mixed enterprises can sell new shares to the public if the government is reluctant to put up the money to buy them itself. But this clearly poses the question of control: the government may want to limit such sales in view of retaining its proportion of the voting stock. Further, private shareholders may not be overly attracted to GCEs' shares – as indicated by a French banker: 'GCEs are sometimes seen as less efficient than private firms and less committed to profit. Therefore, investors feel they will get a better return with private sector investments'. Still, such reservations can be compensated by GCEs' image of stability: GCEs are seen as being secure investments because they tend to have a history of relatively stable payout and because the government is in practice committed not to let them down; even if there is no legal obligation for it to do so (and, in fact, there have been instances in which the government has let a GCE down), stockholders know that chances are very slim that GCEs will be permitted to fail. Therefore, GCEs' shares are seen by the public as secure, conservative, albeit not speculative or glamour issues, and they normally do not encounter major underwriting problems.

2. *Debentures*

GCEs have generally relied heavily on this method and in some countries like Italy it has constituted close to 50 per cent of GCEs' sources of funds in certain periods. In some cases (such as IRI debentures) such securities carry a state guarantee. This makes them more secure and thus more attractive – other things being equal. This can result in a lower interest rate. Further, the company can afford a higher debt ratio because lenders perceive their investment to be secure beyond the level otherwise justified by the assets or the future earnings potential of the firm.

In fact, even where debentures do not carry with them a formal state guarantee, investors perceive the firm as safer than a similar privately owned firm. The rationale is that the government will step in and bail out an ailing GCE and make sure it meets its obligations. This amounts to a *de facto* guarantee by the government. And this too results in lower interest rates and/or higher debt capacity. Still, it is noteworthy that an explicit guarantee does make a difference – as indicated by an Italian interviewee: 'A formal state guarantee may result in lowering the interest rate by as much as half a percentage point'.

This is in fact hard to document in terms of data. Several studies are available but all provide partial information (for example, they are restricted to certain sectors).[12] And they all lack a valid control group: it is hard to compare private and public companies on one dimension, 'other things being equal', precisely because other things are *not* equal. Yet, this conclusion (as well as that of our later discussion on other aspects of debt financing) is corroborated by the findings of the available studies as well as by the experience of practitioners. In the words of one financial executive: 'That GCEs have a higher debt capacity than private companies is obvious: they are perceived as better credit risks. This is not only logically right but is in fact reflected in practice by the market's attitudes'.

GCEs can also use convertible debentures. IRI was the first to use them before the Second World War. This can run into the same dilution of control problems as equity capital: as private investors actually convert their debentures, the equity effectively remaining in the hands of the government may fall beneath a certain threshold, causing the state to lose that share of the voting stock which it deems appropriate for it to have.

Again, the Italian holding companies provide a refinement to debenture financing. The parent can borrow from the public and so can the *Finanziarie* and the operating companies. This multiplies the debt-raising 'agents' and results in a high leverage capacity indeed for the group as a whole.

3. *Long-term loans*

These are long-term credits from financial institutions – banks and other credit organizations.

While in certain countries such as Italy both public and private banks are prohibited from offering medium and long-term loans, in others such as Germany banks do engage in this type of financing. Here there is little question that GCEs are in a better position than private companies: again, the creditor sees them as less of a risk than a similar private firm. A German banker said: 'A banker is primarily concerned with his customer's ability to repay his debts and the tacit backing by the government is an implicit supplementary guarantee of *de facto* solvency. Clearly, we take this into account in our credit policy for GCEs'. As in the case of debentures, this results in a willingness to lend more money at more attractive terms.[13] In fact, bankers feel this advantage is particularly sizeable in the case of companies whose financial position is shaky. In the case of first-rate companies, banks tend to lend at prime conditions anyway. Since banks comply with the directives of the central bank, and given that a central bank would rarely press for explicit special conditions for GCEs via regular banking institutions, banks rarely can go much further than lending at the prime rate. However, in the case of less than truly sound companies, GCEs do have an edge – as reported by a French banker: 'If a company is ailing a banker is concerned that it will not be able to repay its loans and thus he will be careful in extending credit. But if the company belongs to the government the risks are far more limited and the banker is more prepared to make a loan. A GCE tends to be treated as a healthy enterprise even when it is sick'.

Beyond banks, three types of specialized credit institutions are relevant. The first are general in character in that they provide funds to industry with no special purpose in mind. A good example is IMI (Istituto Mobiliare Italiano) established in 1931 for the purpose of providing long or medium-term credit for industry. IMI had a virtual monopoly in Italy until the war and still dominates the field. This type of institution has originally developed in particular where banks were not allowed to extend medium or long-term loans so as to insulate their deposits from the risks of industrial investments. The attitude of this type of institution *vis-à-vis* GCEs is similar to that of other creditors: GCEs are seen as better credit risks and therefore enjoy better conditions.

The second type of credit institution is insurance companies.[14] They too tend to treat GCEs more favourably than comparable private companies in view of the greater safety they provide given the state's implicit backing. Further, insurance companies' funds are usually controlled by law. Thus, the law may require that they put a certain proportion of their funds in investments which give certain guarantees of safety. GCEs may meet such safety standards. 'This is an additional "plus" for us in our relations with insurance companies', said the finance vice-president of a GCE.

The third type are 'special purpose' institutions which have flourished over the years. Examples are the French 'Fond de Développement Economique et Social' – 'the body established after the war to provide public finance for investment projects deemed to be in the national interest'[15] – or the Italian regional institutes, co-ordinated by the Cassa del Mezzogiorno for the purpose of providing funds for investments in the underdeveloped South. Such institutions make funds available for particular types of investments which are considered by the government as desirable. In so far as GCEs are particularly responsive to government planning directives, such institutions are naturally led to have close ties with public enterprises. 'There is a community of goals between them and GCEs which results in privileged relationships; therefore these funds have a greater probability of going to GCEs – other things being equal' – said an Italian interviewee.

When the credit institution is itself a GCE (for example, a state-owned bank or insurance company) one must add to the reasons for giving GCEs preferential treatment on the grounds of their greater credit worthiness the fact that there is a community of goals: the lender and the borrower belonging to the same 'owner', they tend to pursue the same overall ends. Thus – in the words of a French interviewee –

> A state-owned financial institution is more inclined to lend money to a GCE than to a similar private company because it knows assisting the GCE will result in synergy from the viewpoint of the state ... Despite all the allegations that government-controlled banks and insurance companies don't differentiate between private and public firms, discrimination is inevitable. This is normal were it only because a state credit institution should, given the choice, help those companies which are responsive to the same expectations of the collectivity as they are.

Indeed, GCEs enjoy especially good conditions when borrowing from publicly owned sources.

4. *Short-term borrowing*

This refers primarily to bank loans. In certain countries such as Italy, GCEs have made considerable use of this source of funds. In ENI's case, for example, short-term borrowing has represented up to 40 per cent of its new liabilities in one year.[16] Normally, these sources should finance short-term assets or working capital. But in several instances they have in fact financed fixed assets. Not infrequently, GCEs' short-term liabilities are renewed practically automatically, thus effectively becoming long-term liabilities. Normal banking practice generally requires that short-term loans be off the company's books for a given period each year (that is, that the debt be repaid before a new similar loan is extended). In the case of GCEs, this requirement is frequently *de facto* waived. This can either be due to a deliberate choice: if it is believed that interest rates are temporarily high, 'and that it will become cheaper to make long-term loans a year or two later. Alternatively, such borrowing may be regarded as an expedient forced upon an enterprise because of the non-availability of long money at particular times. The evidence would seem to indicate that in the case of the public enterprises short-term borrowing to cover fixed investment was not a deliberate choice'.[17] ENI's experience corroborates this: 'Recent tightness in the financial market . . . when adverse circumstances last year made it difficult to issue bonds, the group turned increasingly to bank loans.'[18]

For much the same reasons as for long-term loans, banks tend to lend GCEs short-term money more readily than to private firms. It is no coincidence that where this is most prevalent is in Italy where the largest banks are not only themselves GCEs but also often belong to the same group as the borrowing GCEs – IRI. Lutz points out that IRI's policy has been consistent in borrowing short only from public-law banks of 'national interest' – in other words its own.[19] An Italian banker thus said: 'While the official policy of IRI banks is to have an independent strategy and operate as other private banks without favouring IRI companies, it is obvious this is really not so'. And again, there is a logic to this: the creditor and the borrower are part of the same group; from the group's point of view the aim is to maximize the results of the whole; this calls for a certain co-ordination, and just as funds are shifted from a profitable IRI enterprise to an unprofitable one, it appears reasonable for a group bank to help a group company.

Again, it is hard to give definitive quantitative data to 'prove' the above. Yet previous studies and our interviews clearly corroborate this. Thus, based on their own research, Posner and Woolf write that 'it is reasonable to assume that they [IRI banks] show more understanding towards the peculiar nature of public enterprise investments than a bank might show towards a private firm'.[20] In fact the private sector constantly complains about unfair competition by GCEs in terms of bank borrowing. And the banks themselves often admit this is true – as reported by one of their executives: 'We favour other IRI companies often less by explicit design as by *de facto* communality of interests'. In this connection, the experience of an executive from a company which had been split up in two, one part remaining in the private sector, the other being taken over by IRI, is revealing. The executive – who had remained in the former – said: 'The divisions now belonging to IRI have terrible results but they have no problems any more in terms of securing bank loans. We, on the other hand, increasingly face short-term financing problems despite our satisfactory performance'.

To what extent does the same occur between GCEs and public banks which are not part of the same group? In the Italian case, non-IRI GCEs certainly benefit from preferential treatment as well – though probably less explicitly. In France, the other country with a vast state-owned banking sector, there is less evidence of this, but in part the reason is that GCEs find alternative means to finance their operations than short-run credits. In the words of a French chief executive: 'In France GCEs borrow less short-term than in Italy because they don't need to; they feel overreliance on short-term financing is unsound policy and they find adequate long-term financing more readily. But in fact, should there be a need to raise such funds, GCEs would benefit from "some" special treatment by government-owned banks'.

5. *Endowment funds or loans by the state*

This ranges from outright capital grants to actual loans.

Capital grants are *de facto* subsidies. They are 'gifts' the state makes to GCEs on which it has no further explicit or implicit claim either in terms of repayment or in terms of any kind of direct financial return on the capital invested (for example, interest or dividends). Such subsidies are given either on a punctual basis or on an ongoing basis. The former case occurs when a GCE is charged with a particular mission (for example, to step in massively in an ailing sector and revamp it completely, or operate an uneconomical aircraft), or when a GCE is in a particular crisis it has to overcome (war damage, for example). They can be born as subsidies or become subsidies as the result of the transformation of a previous liability of the company into a grant; such a debt write-off has occurred, for example, for several British nationalized industries (such as after the Second World War). The latter case – ongoing subsidies – occurs when a GCE witnesses continual or chronic deficits. To keep alive, the company is condemned to receive almost perpetual help from the government. On the whole, among the *faibles contraintes* GCEs with which we are concerned in this study, there are few cases of overtly admitted chronic deficits. Most subsidies are therefore made with at least some hope that in time the receiving GCE will be able to operate economically; consequently, rather than granting continuing subsidies, the government prefers to finance GCEs via some kind of mechanism which will enable it to somehow share in any future profits.

The most straightforward form of such mechanisms is the government loan. In some instances – notably in Britain – state-owned companies borrow from the state as opposed to borrowing from financial institutions. The state receives interest on such loans and the principal is either repaid at the end of a given period or renewed. This, however, is rare on the whole. Usually, loans by the state carry some kind of special feature. 'Otherwise', said a French interviewee, 'there is no logical justification for the state to substitute itself to regular sources of credit; the state normally enters the picture only when regular sources cannot meet the company's needs'.

Thus, in certain cases the interest is skipped if financial results are not sufficient. While the loan carries a normal interest provision, the government can agree on an *ad hoc* basis to pass the interest. This interest can then either be payable at a future date when results make this possible, or be written off altogether. In fact the government can also pass the repayment of the principal. When repayment comes due, the loan can either be extended or even written off (in which case, for all practical purposes, it becomes a subsidy).

While in the above, deferring the payment of a liability or writing it off is the exception, governments also provide financing in which the exception really is interest and even capital repayment.

Thus, endowments are *de facto* capital grants or quasi-grants on which no interest is paid. While subsidies are officially and legally recognized as 'gifts' on which the government relinquishes any further claim either in terms of principal or capital remuneration, endowments are legally considered investments for which the government retains some hope of repayment. A typical instance are the *fondi di dotazione* of the Italian *Enti di gestione*:

> The institutions [the GCEs involved] are legally bound to hand over 65 per cent of their net profits to the Treasury in repayment of the endowment. In practice, few of the institutions which have received endowments have shown profits, either because they were losing concerns, or else because, after servicing their debenture debts, by far the greater part of their remaining profits remained hidden in the accounts of the Institute's [here IRI] subordinate companies and did not appear in the profit and loss account of the parent Institute itself.[21]

Indeed, the vast majority of interviewed companies confirmed that endowments are rarely repaid. Sabena stated: 'Such endowments are provided for in our by-laws. They are theoretically repayable – if we make enough profits in the future we may pay the government back. But this is not an obligation and the endowment does not constitute an incremental liability for which we are responsible. In actual practice, they are nearly never repaid'.

Endowments can be granted at the time when a GCE comes into being, as in the case of the *Enti di gestione*. Such funds are justified when the particular group is given the mission of reshaping a particular sector, which entails massive expenditures (for example, IRI, created in 1933 for the purpose of primarily revamping the country's ailing banking and credit system). Endowments are also granted in the course of GCEs' lives. This happens in crises situations such as after the Second World War when several endowments were granted to cover war damage and reconversion.

Endowments are granted on a regular basis as well. As we will see, GCEs are often expected to undertake projects in the collective or national interest which are of doubtful profitability. The government can then finance the resulting losses via increases in the company's endowment funds. In particular, in recessions, GCEs are often called upon to fulfil a salvage role on a continuing basis (GEPI, whose mission is to be a 'hospital for sick companies', is a case in point). And GCEs frequently carry out high technology programmes which are costly and risky and which call for government financing; again, this is often done via endowments.

Finally, there are special redemption loans – loans which are repayable only under certain circumstances. The commonest are those granted for high-risk long-term ventures which must be reimbursed only if the venture has a favourable financial outcome. For instance, the French government gives *prêts remboursables* to high-technology firms for the development of particular projects.

Such loans bear very low interest rates and are repayable if the project is a success. What is meant by 'success' is not always clear. The usual practice is that repayment occurs when a break-even point is reached. But this too is ambiguous. In some instances, break-even is defined as the point where all costs are met, including financial obligations, that is, interest charges and, where appropriate, repayment of the principal of regular liabilities; here then the government loan takes precedence on equity remuneration or dividends. But the break-even can also be defined as being after equity remuneration. It can indeed happen that dividends are paid before any repayment of the government loan; this occurs particularly in mixed GCEs where it is felt that private shareholders should receive a dividend on their investment. (In fact, several leftist parties are very critical of this on the grounds that public funds are used to pay dividends to private shareholders, while the funds themselves receive little interest and are usually either not repaid at all or repaid after a long period of time when inflation has eroded their value.)

6. *Internal financing*

The main distinctiveness of GCEs here lies in their ability to generate funds through retaining earnings.[22] The first issue is their profit-generating capacity itself. As we will see in the next chapter, many of the actions called for by the tool goal can be detrimental to GCEs' profitability. Further, given their tendency towards high debt ratios, GCEs often have high interest charges which further reduce their profits.

The second issue is GCEs' capacity to retain earnings. There is little question that GCEs can retain a greater share of their profits than private companies.

Here, one must be reminded of the particular sensitivity of European investors to dividends: the European private investor appears more concerned with dividends than with corporate profits in comparison with the US investor. While we have found no empirical evidence of this, this opinion is so widely held by professional finance people and academics that we can safely take it as a postulate. Our interviews have widely corroborated this. A French banker said:

> European investors have not yet really understood that there can be
> an opportunity cost to dividends: if a company can earn a higher
> return on profits it retains than shareholders can by reinvesting the
> dividends they receive, then it is better that the company retain the
> money; the money paid out in dividends could return more to the
> shareholder if retained in terms of capital gains.

And A. F. Tuke, the Chairman of Barclays Bank, presents a similar argument:
'In Europe, investors on the whole are more dividend conscious than in the
US. Clearly, even in Europe there are a number of institutional investors who
don't care about dividends too much. But on the whole, we do have shareholders for whom dividends are essential income. We could not pass our
dividend in any one year'.

Accepting the notion that dividends are a virtual must for private enterprises, GCEs have an advantage in that the government is much less anxious
to receive a dividend. A government does not depend on dividends from
GCEs. It is much more concerned with the performance of GCEs – particularly in terms of their contribution to its own policies. Even for those GCEs
with high autonomy which are driven essentially by the profit goal, the government is relatively uninterested in dividends. Further, the government
tends to encourage profit retention because this is, from its point of view,
often the best form of financing for GCEs: 'Given the problems equity issues
encounter and given the criticism debt financing arouses in the private sector,
internally generated funds are the most desirable form of financing for state
enterprises', said a French government official. In fact, it makes little sense
for the government to receive a dividend if it has in turn to be financed by
external sources – particularly an increase in the equity capital. An Italian
interviewee commented: 'Mixed enterprises provide a good base to show
government's moderation in its dividend expectations: it is always from the
private and not the public shareholders that the pressure for dividends
comes'.

Between potentially lower profits and lower dividends, the latter usually
tends to be a more important factor. True, there are exceptions. Thus, in the
Italian case, former Minister Pieracini estimates that in the period from 1965
to 1969 an average two-thirds of private industrial development was self-
financed compared to one-third for GCEs.[23] But this refers to all GCEs –
those driven by the profit goal and those driven by the tool goal. It is clear
that, given their macro kinds of obligations, the latter can generate lower
profits. Indeed, on the whole, those GCEs which are driven primarily by the
profit goal clearly are able to generate more cash for self-financing than
private firms. As a private sector interviewee said: 'Were we to be
nationalized, we would at least have the advantage of being able to retain
a greater proportion of our profits for self-financing'.

52

7. *International financing*

In general terms, on the international scene GCEs tend to exhibit fewer particularities. Still, four areas should be pointed out where there are distinctive features.

a. Equity   In the case of mixed enterprises, there is often a certain reluctance to allow foreign investors to acquire substantial amounts of the parent companies' stock. It is generally felt that GCEs have a national mission to fulfil and that foreign shareholders should not have a sizeable interest in the company. (In fact, several GCEs have come under the government control to avoid a takeover by foreigners in the first place.) Still, we must say that to date this is a rather academic question; historically, foreigners have rarely expressed interest in purchasing substantial shares of GCEs.

From another point of view, an international joint venture with a GCE sharing the equity of a subsidiary with a private partner may run into problems. From the viewpoint of the private partner, we saw earlier that there can be certain preconceptions which lead private firms to shy away from close ties with GCEs. This can be especially serious when it comes to sharing equity. From the viewpoint of the GCE itself, we will see later that certain overall policy considerations may result in a GCE choosing to stay away from partnerships involving joint ownership of a subsidiary with the private sector. A finance vice-president thus commented: 'This is detrimental to our flexibility; it forecloses one form of MN operation which could otherwise be quite attractive in many instances'.

b.   Debt   There are no sources of debt that GCEs have access to which are not equally available to private companies. The one major particularity is GCEs' greater overall creditworthiness, a plus in all forms of debt financing – debentures, bank loans or credits from specialized institutions (for example, the EXIM bank). International lenders go through much the same reasoning as national creditors; they see GCEs as safer due to government's backup. Again, a formal guarantee is better than a tacit backup. The relations of airlines with the EXIM Bank illustrate this. In the words of Air France's *Directeur général* Gilbert Pérol:

> If we take three airlines which are equal in their financial structure and strength, operating in the same conditions, and one is private, the other a GCE whose debts are not explicitly guaranteed by the state, and the third a GCE whose debts are formally backed by the government, an institution such as EXIM will give the best treatment to the third and the least attractive to the first.

While this is true in general, some variations are noteworthy. GCEs from certain countries tend to be perceived as less secure than others. For example,

Italian GCEs suffer from the national economic and sociopolitical crisis. In the words of an Italian executive: 'Foreign lenders may fear that our government has other things to worry about than to bail out a company with its foreign debts. So these creditors either want an explicit government guarantee or they want to look the company over more closely and see if it can stand on its own feet', Indeed, the financial standing of the company itself has an influence. If a company is strong, creditors will be less sensitive to an explicit government guarantee. The Chairman of Aer Lingus, Patrick Lynch, said: 'We still derive a benefit from a government guarantee on our international liabilities while older and more established state-owned companies often don't any more'. Further, the type of creditor can play a role. Those who are familiar with GCEs tend to be more sensitive to their implicit governmental backup. In the experience of many companies, American creditors, generally less used to working with GCEs, have been quite responsive to explicit state guarantees – particularly as debentures sold to the public are concerned.

c. Special government assistance in certain foreign investments   The best illustrations are provided by investments in the Eastern bloc where several GCEs such as ENI or Renault have a substantial involvement. This can range from mere export or licensing agreements to fully fledged direct investments in production facilities or turnkey operations. In such ventures, the financial support of the government is 'either in the form of guarantees for credits or, in some cases, full financing on a government-to-government basis'.[24] The government sometimes acts as a normal source of financing, lending money for an investment. Or the government can bear part or all of the financial risk (for example, exchange rate risk). Or, and most important, the government can arrange with the host country's government to overcome the problems created by the relative scarcity of hard currency which communist countries frequently have. For instance, if a company has to set up a turnkey operation is such a country, the governments can agree that it will be paid for the plant by its home government on completion or in instalments over the construction period of the plant. The host country government will then pay the home country government back over time (perhaps with the currency earned by the export of the very products of the plant). Still, we should note – in the words of an Italian interviewee – 'that this type of arrangement is not the exclusive prerogative of GCEs; private firms also can enjoy this type of government assistance. (Fiat's turnkey operation in Togliattigrad in the USSR is a case in point) . . . Yet, what is true is that, on the whole, the government is *particularly* inclined to assist GCEs'.

d. Profit repatriation   The fact that GCEs are under less pressure to pay out dividends can enable their foreign subsidiaries to retain a greater share of their profits locally. To quote M. Plescoff, President of Assurances Générales de France: 'Take Brazil; we are the biggest foreign insurance company there; everybody complains about restrictions on profit repatriation; we don't need to

54

repatriate profits because we don't need the cash to pay the dividends private companies have to pay; we are free to re-invest our foreign profits locally if we feel this is the best use we can make of the funds'.

8. *Conclusion*

Two questions have to be asked at the end of this discussion:

(1) On the whole, what is GCEs' access to funds relative to privately owned firms?

(2) What consequences does this have for their MN activities?

Vis-à-vis the first question, at the risk of oversimplifying and bearing in mind that there are several exceptions, three main points can be made:

(1) GCEs tend to have a harder time raising funds via new equity issues because of the general reluctance of governments to put incremental equity capital in the firms or to allow private investors to buy GCEs' shares beyond a certain limit. This can be compensated in part by a lesser need for GCEs to pay dividends and thus retain a greater portion of their earnings. On balance, according to M. Louré, President of Société Générale,

> the advantage of GCEs of having to pay less dividends is more often than not less significant than private companies' advantage of being able to raise incremental equity capital; at least as far as French banks are concerned, the cash savings state banks make in terms of lesser dividends payable are smaller than private banks' gains in terms of the greater amounts of money they receive from their shareholders in the form of issues of new equity.

(2) GCEs have a higher debt capacity than comparable private companies. This is due to the fact that lenders perceive them as better credit risks because they feel the government more or less explicitly guarantees GCEs' liabilities.

(3) GCEs have access to special sources of funds. The best example are state endowments. It is noteworthy that such sources are national sources.

In sum, GCEs have access to greater sources of outside funds than private companies – the disadvantage in terms of incremental equity capital being usually more than compensated by other sources of funds, notably debt financing.

Vis-à-vis the second question, it is safe to say that, contrary to common belief, these differences in themselves do not have a major impact on GCEs' overall MN behaviour. While not truly determining, three implications can be noted:

(1) The overall access of GCEs to greater sources of outside capital results in greater resources available for investments – including foreign investments. When this greater supply of funds does not carry with it any special condition as to its use (for example, a loan for a particular type of investment), growth is facilitated, and with it, international expansion.

(2) GCEs' greater creditworthiness gives them an advantage also in raising debt abroad. This can result in better terms and/or more debt internationally. This can favour MN growth.

(3) the fact that GCEs' foreign subsidiaries can be under less pressure to repatriate profits is an advantage for the development of existing international operations.

These are not negligible factors. They can be an asset in an MN strategy. But they clearly are not important enough in themselves to cause the development of such a strategy in the first place. As one interviewee said:

> GCEs do enjoy certain financial advantages which can help them in certain circumstances in their international operations. But these are not critical enough to give them such a competitive edge in MN operations that they would go MN just because of these advantages. In fact, these advantages do little in terms of modifying their strategic and policy behaviour on the international scene.

Most interviewees agree that financial variables play an insignificant role in causing a GCE to go or not to go MN. One private sector chief executive concluded:

> Particularly in normal, non-recessionary times, large companies can usually get the money they need for good investment projects, especially when these projects are not the most important ones relative to the overall investment programmes of the firm as in the case of most GCEs' international investments; consequently, the advantage of GCEs over private companies in this respect is not truly significant for MN operations. It is not in the area of finance *per se* that you will find the explanation for distinctive MN behaviour on the part of GCEs.

C. R & D

Governments take a general interest in companies' R & D activities whose value they see in terms of byproducts in other industrial endeavours and broader benefits for the nation (defence, for example). Clearly, this is most evident in high technology sectors where the number of GCEs is high (such as the computer or aerospace industries).[25] As we will see in some detail in the next chapter, governments encourage and try to assist the R & D efforts of their companies in these so-called *secteurs de pointe*.

The result is that GCEs have relatively generous R & D budgets and a relative strength in terms of technological knowhow ('relative' to private companies of similar size). Thus for computers 'American firms, particularly in the formative years of the industry, benefited from government development contracts, and European governments have sought to recreate similar circumstances by subsidizing the R & D activities of their firms'.[26] And beyond their own R & D budgets, GCEs frequently benefit from access to outside research centres (for example, nuclear energy or space programmes) which can further strengthen their technological edge.

True, several private firms in such sectors also benefit from this kind of government backup. Yet, not as much – as indicated by a French interviewee:

> It is a matter of degree, but usually the gap between private and public firms on this score is quite big. Private companies which get money from the state would get more were they nationalized. Government backup of GCEs' R & D activities is more systematic . . . Further, a government holds GCEs less accountable for the payoff of the help it gives them . . . It is in fact no coincidence that where the Left wants to nationalize private high technology companies – e.g. aircraft manufacturers – is precisely in France and the UK where the governmental funds committed to such companies are the greatest [this was before the British government's takeover of aircraft producers].

Government assistance is important. High technology sectors are oligopolistic as well as international: one or a few firms dominate the industry not just at home but across national boundaries. Beyond certain forms of protectionism (especially via nationalistic procurement policies of customers), competition is similar everywhere. Further, size is a key factor of success. The magnitude of the projects and the necessary R & D outlays make critical-mass a fundamental condition for being competitive. It is therefore desirable for firms whose domestic market is necessarily limited, to broaden their customer base beyond national frontiers. 'This makes it necessary to be competitive internationally,' said a British executive. Now, for European firms to be competitive internationally is often a challenge indeed; US companies in particular are much bigger, have more experience and can afford to commit far greater resources to R & D. Further, they have traditionally received enormous development contracts from the government, which constitute a primary captive market of tremendous proportions compared to the same markets in Europe. Facing this competition, the governmental help can indeed make a difference – as argued by a French executive:

> Belonging to the government or having the government participate in the capital means benefiting from its backup. This allows the company to commit greater resources to R & D than if it were private. It also means the company can launch bolder projects whose size, sophistication and riskiness it could otherwise not bear. This in turn enables it to produce better, more competitive products which have a market abroad. In many instances, this is a condition for European industry to close at least part of the technological gap with the US and for us to become competitive on world markets.

The first step in internationalization, that is, exporting, is thus helped by this backup. This in turn should eventually induce production abroad.[27] At least where economies of scale are not such to suggest keeping production concentrated in one location, it should be possible and often desirable to produce (or at least assemble) abroad once a solid foothold in foreign markets has been secured through exports. Thus, a French interviewee said: 'The help the government gives us results in a better product which can be sold abroad more readily. It can also result in a competitive advantage in terms of technical know-how which can be exploited abroad via foreign investments'.

We should note, however, that high technology firms are often also prime targets of pressures tending to preserve their national character. For reasons which will become clear in the next chapter, governments frequently endeavour to retain their high technology firms' key activities within domestic frontiers. This then reduces the possibilities these firms could otherwise have to go MN. What this means is that these companies are rather infrequently driven by the profit goal alone; tool goal constraints limit their foreign expansion possibilities. The fact remains, however, that where there are no such constraints, GCEs do have an edge over similar private companies to develop overseas.

D. Labour relations

In Chapter IV we will see that governments frequently expect GCEs to behave in a way which is particularly favourable to their employees. Here we focus on corporate characteristics which derive from the employees themselves over and beyond tool goal requirements. These are then intrinsic features of GCEs apart from any specific macroeconomic or social policy objective.

GCEs' workers adopt a particularly exacting attitude *vis-à-vis* their employers. They fight for higher compensation and benefits – longer leisure time, improved working conditions, greater fringe benefits, higher social benefits. . . And unions frequently insist that GCEs commit themselves to courses of action which will benefit the working classes at large: investments in less-developed areas, hiring in terms of unemployment, expansionist policies during slump periods etc. In fact, collective bargaining between unions and industry representatives often occurs separately for private and public companies. Thus in Italy this has occurred in certain cases as early as 1956 with the creation of Intersind for IRI (Associazione Sindacale Intersind) and ASAP for ENI (Associazione Sindacale per le Aziende Petrochimiche e Collegate a Partecipazione Statale). Agreements which ensue from such collective bargaining are often pacesetters. This is how one scholar has analysed one of the first agreements of this sort:

> Viewed as a step in the modernization of Italy's archaic system of industrial relations this agreement represented a major pace forward. A new form of articulated contract was provided designed to

extend bargaining from the national confederal level down to that of the engineering sector. It also made provision, in accordance with predetermined principles, for limited negotiations at the level of the plant or enterprise. Six engineering sectors were recognized, and within the framework of the national confederal contract, hours, minimum wages, piecework, sick pay and details of job classification were open to enterprise negotiations at this sector level. Provision was also made for union access to managers for negotiation of the method of application of piecework systems and other matters.[28]

Considering that this is all the result of the negotiations relative to a single agreement it is an impressive list indeed!

Another significant example is an agreement concluded in April 1965 which 'gave assurances in principle against victimization on grounds of political or religious opinion or trade union membership. Since the arbitrary exclusion of the unions from the plant has been a major factor strengthening those seeking to instrumentalize the unions for social demagogic ends, these clauses represented a further important step towards a rational collective bargaining structure'.[29] Finally, as pointed out by Kendall, one should note that of the greatest importance was

> the seemingly insignificant clause providing for a union 'check off' from wages. The endemic refusal of . . . workers to pay regularly even an artificially low level of union dues has been a major cause of union dependence on outside subventions. The check-off system by opening the road for the first time towards a substantial degree of union financial autonomy, may well prove to [have been] a further major step towards the provision of an effective system of industrial relations.[30]

Unions have often been successful in obtaining governments' own backing to push forward their demands with GCEs. Thus, the working of the above mentioned articulated contract demanded certain concessions which could be only effectively brought with political support:

> A circular from the Minister of State Holdings . . . proposed to state holding companies that as a matter of public interest greater facilities ought to be accorded to unions in state industry. As a result, clauses providing for the provision of union notice boards, of limited time off for the exercise of union functions and above all for the deduction on individual request, of union dues from wages, were all brought into negotiation and finally incorporated in the new articulated contract.[31]

There are a variety of reasons for such attitudes. First, there is the feeling of many worker-representatives that, since GCEs belong to the collectivity, they should be at the 'service of the people'; they should be concerned principally with the welfare of the working classes and devote their efforts to the betterment of the proletariat's existence. A French interviewee argued:

> Somehow, GCEs have an image of social commitment inherent in their very nature. Because they are not private capitalistic undertakings and because they belong – via the state – to the people, it is tacitly assumed that they ought to do all they can to improve the *condition humaine* around them. And this starts with their workers' interests. Therefore, unions feel all the more legitimized to fight hard with employers for higher pay, social advantages or other types of benefits.

Further, several cases have shown GCEs are frequently less tough in labour negotiations. One interviewee said:

> Is it because public authorities are anxious to keep the temperature cool in their enterprises on the social front in view of avoiding giving other workers any opportunity to build on disturbances to create social unrest in their own right, or because public owners are less defensive about their economic interests than private capitalists? Anyhow, unions have learned that GCEs tend to be less hard in collective bargaining than private enterprises.

Moreover, 'the state itself, under pressure from the political parties, has from time to time given IRI special directions, the net effect of which has been to encourage a pre-existing tendency to make of IRI and Intersind "condition leaders" for the Italian economy'.[32] Indeed, in Italy and elsewhere governments' own policies have encouraged workers in their attitudes. As will be seen in the next chapter, governments often rely on GCEs to undertake socially oriented actions. In light of this, unions are encouraged to feel free to make GCEs their favourite ground to fight for their own demands with the expectation that once their demands are satisfied in GCEs, the rest of industry will have to follow.

Workers' attitudes can restrain MN expansion. First, there can be a financial problem: the demands of workers are frequently costly, which reduces resources available for investment projects, including MN investments. This can be significant when workers' demands increase as soon as there are rumours of foreign expansion: the reasoning is that, since foreign expansion is envisioned, it must mean that the firm has financial resources available; this then triggers workers' demands on the grounds that this is the right moment to formulate new demands.

This hints at the importance of the psychology of labour relations and raises a second and far more critical issue for MN expansion. Particularly in countries where unions are heavily politicized (such as France or Italy), workers believe GCEs ought to be committed primarily to fostering the interests of the national collectivity, their owner. Unions tend to view themselves if not as the sole guardian of such interests, at least as 'co-responsible' of their sponsorship. Consequently – in the words of an Italian interviewee, 'they feel they should fight to maximize the collective interests, i.e. obtain as much as possible for the working classes in general and the companies' employees in particular'. On the other hand, they tend to be mistrustful of GCEs' management just as they are of private companies' management: 'A unionist is always a unionist, said a French GCE executive; be it with private industry or state-owned industry, he will always view management as an enemy'. Unions tend to have a constant worry that management will undertake things which go against the interests of workers to pursue 'para-capitalistic' ends.

In this context, foreign investments can often become a particular target of unions' struggles because they are seen as typical capitalistic endeavours – exclusively profit-motivated. They are seen as entailing few benefits for national workers (the long-term benefits which might ensue are typically not recognized). In fact, they are seen as entailing an opportunity cost for workers: the unions reason that production transferred abroad means lesser domestic production and thus negative consequences in terms of employment opportunities and the like at home.[33] And foreign investments are allegedly designed to diminish workers' control over the company; by expanding abroad, the firm is seen as seeking to decrease its dependence on domestic labour forces, thus decreasing workers' bargaining power. As a French interviewee complained:

> When unions take such a negative view of MN expansion, investing abroad becomes truly arduous. It is not their demands themselves which are the obstacle; though often totally unreasonable, they can be negotiated and they don't in themselves constitute major barriers to MN growth. What is a true problem is their overall attitude: the more a GCE gives in to their demands the more they are reinforced in their contention that GCEs should indeed give priority to social returns to the collectivity and their workers in particular. And the more this kind of feeling is nurtured the more purely commercial endeavours are hard to pursue. MN growth is then a natural to be sacrificed.

III. CONCLUSION

In this chapter we analysed what is distinctive about GCEs' MN behaviour when they are driven by the profit goal. The question which was asked is: if a GCE is free from any obligation to pursue aims imposed upon it by the government and if it can pursue the same ends as a private firm, what is particular about its attitude *vis-à-vis* foreign expansion?

We saw that while the profit goal is the same goal pursued by private enterprise, the actual decisions it leads to vary from company to company as a function of each company's environment and corporate characteristics. In this context, GCEs' particularities can be summarized in five basic points:

(1) In certain instances, governments can act in a way to favour GCEs in their domestic operations (for example, via tariff protection). This can be a disincentive for MN expansion.

(2) Several aspects of GCEs' marketing and goodwill are distinctive. GCEs can enjoy preferential conditions in the marketing of their products at home. This too can be a disincentive to go abroad. Abroad, positive and negative variables tend to even each other out, the former being more important in countries with a socialist bent, the latter carrying more weight where orthodox capitalism is deeply ingrained. Yet, again, this is not truly essential (the most important aspect being the goodwill dimension in co-operative agreements where GCEs may encounter some difficulties in view of their image with certain private sector partners).

(3) GCEs exhibit sizeable differences in the area of finance. On the whole, they are able to have access to greater sources of funds – except via new equity issues. But again, this has limited influence over GCEs' MN decisions.

(4) Certain GCEs have an advantage over private firms in terms of R & D which can enhance the competitiveness of their products.

(5) Where unions are heavily politicized, labour can hinder GCEs' expansion outside national frontiers.

Still, none of the above have a determining effect on GCEs' MN behaviour. This is the main conclusion of this perspective. On the whole, GCEs driven by the profit goal have no special features which cause them to behave much differently than private companies; there is little in their environment or in their own characteristics to suggest that their attitude with regard to foreign expansion should be significantly distinctive.

Having said this, a few qualifications must be made:

(a) Given (1) and (2) above, GCEs may have less reason to be quite as aggressive as private companies in pursuing foreign opportunities.

(b) Given their image, GCEs can have a special attraction for countries with a socialized economic system as opposed to a totally free-market system. And they may be less likely to enter joint ventures with certain private firms.

(c) Given (4), high technology GCEs have an edge which facilitates their entry into foreign markets.

(d) Given (5), GCEs which are in labour-intensive sectors and which are from countries where unions are politicized do encounter difficulties in pursuing foreign direct investment opportunities.

Consequently, certain GCEs (such as those in the *secteurs de pointe*) are in somewhat of a special situation *vis-à-vis* MN expansion. But otherwise, this analysis has not uncovered anything, suggesting that GCEs' MN behaviour is but marginally different from that of similar private sector enterprises.

Yet, this analysis is puzzling on several accounts. First, there are certain anomalies in terms of GCEs' behaviour. True, many GCEs which are free of governmental pressures to pursue tool-goal endeavours do behave internationally in a way similar to their private sector counterparts, successfully exploiting foreign opportunities. Yet, others do not. When asked whether they saw attractive opportunities abroad for their firm, many of these interviewees acknowledged several; and when asked if there were any impediments – particularly coming from the government – for the company to pursue them, they said there were none. Thus, one corporate planner said: 'Objectively all the conditions for us to go MN are there: we have several attractive possibilities overseas [and he listed three]; we have the resources to build on them; we have nothing which stands in the way for us to do so (such as conflicting domestic alternatives or obligations). But we don't. I am not sure why . . .'. And while many GCEs with special characteristics relevant to MN operations do exploit them, we found certain exceptions. Thus a high-technology firm interviewee said: 'Thanks to the state's back-up we have been able to develop products which are quite competitive. But we have yet done little in terms of trying to penetrate foreign markets . . . We just are missing attractive opportunities'.

This analysis is unable to account for such exceptions.

Further, this analysis leaves several issues unresolved in terms of why certain phenomena occur. For instance, why is the government really unprepared to subscribe to new equity issues while it is willing to extend generous loans or even endowments to GCEs? Can one really ascribe state-organizations' inclination to lend preferentially to GCEs just to a 'communality of goals' between creditor and borrower? Is governments' particular assistance to GCEs fully accounted for by the rational reasons offered by this perspective?

Does this traditional kind of an approach uncover all the causes for GCEs' MN behaviour?

NOTES

1. Raymond Vernon, 'International Investment and International Trade in the Product Cycle', *Quarterly Journal of Economics*, May 1966, pp. 190–207; Vernon, *Sovereignty at Bay*, Basic Books, New York, 1971.
2. John Fayerweather, *International Business Management*, McGraw-Hill, New York, 1969, p. 26.
3. John Fayerweather, *International Business Management*, p. 29.
4. 'La France va-t-elle créer une industrie de calculateurs largement française?', *Le Figaro*, 19 April 1966.
5. See: Douglas Lamont, 'Joining Forces with Foreign State Enterprises', *Harvard Business Review*, July–August 1973.

6. Renato Mazzolini, *European Transnational Concentrations*, McGraw-Hill, London, 1974, p. 72.
7. For a description of this agreement, see: Paul M. Goldberg, 'The evolution of transnational companies in Europe', PhD dissertation, Massachusetts Institute of Technology, Sloan School of Management, 1971, pp. 194–200.
8. It is noteworthy that these banks later entered into a co-operative agreement which included two GCEs – the French Société Générale and the Italian Banca Nazionale del Lavoro.
9. See: Stuart Holland (ed.), *The State as Entrepreneur*, Weidenfeld and Nicolson, London, 1972; M. V. Posner and S. J. Woolf, *Italian Public Enterprise*, Gerald Duckworth, London 1967.
10. See: M. V. Posner and S. J. Woolf, *Italian Public Enterprise*.
11. See Chapter I
12. See: Pasquale Saraceno, *Il Finanziamento delle Imprese Pubbliche*, A. Confalonieri, Milano, 1963; Edouard Bonnefous, 'Rapport d'Information' No. 421, Sénat, Paris, 1976.
13. Again, this is hard to quantify precisely. Yet, interviewees were unanimous.
14. See: *La Finanza delle Assicurazioni Sociali in Italia*, Mediobanca, Milano, 1964.
15. Andrew Shonfield, *Modern Capitalism*, Oxford University Press, London, 1965, p. 129.
16. ENI, 'Relazione e Bilancio', Rome, 1962.
17. M. V. Posner and S. J. Woolf, *Italian Public Enterprise*, p. 82.
18. ENI, 'Relazione e Bilancio', Rome, 1963, pp. 83–84.
19. V. A. Lutz, *Italy. A Study in Economic Development*, Royal Institute of International Affairs, London, 1962, p. 272.
20. M. V. Posner and S. J. Woolf, *Italian Public Enterprise*, p. 82.
21. M. V. Posner and S. J. Woolf, *Italian Public Enterprise*, p. 77.
22. Other internal sources of cash such as depreciation are normally closer to what happens in private companies.
23. Ministero del Bilancio, 'Progetto di Programma di Sviluppo Economico per il Quinquennio 1965–1969', Rome, 1965, p. 172.
24. Louis Wells, 'Automobiles', in Raymond Vernon (editor), *Big Business and the State*, Harvard University Press, Cambridge, Mass., 1974, p. 249.
25. See: Nicolas Jéquier, 'Computers', in Vernon (ed.), *Big Business and the State*; Milton Hochmuth, 'Aerospace', in Vernon (ed.), *Big Business and the State*.
26. Nocolas Jéquier, in Vernon (ed.), *Big Business and the State*, p. 223.
27. See R. Vernon, *Sovereignty at Bay*.
28. Walter Kendall, 'Labour Relations', in Holland (ed.), *The State as Entrepreneur*, p. 224.
29. Walter Kendall, 'Labour Relations', in Holland (ed.), *The State as Entrepreneur*, p. 225.
30. Walter Kendall, 'Labour Relations', in Holland (ed.), *The State as Entrepreneur*, p. 225.
31. Walter Kendall, 'Labour Relations', in Holland (ed.), *The State as Entrepreneur*, p. 225.
32. Walter Kendall, 'Labour Relations', in Holland (ed.), *The State as Entrepreneur*, pp. 222–223.
33. The validity of this argument will be discussed in Chapter IV.

CHAPTER IV

The Tool Goal

'There has been a growing tendency to use national enterprises in the effort to solve specific problems as if they were agencies of the State.'[1]

Here we analyse the demands placed on GCEs deriving from the tool goal – the aim of serving as a vehicle to carry out government plans and policies – which have a bearing on GCEs' MN behaviour. The question we ask is what pressures for specific actions come to bear upon GCEs which cause them to take particular attitudes *vis-à-vis* international operations. There are three categories of such pressures: hindrances to MN expansion, driving forces for MN expansion, and pressures for particular patterns of behaviour on an MN scale.

I. HINDRANCES TO MN EXPANSION

There are pressures for national endeavours which stand in the way of MN expansion. And there are pressures against MN expansion *per se*.

A. Pressures for developing at home

GCEs are frequently under pressure to accomplish certain missions domestically which then stand in the way of going abroad. In this context, a government official said: 'MN expansion is not considered bad in itself; but since you can't do everything, you have to choose; given you have limited resources, there has to be a tradeoff between national and international growth . . . Certain GCEs are effectively expected to commit virtually all their resources to domestic development'. This 'domestic imperative' has three facets.

1. *Sectorial policy*

In varying degrees and for varied reasons European governments have a set of policies designed to stimulate and monitor the development of certain sectors.* Where they exist, GCEs in such sectors are under pressure to comply

---

*It should be clear that sectorial policy refers to a set of aims for the sake of that very sector, that is, the government wants that sector to develop in a certain way, and this is an *end* in itself and not a *means* to achieve other objectives (employment, for example).

with government policy. In fact, many GCEs were born precisely for the purpose of carrying out a particular sectorial policy.

What sectors in what countries are the favoured targets of governmental policy? What are the reasons behind such policies? And what influence do they have on GCEs' behaviour? In the context of 'competitive industries' (as opposed to state monopolies) five sectors are critical.*

a. Coal We regard this as a sector *à faibles contraintes* not only because of firm-to-firm competition but also because of competition between coal and other sources of energy. Up to the Second World War, governments' concern with this industry was mostly for its importance as the key source of energy. But since the industry was flourishing there was usually little need for the government to step in and the limited amount of state intervention tended to be based on dogmatic reasons. Even the 1902 creation of DSM in Holland, for example, while reflecting a will to secure national mastery of this source of energy was also inspired by strong nationalistic motives.

As the industry matured, it became increasingly difficult for companies to remain competitive, particularly in view of cheaper sources of energy. Thus a threat emerged of a wave of consolidations, contractions or shutdowns. To avoid massive layoffs, the government stepped in (not necessarily via nationalizations) to assist the reconversion of workers into other sectors (say, via the diversification of their own company – DSM moving into chemicals, for example). Here then, the emphasis was not on sectorial policy as such but on employment.

However, as early as the end of the 1950s, several states became concerned with preserving the resiliency of at least part of the industry as a contingent source of energy. Needless to say, in 1973 such a policy was made far more articulate. In particular, France and Britain have placed a new stress on coal emphasizing effectiveness of production to the detriment of reconversion or gradual phaseout.

This has clearly influenced GCEs' attitude *vis-à-vis* MN operations. When the issue was avoiding layoffs, it is clear that the governments' interest was to preserve domestic operations *per se*. With the growing concern for national energy independence, governments' renewed interest in coal has led to emphasizing national extraction. In the words of a Charbonnages de France executive: 'If our only mission were to supply the French market with the cheapest coal, we would probably do a lot of foreign extraction. But we have to produce *French* coal'. Further, countries prefer to retain their sources of energy for domestic consumption as opposed to exports. In the words of an industry executive: 'Governments prefer that the domestic energy market be supplied as much as possible by national sources. Therefore, we tend to be under pressure not to export our coal'.

---

*This discussion is voluntarily limited to those sectors where there are GCEs and where those firms are prevented from effectively exploiting their MN opportunities by government sectorial policies.

(Having said this, we should note that recently both these countries' governments seem to have changed their policy somewhat; precisely because coal has regained importance as a key source of energy, GCEs in the sector are now expected to make sure that there is an adequate and economic supply for the country. This has led governments to allow companies to become, at least to a limited extent, involved in foreign mining if this is necessary to ensure adequate availability of raw materials.)

b. *Iron and Steel*[2] Several European countries such as Great Britain or Germany have abundant resources in this vital field. Here governments' intervention has been relatively low. Market forces have been sufficient to cause national sources to be the prime supplier of domestic demand: the country's private sector on its own has been able to satisfy the home market at adequate prices. And it has been able to offer satisfactory guarantees in terms of national independence from a political standpoint (given that it is the foundation of heavy industry, governments have always been concerned about being as autonomous as possible in this field, not only in normal times but also in case of crises, such as war). Thus the German government has done little in terms of actual policies for the sector – even in the case of giant GCEs such as Salzgitter. Similarly, the nationalization of British Steel is less due to sectorial policies than to sociopolitical reasons (or economic reasons pertaining to the situation of that enterprise *per se*). In the Benelux countries too, firms have had considerable freedom to formulate their own strategy.

This freedom has enabled GCEs to go abroad when they saw fit. For instance, British Steel estimates its foreign assets to be worth over 50 million pounds. And Hoogovens encountered few obstacles from the Dutch government to proceed with a transnational merger with Germany's Hoesch.[3]

In France, raw materials are also relatively abundant but there is a long *étatist* tradition: 'The steel industry was involved in the French planning process from its inception'.[4] Yet, the government has never felt the need for a GCE (though the Left has asked for several nationalizations). The focus of the government plans has been primarily financial since the industry 'was desperately in need of funds for a reconstruction and modernization ... [It received] the largest share of investment funds secured by any private industry'.[5]

It is in Italy where sectorial policy has the greatest influence on GCEs. The country is poor in raw materials which it has to secure from abroad. In view of enhancing the country's control of its steel supply (both in terms of quantity and prices), the government took the position as recently as the early 1930s that Italy should have a steel industry of its own as opposed to relying on imports from foreign producers. The government realized that because of the size of the investments required and the risks involved as well as the uncertain and long-term nature of any potential return, the private sector could not be relied upon alone to give the country the desirable autonomy in the field.

Thus in 1937 Finsider was created – now one of the major sectorial holdings of IRI – grouping together all the Institute's enterprises in the metallurgical industries. Finsider developed parallel to private enterprise, though faster, up to a point where it now has over 60 per cent of the national steel output. While historically profitable in its own right, Finsider has – in the words of a company executive – 'the mission of making sure that the country's needs are met at appropriate prices . . . We are the guardians of Italy's steel independence'.

In a country deprived of raw materials, the government's aim of independence leads Finsider to go abroad to secure these resources. We will return to this in Part II.

At the other end, through its export subsidiary Siderexport, Finsider sells 450 billion lire annually abroad. This is an attractive incremental activity since on international markets it is free in its pricing, in contrast to domestic sales where prices are often at least indirectly regulated. Yet, Finsider considers this as a marginal part of its mission. Exports are viewed as a safety valve: Finsider usually produces more than the expected demand at home in order to have an excess capacity in case actual demand exceeds forecasts. This excess is exported. By selling its slack on international markets, Finsider can not only meet unforeseen domestic demand but also maintain a constant level of production. Yet, what is important is – in the words of a company executive – 'that these sales are considered merely as a *means* for the company to accomplish its basic mission of securing the smooth supply of steel to Italy more effectively'.

In terms of actual production, all of it takes place in Italy and there has never been any question of setting up production elsewhere. As explained by a Finsider official:

> Even if we thought this could be cheaper either for the steel sold in Italy or for that we sell abroad, we would never consider production abroad. We want to have the highest possible value added at home. Given the aim of national independence, it is felt that everything should be done to use national factors of production. Even if foreign production could be done via wholly owned subsidiaries, domestic production uses Italian labour, plant and equipment and this contributes to our mastery of the production process.

A government official added: 'It is bad enough to be dependent on outside sources for raw materials (and, in fact, we do all we can to control these sources directly ourselves – e.g., do the mining ourselves); beyond this necessary evil, we want as much as possible to have Italian steel for the Italian market'.

c, Oil (and gas) Especially since 1973, all European governments have a more or less explicit policy here. There are three basic types of situations – first, France, Italy and more recently Germany (as well as formerly the UK), which have little resources of their own but which use GCEs to enforce a policy in this sector; second, the UK today, which is increasingly dependent on national resources which it exploits via active government intervention; third, the other smaller countries which rely on the private sector either via foreign MNCs or via national firms (for example, Petrofina in Belgium). Obviously, we are concerned only with the first two where there are GCEs involved.

In the first case, the thrust of the government's policies is to decrease the dependence on foreign suppliers by increasing national independence via national GCEs.

France decided as early as the 1920s that it should reduce its reliance on foreign suppliers via a national enterprise with direct access to sources of oil. It was felt that such an enterprise should be monitored by the state via a participation in the equity. Besides, it was expected that such a participation would strengthen the company's financial standing not only in terms of the actual contribution the government would make in the capital but also indirectly – the presence of the government signalling that the government would back the company in its development, thus attracting private capital in a field where it would otherwise not venture on its own.[6] It is in this context that CFP was created in 1924, with the state holding a minority of the capital 'but exercising a powerful influence on the management'.[7]

Much later, the government felt that CFP was not enough. A second company – ERAP – was created in 1966, with the government as the sole owner. This was consistent with the policy 'first enunciated in November 1964 and taken up again in the FIFTH Plan, aimed at reducing the position of foreign companies in France with regard to the importation, refining and distribution of petroleum, as well as foreign trade in finished products'.[8] Ten years after its creation ERAP was merged with SNPA, of which it previously held 51 per cent of the shares. The new group, Société Nationale Elf-Aquitaine, is owned approximately 70 per cent by the state and is active in the research, transport, production, refining and distribution of oil as well as natural gas, sulphur, chemicals, etc.[9]

In Italy, ENI was founded in 1953, taking under its wing the old state holdings in the oil and gas sectors which had been set up by the Fascist regime.[10] Organized as an *Ente di gestione*, it is composed of a number of companies, some of which are 100 per cent owned by ENI (e.g. SNAM), others being owned partly by ENI, partly by the private sector (e.g. ANIC). Over the years ENI diversified its activities and now, beyond its traditional activities of exploration and production of oil and natural gas, ENI is involved in the transportation and the marketing of these products, in the production and marketing of petrochemicals, in textiles, in engineering activities, etc.

In terms of government policy, the main feature is that in a sense the means engendered the ends. As explained by a government official: 'The new Italian Republic inherited its holdings in the sector from the previous regime. It didn't have a clear notion of what to do with them. At first and for a long time, it was the company which decided what to do. And in fact, it did a lot for the national interest. It is only recently that the government has developed an explicit policy of its own'.

The German government's active involvement in the oil sector is relatively recent. Traditionally 75 to 80 per cent of the German oil market has been in foreign hands. The government had not taken much action until the 1968–69 takeover bid of the major German oil company – Gelsenberg – by CFP.[11] Apparently suddenly preoccupied by the situation, it blocked the merger. After 1973, its policy became specific.

Gelsenberg is now controlled by VEBA – a diversified GCE with its own substantial operations in the oil sector. Besides, VEBA and Gelsenberg together hold a majority interest in Aral – the largest German distribution company. And the state controls 56 per cent of the capital of Deminex – an oil exploration company. The aim is now to consolidate the operations of such undertakings in view of – in the words of a Gelsenberg executive – 'creating one major German enterprise which would have enough weight internationally, in particular *vis-à-vis* OPEC and MNCs'.

Britain was the first country to have a mixed enterprise in the oil sector: 'When Winston Churchill adopted . . . the device when setting up the Anglo-Iranian Oil Company with a 51 per cent government share of the equity before the First World War'.[12] Later this company was to become BP and the share of the government was to decline to 48.2 per cent. Today, after the 1975 arrangement between the Bank of England and Burmah Oil, the State owns 51 per cent of BP (31 per cent owned by the government *per se* and 20 per cent by the Bank of England).[13] The government has the right to put two directors out of seven on the board, who have a veto power (though never used to date). A company executive said: 'In normal times the way we naturally go about our business doesn't warrant any intervention by the government. But it is important for the government to know it has potential control over the company – that it can readily step in any time it needs to'.

In contrast to this traditional situation, the British government has adopted a new attitude in the 1970s – a result of the combined effect of the oil crisis, the exploitation of the North Sea oil and the return to power of the more interventionist Labour Party. This led to the 1976 creation of the British National Oil Corporation whose basic role is to further 'the national interest in development and use of UK Continental Shelf oil and gas resources'.[14] Specifically:

> The corporation combines functions of an instrument of national policy, of a commercial enterprise and of an adviser to the government. The role of the corporation will develop but its present priorities are:
>
> – efficient and commercial management of its equity interests in offshore petroleum exploration, development and production;
> – effective disposition of petroleum available to the Corporation

both from its equity interests and through participation arrangements with other offshore petroleum production licenses, with due
regard both to commercial considerations and to national and
international interests and obligations;
– development of expertise in and knowledge of all aspects of the
oil business, but particularly those relating to the development and
use of resources under the UK Continental Shelf; and
– development of its capability to give informed and expert advice
on oil matters to the Secretary of State as a contribution to the
development of national policy.[15]

Except for the new attitude of the British government geared to the exploitation of the North Sea Oil, these policies have similar motivations. Much of
the reasoning behind the Italian steel policies applies: given the country does
not have raw materials of its own, it wants to have national undertakings
going abroad to seek natural resources in order to enhance the safety of the
country's supply. One government official summarized this attitude:

Oil is a vital commodity both for the life of the economy at large
and for political reasons. When a country has its own natural
resources it may be OK to leave their exploitation to the private
sector because the government can always step in in periods of
crises and take the necessary measures. But when you depend on
foreign sources, you at least have to control the means of exploitation of these resources. Of course, you are at the mercy of foreign
political powers, but government control of the oil-producing
organization is the most you can do to minimize uncontrollable
risks.

Further, governments feel that by having their own enterprise, they are able
to influence oil prices more than otherwise – as argued by M. Logters, President of Deminex: 'By being present through a GCE in the drilling and production of crude oil and by monitoring the sales of this oil, the government
can provide cheaper oil to the country by controlling its prices when this oil is
sold to the market'.
Governments' policies result in both driving and restraining forces for MN
expansion. The former will be discussed in Part II. In terms of the latter,
it is firstly downstream operations which are critical.
GCEs' number one task is to make sure that the country has a safe and
economical oil supply. This means that they should have a substantial share of
the domestic market so that this market is not overly dependent on foreign
companies. An ENI executive said: 'Even if we could earn more money on
international markets we have to first be strong domestically; in this sense we
operate differently from purely private MNCs whose major concern is to

maximize profits on a global basis'. Thus Aral reported that it viewed marketing abroad only as a means of supporting domestic operations:

> We have to have some market penetration in the surrounding countries because otherwise we would lose some of our customers who travel a lot abroad. If Germans cannot find our products in their journey in the neighbouring countries they may well switch to competitors who are international in scope and who are present in Germany as well. It is hard to get these people back once they return to Germany. Therefore, we do invest in international marketing operations but on a relatively limited scale and not on the grounds of making a good investment in itself but as a means of strengthening our domestic operations.

This means that a GCE can only be aggressive abroad once it has a strong position nationally. ENI reported:

> Also due to the fact that historically our government didn't have much of an oil policy, we were able to expand abroad after a certain domestic development. In fact, in more recent years, with our government having a clearer sectorial policy, we have had to shift back to more emphasis on domestic development . . . Moreover, oil companies have to be MN after a certain point. Greater size means economies of scale. Thus, we had to grow to remain competitive. But given the oligopolistic structure of the market, it is difficult to increase penetration beyond a certain level in any given country – even in one's own country. Thus, we had to grow MN. In a sense, we had no choice.

The governments' policies also have implications for refining as well as transport operations which are geared towards national distribution of end products. As much as possible, refineries are located in the home country. In fact, even in the case of MN expansion, GCEs tend to delay investments in foreign refineries and supply foreign markets via national refineries in order to maximize the value added of the firm at home.

In certain cases, GCEs can also be under pressure to 'stay at home' in the case of upstream operations – when there are natural resources domestically which the government wants a GCE to exploit. One interviewee put it this way: 'For reasons of national independence the government wishes national natural resources to be exploited even when it is cheaper to rely on imported resources. When these resources are not otherwise economically attractive enough for a company to exploit them on its own, the government puts pressure on a GCE to do so. This is clearly to the detriment of MN expansion'.

The best illustration is of course Britain's new policy geared towards the exploitation of the North Sea Shelf. The British National Oil Corporation was primarily created to guard Britain's interests in the exploitation of the newly found national oil. True, the corporation has a secondary mission of securing national oil supply *per se* which may eventually lead it to seek alternative sources of crude oil outside the national territory. But its primary aim for the foreseeable future is clearly to monitor the efficient production and selling of the country's own natural resources.

Elsewhere, ENI and ERAP are also under pressure to seek natural resources at home. ENI in particular provides a good illustration – as analysed by Shonfield:

> Its great achievement in the 1950s was the exceedingly rapid development of the newly found reserves of natural gas in North Italy. It is highly improbable that any of the international oil companies . . . would have done the job with equal speed. The other alternative, an indigenous private enterprise organization, could hardly have matched ENI's high-speed performance in bringing to Italian industry all the supplies of the newly discovered natural gas that it could use, in so short a time. The speed with which any normal private business would have set about the venture would have been determined by commercial criteria, such as the desire to husband reserves or the wish not to disrupt other established supplies of fuel, which would have slowed down the process. Indeed, it is sometimes argued that ENI's pace was excessive: the consequence is that known Italian reserves of natural gas are in danger of being exhausted in a matter of a few years. However, those who took charge of Italian gas development were guided by other considerations than this. They were, of course, anxious to make a profit; but their main objective was to apply to the national economy the stimulus of plentiful domestic fuel for industry at a cheap price.[16]

d. Aerospace　High-technology sectors have been the object of government policies for a variety of reasons – military, political, prestige, economic (in particular since they are motors for the rest of the economy). 'Because of the military, technological and social significance of the industry, as well as the high visibility of its end products, the aerospace sector has received more attention from West European governments than its relative economic importance would seem to warrant'.[17]

Hochmuth has given an accurate account of the development of this sector.[18]

> The total aerospace sales of the Common Market, Britain included
> . . . were 3817 million in 1970 . . . Boeing's sales [were] of 3667

Table IV.1 Annual aerospace sales of selected firms, 1971 (millions of 1971 US dollars)

British		French[a]		United States	
Rolls-Royce	$ 650	Aerospatiale	$ 663	Boeing	$3,011
British Aircraft		Dassault-Brequet	316	Lockheed	2,852
Corporation	382	SNECMA	248	McDonnell-	
Hawker-Siddeley	546			Douglas	2,069
Westland	139			United Aircraft	2,029
Total	$1,717		$1,227		$9,961
Total industry sales excluding intra-industry sales	$1,634		$1,418		$20,632

Sources: Annexes I and II of 'Les Actions de politique industrielle et technologique de la Communauté à entreprendre dans le secteur aéronautique', EEC Commission, document III/2457/72-F, Brussels, 21 December 1973. Sales of individual US firms are from Moody's Industrial Register 1972; total US industry sales from *Aerospace Facts and Figures*, 1927–73.
[a]Excluding tax

million for that year. Moreover, at least three other US aerospace firms had sales rivalling this figure, so that US aerospace sales in total came to 24 850 million for 1970 . . . 75 per cent of the aircraft flying on the scheduled airlines of the world . . . were US manufacture. Over 90 per cent of the acquisition costs of such aircraft were embodied in US equipment.[19]

This is corroborated by the figures of Table IV. 1.

This unfavourable market position is compounded by the extraordinary and ever-increasing costs involved in the development and production of modern aircraft – as illustrated by Table IV. 2. As noted by Hochmuth,

European manufacturers have had a decided advantage over the United States with respect to labour costs. But this advantage has been more than offset by the size of the US market, which has permitted US manufacturers to reap the benefits of economies of scale and to spread the costs of the learning process. While the phenomenon of economies of scale is well understood, the import-ance of the learning curve is less well known. Briefly, according to a widely accepted model, the production costs of successive lots of an aircraft can be expected to diminish by a fixed percentage, 20 per cent being a commonly used figure. Thus if the production cost per plane of the first lot is C, the cost of the second lot would be 0.8 C, the third lot 0.64 C, and so on. Clearly, American manufac-turers, with a home market significantly larger than the combined

74

Table IV.2   Aircraft development costs between 1933 and 1974 (millions of current US dollars)

Plane	Time period	Development costs
DC 1/2/3	1933–36	$1.5
Canberra (UK military)	1945–51	50
Caravelle	1953–59	140
Douglas DC-8	1955–59	200–300
Concorde (Anglo-French) (including engine)	1962–74	2400
Boeing 747	1965–69	1000
Airbus A-300 (Franco-German)	1969–74	500

Sources: Peter W. Brooks, *The Modern Airliner* (London: Putnam, 1961), pp. 82, 86; Great Britain, Committee of Inquiry into the Aircraft Industry, *Report*, 1965 (Cmnd. 2853), p. 6; Frédéric Simi and Jacques Bankir, *Avant et Après Concorde* (Paris: Seuil, 1965), pp. 49, 106; R. G. Hubler, *Big Eight* (New York: Duell, Sloan and Pearce, 1960), passim; *Le Monde*, 2 February 1973, p. 8; Commission of the European Communities (Brussels), *A Policy for the Community for the Promotion of Industry and Technology in the Aeronautical Industry*, p. 49 (Annex III).
[a]Excludes engines except where indicated

European home market, could set a lower average price for a given plane. Moreover, because of the national compartmentalization of the European market, European manufacturers have had to export heavily in order to achieve any degree of cost competitiveness. Though total market estimates for different classes of civil airliners have varied considerably, European manufacturers have been forced by US competition to set initial prices which would require sales of 250 to 350 aircraft in order to reach the break-even point. Few European transport planes in the last twenty years have enjoyed this degree of success.[20]

In this context, European industry cannot be viable but with government backup – as explained by an industry official: 'Only if the government clearly commits itself to assisting the industry (e.g. via favourable financial terms, tax reliefs or preferential procurement policies) will national enterprises be able to develop appropriately and hopefully reach a level of efficiency comparable to that of other manufacturers elsewhere'.

The two relevant countries are Britain and France, the industries of which have 'enjoyed substantial government support and are by far the most highly developed in Europe'.[21] Smaller countries have not been able to commit sufficient resources to the industry to capture more than but a few segments of it (some, like the Dutch, quite successfully). And the German industry 'has not occupied a position of great importance in the eyes of successive Bonn administrations'.[22]

France and Britain have major airframe manufacturers (Aerospatiale and Dassault for France, and British Aerospace) and each a major aeroengine manufacturer (Snecma and Rolls-Royce). All are GCEs, except for Dassault. Yet, in June 1977 the French government decided to take a 34 per cent participation in this company as well (which would give it a *minorité de blocage* – effectively, a veto power).[23] This, plus the historical ties between Dassault and the state (primarily a function of the firm's dependence on government financing) may allow one to consider it – in the words of one interviewee – as a 'quasi GCE'. And in fact, Dassault has been under constant threat of nationalization since 1972 ('Dassault, whose financial and political power rests essentially on the importance of the public orders it enjoys, shall be nationalized'.)[24]

The governments have poured substantial amounts of money into these enterprises in the hope that they would give the country a significant and competitive role in the aeronautics field.[25] While Britain witnessed 'an indecisive on-again off-again government which started and stopped too many programmes',[26] France enjoyed a long period of stability and continuity in government policies.

In spite of such differences, the impact of government policies on companies' MN behaviour has been similar. The governments' objective is to encourage the creation of strong national industries. This has hampered the creation of larger European transnational undertakings. A French executive explained: 'In this industry, the urge to go MN does not manifest itself in terms of foreign direct investment. The importance of economies of scale commands that production be concentrated. Instead, what does make sense is to link up with other European companies in view of joining forces to reach the desirable critical mass which it has become impossible to reach within the national context alone'.

The need for transnational concentration has been discussed elsewhere.[27] And a few such linkups have actually occurred.[28] But because of governments' intervention, they have mostly been temporary joint ventures on specific projects and not permanent mergers: given their aim of national independence, governments have prevented firms from seeking permanent arrangements with foreign partners – the only true hope for Europeans to develop a viable industry of their own. As one interviewee put it:

> In this sector government policy is a true hindrance of transnational development. And here more than anywhere else, this development is needed. It is the only hope of being competitive ... This attitude of governments is myopic: to retain national autonomy, they stop companies from going European; but this is threatening for their very survival (even if their life can be artificially prolonged via subsidies) and thus in turn for the country's autonomy.

Hochmuth concludes: 'One is led to the inescapable conclusion that the basic factors in developing a successful aerospace industry are the size of the

home market and . . . the bedrock of government support'.[29] While government backup is necessary to ensure the viability of an aerospace industry, this
backup entails a nationalistic policy which hinders the Europeanization of the
industry and thus its long-term competitiveness.

e. Computers   Jéquier notes:

> Virtually every government in Europe today can claim to have a
> national computer policy. Only four countries, however, – the
> United Kingdom, France, Germany, and the Netherlands – have a
> significant and independent computer manufacturing industry.
> Furthermore, in these countries, the industry consists largely of
> one big nationally owned firm, a limited number of very small
> companies, and one or two big American subsidiaries. National
> policy amounts essentially to a special relationship between gov-
> ernment and the one big national firm.[30]

Among these countries, the Netherlands has left computer manufacturing to
the private sector (via Philips). In Germany, while the government has made
more explicit attempts to devise a sectorial policy, the industry is also in the
hands of private firms (Siemens and Nixdorf). Thus France and the UK are
again the two critical nations.

The situation here is somewhat *sui generis*. The British government has but
a minority interest in ICL (some 25 per cent of the capital through the
National Enterprise Board). While the French government's participation in
CII–Honeywell-Bull is indirect; CII was born in the late 1960s as a result of
the *Plan Calcul* – the government's plan for the development of an independent computer industry. The state's holding in CII was through IDI (the
state's development institute). In 1967, CII was merged with Honeywell-Bull.
The state's holding in the new group now goes through an intermediary
corporation – Compagnie des Machines Bull – which owns 53 per cent of the
capital of CII–Honeywell-Bull, the state owning a share of the capital of
Compagnie des Machines Bull. Still, as argued by Jéquier, these companies
are so dependent on the government for their survival that the sponsorship of
the state clearly goes farther than its actual participation in the capital.[31] As a
CII executive said: 'In the case of CII, for instance, the company was born
through the initiative of the government and the majority of its orders have
traditionally been government-sponsored. In fact, we may well be soon taken
over by the government altogether'. Jéquier thus argues: 'By the early 1970s it
was widely accepted that government had its *mot à dire* in the computer
industry and that national firms, while still partly privately owned, had in fact
become public enterprises'.[32]

The objectives of governmental policy are similar to those in the aerospace
industry. First, political – witness this quote concerning France: 'Our policy of
diplomatic independence would be meaningless if it didn't rest on real tech-

nological capabilities, particularly in the fundamental field of computers'.[33] Prestige is also important; and so are economic objectives: development of such a key *secteur de pointe* is seen as inducing technological progress in industry at large, and these byproducts are often considered as desirable as the results in the computer sector *per se*. These motives result in a policy attempting 'to maintain and develop a nationally owned industry which will also be economically viable in the long run'.[34] The means employed to foster such a policy have been threefold: 'The first was, and still is, financial support to research and development activities of the nationally owned computer firms. The second is the regrouping of national firms to form one single large company capable of withstanding competition on the world market. And the third is preferential government procurement'.[35] The first and third means were discussed in Chapter III; see also Table IV. 3.

The second means – that of national concentration – has been largely fostered in the UK by the IRC, which was instrumental in the successive consolidations which finally resulted in ICL (as illustrated by Figure IV. 1). In France, CII was the product of the union of CAE and SEA; and we saw that CII itself was then merged with Honeywell-Bull.

The consequences in terms of firms' MN behaviour are comparable to those in the aerospace sector: given the aim of making these companies national champions and the means employed, it is clear that foreign expansion is hindered.

Again size is a critical success factor, particularly in terms of R & D and marketing. Except for ICL, no European computer manufacturer is 'capable

Table IV.3   Government support to civilian R & D in the
European computer industry, 1966–75
(millions of US dollars at current exchange rates)

	Yearly average	
Country	1966–70	1971–75
United Kingdom	10[a]	25[b]
France	30	48
Germany	15[c]	44
Total	55	117

Sources: Gaps in Technology: Electronic Computers (Paris: OECD, 1969), Federal Republic of Germany, Ministry for Education and Science, *Zweites Datenverarbeitungsprogramm der Bundesregierung*, 1971; Eric Moonman, ed., *British Computers and Industrial Innovation* (London: Allen and Unwin, 1971); company reports and press releases.
  [a] 1968–70 period.
  [b] Preliminary estimates.
  [c] 1967–70 period.

78

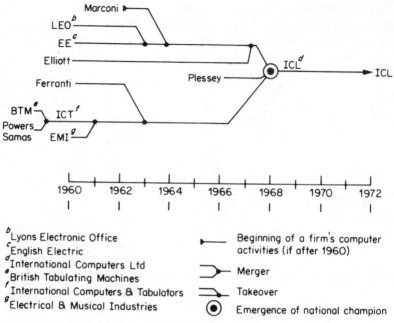

Figure IV. 1: Emergence of a National Champion in the U.K.
Source: Jéquier in Vernon (ed.), p. 215

of matching even the second tier of computer manufacturers in the United States'.[36] And again the solution to secure the appropriate size is transnational concentration: the pressure for size first led to a wave of domestic mergers, but this route is now mostly exhausted; further external growth must now come from the international route. Here too, government policy hinders this process. For political reasons (such as national security) governments insist on retaining the national identity of their firms. And – as alleged by a government official – 'to reap the by-products of R & D, this function must be performed at home; given the intimate relationship between R & D and production, the latter also cannot be done abroad . . . multinationalization of our computer company would result in a dilution of the national scientific patrimony'. Jéquier thus notes: 'In fact, there probably is a basic conflict, if not total incompatibility, between the support given by governments to their national champion and the often expressed need for a "European" strategy based on mergers'.[37]

Indeed, the only significant European transnational linkup has been UNIDATA – a common subsidiary owned by CII, Philips and Siemens – for the purpose of pooling marketing activities and coordinating R & D and production. This is of course far from a merger; and in fact, the agreement turned out to be a temporary one since the companies decided to terminate the venture in 1975.

The EEC Commission has developed its own computer policy.[38] This also highlights the need for this type of 'European' strategy. The first objective of this policy is to favour transnational concentration, which will enable European companies to reach a more competitive size. The second objective is to make sure that the subsidiaries of non-EEC MNCs abide by the Common Market's competition rules. The third is to ban preferential public procurement and establish a true common market. The first and third objective are in conflict with actual national government policies.

An industry executive concluded:

> In high technology industries, it is not enough to commit large resources to a development programme; it is essential to commit them at the right time. In the case of computers it would have been necessary to allocate the resources which are committed now ten years ago. Today there is a great lag to catch up. To succeed in creating a viable industry, two ingredients are necessary: government backup *and* a truly multinational strategy. This means that governments would have to develop a common policy *vis-à-vis* an industry which they would not be able to control individually as they please, since it would be transnational in character. In the eyes of many, this interferes with national sovereignty. I am not sure governments today could take this.

2. *Regionalization policy*

Practically every European country has certain depressed areas which it wants to develop. Governments' aim is to encourage industrial growth. Preference is given to labour-intensive sectors, since the typical problem is underemployment. Particular encouragement is given to investments which can induce other investments – which can 'secure a "multiplier effect" on the activities of other firms and thus on the character of activity in the sector as a whole'.[39] A case in point is an automobile plant which typically engenders other investments in subcontracting fields.

Many countries have used infrastructures and financial incentives to pursue these ends – liberal credit terms, tariff exemptions for machinery imports, lower tax rates etc. Beyond such measures, GCEs are expected to make a special contribution to regionalization policy. As a government official put it: 'Especially those GCEs which can be motors for industrial development (either by just showing the way or by creating a demand for components as well as peripheral activities – e.g. housing) are often under strong pressure to make regionalization policy the prime target of their activity'.

The typical case is Italy's South. The historically depressed character of the Mezzogiorno has been studied in depth.[40] The kernel of the problem lies in overpopulation and *miseria* (extreme poverty, malnutrition, lack of housing, etc.). Confronted with this situation, the government has three principal aims. First, it wants to ensure the location of more investment and more jobs in areas of low employment growth or actual employment decline. Second, it wants to develop self-sustaining industries in the South. Finally, it seeks to modernize agricultural methods.

Pressure is brought to bear upon GCEs to help implement these aims. In 1957, the government passed legislation requiring state holding companies to locate in the Mezzogiorno 60 per cent of the new plant investment and 40 per cent of total investment over a ten-year period ('new plant investment' refers to investments in any new production unit while 'total investment' includes also investments in existing facilities – for example, new equipment in an existing plant).[41] Subsequently, these requirements were raised. Today GCEs must invest in the Mezzogiorno at least 80 per cent of new plant investment and 60 per cent of total investment.[42] It is noteworthy that these are percentages of overall company investments – domestic and foreign combined. Besides, GCEs are pressured to commit themselves to the South beyond this legislation. As an Italian interviewee argued: 'GCEs' decisions have to be approved by the government. This gives it discretionary power over their actions . . . GCEs must conform to government planning . . . In particular, they receive clear directions as to the amount and type of investment they must carry out in the South'.

The success of this commitment to the Mezzogiorno is mixed. On one hand, it is true that GCEs have made substantial investments in the South.[43] 'The South did improve its relative position in some sectors, almost invariably those sectors in which state holdings were heavily represented. Also, as the state's holdings became diversified through the 1960s, more labor-intensive manufacturing enterprises became available for location in the South, including plastics, pharmaceuticals, food processing, aircraft assembly, automobiles',[44] which made a more substantial contribution in terms of employment creation relative to the earlier, more capital-intensive industries. Such investments sometimes not only created employment *per se* but engendered investments by others. An example is Alfa Sud – Alfa Romeo's economy car plant in the Naples area: 'The announcement of the project led Fiat to expand its investments in the South after it first opposed the government project. Pirelli followed Alfa and Fiat with the construction of a tire plant in the region'.[45]

But such investments have also aroused considerable criticism. IRI in particular has been accused of building 'cathedrals in the desert' – large industrial undertakings utilizing sophisticated technologies but unadapted to the local environment. Such investments were capital-intensive and required skilled labour unavailable locally: 'Since the state holdings in manufacturing enterprises were mainly capital-intensive – represented by steel, petrochemicals, heavy engineering and so on – the policy would not be likely to have a significant effect on employment'.[46] Further, these investments are not conducive to attracting other investments since they typically involve specialized and integrated activities. 'On the whole, they have not accomplished much in terms of being motors for the overall development of the South', said a government interviewee. And GCEs' investments in the Mezzogiorno have mostly proven non-viable economically, as reported by an IRI executive: 'Due to their unfavourable position on the learning curve caused by labour's inexperience, to the distance of sources of raw materials as well as from end markets, to the local socio-economic conditions, these ventures are mostly non-competitive costwise'.

True, part of these inefficiencies are being corrected, but now it appears that several GCEs' contribution to the Mezzogiorno is threatened by a deteriorating corporate performance, at least partly the result of precisely the earlier misdirected and disproportionate investment in the South.[47]

In France, regional planning was 'instituted in the 1950s but given promi- nence only in the Fifth Plan . . . It has as its principal object to overcome *le Désert Français*, the rather descriptive name for the phenomenon of economic underdevelopment in the provinces'.[48] There is in fact a state agency, DATAR, responsible for regional planning—'to harmonize the economic development over the whole national territory, and thus help create jobs in depressed areas'.[49]

GCEs are prime tools to implement regionalization policies. Yet, in the past – say up to the mid-1960s – GCEs have not always actively pursued the aims set forth by national planning.[50] Public authorities became concerned that they were not getting the appropriate use out of GCEs. This was one of the major conclusions of the 1967 Nora report – the report to the Prime Minister inquiring into the operations and problems of public enterprises.[51] Now – as reported by a Renault top executive – 'GCEs are under constant pressure to abide by regionalization planning . . . We really can't build a new plant without clearing it with the government . . . Regionalization policy is one of the most important determinants when we decide where to put our new facilities'.

Germany too has regions such as the North-East, Lower Saxony or Schles- wig which have witnessed less industrialization than the rest of the country. 'GCEs have a particular responsibility *vis-à-vis* these regions,' said an inter- viewee from the Ministry of Economic Affairs 'and they are pressured to invest there rather than elsewhere.' Thus, the shipyards are quite active in the Kiel region and Salzgitter AG is the key industry in the Salzgitter area. A good illustration of the effect of regionalization policy is provided by Volk- swagen. Over the years the company was partly denationalized and now the Federal Government and the state of Lower Saxony each have 20 per cent of the shares. But the two governments retain domination of the company;[52] and their influence has been strong in the decisions as to where new plants should be located. A company executive commented: 'We have six plants in Ger- many, five in Niedersachsen and one in Hessen. Each time we talk of a new investment, Niedersachsen puts pressure on us to do it here not just for the employment question but also for the tax returns this produces and all the induced side-effects a new investment triggers'. Thus Wells suggests that 'influence by the Federal Government was the principal reason behind the decision to build a plant in 1958 in Kassel, where there was a large unemployment problem'.[53]

In the UK, GCEs have been used relatively little for regionalization policy. Thus J. Driscoll, Managing Director Corporate Strategy of British Steel, claims that 'management doesn't do anything in terms of particular investments in particular regions which is not commercially viable'. Yet, management does recognize that there is 'some' influence by the government in the sense that between two locations of similar attractiveness to the firm, the company will be sensitive to the national interest in its choice between the two. Further, as one interviewee said, 'a GCE will be especially careful not to fire anybody in a depressed area unless absolutely necessary'.

Among the smaller countries, Ireland is the one with the most serious regional problems. Several parts of the country suffer from severe underindustrialization, and the government is endeavouring to correct this. However, we found that the government takes the position that, given that the country as a whole needs a considerable industrial investment, it is unwise to interfere with GCEs, particularly when they are growing healthily. 'There is always the risk of messing things up in a resilient organization if the government interferes', said a civil servant. 'It is better to leave companies on their own, especially when they are already contributing a great deal to national development'.

The other smaller countries also have some regional problems. On the whole, they too do not have an overall national plan for regional development and tend to tackle each problem on an *ad hoc* basis – deal with each pocket of underemployment with a special plan which often consists of an investment programme for a company negotiated between management and the government. An instance is the Dutch DSM which, as a result of government's influence, concentrates on the South and the North of the Netherlands, which both are less industrialized than the rest of the country and depend largely on DSM for their economic development.

Here too, the consequence of regional policy for GCEs' MN expansion are easy to understand: given GCEs are under pressure to invest in certain areas of the country, they will invest less elsewhere and notably abroad. An Italian government official said: 'You need a certain production level and it makes little sense to go beyond the output you can sell. If you have to locate your facilities for this output at home, there is no room for foreign production facilities'.

Thus regionalization policy particularly restrains labour-intensive GCEs from investing abroad in production facilities. One interviewee said: 'Companies are free of course to have foreign sales subsidiaries and indeed, they are encouraged to, since this should increase exports which in turn should create a greater need for domestic production and thus employment opportunities in less developed regions; but as far as manufacturing is concerned, regionalization policy calls for staying home'. In fact, this has a bearing on foreign assembly operations as well: given that this too involves labour-intensive activities, regionalization policy hinders the development of such operations abroad.

3. *Circumstantial policy*

This refers to *ad hoc* policies dictated by particular socioeconomic needs of a particular point in time. Three areas are especially relevant.

a. The grands équilibres *of the state*   Price stability, full employment and balance-of-payments equilibrium are the pillars of economic stability which are of prime concern to a government.

Over the last ten to fifteen years all European countries have witnessed recessions with rising unemployment. The conventional attitude of governments is then to adopt inflationary policies, increasing the money supply and thus hopefully spurring demand, which in turn is to trigger higher investment and consequently decrease unemployment. Yet, the wisdom of such traditional Keynesian economics has increasingly been questioned, essentially because the expected positive effects of such a policy—growth—were often slower to come than the negative byproducts – rapidly increasing prices. Indeed, 'the stimulation of demand by fiscal [and monetary] policy measures therefore may result in demand-pull inflationary pressure before long-term investment has resulted in production to satisfy the expanded demand'.[54] Thus governments have been inclined to intervene in a more direct and specific fashion. It is in this context that national planning developed by which the government stepped in directly in the industrial development of the nation, attempting to avoid the inefficiences caused by a totally free market economy (for example, bottlenecks in the supply of energy or raw materials) and trying to foster smoother growth with both less unemployment and limited inflation. To implement this, a new set of tools was necessary. GCEs were prime candidates.

In a period of recession, if it appears unwise to adopt inflationary policies to spur the economy, the government may encourage business to invest more than the actual level of demand would warrant. But such 'encouragements' are generally not mandatory. And private firms are more often than not reluctant to abide by them precisely because economic conditions do not justify increased investment. GCEs on the other hand, are expected to comply with government directives closely. In the words of a French interviewee: 'This is so not only to be prime contributors to national policies *per se* but also to show the example to the rest of business . . . If GCEs themselves were not to stick to governments' directives, how could one expect the rest of business to pay any attention to such directives?'

It should be no surprise that where GCEs have been under the strongest pressures is those countries with the deepest and more lasting economic problems. Here GCEs are expected to commit themselves to extensive investment to make up for the lagging activity of the private sector. Just as in the case of regionalization policy, the GCEs which are mostly concerned are those in labour-intensive sectors and those which are in 'driving' sectors – those most likely to be motors for the rest of the economy. While Britain has suffered from severe and lasting problems, it has not traditionally made as much use of GCEs to try and correct them as one might expect. It is Italy which provides the best illustration here, both because it has lived through several severe recessions and has many GCEs in labour-intensive and driving activities. After the so-called Italian miracle, Italy since about the mid-1960s has suffered serious economic difficulties with their origin in the unstable sociopolitical environment. Lately, these have worsened and the threat of the Communist Party reaching power has further deterred private investment. As an Italian interviewee argued: 'GCEs have been under pressure to invest heavily to keep economic activity alive and the unemployment rate at manageable levels to avoid further dangerous unrest, indeed a social explosion'. Beyond making new investments of their own, GCEs have the unrewarding role of absorbing failing companies to preserve employment. In fact in 1971, a special holding company was set up, GEPI, the task of which is 'to increase and speed up the number of rescue operations among ailing companies'.[55]

GCEs which have the task of sustaining the national economic activity cannot be expected to invest extensively abroad. The same argument holds as in the case of regionalization policy: 'One cannot do everything'. Further, as discussed in Chapter III, when GCEs are expected to be heavily involved domestically, each time they contemplate a foreign investment they encounter resistance on the part of their workers and the unions.

In the long run, a policy of investing *a priori* at home and rejecting any international investment opportunity is a threat to the economic standing of the firm – as argued by a British executive: 'With the internationalization of demand and the multinationalization of production, a firm which voluntarily limits its investments to domestic opportunities runs the risk of being undermined by competitors which capitalize on what often are more attractive investment locations'. A Finmeccanica executive said:

> The firm which is free to invest whereever it sees fit is clearly in a stronger long-run position . . . But GCEs today are often seen as having their major responsibility towards investing at home . . . When a firm is in this kind of situation, where it has to give priority to national growth even before it can worry about its profitability, it just can't expand outside national boundaries . . . In the present times of national economic crisis, this may well be our major hindrance for becoming multinational and at the same time this may well be the major threat to our long-term competitiveness.

b. GCEs as 'social pilots' When the government wishes to cause an innovation to happen in corporate practice on the social front, it frequently asks GCEs to put it into practice first. This then serves as a testing ground and as a model for the rest of industry. Examples include longer holidays, more worker participation, better working conditions, etc.

A case in point is Renault, which has always been at the forefront of French social progress. An illustration comes from the legal documents themselves stipulating its nationalization in 1945 and particularly the decree of March 1945 which, among other things, gave the company a *Comité d'Entreprise* – a committee composed of the chief executive and worker representatives, responsible for 'the collective conditions of work and of life of the personnel' as well as other worker-related questions.[56] As Anastassopoulos stresses: 'Renault was the first company to possess such a *Comité d'Entreprise*, which later was made compulsory for all companies – whether public or private'.[57] Renault has continued in its role as social pilot throughout its history. For instance, in 1950 the duration of paid vacation was extended from two to three weeks – a measure which was made compulsory in the spring of 1956 for all companies; and in 1966 Renault granted a fourth week of paid vacation, and again the rest of industry had to follow suit a year later.[58]

Such a method is especially effective when the government wants a reform to be implemented and business opposes it. In such cases, business most often takes the stance that a particular benefit to workers (say, an additional vacation week) is unbearable for industry. Rather than engage in an often distressing argument with business or to force a reform upon firms via legal action, the government finds it simpler and less disruptive to enforce the reform by having GCEs adopt it first. If successful, this usually indicates that the reform is, in fact, bearable. And it forces the generalized adoption of the reform, since workers in other firms fight to obtain the same treatment as their peers in GCEs.

Moreover, the government is especially anxious to keep the social climate as good as possible in GCEs and thus is inclined to look upon worker demands more favourably than do private employers; GCEs tend to be perceived as 'thermometers' of worker satisfaction and if, say, a strike develops in the public sector, it is likely that the unrest will spread to the rest of the industry, while if GCEs' workers are 'peaceful' chances are that social tensions will be relatively low. Therefore, 'GCEs are encouraged to give in more easily to workers' pressures in order to keep them calm', as a French interviewee put it. In fact, as an Italian executive pointed out: 'Since workers in GCEs often tend to have higher expectations than those of private enterprises, GCEs are under double pressure to be strongly socially committed: higher workers' demands as well as governmental pressure to keep a particularly good social climate, which also calls for higher benefits'.

The consequences are similar to those of worker attitudes discussed in Chapter III. The pressure for social progress is not in itself a real restraining force for MN expansion. Rather, the problem is one of competition for resources: several interviewees have argued that whenever a GCE builds up a cash flow of some importance, pressure builds up to commit this money to improvements in workers' conditions. One interviewee said:

> It should be clear that the issue is not real competition for funds in the context of a specific choice between two clear alternatives – a given expansion project abroad and a specific social investment domestically. Rather, it is much more a matter, so to speak, of corporate philosophy. In several instances, a clear choice appears to be made on the part of government to pressure GCEs to generally devote their best efforts to social progress. In such cases, overall corporate resources tend to be devoted with a clear preference to such ends, to the detriment of more potentially financially rewarding alternatives, among which MN expansion would often be a prime candidate.

And a Belgian executive added: 'It is really a matter of corporate "state of mind": do you want to emphasize growth and profitability or social progress? In many cases, GCEs tend towards the latter . . . This involves an opportunity cost for MN expansion'.

c. Special interventions in the economy   A government can ask a GCE to accomplish a specific task at a given time. Three types of instances are noteworthy.

The first is the restructuring or reconversion of a sector. The government may feel a particular sector is weak, because perhaps it is too fragmented or because not enough funds are committed to R & D or new equipment. If it feels that sector is critical for the country (for military reasons, for instance), it may decide to step in and reorganize it. It may do this via one or several GCEs. We should point out that usually there is no will on the part of government to actually control the sector involved. It is only because it considers the private sector is not doing what it thinks it should that it asks one of its companies to intervene. (In fact, it is quite conceivable that, once the reorganization is accomplished, the GCE will step out from the sector*.) A good example of this type of intervention is provided by EFIM – as reported by Dr Ducio Valori: 'Over the years we have been asked to get involved in a variety of industries. An instance is the railroad equipment industry, which we were asked to try and turn around. The motivations were a mix of the feeling that the sector was important for the economy at large and the desire to preserve jobs. If we succeed, we may well get out of this sector'.

---

*Yet this is relatively rare in practice because the government tends to step in primarily in ailing sectors and is often unable to turn them around and make them attractive enough for private enterprise; further, when such a turnaround does occur, this runs into political problems such as leftist criticisms that the government allegedly gives industries which have benefited from the injection of public resources away to private capitalists who unduly benefit from the returns which should in fact accrue to the collectivity.

The second instance is reinforcing competition. As argued by Holland, antitrust policy is not always effective in oligopolistic situations, particularly in inflationary conditions in which 'a dominant company may not draw government attention to no-entry or elimination prices . . . by simply holding [prices] stable at a time when the rising costs of inputs for itself and its competitors reduces actual or potential profit margins, only raising them after it has deterred entry or taken over the competitor concerned'.[59] Further, given that antitrust legislation is far from stringent (especially when compared to the US), governments lack the legal tools to monitor free competition. Therefore, they have not infrequently resorted to GCEs to check antitrust abuses. By controlling the key firm in an industry, the state can 'mobilize the oligopolistic mechanisms concerned in its own and thus the public interest'.[60]

'To the extent that the state controls the investment and pricing behaviour of a leading firm through total or partial share ownership, and inasmuch as that firm is a market leader within a given sector, the state is enabled to influence the prices within that market and to keep them competitive over the long run'.[61] This method is especially useful when a particular industry is controlled by a foreign company. In such instances, the government is even more powerless to monitor the behaviour of the firms directly. So, rather than attempting to force the industry to follow a given behaviour, it is easier for the state to intervene directly in the market via a firm of its own. This then involves the creation of a new activity in the field. This is what happened for example in the case of the Italian market for flat glass. The market was dominated by three giants BSN, Saint-Gobain and Pilkington. In the 1960s it became apparent that the Italian market was supplied at higher than normal prices. Thus EFIM decided to enter this market on its own and supply it at more reasonable prices. Interestingly enough, there have been speculations that, given its lack of 'experience' in this field, EFIM was pricing its glass at levels which were too low to enable it to make a profit, indeed to break even.[62] It did so essentially to oblige its competitors to bring their prices down and not to itself capture a major position on this market.

The third instance is coping with MNCs. The pros and cons of MNCs for a host country are well known. The pros include the transfer of technical and managerial know-how, the fact that MNCs are often good exporters (that is, they export a good deal of what they produce locally, which entails positive balance-of-payments effects) and their contribution to regional development, which can normally be considered positive.[63] But MNCs also pose a number of problems. These include the risk of transfer price manipulation in view of minimizing taxes due to the host country, the possibility of speculation against the national currency, the fact that often little R & D is actually done locally, the threat of increased competition for local companies with the consequence that their growth may be jeopardized and the overall threat to national sovereignty (that is, key sectors controlled by foreign firms whose decision centers are located abroad).[64] Further, MNCs have a history of frequently disrupting the local socioeconomic environment by rash decisions such as abrupt layoff decisions.

In this context, governments have increasingly tried to monitor foreign investments without losing the benefits thereof. This frequently involves GCEs.

Thus, joint ventures are frequently encouraged between an MNC and a local firm. This allows the preservation of most of the benefits of foreign investment while checking at least part of the negative byproducts of MNCs going it alone. In several cases, local partners can be found in the private sector. But in others, private firms are just not available. For example, in high-technology sectors, private firms are often just not prepared to commit the necessary funds and face the risks involved. A GCE may then be asked to step in.

A GCE is in fact a greater guarantee for the government than a private firm. A GCE is more reliable in terms of the avoidance of improper practices such as transfer pricing manipulation or undue layoffs.

> In general, such joint ventures ensure a much more effective sur-
> veillance of the partner's activity than is possible for a part-time
> state nominee on a multinational's board. Continual participation
> in management decision-making at all levels can permit the
> scrutiny of proposals before they have become company policy,
> and thus anticipate rather than react to investment decisions once
> they have been taken.[65]

In other instances, a GCE's intervention may take the form of bailing out an ailing subsidiary of an MNC. As mentioned earlier, MNCs have often proceeded with disruptive shutdowns. Further, they have used the weapon of such closures to bargain with local authorities and unions ('They actually blackmail you', said a British unionist). As a response, a government may ask a GCE to be prepared to step in and take over the plants which an MNC might close. An Italian interviewee said: 'The fact that they [the MNCs] know that there is a competent GCE ready to step in in the case of misconduct or threat thereof, is a major deterrent for using this type of argument [that of threatening to close a plant] in the bargaining processes with local admini-strations and employees'.

Finally, a GCE many be asked to stop the takeover of a national company by an MNC. A GCE may pre-empt the company before the MNC's takeover bid has succeeded. Monotti's findings illustrate this:

> IRI secured control in the later 1960s of two of the main national
> food processing and distributing companies which were threatened
> with takeover by US companies. In these and other cases, such as
> the Innocenti steel and motor vehicle company, IRI no doubt
> benefited in part from the desire of firms to remain Italian, and
> also from the concern of their unions that the companies should
> not pass outside Italian control.[66]

An alternative tactic is for a GCE to secure a joint venture takeover with a national private company. This tactic was used in the case of Westinghouse's bid for key Italian firms in electromechanical engineering, and, particularly, nuclear power plants. Again, IRI stepped in and proposed an agreement between its own electromechanical engineering companies and Fiat.[67] This kind of tactic too can work as a persuasive device to deter an MNC from trying to take over a national company even before the local bid agreement is carried though: as Holland found, a GCE's 'backing for a threatened company tends to be sufficient to ensure that a multinational challenger calls off his bid'.[68]

The implications of this are once more that MN expansion is hindered. An interviewee argued: 'It is true that each of these interventions is a one-shot deal which, once accomplished, does not require continuing commitment. But the problem is that there is always a new task to accomplish. Thus, our commitment to one-shot deals often becomes a permanent one.' Indeed, we found many GCEs which reported they had 'always one of these *ad hoc* missions to pursue', as one president said, 'with the result that this has become a permanent feature of our life'. In these cases, it is clear that other ventures are deterred. Particularly the task of coping with MNCs' results in GCEs often finding themselves owning new productive capacity which might not necessarily be warranted. As an Italian interviewee put it: 'These special interventions in the economy usually result in an increase of our production potential. Our problem then is to find the markets on which to unload this capacity. But rarely is there room for incremental production abroad'. So, not only do these tasks limit the resources for foreign investments, but they also frequently limit the use of such investments in the first place.

B. Pressures against MN expansion *per se*

GCEs are also hindered in going abroad by certain policies against MN expansion as such – governments exerting pressure on GCEs not to invest abroad in view of avoiding certain perceived negative consequences entailed by foreign investment *per se*. There are two broad categories of pressures.

1. *Pragmatic motives*

Governments may feel foreign investment is bad because of tangible, practical negative effects it has on the country's economic and social situation. Specifically, governments may see negative effects in terms of balance of payments and employment. In Stobaugh's words, governments' attitude rests on the following reasoning or theory:

> [The] theory holds that the multinational enterprises are free to locate their plants in countries with low labor costs and sell the resulting products in other countries with the largest markets and highest prices. Those subscribing to this theory assure that the . . .

> multinational enterprise could retain its markets by expanding
> production in the [home country] but, instead, chose to expand
> abroad. An analysis based on this assumption typically shows that
> the effect of a foreign direct investment on the [home country's]
> balance of payments is negative, primarily because of the loss of
> ... exports [for the country].[69]

Further, in this view, foreign direct investment also entails negative employment effects for the country: given that a company chooses to make a foreign direct investment as a substitute for exports which would be supplied by nationally produced goods, the foreign-produced goods entail an opportunity cost in terms of domestic production and employment: 'Since there is a strong relationship between trade and employment, it might be expected that if a foreign investment had a negative impact on the [home country's] balance of payments because of lost ... exports, then ... employment would be reduced'.[70]

Countries with balance-of-payments and employment problems have therefore adopted measures to spur exports and limit foreign direct investment. They have devised incentives such as export credits (financing at favourable terms for the exporting firm) or fiscal advantages; governments have also created special agencies to assist firms in their exporting effort (for example, the French BFCE or COFACE). Such measures are a deterrent to foreign direct investment, in that firms being able to serve foreign markets via cheaper exports are less inclined to set up production facilities abroad. Further, governments can use measures such as exchange controls, which also temper foreign investments since firms are unable to export capital for such projects.

Obviously, such measures are only partially effective. Export incentives indeed distort the normal economic forces in favour of exports and thus decrease the relative attractiveness of the foreign investment route. But on the whole, they at best delay foreign investment. In fact, given foreign markets conquered at first via exports typically call for direct investment in order to be retained, the higher exports engendered by export incentives in time actually should call for greater foreign investment.[71] It is at least safe to say that, over time, higher exports do not result in significantly lesser foreign direct investment. Further, measures designed to limit direct investment via exchange controls can only hope to have a limited impact: if a firm cannot export capital, it will raise it locally or on international capital markets.

The government therefore cannot hope to stop foreign investment through such policies. This puts a particular burden on GCEs. In fact, GCEs are often under a double pressure. On one hand, the government does not want GCEs to add to its problems and thus exerts pressure on them not to go abroad as an end in itself. On the other, it wants GCEs to serve as an example and is thus especially concerned that they abide by its antiforeign investment policies. An Italian executive stated:

Italy today has high unemployment and balance-of-payments deficit. The private sector is insensitive to governmental directives; it has never taken them seriously anyway, and today there is a further confidence problem both in the country's future and in the government; the result is that industrialists have only one concern – export capital to safer places. This is obviously the contrary of what the government seeks when it wants to discourage Italian investment abroad. So only GCEs are left to help put the governmental policies into practice because they are the only ones which the government can coerce. In this situation, for a GCE to make a foreign investment requires considerable justification in terms of showing that the investment is an absolute necessity not only from the company's viewpoint but also from that of the country.

2. *Dogmatic motives*

A government expects a certain type of behaviour from a GCE not because of practical economic needs but because of general principles about what it thinks corporate behaviour ought to be. There are essential motives to be identified.

a. Sticking to the corporate mission Several GCEs have a well-defined activity, either explicitly (for example, in their nationalization act or their by-laws) or implicitly (as a tacit understanding between the management, the government and the public at large). Often the government insists that the company abide by this definition 'as a matter of principle' and this limits diversification. Such a limit can apply both to product and geographical diversification.

A good illustration is provided by natural resource industries where the natural resources are on the national territory: GCEs in such industries are frequently expected to refrain from becoming active abroad. The difference with sectorial policies is precisely that here there are no such policies. As a German executive put it: 'Firms pursue a particular product market strategy and not another, in view of "values" – subjective preferences of the government – and not in view of any concrete objective to pursue'. For example, Charbonnages de France and the National Coal Board were until recently hindered in investing abroad in mining operations. It is only a few years since, due to the intensification and internationalization of competition in the coal sector, these companies were granted the possibility of becoming involved in mining abroad, though even now explicit government authorization is normally required.[72] In particular in the UK, the 1946 Coal Industry Nationalization Act clearly limits the production activities of the Board to Great Britain (though the 1949 Coal Industry Act removed these restrictions subject to consent being granted by the responsible government minister by means of a statutory instrument; and the Coal Industry Act 1977 spells out the relaxation of the 1946 Act in more detail and simplifies the procedure of the minister granting consent for the Board to go abroad).

In Germany, companies such as the Bayerische Braunkohlen Industrie or Rheinische Braunkohlen Werke 'could never – in the words of Herr Oetel, a *Vorstandsmitglied* of the former company – dream of either diversifying in other products or become active in other areas, because we know we are expected, on principle, to fulfil a very specific mission which forecloses any possibility of becoming active in other fields'.

Another illustration is provided by companies which, although in the competitive sector, provide a service to the public. The best instance is airlines. Airlines are under increasing pressure – from a microeconomic standpoint – to enter into so-called 'ancillary' activities. These include hotels, catering, or even the computer industry. Such activities are attractive because of their synergistic fit with the main activity of the company. Many airline executives complain that their government creates difficulties when they contemplate a diversification move, on pure dogmatic grounds. 'There seems to be some kind of magic stigma about sticking to flying airplanes and we have a hard time doing other things even if they are related to flying aeroplanes and if they make obvious economic sense', said one company president. And another interviewee added: 'Clearly this does not mean that airlines cannot engage in any diversification. Indeed, they do. But the point is that they are *limited* in their diversification by governments' *a priori* principles'.

Foreclosing diversification in general also limits diversification abroad. In the case of airlines this is especially critical because of the natural international character of most diversification moves (for example, investment in a hotel chain usually results in the majority of the investments being abroad).

b. Restraining international development per se   In several instances, governments are dogmatically opposed to MN expansion *per se*. A Belgian executive said, 'Clearly, there is always the presumption that concentrating on domestic activities will do more for the country's economy and workers; but this notion is so intuitive and vague that it is as if "staying home" should be taken as a principle of good conduct in its own right which requires no explanation'.

A good illustration is provided by 'special purpose' financial institutions which can be hindered in developing their activities in an international sense. Examples include IDI (the French Institut de Développement Industriel) – a government-controlled institution involved in financing companies with a high growth potential – or other comparable organizations such as the Irish Industrial Credit Company or the Société Belge d'Investissement. While such institutions are naturally constrained by the national plan, they are in addition constrained by dogmatic motives: whereas the plan could in fact conceivably lead them to legitimately engage in international operations, they usually do not. Thus, an Irish interviewee said: 'Only in exceptional cases would the Industrial Credit Company get involved in financing a firm which is multinational in scope'. Société Belge d'Investissement has only recently engaged in such ventures and even here only as a partner with private financing houses (particularly the Lambert group). One interviewee said:

> We have to operate in the national context beyond the require-
> ments of the Plan. Not only would it be inconceivable for us to
> take a participation in a foreign firm, but it would also be difficult
> for us to finance a firm with sizeable growth outside the country.
> We would be accused of failing in our mission of helping the
> growth of national industry even if we could demonstrate that the
> firm's international growth in fact helps its domestic development.
> It is a tacit rule of good conduct that companies such as ours
> *should* have a national scope.

c. Hindering the growth of the public sector   Conservative governments typically have not helped the development of GCEs and have often tried to limit their opportunities for expansion relative to the private sector. Thus the German Christian Democrats (CDU) have traditionally tried to limit the scope of the public sector and in fact have partially turned certain companies back to the private sector by selling shares to the public (for example, Volkswagen or VEBA). In the words of Dr Konrad Ende, *Vorsitzender des Vorstandes* of Deutsche Schachtbau und Tiefbohr GmbH, 'The CDU has never liked GCEs. Particularly as long as Erhard was in power, GCEs were black sheep. He didn't want GCEs and never really worried about them. He deliberately penalized them by neglecting them'. In the UK too the Tories have frequently favoured private industry *vis-à-vis* GCEs. For example, in the airline sector, the now merged BOAC and BEA have often complained that private airlines were being favoured. In the words of the British Airways' Chairman, David Nicolson: 'The conservative government favoured the private sector. It wanted it to grow and didn't want the public sector to become too big. For instance, the guidelines the government gave to the Civil Aviation Authority were to give preference to private companies for the allocation of new routes'.

Hindering GCEs' expansion in general is also clearly detrimental to their MN expansion. In fact. as noted by a German interviewee, 'it frequently happens that when the government is anti-GCEs it is especially concerned that they don't expand overseas. Abroad, it feels it can't control them as readily and that their growth may therefore go unchecked'.

II. DRIVING FORCES FOR MN EXPANSION

There are government pressures for GCEs to develop abroad both for sectorial motives and for macro or national motives.

A. Sectorial policy

Just as sectorial policies call for a certain type of domestic development, they can also call for a certain type of international expansion. The key sectors are those involving natural resources: when a country has no natural resources of its own in a sector which the government considers vital either for economic or for political reasons, it encourages the relevant GCEs to become directly involved in the extraction abroad of these resources.

1. *Iron and steel*

Italy provides the best illustration. As discussed earlier, Finsider has been successful in developing a modern, large and efficient steel industry in a country practically devoid of natural resources. While Finsider has built several integrated plants in Italy in which the full production process takes place, it must seek the necessary raw materials abroad – notably iron ore and coking steel. For the procurement of such raw materials, two main routes are available: either buy them on international markets or get involved in the mining via direct foreign investment in such activities. The former requires little investment. Given the pressures GCEs are under to develop at home, one might expect that Finsider would have taken this route in order not to divert financial and human resources from its national responsibilities. Yet, the latter route was chosen. The reason is that this maximized the government policy's objective of giving the country the highest autonomy possible in terms of steel production: by getting directly involved in mining, the company reduces its dependence on the whims of the international markets for raw materials. As a company executive put it: 'Such involvement is considerable because today if one wants to have a safety in raw materials' procurement, one has to have a direct stake in mining or at least be a key element in the financing of the mining operations'. Clearly, this does not foreclose the possibility of a crisis in the supply of raw materials, since the mining occurs in a foreign nation state which can, at any time, block the mining process. But this at least minimizes the risks as much as possible – as argued by a government official: 'Given Italy has little raw materials of its own, the most we can do to monitor our supply is to secure direct influence over the mining. While this does not protect us from political action by the foreign country involved, it at least gives us some control over the economic variables – the market forces which otherwise have a bearing on the supply of raw materials'.

The aim of achieving autonomy by securing control of the sources of raw materials is in fact a very strong driving force for MN expansion for companies such as Finsider. It is not only stronger than the tool goal pressures which call for staying home, but also constitutes an active driving force for MN expansion beyond what would be called for by the profit objective alone. If Finsider were only concerned with maximizing its own profits, it would not have insisted as much on getting involved in foreign mining. Company executives argue that from a purely business point of view, being dependent on independent foreign suppliers is in fact not a major risk. In the words of one of these men:

> A company which is only concerned with its own economic performance will not be concerned with controlling its sources of supply. The investment is not always worth it, in that the risks you eliminate are really not major ones relative to the importance of the investment. But from the country's point of view, the value of reducing such risks is much greater and does justify the investment.

2. Oil

Again, a country with no crude oil of its own can either rely on free market forces – that is, depend on private MNCs – or devise an oil policy which attempts to give the state more of a direct handle on the oil supply. The larger European countries have opted for the latter alternative (the UK's policy is now geared primarily to the exploitation of its North Sea reserves).

This policy means that the relevant GCEs must not only be active in downstream operations but also be directly involved in upstream operations – exploration, drilling and production of crude oil. This involvement has been considered even more vital than in the steel sector. While in the case of steel it is possible to buy the raw materials from a relatively broad range of sources in a relatively competitive market, in the case of oil, world markets are quite oligopolistic with a few giants – 'the seven sisters' – effectively controlling the market, including the sources of raw materials. A company not involved in upstream operations has inevitably been dependent on foreign suppliers which are cartelized. While this situation has evolved in recent years with oil-producing countries taking a more active role in the production of crude oil, traditionally this is the situation with which most states have been confronted. Their response has been to press their GCEs to get involved in upstream operations. In the words of an oil company president: 'It is worth emphasizing that in the case of oil, this was of special importance: countries were not only dependent on foreign raw materials but also on foreign economic entities to extract and supply them. While the first dependence is inevitable, the latter can be reduced'. In the words of a French executive: 'We can at least control the exploitation of the resources. This is a sizeable risk-reducing element. Further, this can also reduce the political risk by enabling us to have direct relations with the local authorities. At least, we are better informed about these relations and maybe we are also able to have better relations than private MNCs'.

Probably the most experienced company in this category is CFP. ENI is also quite active. After the early years during which exploration and production were concentrated on the national natural gas fields (such as the Po valley), ENI turned increasingly to exploration and extraction abroad. And notwithstanding the relatively recent German policy, Deminex is giving priority to 'securing crude oil for ourselves – finding it, drilling it and processing it', as its President, Dr Logters, said, while Gelsenberg's only major foreign investments are in the crude-oil-seeking area – particularly in Libya.

It should be pointed out that again the policy of securing independence can be a strong force in shaping GCEs' MN behaviour – as suggested by one chief executive:

> If GCEs didn't have the aim of being present as much as possible in all the phases of the production cycle, they would most probably invest less in foreign activities and rely more on foreign producers for their crude oil supply. In many cases this would be more efficient from the company's own economic standpoint. The real value of direct access to sources of raw materials is to the country.

In this connection, an executive of the privately owned Petrofina posed an interesting issue:

> From our point of view, GCEs' behaviour is hard to predict because they obviously don't always operate according to economic criteria, particularly when upstream operations are involved. For example, ENI invests in certain African countries when everybody else is thinking of getting out because of political risks – particularly nationalizations. They seem to have a propensity to take risks which are unjustified by the expected returns.

This question was subsequently taken up with GCEs and ENI in particular. The explanation is clear:

> GCEs don't always operate according to microeconomic criteria [said one interviewee]. In the case of investments in upstream operations, the expected returns are not just in terms of corporate financial results. The emphasis is much more on increasing the national autonomy . . . What such investments do for the country is much more than what they do for the company; and the risks involved are well worth taking from the national viewpoint.

B. Macro or national motives

For macro economic as well as for political reasons the government may ask a GCE to go abroad.

1. *Economic reasons*

There are several instances in which a government can wish that certain investments be made in given foreign countries. While this can occur via private enterprises, GCEs are often the prime vehicle for such investments.

The best illustration is provided by several countries' relations with oil-exporting nations. After the 1973 oil crisis especially, governments have found it increasingly desirable to pay the more than quadrupled oil bill with other means than hard currency – industrial investments in particular. From the host country's viewpoint, this is attractive since it brings badly needed know-how. From the home country's standpoint, this is also attractive since it enables it to exploit its comparative advantage – to pay with technology and managerial resources.

The companies which are prime candidates are those where the activity is most germane to the oil-exporting country's development requirements. These are first activities directly connected with oil – for example, construction companies and suppliers specialized in refineries. And given the aim of reaping the benefits of integration, ancillary activities such as petrochemicals, synthetic fibres and engineering are important – since local governments are eager to exploit their resources both *in loco* and on their own. But oil-exporting countries are also anxious to broaden their industrial base and create a wide range of manufacturing activities. Particular emphasis is given to manufacturers of key products for the national development (for example, construction equipment) and to investments which can in turn induce economic development (such as the car industry). Besides, there is often a concern for military and prestige considerations which can be conducive to high technology-type investments.

Beyond foreign direct investment as such, oil-exporting nations seek to participate in the transfer of technology by some form of association with foreign companies, for example, joint ventures between a foreign company and local capital (private or public). Another form of association is the contracting of foreign firms to develop a project which in time will be turned over to locals. Turnkey operations are a case in point.

Oil-importing countries try to use their GCEs to meet the expectations of oil-exporting nations. The best instances are found where there is a large variety of GCEs to undertake a wide range of investments. France is a good instance not only because it has a vast public sector but also because its balance of payments has been under particular pressure after the oil crisis – as explained by a Renault executive:

> France has been particularly motivated to pay in other ways than through currency. So the government has encouraged industry to invest in oil-exporting countries. True, private companies have also participated in this effort. But GCEs have a clear role as leaders . . . Very often when the government wants a certain pattern of investment to develop, it comes to GCEs first. We are expected to open the way; then the rest of industry will follow.

Another GCE executive said: 'Private companies abide by government policies *if* they find that this is good for them . . . But *we* can be persuaded to make an investment even if it is not as attractive for us as we would like it to be'.

Another instance is Italy. The country has the most diversified public sector in the EEC, which can offer a broad spectrum of investments indeed. First, ENI itself is involved in a variety of endeavours going from petrochemicals to textiles. Then, the other state holdings combined – IRI, EFIM, GEPI – offer an almost complete range of industrial activities. And, as Dr Romolo Arena, IRI's *direttore centrale*, said: 'Our diversified activities can offer an appealing package indeed for an oil exporting country; but beyond this, we can be useful because of our experience in developing backward regions; our experience in the Mezzogiorno is directly applicable in many instances to the problems of an LDC; this makes us particularly attractive for OPEC nations'.

This is what an Italian interviewee termed 'conglomerate strategy of GCEs'. GCEs belong to the same owner – the state – and it is its benefits they must maximize. From the state's viewpoint, the performance of the public sector in general – and not solely in financial terms – is more important than the performance of the individual GCEs. 'Therefore, coordination among GCEs is warranted not just in view of economic results but also in terms of socio-political benefits', said our interviewee. Since most European states have oil GCEs of their own, there is an opportunity to coordinate the 'give and take' with oil-exporting countries – the needs of the oil companies and the offerings of the other GCEs.

Again, Italy is a good illustration. Here there are considerable opportunities to pursue this policy not only because of the breadth and depth of the public sector but also because of its setup. The IRI holding company structure is designed to leave the individual operating companies considerable freedom in the conduct of their daily affairs, while allowing the parent to monitor their strategic choices. This sets the grounds for coordination of the group's activities. To take a domestic example, in the case of the development of the Mezzogiorno, IRI's effort can be effective if coordination takes place among its various sectors. Thus, Finsider's steel plants have to be complemented by mechanical construction plants which use this steel; Finmeccanica's Alfa Romeo plant in the South, for instance, can do just that.[73] This approach is not only good for the company in view of the resulting synergy, but is also desirable for the region since it extends the scope of the investments with the consequent employment benefits. Beyond the structure of GCEs, there is a ministry for state holdings whose role is to plan and control the doings of GCEs. It has the power to monitor their strategic choices and thus to coordinate them. In particular, *vis-à-vis* foreign expansion, it can make sure GCEs do not 'go it alone'. In the words of a direct collaborator of Italy's Minister of State Holdings, Antonio Bisaglia: 'Our duty is to make sure that these enti don't move in Italy and especially abroad, each one on its own. They must go abroad with one common policy. Particularly with IRI and ENI, we must coordinate the latter's activity as a "taker" with the former's activity as a "giver"'

This system has been taken as a model in several instances. Thus, the Rapport Nora calls for a comparable set-up for France:

> Sectoral holding companies should be established, and the possibility of a central holding organization on the lines of the Italian IRI be considered. If such a central holding mechanism were established, rather than a variety of separate holdings at the sectoral level, the government could use the state companies more effectively as instruments of national planning. At the same time, the principle of the state-holding organization would overcome the confusion that might arise from maintaining central planning and decentralized public enterprise side by side.[74]

2. *Political reasons*

A government can ask a GCE to make a certain investment in a given country in the context of its foreign policy – to contribute to the development of good relations with that country. A German interviewee said: 'When the government wants to foster its relations with a country, it often finds it desirable that these relations materialize in mutually beneficial economic actions such as an increase in trade or – more significantly – actual industrial ventures in that country'.

True, private companies may feel this type of pressure from the government as well. But when a government tries to initiate a flow of investments in a country especially, the first projects are typically of uncertain profitability. Therefore, private business is quite reluctant to abide by the state's pressure. 'GCEs are once more the only ones to serve the state faithfully', said a French interviewee, 'since we are the only ones which *must* comply with the government's directives'.

There are many instances of such politically minded ventures. Thus, Renault's involvement in Canada in the 1960s was consistent with the government's desire to develop preferential ties with this country.[75] Similarly, in Germany when the Brandt administration launched its Ostpolitik, the government encouraged German industry to become involved in Eastern countries. Private industry went along with this policy, but interviewees feel that while private firms thought twice before embarking on such ventures and were naturally made cautious by their concern for their economic performance, GCEs were more prepared to just comply with government pressures. And the French government asks its GCEs to make a particular effort to locate some industrial investments in its ex-colonies with which it maintains friendly ties.

Such political pressures can also occur in service industries. For example, airlines are asked to operate certain uneconomical routes. Thus, when Air France opened its Paris–Peking route it was the time when France was establishing diplomatic ties with Red China. When Ireland joined the EEC, Air

Lingus was asked to open a second daily flight between Dublin and Brussels 'so that civil servants may go to Brussels in the morning and return in the evening'.[76] Further, several interviewees referred to a hypothetical instance: should the North Atlantic route become even more unprofitable, it would be conceivable that on pure economic grounds an airline would contemplate reducing its flights on this route dramatically. Reflecting management's views, one interviewee said: 'In such a case the government would invariably step in and practically force us not to do so, given the political importance of this route'.

Pressures for foreign investment can be exerted on GCEs on the basis of the sheer political power such investments yield. An illustration was furnished by a French oil company which reported the government encouraged it to broaden its scope to MN dimensions and also to secure access to crude oil 'in order to establish France's role in the vital field of international distribution of energy'.

III. PRESSURES FOR PARTICULAR PATTERNS OF MN BEHAVIOUR

Government policies result in pressures on GCEs to have a particular *modus operandi* on an international level. Four points are in order.

A. Abiding by general government policies and regulations

GCEs have to stick to general rules of conduct advocated by the government especially closely.

1. *Hedging and speculating*

An MNC can hedge against a devaluation or a re-evaluation by either delaying or accelerating payments in the currency concerned. This is the technique of so-called leads and lags by which a company pays its liabilities in a currency expected to revalue faster and delays its receipts in such a currency until the re-evaluation has occurred; and delays the payments in a currency expected to devalue while trying to accelerate its receipts in such a currency until the devaluation has occurred. This obviously makes sense from the company's point of view. But from the country's point of view this is disruptive because it puts further strain on its currency (in particular 'the withholding of payments . . . can contribute to the necessity for a devaluation which otherwise might be avoided precisely by reducing the value of registered exports during a critical period'.[77]) This in fact can be even worse when MNCs go beyond hedging and begin speculating: if a currency is under pressure to revalue, for instance, MNCs may buy massive amounts of it in the hope of its appreciation. But by so doing they increase the demand for that currency and thus put upward pressure on it, which ultimately results in a revaluation. This is a self-fulfilling prophecy.

Governments try hard to dissuade companies from engaging in such trans-actions when their currency is under pressure. But this is hard to enforce. For intrafirm payments in particular, 'it is virtually impossible for anyone outside the company to know to what extent such practices are being employed, and to what extent explanations of other reasons for such withholding of pay-ments are valid'.[78]

The situation is different when the government is the owner. What is the attitude of the government *vis-à-vis* GCEs: does it allow GCEs to pursue their micro interests and protect themselves against currency fluctuations or does it expect them to help it pursue its macro aims and refrain from protecting themselves in view of its fight for its currency's stability?

On the whole, governments tend to take the former attitude. It appears that only when two elements are combined does the government take the latter – when the national currency is under chronic pressure and when the public sector is vast enough and sufficiently widespread internationally to make a difference if influenced, that is, have an impact on the currency if it manages its finances one way or another. Italy is currently in this situation: due to the deteriorating socioeconomic situation, the lira has been weak for many years – and the public sector is big. An official from the Bank of Italy said: 'An intervention in GCEs' financial management can unquestionably have a noticeable impact on the balance of payments. Indeed, when the pressure on the lira is particularly strong and when we intervene to sustain its value, GCEs are asked to cooperate by not putting further strain on the national currency'.

But on the whole, GCEs feel they are relatively free to hedge against currency fluctuations. 'The government understands this is sound business practice', said a British interviewee. 'Except for extreme situations, protecting oneself is regarded as legitimate', said a French interviewee, 'otherwise we would be too much at a disadvantage *vis-à-vis* private firms'.

On the other hand, speculation as such is banned. Interviewees were unanimous in saying that this behaviour is considered improper and that a government will stop a GCE from trying to make a profit by exploiting the national currency's weakness. A French interviewee said:

> The government believes that this is first of all not our business; we are to make a living by manufacturing and selling goods, not by gambling in financial deals of this sort; in fact, an important con-sideration is the risk of being wrong – everybody wants to avoid the risk of being embarrassed by losses in this kind of game. Sec-ond, and even more important, by speculating we go in a sense against our own interests. We are part of the state's apparatus and speculating means we go against the state . . . It is not only immoral but also a contradiction for a GCE to speculate against its own country's currency.

102

2. *Transfer pricing*

MNCs have come under repeated criticism for manipulating transfer prices in view of minimizing the firm's tax liability – 'the fixing in intra-firm transactions of low prices in high tax areas and high prices in low tax areas'.[79] This makes good sense for the company but is hard on governments. Again, in the case of private enterprise, while 'in principle it should not be impossible for a government to distinguish such practices by examining a company's books . . . in practice it is almost impossible for anyone outside of the company'.[80] This is particularly so when the goods transferred have no market value.

Here, too, the situation is different when the government is the owner of the firm. GCEs are to maximize returns to their owners; it therefore makes little sense for them to distort the rules of the game set forth by the owner himself. Besides, there is no reason to reduce tax payments to the state in order to increase dividends (present or future) to the shareholder, which is again the state: 'The logic of public ownership of an enterprise forecloses any attempt to try and get around taxes', said a French interviewee. A German interviewee added: 'GCEs should abide by governmental directives first in view of the contribution this makes in itself to the implementation of the policy in question, and second, to show the good example to others. GCEs have to be irreproachable in their fiscal behaviour'.

B. Financial policies specific to GCEs

Beyond expecting GCEs to abide by its general policies, a government may ask public enterprises to adopt a particular pattern of behaviour to help it implement a given aim. Specifically, it may pressure GCEs to raise at least some of their debt capital abroad. Raising money abroad reduces the need to export capital for foreign investments; besides, raising money abroad for domestic investments actually brings currency to the country. This has obvious positive effects on a balance-of-payments deficit.

Italian GCEs, and IRI and ENI in particular, have been asked to borrow heavily on international markets, both on short-term eurocurrency markets and on long-term foreign bond markets. As one executive said: 'In view of the weakness of our currency, this makes sense since it brings hard currency to the country. Furthermore, this policy has the added advantage of freeing our thin national capital markets for the private sector whose medium and small firms in particular do not have enough international standing to be able to borrow readily abroad'.

A study by a French Marxist economic journal corroborates this.[81] It analyses the evolution of the foreign debt issues of nine major French GCEs over twelve years. It shows that 'while the foreign debt issues are practically negligible until 1967, they begin to become important starting in 1969. From 1969 to 1973 they represent 17 per cent of the total long-term debt issues of these firms and in 1974 they represent about 75 per cent'.[82] It is noteworthy that

1974 is a year in which France witnessed a particularly serious balance-of-payments deficit. The study goes on to comment that 'this situation is imposed by the Finance Ministry: it corresponds both to a wish to preserve French savings for the monopolies [in the Marxist jargon, large capitalist enterprises allegedly dominating the national economy] and to impose on the public sector the chore of "defending the franc", which means in today's situation, to find foreign currency'.[83]

Leaving aside ideological overtones, it is clear that such a policy has its logic from the government's point of view. From the firm's point of view, however, this can constitute a particular burden, especially if the funds raised abroad are to be used for domestic purposes. The company is then exposed to the risks of exchange rate fluctuations, particularly since this policy is used when there is downward pressure on the national currency: if a GCE borrows in a foreign currency for domestic purposes it will convert the funds into national money. If the national currency devalues before the loan has been repaid, repayment will cost more in proportion to the rate of the devaluation.

C. Circumstantial policies

Circumstantial policies can also affect GCEs' attitude *vis-à-vis* existing MN activities.

If the state is confronted with a difficult socioeconomic situation calling for particular actions by industry, it may not hesitate to ask GCEs to undertake such actions even if this is to the detriment of the firms' own economic standing and its MN posture. A government may ask GCEs to contract their foreign operations in order to devote their resources to national operations. While this happens primarily in crisis situations and thus tends to be a relatively rare event, the fact remains that GCEs' foreign operations can always be modified, sometimes dramatically, by governmental policies regardless of the costs involved. Two examples will illustrate this.

Prior to 1974, Renault was producing certain models of its cars in Spain. In particular the 'R12 Brake' was manufactured in Spain for the entire European market. When the oil crisis broke out and entailed a slackening of the demand for automobiles, Renault did not hesitate to compress the Spanish operation, including a contraction of the work force, to transfer production to France 'in order to allocate – in the words of a representative of the Ministère du Développement Industriel et Scientifique – the production among domestic plants; this was necessary to minimize disruption of national production, especially in terms of avoiding reductions in employment at home'. As it turns out, this did not involve major costs to the firm; yet the prime consideration was employment in France, and had the costs been higher, the chances are that the same policy would still have been followed.

Another instance involves ELF-ERAP and was reported by an interviewee from a competing firm. When the 1973 oil crisis broke out ELF-ERAP was the first to withdraw from a number of foreign markets in order to save the oil it had

access to for France. Our interviewee said: 'Apparently the French government gave almost immediate instructions for ELF to stop selling abroad and to
channel its oil to the national market'. Again, national reasons were stronger
than any microeconomic rationale which probably would have called for a bit
more subtleness *vis-à-vis* foreign markets, were it only to preserve their loyalty
in view of a possible (and likely) wish of the company to come back to these
markets at a later date.

These two cases show that for GCEs the profit goal can truly become a
secondary aim relative to the tool goal, not only in terms of new investment
decisions but also as a guiding principle for ongoing operations. Indeed, as a
French interviewee put it: 'When governmental pressures are strong, the
notion of maximizing profits on a global basis can really become meaningless;
in crisis times, only the reason of the state counts'.

D. Going European

A government can pressure a GCE to give its MN expansion a European
twist. It is noteworthy that rarely does this occur unless it has been decided
that MN expansion *per se* will be pursued. Thus, pressure to go European is
much less a driving force for MN growth as it is a pressure for MN expansion
to take a particular form.

A government can exert such pressure in order to foster EEC integration.
This corresponds to the fairly traditional argument that – in Reuter's terms –
'It is industrialists who will create Europe':[84] Europeanization of business will
be a motor for the unification of Europe. A government may thus ask a GCE
to select European locations for their foreign investments or European partners for transnational joint ventures. The assumption is that this will foster
EEC integration not only by actually making a contribution to the Europeanization of business *per se* but also by serving as an example or stimulus for the
rest of industry.

Moreover, a government can wish the Europeanization of a specific sector.
In particular, for fields which are critical from an economic or political standpoint, a government may insist that enterprises develop in a European
context. For instance, in the case of military equipment manufacturing,
governments may prefer for security reasons to see intra-European rather
than global development. The same is true in the case of energy. The argument is that, given certain sectors call for international co-operation anyway,
this might as well occur in a European context: certain fields must be
developed on a transnational scale in view of the magnitude of the projects involved; co-operation in a European context then causes fewer draw-
backs from a political standpoint than co-operation with non-EEC partners;
from the viewpoint of national independence, co-operation at the European
level occurs in a context in which there is at least some degree of political
co-ordination among partners' states and in which the parties involved are
bound by some kind of common interests. Such cases are well documented

elsewhere.[85] In the words of an interviewee: 'A good illustration is the aircraft industry. Since there must be co-operation across frontiers, it should take place in the context of the EEC . . . For instance, projects such as the Airbus have been developed purposely in the European framework, consistent with the aim of fostering the development of a *European* aerospace industry'.

IV. CONCLUSION

In this chapter we analysed the various types of pressures which come to bear upon GCEs' MN behaviour, which derive from governments' aim to use public companies to implement their sociopolitical and economic plans. Of course each pressure applies differently to different GCEs – most pressures applying to certain GCEs only. Each GCE is subjected to a special mix of pressures and to understand and predict the behaviour of an individual GCE one has to ask which particular mix applies to that particular GCE. This discussion has uncovered the various pressures and their consequences for MN strategic and policy decisions, which can make up this mix.

Three observations are in order.

(1) Restraining forces for MN expansion are greater than the driving forces. First, pressures hindering MN growth are more numerous than those calling for such growth. Further, they tend to represent issues of greater concern to the government. Thus, the benefits to the collectivity from GCEs' contribution to regionalization policy are greater than those accruing to the nation's foreign policy from GCEs' investments in countries with which the government tries to improve relations.

Moreover, restraining forces for MN expansion tend to derive from more ongoing government policies while the driving forces tend to derive from passing national concerns. For example, the concern for regional development typically is a constant for any government in a country with regional problems. Such problems take decades to be solved (assuming they can be solved) and have virtual permanent status on governments' agendas. On the other hand, driving forces most frequently correspond to transient problems which arise at a particular point in time and which can either be solved relatively quickly or simply lose their relevance because of a change in the political or economic scene. For instance, we saw that in the years immediately following the oil crisis, governments were eager to see national firms invest in oil-producing countries. Soon, however, it became apparent that several of these countries did not offer the anticipated opportunities for industrial investment either because they were not pursuing development programmes amenable to the kinds of investments which national companies could undertake efficiently or because those investments which actually did take place were not yielding the expected results (for example, did not help the oil-importing country significantly in its payment obligations to the oil-exporting nation). Thus, governments are tending to de-emphasize the importance of investments in certain of these countries and to relax the pressure on GCEs to become involved there.

(2) The importance of the state's policy. According to the country's needs and the government's inclinations, the state's ends can vary considerably, which in turn results in differing mixes of pressures on GCEs. To explain a GCE's decisions it is indeed essential to examine the political line followed by the nation.

The situation of certain countries and the type of government in power can result in a high priority given to national policies calling for GCEs to engage in actions whose scope is domestic. In general, the greater the domestic socioeconomic problems, the more will this be the case. Italy provides the best illustration: the deep recession plus the chronic Mezzogiorno problem are putting high demands on GCEs to develop at home and in the South in particular. Such pressures are all the more acute when the government in power has a leftist bent since such a government will be especially sensitive to the social problems created by this kind of situation. In the same context, a socialist government wishing to promote industrial reforms may apply pressure on GCEs to stay home and serve as leading implementers of such reforms. Conversely, certain countries may decide to give priority to policies calling for GCEs' actions which are international in scope. For example, when the Gaullist government decided, in the context of its aim of enhancing 'national independence', that France needed to increase its autonomy in energy, there was considerable pressure on the relevant GCEs to develop multinationally to secure direct access to sources of raw materials unavailable at home.

(3) Importance of company characteristics. According to what aims a government pursues, certain GCEs are more relevant than others. Certain GCEs lend themselves to the implementation of domestically oriented policies only, while others can effectively accomplish internationally oriented missions. If a government is concerned, say, with promoting industrial investment in oil-producing countries, certain non-diversified, vertically integrated, primary-sector GCEs (for example, Charbonnages de France) are not appropriate, since their field of action is both too narrow and unadapted to oil-selling countries' requirements. On the other hand, a multisectorial group of the IRI type is naturally a prime candidate in this context. To understand which GCEs are pressed to go abroad, one must ask which GCEs have a scope and competences which make them best fit to carry out government's international policies.

In sum, this perspective suggests that:

(1) From the viewpoint of strategic decisions, GCEs which are driven by a strong tool goal are in general more likely to stay home than to expand abroad. This is due to the numerous and compelling demands for action they are to satisfy domestically, and to a number of pressures against foreign investment as such.

Still, for several GCEs this is not the case. On one hand, restraining forces for MN expansion do not apply to certain GCEs – either because their government just has no policy really requiring the use of GCEs or because their own characteristics and scope do not match the particular plans of the state. On the other hand, certain GCEs are expected to accomplish particular MN missions – their contribution abroad is valued more than their contribution at home; pressures for them to play a role internationally are then greater than the domestic imperative. But these tend to be more the exception than the rule. To repeat, the tool goal results mostly in hindrances to MN growth.

(2) From the viewpoint of policy decisions, the *modus operandi* of GCEs exhibits certain particularities on an MN scale. Thus, their financial and accounting management is especially sensitive to governmental directives and so are their resource allocations – the management of their MN operations is firstly responsive to the needs of their country.

Yet, in many dimensions GCEs' ongoing behaviour does not appear to show particular traits. Indeed, this analysis has uncovered but a limited set of governmental aims and policies calling for distinctive patterns of MN behaviour. For the rest, this view's logic suggests that GCEs behave according to the profit goal: in the absence of any particular government demand, GCEs, left on their own, behave like other MNCs. In particular, this approach says little about how a GCE behaves in host countries – its attitude towards local norms and regulations, labour, host government policies, expectations, taxes, etc. Here, we must then infer that GCEs behave like private companies: they pay no particular attention to things other than their financial returns (for example, show special socially responsible attitudes towards the local environment) beyond what is minimally required to remain in business.

Yet, even more than at the end of Chapter III, we are left with questions concerning this account. These fall into two categories.

1. *Anomalies in GCEs' behaviour*

We observed a number of instances in which GCEs' actual behaviour seems to depart from what would seem rational behaviour given the aims pursued. In particular:

(1) While the majority of GCEs do exhibit a commitment to investing preferentially in depressed areas, several GCEs, which have all the characteristics to be prime implementers of regionalization policy and which are under no other governmental pressures which might be conflicting with such policy, in fact do not appear to conform to it. In particular, DATAR reports that several French GCEs did not abide by its directives.[86] And in Italy, notwithstanding clear legislation, several GCEs – food companies and ENI companies in particular – have invested little in the Mezzogiorno while continuing expansion in the North.[87] And we found several cases where GCEs under pressure to invest at home in fact pursued MN opportunities.

How can this happen? How can a GCE depart from government directives? Why do certain GCEs clearly abide by government policies and why do others not?

(2) Attempts to co-ordinate the actions of various GCEs have often at best been marginally successful. To take an example used in this chapter, Alfa Sud, which was to match Finsider's steel production in the South, was in fact located suboptimally from the viewpoint of synergy between the two operations – as reported by Alfa's President Giuseppe Luraghi.[88] And Holland found that the timing of Alfa's operation was so bad as to put the entire venture into jeopardy.[89] Both these errors were so gross as to be obvious to anyone.

The same is true internationally. Despite certain undeniable successes in the context of 'GCEs' conglomerate strategy', many interviewees pointed out that such ventures only scratch the surface of what could be done in this context. An IRI interviewee said:

> Given our balance of payments problems and given the magnitude of our public sector, we have a far greater potential for investments in OPEC countries than what we do in fact . . . The main culprit for this is the lack of co-ordination between various GCEs, due to the state's lack of effective monitoring, which in turn is due to the lack of continuity in governmental leadership and to the bureaucracy's inefficiency. GCEs are thus pushed into investments in OPEC countries in a disorderly fashion, with no coherent policy to co-ordinate their investments and the activities of the resource-seeking companies.

And another interviewee said: 'We know it is desirable to invest in oil-exporting nations and so does the government. But we in fact do relatively little of this. We are not optimizing because we are left on our own to make these decisions, with no central plan . . . The reason is a lack of guidance from the state due to the political and public administrative chaos in which the country finds itself'.

A French interviewee's comments were also revealing:

> Consistent with our *étatist* tradition and given our requirements in terms of oil imports, the state has devised plans for industry to go to oil-exporting countries. Yet, this does not occur as effectively as it should. GCEs really don't 'attack' such markets in a well-co-ordinated fashion. And they are far from aggressively exploiting all the potential opportunities which exist there . . . The problem is that the government, while having done considerable analysis of the problem France faces *vis-à-vis* oil-exporting countries and while being aware of what French industry should do in this context, does not take active steps to cause industry to actually

accomplish what it should. In particular, it doesn't seem to use GCEs. Public companies in fact seem to be left pretty much on their own, with little attempt by the state to cause them to invest in oil-exporting countries as aggressively as it seems they ought to.

How can such irrational and inconsistent behaviour be explained? Given the unitary character of the government and GCEs, how can there be a lack of co-ordination? These interviewees refer to an absence of coherence in decisions and actions: how can this misplanning and misimplementation be accounted for?

(3) There appear to be breaches in the coherence of certain sectorial policies. Thus, in high technology the public sector does not always seem to pursue a strategy consistent with the aims of national or European autonomy. A good illustration is the French computer industry. In the early 1960s France had a relatively significant computer company – Bull. Confronted with financial difficulties, Bull (whose technical capabilities were high) sought government help. This was denied it and Bull was forced to come to an agreement with GE (followed later by a takeover). And at the same time the government launched its own computer program – the *Plan Calcul* – which was to result in CII. As noted by Jéquier:

> The French government could have helped Bull through this critical phase and thereby prevented a takeover. The sums of money which Bull required were at any rate smaller than the later investments made by the government in the *Plan Calcul* ... The real issue was the absence of a clear-cut policy which could have justified direct support on the part of the government and allowed decisions to be taken at very short notice.[90]

Later, in the early 1970s, the government showed some reluctance to permit its company, CII, to become too involved in the European co-operation route in the context of UNIDATA. Yet, in 1976 it suddenly allowed CII to merge with an American company – Honeywell – a merger which was in fact more of a takeover. (The irony of the story is that Honeywell had inherited Bull's assets from its takeover of GE's computer interests; the French government therefore now has a stake in Bull, which it originally refused to help, through its holding in CII–Honeywell–Bull.)

Again, how is such inconsistency possible? Why refuse to help Bull while creating a new company whose results were clearly going to be lesser than those Bull might have reached had it been given the resources invested in CII? Why did the government forbid CII to pursue a European policy, while at the same time claiming it favoured such a policy, and then allow a link-up with a non-European partner?

(4) While the logic of this approach suggests that GCEs comply with the letter and with the spirit of government policies, there is evidence that they

often do not – notably in terms of their MN *modus operandi*. Thus one interviewee reported a specific instance of a joint venture between an MNC and a GCE in which transfer prices were manipulated to minimize taxes due to the GCE's home country. Besides, several GCEs have been accused of speculating against their national currency.[91] And while several GCEs do indeed comply with government's requests to raise capital abroad in times of balance-of-payments crises, others which clearly could actually do not.[92]

How can a company go against its own interest: if it is true that a GCE is an integral part of a whole which is the state, how can it be permitted to injure the state's rights? Surely this is a self-defeating purpose? Is the government not going against itself?

(5) While this view suggests that GCEs behave in host countries like other MNCs, we found many which seem to show special sensitivity to expectations of the local society. Whereas several GCEs do not, others clearly appear to exhibit the same concern abroad as they do at home for their employees' wellbeing, for local government expectations, in their hiring and firing practices, etc.

Why? What reasons do such GCEs have to act in this fashion when they are under no pressure from their government to do so? Why do they not just go after the best possible economic performance? And why do certain GCEs behave like this while others behave like private companies?

2. *Puzzling explanations of GCEs' behaviour*

In many ways, the explanations offered by this view of GCEs' decisions and actions appear troublesome. Thus:

(1) This analysis more or less explicitly assumes that the government has full control over GCEs – that the enterprises are perfectly docile and prepared to subordinate their micro interests to the higher interests of the state. So, it at least tacitly assumes that the government is able to cause GCEs to invest consistently where, when and how it sees fit; that it can totally monitor GCEs' *modus operandi*. Indeed, the question of the effectiveness of government controls does not come up.

Is this realistic? Can one assume that GCEs' management has so little initiative of its own, or at least that it is always so eager to sacrifice its own aims? Can the government truly accede to and digest all the information necessary to monitor GCEs' financial policies? For instance, the argument was made that hedging against currency speculation is legitimate but speculation is not; but can this distinction always be made clearly in practice? Does the transparency between GCEs and government exist to the extent implied by this approach?

(2) In high-technology sectors in particular, governments have hindered transnational concentration so as to preserve the national identity of the firms involved in view of their national independence. Yet, it has increas-

ingly become obvious that this is a shortsighted policy: unless they develop on a European scale, certain sectors will just not develop efficiently at all. This view appears to be recognized in government circles themselves. Still, nationalistic attitudes seem to prevail.

How can such a myopic line be maintained?

(3) Several 'imperfections' were noted in the way GCEs implement government policies. Thus, we saw that Italian GCEs often make awkward capital-intensive investments in the Mezzogiorno, instead of badly needed labour-intensive investments. The Rapport Nora itself noted that GCEs did not truly abide by the government's plan.[93] This analysis offers no satisfactory explanations for such happenings, nor does it help us understand the specifics of certain decisions. For instance, given that a GCE complies, say, with regionalization policy objectives and commits itself to develop in depressed areas, how does it actually pick a specific investment location and project?

(4) We saw that the government frequently hinders foreign investment in order to preserve domestic employment and for balance-of-payments reasons. This attitude, in fact, is detrimental and counter-productive. From the company's point of view, it is clear that not making an economically desirable investment can only weaken it. In Stobaugh's terms: 'If firms failed to invest abroad, then they would retain less of the world market'.[94] Beyond the opportunity cost of not making an attractive investment, this weakens the enterprise's overall position. First, an incremental profitable investment makes a contribution to the firm's fixed costs and generates funds which can be allocated, say, to R & D. Second, such an investment has a synergistic effect on overall operations. It entails greater sales and market share, and thus greater 'experience' which in turn increases the firm's operating efficiency. Over time, this may jeopardize the firm's overall performance, including domestic operations.

From the point of view of the government, restricting foreign investment is also a questionable policy. To the traditional theory that foreign investment is bad for the country's balance-of-payments and employment situation, Stobaugh opposes another theory:

> Management of the . . . multinational enterprise prefers to invest [at home] but at times is forced to invest abroad in order to serve a market, and if this were not done, then foreign firms would invest and capture the market. Studies assuming that this theory is correct typically show that foreign investments . . . have a positive effect on the balance of payments . . . because they increase . . . exports . . . [Thus also] employment would be increased.[95]

This has a number of implications. First, given 'companies usually make [direct foreign] investments in self-defense, to protect their markets abroad'[96], hindering foreign investments appears a self-defeating purpose; by so doing, the government does not succeed in enhancing domestic production (via exports) since the export route does not permit holding on to foreign markets; eventually, the company involved will lose the foreign markets altogether with the related opportunity cost for the company itself and with no benefit for the home country. In addition, the loss of overall competitiveness of the firm is clearly counter-productive for the country also. Second, foreign investments result in positive effects in the home country's job growth and balance of payments. Foreign investments provide jobs for national production workers in three major ways: manufacture of capital equipment to be used in the new plants overseas; production of components to be processed further at foreign plants; manufacture of goods that would not be sold abroad unless the company were established there as well (so-called 'associated' exports).[97] These three kinds of production also result in incremental exports which, together with dividends, royalties and management fees from foreign investments, have positive effects on the home country's balance of payments.[98]

The empirical evidence for this theory is not definitive.[99] In particular, the data available concerns the US and US MNCs. Yet, there is certainly a lot of general truth in this conception. And we found that more or less explicitly, many interviewees – notably within government – shared a similar view. Typical of these, an Italian interviewee said: 'If pressed too hard, regionalization policy is often a self-defeating purpose over time. Pressure on companies not to invest in foreign plants frequently threatens their long-term ability to serve the very purpose behind these pressures: companies over-invest domestically and thus lose their competitiveness, which undermines their long-term ability to grow healthily – including domestic growth'.

Yet, the government persists in exerting pressures for GCEs to stay home. How can this be explained? The advantages of such a policy advanced by the government are too limited and too short-term in light of the usually obvious high costs it entails in the long run. Could there be other reasons for GCEs to pursue domestic ventures so consistently?

NOTES

1. Raymond Vernon, *Big Business and the State*, Harvard University Press, Cambridge, Mass., 1974, p. 3. For details on the use of GCEs for the implementation of government plans, see: Andrew Shonfield, *Modern Capitalism*, Oxford University Press, London, 1965; Stuart Holland, *The State as Entrepreneur*, Weidenfeld and Nicolson, London, 1972; and Stuart Holland, 'Europe's New Public Enterprises', in Vernon (ed.), *Big Business and the State*.
2. For detail see: J. E. S. Hayward, 'Steel', in Vernon (ed.), *Big Business and the State*.
3. See: Renato Mazzolini, *European Transnational Concentrations*, McGraw-Hill, London, 1974.
4. J. E. S. Hayward, 'Steel', in Vernon (ed.), *Big Business and the State*, p. 266.
5. J. E. S. Hayward, 'Steel', in Vernon (ed.), *Big Business and the State*, p. 268.
6. Andrew Shonfield, *Modern Capitalism*, p. 82.
7. Andrew Shonfield, *Modern Capitalism*, p. 185.

8. Charles-Albert Michalet, 'France', in Vernon (ed.), *Big Business and the State*, p. 112.
9. See: Philippe Simonot, 'ERAP fusionne avec Aquitaine', *Le Monde*, 11 January, 1976, pp. 1 and 21.
10. See: Vera Lutz, *Italy: A Study in Economic Development*, Royal Institute of International Affairs, London, 1962, Chapter 12.
11. See: Renato Mazzolini, *European Transnational Concentrations*, pp. 80 and 84.
12. Andrew Shonfield, *Modern Capitalism*, p. 82.
13. The British Petroleum Company, 'Annual Report', London, 1977.
14. The British National Oil Corporation, 'Report and Accounts', London, 1977, p. 4.
15. The British National Oil Corporation, 'Report and Accounts', London, 1977, p. 4.
16. Andrew Shonfield, *Modern Capitalism*, p. 184.
17. Milton Hochmuth, 'Aerospace', in Vernon (ed.), *Big Business and the State*, p. 146.
18. Milton Hochmuth, 'Aerospace', in Vernon (ed.), *Big Business and the State*.
19. Milton Hochmuth, 'Aerospace', in Vernon (ed.), *Big Business and the State*, p. 146.
20. Milton Hochmuth, 'Aerospace', in Vernon (ed.), *Big Business and the State*, p. 152.
21. Milton Hochmuth, 'Aerospace', in Vernon (ed.), *Big Business and the State*, p. 146.
22. Milton Hochmuth, 'Aerospace', in Vernon (ed.), *Big Business and the State*, p. 147.
23. In fact, at the end of that year it became apparent that there were difficulties for this decision to be implemented (see: *Le Monde*, 24 November, 1977).
24. *Programme de Gouvernement du Parti Socialiste et Programme Commun de la Gauche*, Flammarion, Paris, 1972, p. 71.
25. Milton Hochmuth, 'Aerospace', in Vernon (ed.), *Big Business and the State*.
26. Milton Hochmuth, 'Aerospace', in Vernon (ed.), *Big Business and the State*, p. 168.
27. Renato Mazzolini, *European Transnational Concentrations*.
28. Renato Mazzolini, *European Transnational Concentrations*.
29. Milton Hochmuth, 'Aerospace', in Vernon (ed.), *Big Business and the State*, p. 169.
30. Nicolas Jéquier, 'Computers', in Vernon (ed.), *Big Business and the State*, p. 201.
31. Nicolas Jéquier, 'Computers', in Vernon (ed.), *Big Business and the State*.
32. Nicolas Jéquier, 'Computers', in Vernon (ed.), *Big Business and the State*, p. 210.
33. 'La France va-t-elle créer un industrie des calculateurs largement française?', *Le Figaro*, 19 April, 1966.
34. Nicolas Jéquier, 'Computers', in Vernon (ed,), *Big Business and the State*, p. 203.
35. Nicolas Jéquier, 'Computers', in Vernon (ed.), *Big Business and the State*, p. 203.
36. Nicolas Jéquier, 'Computers', in Vernon (ed.), *Big Business and the State*, p. 199.
37. Nicolas Jéquier, 'Computers', in Vernon (ed.), *Big Business and the State*, p. 210.
38. See: Altiero Spinelli, 'Pour une stratégie communautaire en matière d'informatique' (statement before the European Parliament), *Bulletin des Communautés Européennes*, Vol. 2, 1972.
39. Stuart Holland, *The State as Entrepreneur*, p. 26.
40. See: Friedrich Vöchting, *La Questione Meridionale*, Istituto Editoriale per il Mezzogiorno, Napoli, 1955; Gabriele Pescatore, *Interventi straordinari nel Mezzogiorno d'Italia*, A. Giuffrè, Milano, 1962.
41. See: Kevin Allen, 'Regional Intervention', in Holland (ed.), *The State as Entrepreneur*, pp. 165–183.
42. Law of 6 October, 1971, No. 853 which amends the Law—'Testo Unico'—of 30 June, 1967, No. 1523. See also Law of August 12, 1977, No. 675.

114

43 See: Stuart Holland, *Regional Underdevelopment in a Developed Economy: The Italian Case*, Vol. V, Regional Studies, London, 1971.

44. Stuart Holland, 'Europe's New Public Enterprises', in Vernon (ed.), *Big Business and the State*, p. 33.

45 See: Louis Wells, 'Automobiles', in Vernon (ed.), *Big Business and the State*, p. 242.

46. Stuart Holland, 'Europe's New Public Enterprises', in Vernon (ed.), *Big Business and the State*, p. 33.

47. Lloyd Musolf, *Mixed Enterprise*, Lexington Books, Lexington, Mass., 1972, p. 36.

48. Lloyd Musolf, *Mixed Enterprise*, p. 36.

49. Jean-Pierre Anastassopoulos, 'The Strategic Autonomy of Government-Controlled Enterprises Operating in a Competitive Economy', PhD dissertation, Graduate School of Business, Columbia University, New York, 1973, p. 272.

50. See: Stuart Holland, 'Europe's New Public Enterprises', in Vernon (ed.), *Big Business and the State*.

51. Groupe de Travail du Comité Interministériel des Entreprises Publiques, 'Rapport sur les Entreprises Publiques', La Documentation Française, Paris, 1967.

52. Louis Wells, 'Automobiles', in Vernon (ed.), *Big Business and the State*, pp. 240–241.

53. Louis Wells, 'Automobiles', in Vernon (ed.), *Big Business and the State*, p. 241.

54. Stuart Holland, *The State as Entrepreneur*, p. 11.

55. Romano Prodi, 'Italy', in Vernon (ed.), *Big Business and the State*, p. 49.

56. Jean-Pierre Anastassopoulos, 'The Strategic Autonomy of Government-Controlled Enterprises in a Competitive Economy', p. 250.

57. Jean-Pierre Anastassopoulos, 'The Strategic Autonomy of Government-Controlled Enterprises in a Competitive Economy', p. 251.

58. Jean-Pierre Anastassopoulos, 'The Strategic Autonomy of Government-Controlled Enterprises in a Competitive Economy', pp. 285–286.

59. Stuart Holland, *The State as Entrepreneur*, p. 36.

60. Stuart Holland, *The State as Entrepreneur*, p. 36.

61. Stuart Holland, *The State as Entrepreneur*, p. 36.

62. See: The Boston Consulting Group, 'Perspectives on Experience', Boston 1971.

63. Stuart Holland, *The State as Entrepreneur*, p. 27.

64. See: Raymond Vernon. *Sovereignty at Bay*, Basic Books, New York, 1971.

65. Stuart Holland, *The State as Entrepreneur*, pp. 33–34.

66. Carlo Monotti, 'L'Institut Italien de la Reconstruction Industrielle poursuit sa politique de dissuasion à l'égard des investissements étrangers', *Le Figaro*, 15 September, 1970.

67. Carlo Monotti, 'Les investissements de Westinghouse en Italie bloqués par l'Institut de la Reconstruction Industrielle', *Le Figaro*, 9 September, 1970.

68. Stuart Holland, *The State as Entrepreneur*, p. 33.

69 Robert B. Stobaugh, 'U.S. Multinational Enterprises and the U.S. Economy', Graduate School of Business, Harvard University, Boston, 1972, p. 1.

70. Robert B. Stobaugh, 'U.S. Multinational Enterprises and the U.S. Economy', p.1.

71. See: Raymond Vernon, *Sovereignty at Bay*, pp. 65–112.

72. Charbonnages de France, 'Rapport de gestion', Paris, 1976, pp., 37–38.

73. See: Avison Wormald, 'Growth Promotion: The Creation of a Modern Steel Industry', in Holland (ed.), *The State as Entrepreneur*, pp. 98–99.

74. Stuart Holland, 'Europe's New Public Enterprises', in Vernon (ed.), *Big Business and the State*, p. 36.

75. See: Jean-Pierre Anastassopoulos, 'The Strategic Autonomy of Government-Controlled Enterprises Operating in a Competitive Economy'.

76. It should be pointed out that the government gave Aer Lingus a financial guarantee to cover any incremental losses this would entail: if the load factor on that particular flight fell below a certain commonly agreed upon level, the government would pay the company the difference between the revenue generated by the actual passenger traffic and the revenue which would be generated by passenger traffic at the agreed upon load factor level.

77. Stuart Holland, *The State as Entrepreneur*, p. 28.

78. Stuart Holland, *The State as Entrepreneur*, p. 28.

79. Stuart Holland, *The State as Entrepreneur*, p. 27.

80. Stuart Holland, *The State as Entrepreneur*, p. 27.

81. 'L'internationalization des Entreprises Publiques', collective authorship, *Economie et Politique (Revue Marxiste d'Economie)*, October 1975, pp. 105–118.

82. 'L'internationalization des Entreprises Publiques', p. 116.

83. 'L'internationalization des Entreprises Publiques', p. 116.

84. Quoted in André Marchal, 'Nécessité économique des fusions et concentrations intracommunautaires', *Revue du Marché Commun*, No. 109, January–February 1968, p. 44.

85. See: Milton Hochmuth, *Organizing the Transnational*, A. W. Sijthoff, Leiden, 1974; Christopher Layton, *European Advanced Technology—A Programme for Integration*, Allen and Unwin, London, 1969.

86. See: Jean-Pierre Anastassopoulos, 'The Strategic Autonomy of Government-Controlled Enterprises Operating in a Competitive Economy', pp. 272–273.

87. Reported by CGIL.

88 Giuseppe Luraghi, 'Alfasud—Mezzogiorno di fuoco', *Espansione* (Documento), No. 64, 1975.

89. Stuart Holland, *The State as Entrepreneur*, pp. 110–112.

90 Nicolas Jéquier, 'Computers', in Vernon (ed.), *Big Business and the State*, p. 214.

91. A case in point is Renault's Swiss financing subsidiary—Renault Finance.

92. Several IRI companies in particular.

93. Stuart Holland, 'Europe's New Public Enterprises', in Vernon (ed.), *Big Business and the State*, pp. 34–35.

94. Robert Stobaugh, 'U.S. Multinational Enterprises and the U.S. Economy', p. 6.

95. Robert Stobaugh, 'U.S. Multinational Enterprises and the U.S. Economy', p. 1.

96. Robert Stobaugh, 'How Investment Abroad Creates Jobs at Home', *Harvard Business Review*, September–October 1972, p. 118.

97. Robert Stobaugh, 'How Investment Abroad Creates Jobs at Home', p. 119.

98. Robert Stobaugh, 'How Investment Abroad Creates Jobs at Home', p. 120.

99. See: Robert Stobaugh, 'U.S. Multinational Enterprises and the U.S. Economy'.

CHAPTER V

An Organizational Process Approach

The traditional way of thinking about organizations as rational decision-makers – centrally co-ordinated, perfectly informed and value maximizing – must not make one lose sight of the fact that this is a simplification: organizations are really conglomerates of loosely allied suborganizations, each having a life of its own. Top management is indeed the formal leader of the whole. Yet, when it makes decisions it is dependent on the workings of the suborganizations for both the decision-making *per se* and the implementation of decisions: for the detection of a problem, it depends on organizational sensors and for its solution it depends on information it receives from the organization. For the accomplishment of its decision, it has to rely on the actions of the organization, which it triggers through conventional signals conveying authority via generally predetermined channels and which enact more or less fixed and well-defined actions by suborganizations. Therefore, the decisions and actions of an organization can be thought of in terms of an alternative framework – as outputs of units functioning according to standard patterns of behaviour.[1]

We will discuss this framework here. In Part I, we will briefly discuss the limitations of the traditional view and provide some background for the development of our own process approach to strategic and policy behaviour. This part assumes the reader is fairly conversant with the basic thrust of previous theoretical constructs which we refer to in this chapter. For the reader who is not, the Appendix surveys this literature. Part II develops our framework of analysis for strategic decisions, and Part III that for policy decisions.

I. BACKGROUND

A. Appraising the traditional approach

The traditional approach is appealing by its rigour. By making a few assumptions about comprehensive rationality, the analyst achieves considerable intellectual elegance and powerful logical interpretations about corporate actions. As Harsanyi notes: 'The concept of rational behaviour is often a very powerful explanatory principle because it can account for a large number of empirical facts about people's behaviour in terms of a few simple assumptions about the goals (or ends) people are trying to achieve'.[2]

By reducing the actions of an organization to the behaviour of a unitary rational decision-maker, the traditional approach enables one to get a quick reading on some of the more basic forces underlying an organization's broad pattern of behaviour. When the analyst puts himself in the shoes of the organization, he can think in terms of what the organization's course of action should be if objectives are to be maximized; he can approximate what the optimal strategic behaviour should be. He then can reason that this optimum will at least be partly reflected in the actual behaviour of the organization.

Further, this approach is appealing by its ease of use. Its reliance on a relatively simple inference pattern permits explanation or prediction of the behaviour of an organization without the need of much touchy inside information. Thus, an analyst can account for a firm's behaviour if he knows what the environmental conditions are, what resources the company has and what the strategists' values are.[3] The exercise does not require any deep knowledge of the firm's organizational structure or internal processes; it can therefore be performed with information often mostly available from public sources.

Yet, this approach has severe limitations. These have been pointed out repeatedly and are summarized in the Appendix. Here it should suffice to point out that the two fundamental assumptions on which the traditional approach rests are fallacious.

First, neither people nor organizations really behave rationally.

> Most theories of individual and organizational choice employ a concept of 'comprehensive rationality', according to which individuals and organizations choose the best alternative, taking account of consequences, their probabilities, and utilities . . . Such choices require: (1) the generation of all possible alternatives, (2) assessment of the probabilities of all consequences of each, and (3) evaluation of each set of consequences for all relevant goals.[4]

In reality, all the alternatives are not known, and neither are all the possible consequences attached to each alternative nor the probabilities of possible outcomes. Besides, the human mind does not have the computational capabilities to appraise the relevant data were they available. Also, because the necessary data are not available to the decider and in view of the limits of his analytical abilities, he cannot maximize – select the best of all possible courses. Instead, he seeks to 'satisfice': he does not seek to deploy all his efforts to try and achieve the best possible results but he is willing to settle for solutions which are 'good enough'.

Second, organizations are not monoliths behaving as unitary agents but rather aggregations of suborganizations more or less tightly knit together by agreed-upon procedures. An organization is really a complex social structure composed of a variety of units often having considerable autonomy and being but imperfectly related to the whole. This implies that the traditional view of the organization as having aims which are the expression of its fundamental direction or mission is misleading. In practice, organizational goals are much less predetermined in terms of clear ends of the whole and much more the outgrowth of agreements among organizational units. A corollary has to be an inherent potential for conflict about goals within an organization.

This raises the problem of the limits of strategic and policy decisions. In the conventional view, a firm chooses to pursue whatever alternative there is which is most attractive. And the postulate of monolithism allows one to assume that the total enterprise will abide by the central plan geared to the pursuit of that alternative and permits one to ignore the possibility of distortion in the implementation of such a plan. Yet, the realization that an organization is in fact an aggregation of semi-autonomous units uncovers the weakness of this view. The complexity of the organization's task requires the splitting up of this task into subtasks and the assignment of these subtasks to suborganizations which tend to acquire a certain independence and discretion of their own. To ensure an acceptable level of co-ordination and consistency throughout the organization, standardized processes are developed. But these processes are really a two-edged sword: on the one hand they allow a certain – though limited – coherence within the organization but on the other hand they constrain the range of possible actions available to the organization; because the organization is dependent on them for its functioning, what it can do is really limited by the scope of the existing organizational processes. The conventional view says little about this.

B. Organization theory

Several authors have criticized the traditional approach and proposed alternative models of organizational decision-making. This literature is surveyed in the Appendix.

Probably, the most articulate pieces to date remain *Organizations*[5] and *A Behavioral Theory of the Firm*.[6] But what is the relevance of this work, and that of Cyert and March (and their followers) in particular, for strategic kinds of decisions?

One of the most representative critics of the Cyert and March model as a way of explaining strategic behaviour is Igor Ansoff: 'Cyert and March concern themselves exclusively with operating problems; their firm keeps its organization intact and its product-market posture constant'.[7] Their model's emphasis on standard patterns of behaviour, according to Ansoff, sheds considerable light on how a firm's tasks are organized within a pre-established product-market scope. 'By contrast, strategic decisions are not self-regenerative; they make no automatic claim on top management's attention. Unless actively pursued, they may remain hidden behind the operations problems'.[8] Thus, Ansoff argues, the theory is able to account for a firm's overall behaviour when this behaviour is made up exclusively of operating decisions – when no decisions are made about the firm's strategic posture.

Another, though less explicit, critique comes from Simon in his discussion of types of business decisions.[9] He distinguishes between programmed and non-programmed decisions.

> Programmed decisions are repetitive and routine, decisions which a firm is accustomed to take at regular intervals and for which it will usually have developed some form of systematic procedure ... Non-programmed decisions, in contrast, are novel, unstructured and usually very significant. Here management is called upon to respond to very uncertain decision situations where no procedures for choice exist and where it has to rely on its own capacity for intelligent, adaptive, problem-oriented action.[10]

There is in fact a continuum between the two; decisions which fall initially into the non-programmed category will become programmed if they recur a number of times in comparable conditions. Procedures will be developed for dealing with them, which will standardize the way problems are handled.

Programmed decisions are made mostly according to habit: a problem is approached in a given way because it has always been approached that way. And standard operating procedures are developed for 'introducing newcomers into the decision-making norms and habits of the organization, and for reminding old hands of the commonly used methods for solving particular problems. Where programmes for solving problems are not written down, then organizations may secure uniform behaviour patterns through developing common goals, norms and expectations in their staff'.[11] Non-programmed decisions are, virtually *ex hypothesis*, far less systematized: 'There have been far fewer techniques available in the non-programmed area'.[12] These decisions rely much more on judgement and do not lend themselves to standard solutions. It is clear that the basic focus of Cyert and March is on programmed decisions and not on non-programmed ones.

The Cyert and March model *per se* indeed does not directly apply to strategic decisions. True, it acknowledges the possibility of shifts in the firm's field of action, but they conceive of this only as the product of a dramatic, exceptional, usually negative event. Otherwise, change is essentially seen as a gradual process which can only come about slowly as an organization improves its *modus operandi* incrementally over time. The emphasis is on the construction of 'reasonable, short-term models [of the behaviour of the firm] in which a few specific types of goals are taken as given'.[13] Cyert and March say little about the long-run process of 'normal' – in the sense that it is not due to a dramatic event – change in the basic scope of the firm. In particular, they neglect environmental changes which call for a shift in the firm's strategy (indeed, their definition of an organization as a coalition excludes any consideration of the environment as such since 'any one that has some influence on the decision is included as a participant');[14] further, they do not consider internal forces which also may call for a shift in strategy.

Yet, our argument is that this approach lays the grounds for a new look at strategic decisions – a process-oriented approach.

A number of frameworks have been put forward to describe the phases of decision-making – from Dewey's five-phase framework[15] to Simon's intelligence–design–choice trichotomy[16] and Mintzberg *et al.*'s routine-oriented identification–development–selection framework.[17] Our contention is that, whatever categorization is actually used, the various phases of decision-making can most usefully be analysed as interrelated processes; and therefore, organization theory provides a strong base for the development of a theory of strategic behaviour. We argue that while the outcome of a strategic decision may well be different each time, the way a course of action is first elicited, then formulated and approved and finally implemented, is determined by organizational procedures and thus amenable to a behavioural process type of explanation.

This is all the more true for policy decisions. These are not routine decisions. Still, decisions about the fundamental *modus operandi* are partially able to be programmed: they tend to be recurring; and while they rarely occur in the same circumstances and are thus different each time around, they do take place in the context of problems which are of a relatively constant nature. Thus, the way a firm secures its long-term financing is in great part a function of organizational policies (explicit or implicit); each time a firm goes to the capital markets, a comparable series of steps takes place. Therefore, policy decisions are amenable to a process type of analysis.

Others have in fact built on organization theory to look at unstructured decisions. The most elaborate formulation here is probably Allison's process-oriented model.[18] As Allison himself notes: 'This formulation's debt both to the orientation and insights of Herbert Simon and the behavioural model of the firm formulated by Richard Cyert and James March is considerable. Here, however, one is forced to grapple with the less routine, less quantifiable activities of the less differentiated elements in government organizations'.[19] Allison's work sheds considerable light on how an organization reacts when confronted with an abrupt happening requiring that dramatic steps be taken immediately. Yet, just as strategic decisions are different from operating decisions, strategic decisions differ significantly from the decisions Allison focuses upon. It is worth repeating what was pointed out in Chapter I. Allison deals with the governmental setting and not with the micro setting of the firm. Allison's model is useful for the analysis of organizational behaviour in the case of a clear *crisis*, that is a *recognized dramatic* event calling for *immediate specific* action. Relative to this, corporate strategy exhibits two fundamental distinctive features: (1) the focus is on the *long-term general direction* taken by the organization (so to speak, its *raison d'être* over time); (2) far from being a set of short-term actions, it is a continuing and evolving process. Thus the two types of decisions have totally different characteristics and the crisis decisions model cannot be applied to strategic and policy behaviour. This is well illustrated by the decision-need identification phase. In a crisis, the need for a decision becomes apparent as unequivocally as it is sudden, and single stimuli (or signals) are typically sufficient to bring the issue requiring action to deciders' attention.[20] In strategic decisions, on the contrary, there is no immediate pressure to make a decision. In fact, the strategic behaviour of a firm is often characterized by non-decisions in that nothing is done in terms of explicitly changing the current strategic posture. And indeed, a major issue in these kinds of decisions is how the current strategy is called into question – how the need to make a decision becomes felt in the first place. This will become clearer below.

While exhortations towards a descriptive process theory of strategic and policy decisions are becoming increasingly frequent,[21] there have been few attempts to date to actually develop such approaches. Aharoni has focused on the way companies make their foreign investment decisions;[22] Bower has looked at the capital allocation process of a large diversified company;[23] and Mintzberg et al. have analysed the decision process in terms of a field study of 25 unstructured problems together with a review of the related empirical literature.[24] While these authors also develop theory, none of these formulations – as they themselves would probably acknowledge – can be considered as definitive. There is a clear need for more precise theory on how strategic and policy behaviour occurs.

In fact, we need two separate, although related, frameworks – one for strategic, the other for policy decisions. A further particular feature of our approach is worth pointing out. In this study we deal not just with intraorganizational processes but also with interorganization processes: we are concerned with what happens within the organization whose behaviour we are interested in – a GCE – and with what happens within another organization – the government – as well as with what happens between the two. If we were to stick faithfully to the Cyert and March definition of an organization as a coalition, such a distinction would not be necessary since they include anybody who has influence on the organization as a participant of the coalition. Yet, as suggested earlier and as we will see further below, for us such a view is an oversimplification: it neglects to focus on the role of the environment *per se* and neglects to distinguish precisely between the role of outputs emerging from the firm itself and those stemming from that exogenous system represented by the government.

II. AN ORGANIZATIONAL PROCESS APPROACH TO STRATEGIC BEHAVIOUR

We now turn to the formulation of a process view of strategic decisions. We will first discuss in what basic way strategic behaviour is the product of organizational processes. Further, we will analyse in some detail particular aspects of this approach. We will then see the implications of our conception: there are severe limits on what an organization is able to accomplish from a strategic viewpoint. We will conclude with on what to focus to understand and predict strategic behaviour.

A. Strategic behaviour as output of organizational processes

Strategic behaviour is the product of organizational processes in five main ways.

1. Decision-need identification

The information which causes a problem or an opportunity to be identified which may cause a change in strategy, is collected and distilled according to certain agreed-upon procedures. Procedures are designed to gather, formalize and transmit data according to standardized patterns, in other words collect and process that particular type of information for which they are programmed; the way the information is presented is equally determined by routines which thus clearly influence the message conveyed by the information; and processes are responsible for appraising the information. Mintzberg *et al.* found that 'the need for a decision is identified as a difference between information on some actual situation and some expected standard'.[25] This is comparable to Bower's concept of discrepancy: 'The first step in a long process which ends with the expenditure of capital funds, begins when the *routine* demands of a facility-oriented job indicate the need for a new facility'[26] – when there is a 'discrepancy' between performance expectations by the organization and actual results (or the results which are forecast given the type of activity in which the organization is currently involved). The identification of such differences or discrepancies rests upon routines and so does the determination of the standards: standards evolve from a process – as Pounds found, they are based on past trends, projected trends, standards in some comparable organization, the expectations of other people, and theoretical models.[27]

A company therefore is sensitive to certain opportunities and problem areas but not all. A threat or an opportunity in an area in which organizational processes do not gather information may remain long uncovered. Consider the following hypothetic example of an airline. The organization's procedures geared towards monitoring competition may focus on other 'people carriers' – other airlines, railroad or shipping companies, etc. Yet, if the majority of its passengers are businessmen, such information may be but partially relevant in the long run: businessmen travel to communicate with other businessmen, and the airline's competitors of tomorrow may well be 'communications companies' such as IBM or Xerox, which may enable people not only to talk to each other over long distances, but also to communicate visually – see each other and pass around documents; indeed, meetings might be held with participants being at a distance of thousands of miles. This may reduce the need for actual face-to-face encounters and thus make a lot of travelling redundant. Yet, the typical airline data collection procedures about competition usually do not focus on the Xeroxes or IBMs, and competitive threats outside of people – transportation industries will not appear until they have actually bitten off a sizeable share of the company's market.

GCEs have processes to identify certain issues in the environment – given opportunities and threats coming from market, competitive, technological variables. And they have processes to capture signals from the government – procedures by which particular governmental demands are channelled into the organization.

2. Search for alternatives for action

Processes are responsible for finding solutions. Set procedures trigger search and direct search towards particular areas. Not all theoretically possible avenues are considered. Rather, the actions which are contemplated are a limited set of alternatives selected according to a particular routine. This procedure seeks to follow known paths – the range of actions considered and the way these actions are investigated are outputs of set organizational processes. Indeed, organizations tend to accept precedents as binding and look at existing standard procedures as constraining guidelines in any problem-solving situation.[28] Thus the environment is scanned for familiar courses of action and alternatives are appraised according to pre-established criteria. As found by Aharoni: 'Investment decisions in business are based on the alternatives which are known to exist, or those which have emerged from previous activities of the business unit'.[29] 'Existing organizational routines for employing present physical capabilities constitute the range of effective choice open to . . . leaders confronted with a problem'.[30] In most enterprises, the possibility of looking for an investment opportunity in which they do not already have operations rarely comes up. Thus, for foreign investments: 'First, many organizations lacking the precedent of a foreign investment experience would refuse to consider such a possibility. Second, when such a possibility is considered, many previous policies are taken as given and become constraints in the decision process'.[31]

This means that there is a built-in tendency for companies to preserve the *status quo* in their strategic posture. Indeed, the decision to go MN is a case in point: for many enterprises which do not already have MN operations, the possibility of looking for an investment opportunity abroad rarely occurs to them; when they look for alternatives for change in their strategic posture, foreign investments are seldom considered. Yet, obviously, companies do occasionally change their strategy; MNCs have all made their first MN step. This means that at one point, certain organizational constraints will not be binding and can be changed: thanks to a particular occurrence, a new path will be pursued. This too, however, depends on a process: either a drastic event or a strong force will cause the search for alternatives to look for new courses of action; but this occurrence is itself internalized by the organization

via procedures which filter its impact. For instance, a foreign direct investment may be considered in view of preserving a market position in a foreign
country currently served by exports; this can be triggered by import restrictions imposed by the foreign country; for the decision to be made to consider
investing in a local manufacturing facility requires a realization of the implications of the export restrictions, the evaluation of the consequences for the
overall organization and the formulation of alternative actions. Such steps
are outputs of organizational processes.

We shall return to this.

3. Investigation of courses of action

Just as the alternatives which are considered are a limited set, the information
which is analysed to appraise an alternative cannot be complete. While there
are a multitude of factors which could be considered to gauge a given course of
action, it is practically impossible to look at all of them given time and money,
as well as analytical capabilities, are limited. Thus, decisions have to be made
on the basis of partial and selected information. And there has to be a procedure for gathering certain data rather than others. Thus, an investigation is
carried out in successive phases with built-in checkpoints and data are collected, scrutinized and evaluated according to distinct patterns: information is
increasingly elaborate as one goes on in the process, and more and more
precise rules are used to evaluate it.[32] As mentioned above, for an alternative
to be considered which calls for a radical shift in the company's strategy, a
dramatic occurrence is necessary. The strength of this occurrence will be felt
also in the investigation process. Thus, if a powerful ministry requires a GCE
to become involved in a particular country, the investigation processes will
reflect the weight of the initiating force. The force may be so strong that the
initial phases of the investigation process are skipped altogether (for example,
the analysis of general data about the overall macroeconomic and sociopolitical situation of the country are disregarded).

4. Reviews and approval

It is hard to determine at what point and by whom a decision is made.* A
decision to follow a particular course of action evolves over time as resources
are allocated to define and refine the particular course of action and to
analyse its desirability. In other words, decisions themselves are outputs of
organizational processes: the very conception and elaboration of an alternative involve a progressive decision to pursue that very alternative; as a course
of action is investigated, there is a cumulative process of individual and organ-

---

*Bower's findings are germane to this discussion; Bower sees the process by which the technical
and economic content of a plan or project is determined as quite separate from the process by
which plans and projects are approved.[33]

izational commitments to pursue that particular course of action. The key issue is not who made a particular decision to allocate certain resources to a given action, but what conditions created commitments resulting in the acceptance or rejection of that action.[34] Aharoni's findings are significant:

> The very fact that an organization is making an investigation creates new commitments. Some of these emerge because money and time are spent; executives apparently find it hard to look at this investment of scarce resources as a sunk cost. They resist the idea of abandoning the project. They feel an urge to persist, to find ways to overcome difficulties and 'to make a go of it'.

> Thus one executive, when asked to estimate the cost of investigating a foreign investment, added the following revealing comment:

>> When the negotiations become complicated, you get in deeper and deeper. You want to protect your initial investment, so you continue . . . By that time you are stuck and have to go on. You have spent $25.000 and you do not want to lose it, so you invest another $10.000 to continue the negotiations, and then you are in even deeper . . .

> Commitments are created not only by financial investments. They may also emerge because of a psychic or social investment. Thus, the fact that a certain group of people – inside or outside the investigating organization – knows that an investigation is being carried on may also cause a feeling of commitment. It may be felt that once the investigation has begun, a decision to reject the investment proposal may create some psychologically or socially undesirable effects.[35]

Moreover, a particular course of action has to be reconciled with the overall posture of the enterprise – the validity of an alternative needs to be checked recurrently in the course of the investigation. The checking occurs according to set routines and can result in modifications of the alternative. For GCEs this occurs at three levels. First, within a company there is a reviewing process involving various echelons of the organization. An alternative is appraised at various points of the investigation process and modified where necessary, particularly as its congruency with the perceived posture of the firm is concerned. Second, within the government, various parts may take a different view of foreign investments and established procedures are typically used to review a GCE's proposed course of action. Third, between the GCE and the government a consensus has to emerge about the strategy the company will pursue. This is achieved through routines by which the company submits its proposed plan (not necessarily in a formal way) and the government either gives its approval or asks for certain modifications or rejects the proposal altogether. In fact, here (as well as in the case of the intracompany process) true evaluation of an alternative rarely occurs when it has reached the final stage of a formal proposal; rather, particularly for large GCEs, there is an elaboration of a course of action between the company and the government, and a strategy is really an outgrowth of exchanges between the company and the government. Such exchanges are made according to set procedures which themselves have a bearing on the ultimate strategy of the firm. The more numerous and stringent the checkpoints in the formulation process of a proposal, the more consensus and commitments are built up around it and the more the final formal approval is assured. (As a consequence, there are few cases of government intervention to alter the strategy of GCEs: on the one hand, companies tend to engage in actions or make action proposals only when they are confident these will be approved; on the other, governments feel compelled to back the company up and look upon commitments built up during a strategy formulation process as binding for the enterprise.)*

5. Implementation

The accomplishment of an action plan rests on set procedures. The traditional treatments of decision-making stop at the point of approval or actual choice. They assume that action will indeed follow decision faithfully. There is therefore no need to provide for distortions between the formulation and the implementation of a plan. Yet, the current process approach suggests that decisions are rarely accomplished as intended. Given organizations are aggregations of semi-autonomous and imperfectly co-ordinated units, one cannot assume that decision and action necessarily match each other. To truly understand organizational behaviour, one has to include explanation of what happens to a decision between the point it is taken and the point it is carried out in practice.

Organizations have a limited range of things they know how to do – they know how to do what they have been doing already. More specifically, organizational units have a finite number of repertoires they know how to perform – routinized programmes of action which they have learned 'by doing', by accomplishing certain types of tasks over and over again. Over time, via a process of incremental learning whereby organizational units change adaptively as the result of experience,[37] relative efficiency is reached, that is suborganizations adopt patterns of behaviour which are rather effective given the subtasks they are expected to perform. This, however, is only true until the overall posture of the total organization remains stable. But when a new path is sought, organizational units will, at least initially, perform according to patterns of behaviour with which they are familiar. Considerable distortion can therefore result between plan and action: 'Projects that demand that existing organizational units depart from their established programs to per-

---

*Bower found that a proposal is practically never turned down when it reaches top management for approval.[36]

form unprogrammed tasks are rarely accomplished in their designed form. Projects that require coordination of the programs of several organizations are rarely accomplished as designed'.[38] Plans calling for a change in the posture of the total enterprise are thus under special threat of being distorted because they imply that all organizational units conform to that plan in a coherent and consistent fashion.

B. Key characteristics

In this section we examine in further detail four fundamental features of the process approach.

1. Actors

The deciding and acting agent is not a black box – the firm *per se* – but an agglomeration of more or less tightly knit suborganizations. To explain the behaviour of an organization, one needs to disaggregate this conglomerate and study the processes by which its various parts function and relate to each other.

Organizations factor their task – split problems up and assign parts to various suborganizations. This involves decentralization and delegation of power. This means suborganizations are granted some latitude to decide what to deal with and how:

> Factored problems and fractioned power are two edges of the same sword. Factoring permits more specialized attention to particular facets of problems than would be possible . . . if leaders tried to cope with the problems by themselves. But that additional attention must be paid for in the coin of discretion for *what* an organization attends to and *how* organizational responses are programmed.[39]

Responsibility for a particular aspect of a problem encourages parochialism within suborganizations as well as perceptions which are particular to each suborganization, that is, suborganizations tend to have their own relatively personal propensities as to which issues they perceive as important. While this originates in the distinctiveness of their own special responsibility, other factors enhance it such as the particular selective information available to the suborganization or the distribution of rewards by the suborganization.

The traditional approach considers a GCE and the government as a single decider. It assumes that a GCE and the government ultimately agree on a set of corporate objectives to be pursued – a vector in which profit and tool goals are reconciled. Here, instead, a GCE and the government are seen as separate. And each is seen as made up of a variety of suborganizations of its own. The analyst must understand the interplays between GCEs and the government, and he must understand the workings of the government and of GCEs: how state agencies, departments, ministries, and how company divisions, departments, subsidiaries, work and interact. Depending on the aim of the analysis, one may need to go quite far in the degree of disaggregation of an organization – for example, identify several component units within a particular company division.

The government and the various units that compose it, and the GCEs and the units which compose them, all have a certain autonomy. The government clearly has power over GCEs but this power is limited by the scope of the procedures available to actually monitor GCEs. And if one considers the total task of the government, it is clear that GCEs' activities constitute only a part thereof and that their administration must be delegated to those in the companies themselves. Since their doings are part of the overall doings of the state, GCEs can be considered as having a share of the influence on the total activities of the state. Further, each organization has its set of priorities. The government and its components are responsible for overall results in terms of national socioeconomic development. Each government organization puts national results in the area for which it is responsible before individual corporate results and is inclined to use GCEs for the purpose of achieving national ends. On the other hand, responsibility for the conduct of GCEs leads their management to develop its own propensities – emphasizing performance *per se* somewhat losing track of a more global mission of contributing to the country's macroeconomic growth. Still, GCEs' propensities can be influenced by government; for instance, governmental pressures to focus on national issues may result in management having a particularly domestic outlook.

2. Goals

The goals of an organization which are the actual guides for action are usually not stated in a formal fashion: while organizations may have official objectives, these objectives have rarely much to do with what the organization pursues in practice. Rather, an organization's actual goals are outgrowths of constraints which determine levels of acceptable performance. 'Goals of a business firm are a series of more or less independent constraints imposed on the organization through a process of bargaining'[40] among suborganizations with disparate demands. In this study, constraints emerge from a mix of expectations and demands of suborganizations within GCEs and within government. Thus, an agency responsible for regional development may demand a given level of investments in certain areas; a government department for foreign trade may expect a certain level of sales on foreign markets; management of a GCE may want a certain R & D commitment in order to preserve the long-term competitiveness of the firm *vis-à-vis* international competition.

Such constraints are elaborated over time and represent a quasi-resolution of conflict: given the form of the goals and the way they are developed, conflict is never totally resolved – rather, organizations strive with considerable goal conflict within them. Organizational slack absorbs inconsistencies within the organization. Sequential attention resolves conflicts among goals: since organizational tasks are factored to suborganizations which act in quasi-independence from each other, each suborganization can pursue its own sub-goals which are not necessarily consistent with other suborganizations' goals. Thus, seen from an overall organization point of view, not all demands receive attention at the same time. Therefore, organizations can live with conflicting goals because they rarely look at incompatible expectations simultaneously.

In the particular context of this study, government organizations may expect GCEs to go in different directions which are both inconsistent among themselves and inconsistent with the expectations to be found within the companies themselves. Given decentralization, management *de facto* often has a relatively free hand in pursuing its own goals while government organizations may receive occasional satisfaction for their own demands when they exert pressure for them. (Goals not emerging from management are pursued only when suborganizations responsible for them *actively* pursue them.)

3. Search

Beyond what was said earlier, two questions regarding search need to be asked.

First, *when* does search for a new strategic action occur? As other forms of organizational search, strategic search is problemistic search: it is stimulated by a particular problem and motivated to find a solution to that problem. Yet, the 'problem' is not necessarily represented by a crisis or a threat thereof; it can be how to capitalize on an opportunity.* Specifically, search can on the one hand be triggered by a sizeable deterioration in the organization's health (for example a negative evolution in financial performance) or at least symptoms that such a deterioration may be coming. Thus, the realization that the product line is maturing may trigger search for new product areas. The realization that foreign markets currently served by exports may be lost to local producers may induce search for ways of retaining those markets, which may ultimately result in an investigation of the possibility of a foreign direct investment.

On the other hand, search can be triggered by an opportunity—how to exploit an attractive investment possibility lying outside of the current scope of the firm. Such an opportunity can be identified, and search to exploit it initiated, from within the organization. A particular organizational unit may perceive an opportunity and push for its pursuit. Search can also be motivated by an outside force which has influence on the organization. Thus, in the case of GCEs, the government may ask a company to engage in a new type of activity; this may trigger search for a course of action which will enable the company to become involved in this activity.

*This is consistent with Carter's findings—stimulus of search for strategic alternatives can be goal-oriented and positive as well as problem responsive.[41]

Anyway, triggering search for a new course of action in non-crisis times when the organization's health is good requires a strong initiating force. So, if a proposal for investing in a country comes in at a time when results of the current product-market scope are worrying, it will have more of a chance of being investigated than if business is already booming for the firm. In this latter case, only an especially influential force will be able to cause the proposal to be considered seriously at all.

To identify the problem which will eventually motivate search, organizational sensors are needed. These are standard procedures to collect information about performance of the firm: detect threats given the current strategic posture and detect opportunities represented by alternative actions. Such sensors are not all-encompassing; they are bounded in that they are selective as to which problem they are geared to identify or not.

The second question is *how* does strategic search occur? The way search is carried out and its stopping point are largely determined by organizational procedures. The way alternatives are looked for, the way the investigation process is conducted and the way alternatives are evaluated are dependent on routines. Further, search is simpleminded: it looks first at the neighbourhood of problem symptoms, then at the neighbourhood of the current alternative. This means that given that a strategic problem arises, search for alternatives to solve it will start by looking for a similar problem which was encountered in the past and go on by looking at what courses of action were used to solve that problem previously. Yet, given the non-repetitive character of strategic problems, only rarely can familiar problems be found, in fact. So familiar solutions are applied to new problems: search looks for solutions within a rather limited range of alternatives for action known to the organization. Whatever the newness of the problem, the range of effective options tends to be limited to what the firm has done already or at least done partially in similar fashion.

The search process and its routines are fairly stable over the short run. They reflect biases and experience of various parts of the organization. Yet, they do evolve gradually over time. Just as organizations better their overall *modus operandi* as they build up operating practice, the strategic search process improves progressively as organizations assimilate new situations and learn how to deal with particular types of problems.

Solutions are generally sought in a repertoire of known alternatives, and the routines for investigation and evaluation, while improved over time, normally do not change radically. Confronted with a deterioration of the effectiveness of part of its strategy, the organization will tend to seek to correct it with a course of action which was experienced elsewhere; confronted with an opportunity, it will tend to seek to exploit it via courses of action which have been used before.

As noted earlier, for a radically new area of activity to be pursued, a strong force must intervene to trigger search around a problem which normal sensors would not pick up. This does not mean, however, that this force will necessarily have a bearing on what alternatives will be considered. Even when a new type of problem is raised by a force, that problem will be solved via conventional routes unless a force acts also on the search process *per se*. In other words, for a new route to be pursued, an initiating force has not only to cause the *need* for the strategic change or innovation to be felt but also does it have to actively promote the *change* – the new route itself. It is only when a solution has been applied at least once that it becomes part of the standard search process.

A new type of strategic action will usually be tied to a particular project. The first foreign investment is a case in point[42]: even in the case where a company is confronted with a rather general type of problem resulting in the consideration of foreign direct expansion (for example, the domestic market is saturated, foreign opportunities appear to offer new growth possibilities), the first foreign investment analysis will be a specific one (for example, a particular plant in a particular country). Later, as the company builds up experience in this type of operation, the alternative of foreign direct investment is included among those which might be considered in a regularized search process, and standard procedures are developed for the investigation and appraisal of this kind of action.

4. Leadership

What is the role of top management in such a standardized world? Contrary to what is hypothesized by Cyert and March, we do not rule out top management's influence over the organization's behaviour. In the context of strategy, top management has three major roles.

(1) Top management has a key function as an initiating force. This has been termed 'top management's substantive interventions'.[43] While strategic behaviour does rely on set processes if the organizations's scope and posture are to remain unchanged, a shift in strategy must be originated by active intervention of the organization's leadership. This is the case when a new type of opportunity or threat is to be uncovered ('new' in the sense that it lies outside the reach of what existing routines are programmed to detect) and when a new solution is to be pursued. Particularly when top management involves itself in the development of the specific action plan, it heavily tints the output of the search process: if a strong force suggests a particular solution, chances are substantially increased that the solution will be selected. Indeed, if top management suggests a solution, it may well be weighed on its own merits and never be appraised against other alternatives. As Aharoni found, a strong initiating force can propel an organization at a distance 'along the road to investment, causing it to ignore unfavourable circumstances that are uncovered or even to skip the first stages of the investigation entirely'.[44]

(2) Top management over time can have a determining impact on the shape of the processes. As Bower has shown, a key function of an organization's leadership is to shape and reshape the structure in a way to cause

subunits to behave in one particular way rather than another.[45] Managing the 'structural context' – the formal organization, the information, control, measure of performance, and reward and punishment systems – thus becomes a key to influencing the strategy.[46] Actions by top management 'to reorganize to give more attention to . . . or to deal more effectively with . . . ' are illustrative of this kind of function.

Top management can monitor the routines on which strategic decisions are based. Information gathering and processing as well as alternatives generation and analysis are conducted according to standardized procedures. While persistently controlling them is impossible, top management can promote and influence the organizational learning of these procedures.

(3) The third role of top management is the decision itself to pursue a course of action. As we saw earlier, such a decision is not made at a particular point in time by a particular person. Rather, commitments are built up around a particular strategy as its feasibility and attractiveness is investigated and analysed. Top management has to give its approval for such investigation and analysis. It thereby has a bearing on the decision process in that the more outlays it allows for the investigation of a course of action, the more the organization will be committed to it. And the more it allows the process to go on, the more will it have to back up investigators in the commitments they make. Since investigators know they have to get top management's periodical endorsement precisely to avoid making commitments which might be inappropriate, they in fact enhance the pressure for approval by top management. By giving its approval, top management itself makes commitments. Consequently, top management is indeed part of the decision process.*

In the specific context of this study, a critical question is that of who represents ultimate leadership – GCEs' top management or key sponsoring government units. Two views would be possible. The first considers the GCE as *the* organization and looks at the government as part of the external environment; even if the government is itself an organization, it can still be viewed as part of the outside world in which the acting agent—the GCE—functions. The second considers the government as the organization and looks at the GCE as a suborganization.

In fact, the appropriate view appears to be a blend between these two. Our focus is on the actions of the GCE. It is its behaviour in which we are interested, its strategy we are to explain. Yet, the GCE is indeed part of a broader system which can have direct influence over it. Contrary to the overall environment, the government can take steps to cause a GCE to take a given course of action. Indeed, the government has a direct say in the decision process. Therefore, while the GCE's strategy *is* what we are to understand, we see the GCE as part of a

---

*A parallel can be drawn between this and Bower's conception of what he refers to as impetus – 'the force that moves a project toward funding . . . [or] the willingness of a general manager . . . to commit himself to sponsor a project . . .'.[47] Bower sees the need for an impetus for a project to be approved: 'The general manager in question must sponsor the project and shepherd it successfully through the rigors of whatever screening the organization imposes'.[48]

larger organization: to understand a GCEs' behaviour, we must understand how the government's units which have a bearing over it function.

Therefore, beyond the role of GCEs' top management *per se*, we must ask what role key government units play in terms of leadership.

(Before going on, we must specify that when we use the term 'government' here we really mean organizations within the state – ministries, agencies, departments, etc. When we talk of the government we in fact refer to those state organizations which are relevant in a particular situation, that is which have a concern for the particular strategic decision under consideration.)

Governments can play the role of an initiating force. As top management, the government can 'create a problem' which will lead to search for strategic action. This can arise either in the context of an opportunity or in the context of a performance failure or threat thereof. In most cases, it is not the government which raises problems of microeconomic nature (for example, raise questions concerning the financial results of a GCE); corporate management is generally aware of such problems before government. Rather, the problems raised by government mostly concern macro socioeconomic issues. This does not mean that the government cannot raise opportunities which are attractive also from the microeconomic viewpoint, but simply that the government's motivation in proposing the opportunity is primarily geared to broader concerns. For example, a regional development agency can ask a company to invest in a depressed region in order to promote employment; yet, in so doing, it can create an attractive opportunity for the firm itself: it can, for instance, provide financial or fiscal incentives which can make investments in that area quite appealing.

The government can merely pose a problem and leave it to the GCE to devise the solution. Or it can pose the problem *and* suggest the solution. For instance, it may not just exert pressure for a GCE to invest in a particular area, but also propose a specific project (for example a particular plant in a particular location). In fact, the majority of the actions initiated by the government are of the positive kind – that is, opportunities to undertake certain endeavours – posed in conjunction with a particular solution.

Moreover, the government has a role in terms of a commitment build-up process: top management of a GCE tries to periodically consult with government to inform it of its decisions and actions in order to secure approval and back-up for the company's strategy. By periodically consulting with relevant state-organizations, top management gradually converts them to its strategy; as the process evolves they find themselves co-opted and compelled to look on management's commitments to a particular course of action as binding for the GCE involved.

Yet, the role of the government here is not limited to that of reinforcing top management in its decisions. Top management normally decides to pursue courses of action which it knows will be more or less explicitly approved by the government. It is therefore careful to identify and be responsive to whatever inclinations the government may have about the company's strategy.

Thus, there are two sides to the coin in top management's consultations with the government: beyond the commitment build-up process, these consultations serve the purpose of providing top management with information which enables it to align the company's actions to government expectations.

C. Limits of organizational action

A number of organizational factors tend to limit the range of options effectively available to an organization and to restrain its flexibility.

1. Goals as constraints

Organizational goals tend to be formulated as constraints imposed by suborganizations – component organizations' expectations often conflicting among themselves and but partially reconciled: 'Incompatible constraints are attended to sequentially, the organization satisfying one while simply neglecting another'.[49] Component organizations tend to be imperialistic, that is each unit is preoccupied with increasing its scope in terms of its budget, manpower or territory; it also aspires to increase the range of its influence in terms of making sure that its own demands are satisfied as much as possible. There is therefore a more or less explicit struggle among units for the acceptance of each unit's constraints. Moreover, since an organization's goals tend to emerge from constraints laid down by component organizational units, the organization's goals usually only go so far as the demands of its components. If a particular course is not advocated by such and such a unit, it will simply not be included in the normal decision process; unless actively promoted by an initiating force, if no unit pushes for a particular action, the action will just not be contemplated.

There is a variety of units both within GCEs and outside them – notably in government – which have expectations about their behaviour. GCEs' goals partially reflect these expectations – those which are either not in conflict with other expectations, or those which are advocated by the most influential organizational units. Anyhow, a GCE's goals are limited by the particular demands of the units which have a bearing over it. In fact, suborganizations 'are often created in order to pay special attention to a neglected aspect of a problem'.[50] This means that if the wish emerges – often in top management itself – that a given type of activity receive particular attention and be considered as part of the normal pattern of behaviour of the organization, a special unit responsible for that type of activity may be created. This increases the range of options available to the organization, for the new unit will time and again propose an alternative for action falling in the field of activity for which it is responsible. This will also affect the probabilities of organizational choice in that the unit will also generate data tailored to make the selection of its proposed alternative more likely. For example, if say, a chief executive feels his company should pursue foreign opportunities more actively, he may create an international division. This will cause the company to look at the foreign investment option more regularly and thus increase the number of alternatives considered when a strategic problem arises. Yet, because of its outputs (in terms of the information and estimates it will produce), the setting up of such a division is in itself a commitment to international expansion: 'The very creation of a particular division in an organization devoting all its time and energy to international operations creates forces that will drive the organization towards increasing involvement and expansion of this field'.[51]

2. Organizational momentum and inertia

Change in an organization's strategic scope is slow to come about. Behaviour at point t is largely determined by behaviour at $t - 1$ and behaviour at $t + 1$ will tend to only be marginally different than at t. Thus, when a company follows a certain pattern of behaviour, change will tend to occur well after the point where costs are greater than benefits. Thus also, when a company follows a particular course, a change in the environment (such as a change in competition, demand, or supply of raw materials) will tend to cause a change in strategy only much later than the environmental change; usually, only when considerable and repeated data have been channelled into the organization indicating that change is warranted, and when all the relevant processes have been accomplished, will change come about. By that time the 'optimal' point for change will typically long have passed.

Change is all the slower to come about when the procedures involved are numerous and complex. If a proposed change in strategy has to be approved by many organizational units, then the process of change will be more cumbersome. The pace of change will also be affected by the review procedures themselves – the efficiency with which reviewing units operate. Further, the pace and effectiveness of change is dependent on the degree to which the proposed change effects the demands of many suborganizations. A shift in strategy entailing the discontinuance of a particular course of action will be all the more difficult to accomplish when it entails upsetting the expectations of several suborganizations which were satisfied up to that point. Also, if a new proposed strategy has an impact – as positive as it may be – on the expectations of several suborganizations, then its adoption will be cumbersome because each suborganization will want to make sure that its own expectations are met as far as possible. This means that if a course of action is contemplated which promises benefits to several units in terms of the satisfaction to new demands, then its formulation and approval process will be slow because the various units concerned will want to be consulted and be part of the process.

Therefore, in the case of GCEs, strategic change is slow. Given the number of suborganizations within the companies (for example, in the IRI type of organization) and in the government which are concerned by their decisions and actions, change has to go through a great number of procedures. Besides, given the complexity of the relationships among the various suborganizations (as well as often the intricacies entailed by suborganizations), these procedures are frequently accomplished with great sluggishness. Further, the major problem is often represented by the need to co-ordinate the aims of the various suborganizations involved. A change usually entails giving up a certain course of action. This in itself often requires the agreement of a variety of organizational units. Then, the formulation of the new course of action also calls for co-ordination among a variety of units which all have a role in the development and adoption of the course in question. This problem can be expected to be most acute when the strategies of a variety of GCEs is to be co-ordinated.

3. Organizational feasibility

We saw that there is a considerable gap between what a rational unitary decision-maker might plan to do and what a conglomerate of semi-feudal, loosely allied suborganizations can in fact decide. Yet, there are further limits on what can be expected in terms of *action*: not only do organizational processes limit what strategy can be formulated, they also limit what can actually be accomplished in terms of implementing a strategic plan.

First, when the degree of innovation is high, a strategy is hard to implement. When a new pattern of behaviour is to be pursued, leaders can expect that the plan will be considerably distorted. Specifically, subunits will more or less systematically seek similarities between the actions called for by the new strategy and actions which were previously accomplished in the context of different strategies. Therefore, the accomplishment of the plan will not follow 'optimal' paths; rather, it will follow paths which will emulate patterns that each unit will have followed under a past strategic plan, even though such a plan may be quite dissimilar from the one to be pursued now. It is only with experience of a given type of strategy that subunits learn how to develop appropriate patterns of action tailored to this strategy. For example, when a company first expands abroad, the way it goes about it in practice (such as the way investigation of investment opportunities is conducted) will be far from being adapted to foreign investments; the strategy of foreign expansion will thus be accomplished suboptimally since it will be implemented according to procedures directly borrowed from domestic operations.

Second, the extent to which a strategy calls for the co-ordinated action of many units complicates implementation. If a plan can be handled in quasi-independence by one or few units, it will be accomplished more effectively than if it requires the concerted action of several units. To ensure co-ordinated action, procedures are necessary; but again these procedures are necessarily limited in terms of what they can co-ordinate. If a new type of strategy is to be pursued, very often existing procedures are unable to ensure proper co-ordination.

The organization's structure is a critical variable. Consider, for instance, a strategy of foreign expansion. If a company is organized with an international division, the strategy will be implemented relatively smoothly because it will be handled for the most part autonomously by the division without need for much concertation with the rest of the organization. (This will be so especially if the strategy is an incremental one, that is if it does not affect the rest of the company's operations, thus not impairing previously satisfied constraints.) On the other hand, if the company is organized, say, functionally with no separate unit for foreign operations, the entire organization is likely to be affected by the strategy. Extensive co-ordination will be required among suborganizations and one may expect considerable inefficiency in the strategy's implementation – especially if the strategy is a new one for the firm.

In the case of GCEs the problem is further complicated by the fact that the relevant organizational units are often not only within a particular GCE but also outside. A GCE's strategy often requires the co-ordination with governmental units and/or other GCEs. Once more, since the co-ordination procedures are generally limited, concerted action is frequently inefficient and rarely accomplished as designed. Therefore, the possibilities for co-ordinated action between several GCEs and government are *de facto* more limited than what appears theoretically possible.

D. Conclusion

The pre-eminent trait of organizational activity is its programmed character—the extent to which behaviour is the product of set processes. To understand corporate behaviour one must understand these processes. While the traditional approach invoked postulated objectives to account for companies' actions, here the focus is on standard operating procedures and routines which vitally condition what a company does and does not do.

For familiar courses of action, 'the best explanation of an organization's behaviour at t is $t-1$; the best prediction of what will happen at $t+1$ is t. [The process view's] explanatory power is achieved by uncovering the organizational routines and repertoires that produced the outputs that comprise the [firm's behaviour under consideration].'[52] If an organization takes a certain action today, its component units must have taken in the past, in comparable circumstances, an action only slightly different from today's action. Thus, to understand what will trigger strategic search, one has to look at what information organizational routines are designed to collect and process. To understand what alternatives will be considered in given circumstances, one has to look at what past circumstances are closest to the present ones and what was done then, etc. Similarly, to predict a firm's behaviour in a given situation, one has to look at past behaviour in a similar situation. For example, if one asks what will a multinational do, say, if exports to a particular country decline, the most likely answer lies in the company's behaviour when it faced comparable export declines in other countries.

For new types of courses of action, one must still consider what processes lead to a particular output. But for a new kind of problem or opportunity to be identified and for a new kind of strategic alternative to be considered and pursued, an initiating force must actively intervene in the decision process. Therefore, one must uncover which of these forces have influence to cause an organization to look at new types of strategies; and one must analyse to which particular issues various key forces are likely to be sensitive and which particular courses of action they are likely to be inclined to promote. Yet, one must not lose sight of the fact that, while forces can indeed provide the impetus for new problems or opportunities and courses of action to be considered, their influence beyond that is critically conditioned by existing organizational processes; once a force has introduced a new idea, standard procedures take over and the force can have but limited – if any – impact on what is done with its idea. (Nowhere is this more striking than at the implementation level: the actual moves which are taken 'in the field' to accomplish a plan are generally exclusively the products of set routines.) And such procedures yield actions at point t which closely resemble actions at $t - 1$. Therefore, to understand why a strategy – no matter how novel – is actually formulated and carried out the way it is, one is still forced to focus on the existing organizational processes.

III. AN ORGANIZATIONAL PROCESS APPROACH TO POLICY BEHAVIOUR

The following section concerns a firm's basic *modus operandi* – the way a company conducts its ongoing affairs. As suggested above, a framework focusing on policy decisions can draw more readily on existing organization theory – March and Simon, and Cyert and March in particular. Further, several of the concepts assumptions and propositions discussed in the context of the strategic decisions framework apply here. Therefore, our discussion will be relatively short.

A. Policy behaviour as output of organizational processes

The ongoing behaviour of companies is a product of established routines and standard operating procedures. The actual conduct of existing company activities is a process. In a manufacturing concern, the acquistion of resources (human and financial as well as plant and equipment) and their allocation as well as the marketing function are all the product of set procedures. Each suborganization follows certain rules of behaviour which determine its actions in a fairly stable way. In the case of an MNC, the management of the various subsidiaries is subjected to certain given routines. In the case of GCEs, the companies behave within certain guidelines set by government.

Processes determine the co-ordination between various suborganizations. Thus, relationships between subsidiaries and headquarters in a diversified company are specified in terms of more or less explicit standard norms. Such relationships come down to two basic types of interactions. First, the monitoring of operations by headquarters. Central management needs to control the doings of subsidiaries. For this, a number of standard tools are available which gather and analyse data about subsidiaries' performance. But this control function is dependent on processes which are necessarily limited in their scope, that is, partial information on partial elements of the subsidiary's actions. Second, centralized resources and centralized resource allocation. The former refers to payments from subsidiaries to the parent company (such as royalties or dividends); this is clearly related to the control function. The latter is the distribution of resources by headquarters. Again, this is accomplished through prespecified rules and procedures. Furthermore, various units of an organization relate to each other frequently. Here too, such relationships are dependent on standard procedures (for example, rules setting transfer prices between divisions). In the case of GCEs, processes are responsible for intracompany relations (particularly critical in the case of the IRI types of structures) as well as for relationships between GCEs and government.

Given that the tasks of organizations have to be carried out by a large number of individuals in a concerted fashion, it is necessary to have certain rules of conduct to permit co-ordination among the various subtasks. These rules tend to be fairly straightforward to facilitate their learning and their application and they tend to be relatively stable or standard. While these rules are necessary to co-ordinate the doings of an organization, they tend to introduce a certain bureaucratic heaviness or rigidity and sluggish formalism in its behaviour.

B. Key characteristics

Six basic features about this process view are noteworthy.

1. Actors

As in the case of strategic decisions, GCEs and government are viewed as two distinct organizations, each with its own aggregation of component organizations. The analysis of policy decisions may require that GCEs and the government be broken up in different and usually smaller pieces than for the analysis of strategic decisions. This reflects the different nature of the interactions between government and GCEs for different classes of decisions. Strategic scope decisions involve for the most part exchanges between top management and high-ranking government officials (although not exclusively so, as far as the government side is concerned). On the other hand, given their often more specific and technical nature, operating policy decisions frequently involve a larger spectrum of people within companies and government. Thus, the analysis must go into a more minute splitting up of the relevant units.

Suborganizations develop their own perceptions and biases about what things are important and how things should be done. Given the frequently specialized nature of their job, organizational units often have a particular tendency to develop their own idiosyncrasies; technical data available to the unit, recruitment of specialized personnel or tenure of individuals in the unit reinforce the 'personalization' of suborganizations' attitudes.

2. Goals

Again, we find generally implicit goals emerging from within an organization as a set of constraints defining acceptable levels of performance, imposed on the organization by various organizational units. Again, since many of these constraints cannot be reconciled, substantial conflict subsists in organizations. Slack enables organizations to survive despite inconsistencies among participants' aims. The fact that goals are attended to sequentially permits goal incongruence.

3. Uncertainty avoidance and standard scenarios

While uncertainty is a constant feature of the environment in which organizations must live, they constantly seek to avoid it.

> They avoid the requirement that they correctly anticipate events in the distant future by using decision rules emphasizing short-run reaction to short-run feed-back rather than anticipation of long-run uncertain events . . . They avoid the requirement that they anticipate future reactions of other parts of their environment by arranging a negotiated environment. They impose plans, standard operating procedures, industry tradition, and uncertainty absorbing contracts on that environment.[53]

Organizations and suborganizations do not plan when this requires making conjectural hypotheses about the future. They only revert to planning when this helps them reduce environmental uncertainty; planning serves to arrange a negotiated environment, that is, to regularize relations with other agents with which the organization or suborganization has to deal. In a business enterprise, the environment of organizational units is represented by the outside scene in which the enterprise functions – the market, competitors, sources of supply, etc. But from the point of view of a particular suborganization, the environment is also represented by other organizational units with which the suborganization has to deal. In the case of GCEs, organizational units also have to relate to government. Each unit endeavours to stabilize the environment around it by standardizing relations with it. Vis-à-vis the outside environment, stabilization occurs through procedures such as supply contracts or contracts with customers or more or less explicit agreements with competitors. Vis-à-vis the internal organizational environment, stabilization occurs in terms of arrangements such as agreed budgetary splits, accepted areas of responsibility and established practices. Such arrangements occur both within a particular GCE and within the government (say, between various government departments). And similar arrangements occur between GCEs' units and government units.

'Where the . . . environment cannot be negotiated, organizations deal with remaining uncertainties by establishing a set of standard scenarios that constitute the contingencies for which they prepare'.[54] Organizations develop a set of programmes which constitute patterns of behaviour to follow when the organization is confronted with a particular occurrence outside of the negotiated environment. Here too organizational units have a set of programmes tailored to deal with uncertainty *vis-à-vis* the outside as well as the inside organizational environment. For example, an MNC will usually have a standard set of reactions in the case of a devaluation (or a threat thereof) in a country in which it operates. And a division will have a standard behaviour in case of an overall corporate budgetary crunch.

4. Search

The uncertainty-avoidance mechanisms used by organizations are limited. Programmes are necessarily limited. And certain events cannot be foreseen and thus cannot be constructed as possible scenarios. Therefore, there are instances in which an organization finds itself confronted with unexpected situations and unforeseen problems. Here organizations engage in search. Search is motivated and problem-oriented. It is simpleminded – first the neighbourhood of the symptom is searched, then the neighbourhood of the current alternative. Patterns of search reflect biases such as the origin or training of constituent parts of the organization as well as organizational communication patterns.[55]

5. Organizational learning and change

Organizational processes are basically stable. Normally organizations learn incrementally in that they build on existing processes and improve them and refine them as they acquire experience with a particular kind of activity and as they assimilate ways of adapting to new situations. Yet, dramatic change can occur in certain instances. These include marked changes in the budget – either increases or decreases – a dramatic performance failure or a change in management. In the case of GCEs, if a company fails to live up to certain standards, the government will normally demand change; management will then either comply or be replaced with a new management team committed to change.

6. Leadership

Again, the need to decentralize runs headlong into the need for co-ordination.[56] The need for co-ordination as well as the importance of certain overall policies guiding the behaviour of organizational units call for the involvement of leaders. The way a suborganization behaves, its propensities and operating procedures can be influenced by leaders' intervention. Yet, this influence is necessarily limited, and central and persistent control is impossible given the complexity of the task to be accomplished by the organization (that very complexity which calls for decentralization in the first place). Thus, leaders can in certain instances step in and modify the operating routines of an organization, but on the whole this happens rarely. 'Existing organizational orientations and routines are not impervious to direct change. Careful targeting of major factors that support routines – such as personnel, rewards, information, and budgets – can effect major changes over time. But the terms and conditions of most . . . leadership jobs – [often] short tenure and responsiveness to hot issues – make effective, directed change uncommon.'[57]

Where the influence of leaders can habitually be greater is in the behaviour of an organization *vis-à-vis* an unexpected event. Here there are two possible cases. The first is that of an event which is a departure from the normal course of things in the organization's life but which is contemplated *ex ante* in terms of contingency programmes for that particular type of event. Here, leaders can trigger one programme rather than the other. (Leaders can also make marginal changes in the implementation of a particular programme's routines.) The second case is that of a totally unforeseen event for which there is no contingency programme. Here leaders can intervene in the search process. As for strategic decisions, leaders can have a role as an initiating force suggesting one solution rather than another. Further, over the long run, leaders can influence the development of new programmes for different types of contingencies.

On the whole, the role of government leaders in the *modus operandi* of GCEs is clearly even more limited than their role in strategic decisions. Policy decisions tend to revolve around rather technical issues which are of little concern to them. Still, there are exceptions – decisions having relevance for macroeconomic or sociopolitical questions. Further, government suborganizations responsible for a particular area do take an active interest in GCEs' policy decisions. For example, a country's central bank can exert pressure over GCEs to adopt a particular policy *vis-à-vis*, say, currency speculation.

C. Limits of organizational action

Several factors restrain the versatility or adaptiveness of an organization's *modus operandi*.

1. Goals

Organizational goals are constraints imposed by suborganizations defining acceptable performance levels. The actual behaviour of GCEs takes some of these constraints into account – not all, since certain expectations are in conflict with each other. 'Central among these constraints is organizational health, defined usually in terms of bodies assigned and dollars appropriated'.[58] Each suborganization strives to improve or at least to keep constant its 'health', that is, to maintain or increase its importance or imperialism. Three consequences ensue.

First, there is a tendency in organizations to constantly do a bit more of what is currently being done. Organizations have a propensity to repeat what they are doing, each time with a bit more emphasis (more exployees, for example). Thus, budgets change incrementally; to prepare their budgets, organizational units tend to take last year's budget as a base and adjust it upwards. Therefore, in terms of their ongoing activities, organizations are dynamic or at least mechanistic institutions: due primarily to the imperialistic mood of component organization units, there is a natural evolutionary bent built into organizations.

Second, change is much easier if it entails an increase in organizational health rather than a decrease. A change in an operating policy will be all the harder to accomplish if it entails a reduction of certain suborganizations' budgets or ranges of activity.

Third, if a change in an organization's *modus operandi* is to be implemented that entails a broadening of the organization's activity and an increase in the overall budget, there will be a struggle among organizational units to secure jurisdiction over the new activity.

2. *Organizational biases*

Organizations and suborganizations develop relatively stable cultural patterns; that is, propensities about perceptions, priorities, values and generally attitudes *vis-à-vis* the way to carry out their operations. Such propensities are influenced by things such as recruitment of personnel into the organization, tenure of individuals in the organization, training of such individuals; they also depend on patterns of communication within the organization, distribution of rewards, group pressures within the organization. They are reinforced by organizational parochialisms and by outside pressures (for example, suppliers or customers influence and are influenced by and reinforce such propensities). Such propensities are developed in the context of a particular activity but are most often transposed with little change to new activities. Therefore, unless there is an explicit intervention by an authoritative source either from within or from without the organization or suborganization, new activities are implemented according to existing cultural patterns, only marginally adapted from existing activities.

In the case of GCEs, a company develops certain cultural biases in the context of a certain type of activity – say, domestic operations. Interfaces with ministries or government agencies have an influence on the firm's *modus operandi* just as other things do, such as the rewards for pursuing certain patterns of action, or pressures say from other GCEs (suppliers, for example).

144

When the firm engages in new types of activities – say MN operations – it will initially normally transplant these propensities to the new activity without questioning them. Only a dramatic performance failure or the conscious intervention of a force will cause the organization to radically revise its assumptions and attitudes. Otherwise the evolution and adaptation of its *modus operandi* will be but a gradual one.

3. Organizational feasibility

There are severe limits on change in a company's policies. First, in terms of what can be planned: normally, if a change is to affect several interrelated suborganizations, there is a need for a consensus to be reached on the very notion of the change, which can be a cumbersome process. Again, for GCEs, if a change in operating procedures is of concern to the government, the consensus-reaching process can be all the slower since governmental units also have to get involved. Second, in terms of implementation: once a change in an organization's *modus operandi* is decided upon, its accomplishment is typically cumbersome and unfaithful relative to what was planned. To illustrate this point, Roosevelt noted:

> The Treasury is so large and far-flung and ingrained in its practices that I find it almost impossible to get the action and results I want . . . But the Treasury is not to be compared with the State Department. You should go through the experience of trying to get any changes in the thinking, policy, and action of the career diplomats and then you'd know what a real problem was. But the Treasury and the State Department put together are nothing as compared with the Na-a-vy . . . To change anything in the Na-a-vy is like punching a feather bed. You punch it with your right and you punch it with your left until you are finally exhausted, and then you find the damn bed just as it was before you started punching.[59]

It is difficult to change an organization's way of doing things in the context of existing endeavours. And the problem exists also in the context of new endeavours: when an organization enters new fields of activity it tends to apply its usual way of doing things even if the new activity is totally different – to change this is typically arduous.

Assuming some change can be achieved, it is usually difficult to achieve the particular kind of change which is desired. Organizations' reactions are rough approximations of what is originally intended by policy directives. Change in the *modus operandi* of organizations is rarely accomplished as desired, especially when implemented for the first time. This is indeed a delicate issue in operating policy decisions which require certain steps to be taken by many organizational units. The difficulty then is to achieve the proper emphasis in the change throughout the organization; that is, avoid the fact that certain units overreact while others virtually ignore the policy change. To illustrate, consider the MN activities of GCEs; if the finance ministry wants a change in the companies' international financial policies, the ministry has to make sure that whatever organization is responsible for monitoring the change in the various GCEs does so in a consistent fashion for all GCEs involved (for example, that the various civil servants engaged in the control of the policy implementation have a common attitude for the various GCEs concerned); and control also has to be exerted on the way GCEs actually react to the change, in other words, that they in fact comply with the directives in as uniform a fashion as possible.

D. Conclusion

To understand the reasons for an organization's *modus operandi* one needs to look into past behaviour and uncover the underlying processes of this action; to predict future behaviour one has to analyse present behaviour. At any point in time an organization is an aggregation of organizational units, each having its goals, procedures and programmes. The nature of organizational behaviour depends on the characteristics of the established processes. In the case of a contingency for which a set of programmes is available, the organization's behaviour depends on the choice made by leaders of a particular programme as opposed to others. In the case of a totally unforeseen situation, an organization will search a course of action among those courses of action it followed in the past; it will tend to adopt that course which it pursued in that situation familiar to it which most closely resembles the current situation. Leaders can but partially influence the choice of such a course and but partially cause that course to be adapted to the current situation.

In the following two chapters we take a process approach to GCEs' MN behaviour. Under this approach, to explain GCEs' MN behaviour calls for analysing what procedures and routines underlie organizational decisions and actions. As suggested by this chapter, a fundamental distinction this view makes is between actions which are familiar to the organization and actions which are entirely new to it: the process approach conceives of organizations as having an inherent tendency towards perpetuating the *status quo*; therefore, organizations are seen as being inclined towards pursuing familiar courses of action; for novel courses of action to be pursued, the intervention of a force which modifies the normal decision-making process is necessary. Accordingly, our discussion on GCEs' MN behaviour will have two parts: in the first we will examine how GCEs with little or no MN experience take their first steps towards international expansion; in the second we will focus on MN behaviour in the context of GCEs which already have international operations. (It should be clear that rather than an experience/no experience dichotomy we are really faced with a continuum – many companies having *some* MN experience. Yet, for purposes of analysis, it is convenient to consider two opposing cases – GCEs with no MN activities and GCEs which are MNCs.)

In Chapter VI we focus on GCEs' initial MN moves – essentially the strategic decisions a GCE makes to go MN in the first place. Such decisions are a continuum out of which behaviour emerges gradually; the various components of the decision process cannot be clearly separated in independent parts – they are in fact interrelated parts of a single process. Yet, there *are* certain distinct elements which, though intertwined (and in fact usually occurring, at least partially, simultaneously), can be distinguished:

(1) *Problem identification:* a problem can either be a performance failure (or threat thereof) or an opportunity – how to exploit it. A problem can be identified by existing organizational procedures or raised by a force. Since neither such procedures nor forces can ever be all-encompassing, firms are sensitive to certain problems only. Problems are raised not by the organization as a whole but by suborganizations with limited foci of attention. Therefore, problems usually concern but part of the organization's performance.

(2) *Search:* which solution to a problem is adopted depends on the company's past experience, unless a new alternative is imposed for consideration by a strong force. A solution is not necessarily an explicit formal plan. Still, a solution *de facto* is a detailed course of action – the behaviour actually followed by a company when a problem has been identified.

Where the solution starts and the problem ends varies considerably. Sometimes the problem is negative results in existing operations; the solution then can be MN expansion. (The problem can also be an opportunity abroad which the company does not see; there is then no need for a solution.) Or the problem can be, given the company wants to go MN, how to do so; the solution then is a particular strategy (where to invest, when, how – for example with what people, financial resources or partners). Still, the problem can be how to go MN in a particular way (say, in a particular country); the solution then is a strategy tailored especially to that particular form of MN expansion. Anyhow, even when the solution starts with the decision to go MN as such, it cannot stop there; it must address specific questions – define a precise strategy in terms of where to invest, when, how, etc.

(3) *Approval:* while there are formal procedures by which decisions are taken officially, in practice they do not have much direct relevance on the adoption of a course of action. A given course of action is adopted at no particular point but gradually as commitments are made during its very elaboration and evaluation. Yet, formal procedures can have an important indirect impact on the adoption of a certain course. Thus, if a lot of work has to be done in order to get a proposal through a formal evaluation body, there will be all the more commitment generated to back the proposal.

(4) *Action:* because organizations are loosely allied conglomerates of suborganizations, they are blunt instruments. They distort decisions – they do not accomplish a plan as formulated. To analyse organizational behaviour com-

pletely we have to include an explanation of what happens to a decision at the actual implementation level.

In Chapter VII we focus on GCEs with MN experience – with existing international operations. We focus on their MN strategic decisions – the way they decide their major resource allocations on an international scale (such as new foreign investments). We will take the same approach as for GCEs with no MN experience – analysing problem identification, search, approval and action. In fact, we will limit ourselves to pointing out what is distinctive about these companies relative to GCEs with no MN operations.
We then look at the *modus operandi* of these companies. Our focus is, given it has foreign activities, how does a GCE organize its affairs multinationally? What differentiates GCEs from private MNCs? These policy decisions are relevant only for those GCEs which have at least some MN experience: a company with no international operations clearly cannot have a *modus operandi* for such operations. (Still, it will be useful to distinguish between companies with recent and limited MN activities and those with well-established and extensive MN activities.)

The ongoing behaviour of GCEs is an output of organizational processes. As such this behaviour has distinctive characteristics. First, behaviour tends to be rather fixed, at least in the short run. What this means is that organizational processes are basically stable over a short period of time; generally speaking, regardless of the context in which they take place, processes tend to follow the same archetypes. Over time, organizational processes are developed according to certain patterns reflecting the organization's and sub-organizations' culture and biases, and which are reinforced with experience; these processes then occur following basically the same pattern in any situation, including situations which are quite different from those in which they were developed in the first place. Therefore, at least initially, GCEs in their MN activities have a tendency to borrow operating policies from domestic operations.

While processes are basically fixed over the short run, they do evolve gradually over the long term. With time and experience, a company learns to adapt its operating procedures to a new situation. Thus, GCEs with extensive foreign activities have developed processes tailored to MN operations. On the other hand, if a force intervenes, change can take place in an abrupt fashion. Yet, there are limits to the effectiveness with which such changes can take place.

APPENDIX

This appendix is in two parts. In the first we discuss in greater detail the criticisms directed at the traditional approach. In the second we survey the body of theory which has emerged from such criticism and which has provided the foundation for our own process approach.

A. Limitations of the traditional approach

These limitations can be thought of in two sets: the first has to do with the assumption of comprehensive rationality; the second with the assumption of monolithism.

1. Comprehensive rationality

Simon has argued that comprehensive rationality requires 'powers of prescience and capacities of computation resembling those we normally attribute to God'.[60] Specifically, five basic faults can be found with this notion:

(a) It assumes that all alternatives are known. In fact, this is clearly not so. In the traditional approach 'the number of alternatives [a decider] must explore is so great, the information he would need to evaluate them so vast that even an approximation to objective rationality is hard to conceive'.[61] He thus necessarily has to draw from a limited range of alternatives.

(b) It assumes that the consequences of each alternative are known. In fact, this is not the case. In most decisions it is practically impossible to anticipate all the possible effects of a particular course of action.

(c) It assumes that the probabilities of each outcome are known exactly. This means that to each possible alternative corresponds a set of possible consequences with a probability distribution attached to them; thus, the decider knows with certainty the expected value and standard deviation of each alternative. This is not so in reality. Decisions have to be made on the basis of imperfect information, particularly as far as estimates about the likelihood that a choice will yield one particular outcome rather than another.

(d) It overestimates the computational capabilities of the human mind. It assumes that all alternatives are contemplated and all possible consequences of each alternative evaluated in terms of their payoff and likelihood of occurrence. This clearly involves extremely elaborate computations. Even a computer would have a hard time since alternatives cannot usually be appraised in terms of one or even a few quantitative parameters. (Forrester notes that 'strategic problems are perhaps of the hundredth order of complexity while the most sophisticated computers are presently capable of only the tenth order'.[62]) Indeed, in practice, decisions have to be made on the basis of usually crude approximations of the attractiveness of the contemplated alternatives (themselves a restricted set of all the theoretically possible ones).

(e) It rests on the concept of maximization. Rational choice is a simple process: it merely consists of selecting that course of action whose consequences optimize the decider's payoff function. But this requires that all options be evaluated systematically. Since this is not possible in fact, a criterion other than maximization has to be used. In practice, choices are made on the basis of 'satisficing': the first contemplated alternative is chosen which appears to meet a certain arbitrarily predetermined threshold of attractiveness.

2. Monolithism

The traditional view focuses on the motivations and actions of the organization as such, and to explain its behaviour it imputes to it a 'mind' which is able to make global decisions for the total organization and to cause the organization to implement these decisions with absolute coherence and responsiveness. In practice, this conception is deficient.

Given the magnitude of the mission they are to perform, organizations must break up the problems they are confronted with into various subproblems which they ascribe to a variety of component units. An organization is therefore not a monolith but a constellation of suborganizations, each with a substantial degree of autonomy of its own.

The traditional view assumes that an organization has clear aims which reflect explicit decisions about what to do in the most basic sense (for example, choice of the firm's field of activity) – aims defined by the 'central mind' and providing strict direction to the total organization. But given the fragmentary character of organizations, each unit must in fact have its own demands and what the organization actually does must be the product less of central choices than of the interplay among such units.

It follows that conflict must frequently emerge within organizations. The traditional view's assumption about unity in the organization leads the analyst to pass over the fact that there can be absence of consensus about the ends to be pursued. In reality things are different. A good illustration is the resource allocation decision among several divisions. The conventional analyst will assume that resources will be allocated from the top so as to balance the growth of the various divisions in a way which will maximize the long-run performance of the whole. He sees this as a rational process and makes no room for conflict. If it makes sense to allocate more funds to one division at the expense of another, he will assume everybody – notably the latter division – will accept this if it indeed is expected to maximize the results of the whole. In practice, of course, there really is competition among divisions; each division has goals of its own and funds are allocated on the basis of a bargaining process in which the rationale of superior interests of the total organization often has limited weight in the face of each division's demands.

Given the fragmentary nature of organizations and their inherent multiplicity of demands, one has to question their ability to achieve true consistency and coherence in their behaviour. The traditional view does not have this problem. The assumption of monolithism enables one to postulate that all the actions of the organization are perfectly coordinated by the 'central mind': since this central mind is rational and has absolute power over the various components of the organization, no provision is made for inconsistencies. Given this attribute of oneness, the analyst does not have to ask himself how co-ordination is enforced. But things are different if we relax the assumption of monolithism. It is clear that top management is not responsible for all the organization's actions. Top management's jurisdiction is limited since there is

150

an inevitable delegation of authority and decentralization. And there have to be a number of accepted processes to ensure co-ordination among the various suborganizations as well as the channelling of whatever authority top management has. Indeed, the functioning of an organization depends on such standard operating procedures. But this in turn means that what an organization can do is confined by the range of such procedures: co-ordination is purchased at the price of limitations on the sphere of activity actually open to an organization.

The assumption of unitary behaviour causes one to overlook the fact that the demands of suborganizations put limits on the coherence of organizational behaviour as well as the fact that these demands plus the existence of set processes have a determining influence and put strict limits on an organization's actions.

B. Organization theory

Given the limitations of the traditional approach, a body of literature has developed commonly referred to as 'organization theory'. By drawing on a multiplicity of human sciences such as psychology or sociology, this literature attempts to explain the behaviour of organizations, avoiding the pitfalls of the conventional interpretations. It focuses especially on the limits of human intellectual and psychic capabilities and on the conception of organizations as fragmentary entities.

Organization theory is a relatively young science. As noted by James March: 'The field as a more or less identifiable cluster of research interests within a number of social sciences dates for most purposes from a group of books written between 1937 and 1947 – Barnard, Roethlisberger and Dickson, and Simon'.[63] The evolution of organization theory can be thought of in three stages.

> Chester Barnard's *The Function of the Executive* and Herbert Simon's *Administrative Behavior* mark the beginning and the end of the decade of definition of organization theory as a semi-discipline. The second decade witnessed an enormous increase in effort devoted to the systematic study of organizations. Many of the 'discoveries' of that decade (and of earlier periods) are summarized in a logically ordered, propositional form by March and Simon in their path-breaking book *Organizations*, published in 1958.[64]

The third stage is marked by the 1965 publication of the *Handbook of Organizations* under the editorship of James March, which attempts to 'summarize and report the present state of knowledge about organization'.[65] The *Handbook* in fact can be viewed as a synthesis of the various areas of study which are relevant to the understanding of how organizations function – economics, psychology, sociology, industrial relations etc. The chapter headings indicate that the range of subjects relevant to organization theory is broad indeed: management theory, economic theories, organizational growth and development, communications in organizations, organizational decision-making, interpersonal relations in organizations, organizational control structures, the comparative analysis of organizations.[66]

For our purposes, the relevant focus of organization theory is that concerned with the decision-making process in organizations. This stream of thought is best represented by Herbert Simon and his followers and often co-workers – particularly his colleagues at Carnegie, foremost among whom is James March. Simon's path-breaking work 'is motivated by the attempt to understand the basic features of organizational structure and function as they derive from the characteristics of human problem-solving and rational choice'.[67]

The starting point of Simon's approach is the concept of 'bounded rationality'. As we saw earlier, it is unrealistic to assume comprehensive rationality. Decisions are in fact taken in conditions of restricted intelligence – imperfect information and limited analytical capabilities. An essential step in the application of this concept is the 'replacement of the goal of maximizing with the goal of "satisficing", of finding a course of action that is "good enough"'.[68] Given this goal, the decider arbitrarily selects a level of performance to be reached. He will not be concerned with improving performance beyond that level once he has found a course of action which enables him to reach it. Thus, performance does not have to be 'as good as possible' but merely be 'adequate' – in other words, meet a certain standard. Over time, this level of performance can change: if it is always reached easily it will be revised upwards; if one frequently fails to meet it, it will be revised downwards.

In such a process the search procedure for alternatives is quite important. In comprehensive rationality the search procedure is irrelevant: since all alternatives are presumed to be examined, it is the 'best' alternative which will be chosen. But here, since the first satisfactory alternative is selected, the order in which alternatives are considered is essential. In organizations, alternatives are turned up by relatively predictable procedures: individuals and organizations develop set action programmes for various recurring situations as well as standard sequences by which each of these programmes is considered.

Further, problems are so complex that only a few aspects of a problem can be handled at a time. Thus, problems are split up into semi-independent parts which are attended to one by one. Similarly, action problems are designed to deal with one part each. Organizations assign semi-independent parts of a problem to semi-independent units within the organization. The way an organization is structured thus reflects the way problems are split up. But the structure itself affects the factoring of problems as well as the action programmes designed for these problems. Therefore, 'to predict the short-run behaviour of an adaptive organism, or its behaviour in a complex and rapidly changing environment, it is not enough to know its goals. We must know also a great deal about its internal structure and particularly its mechanism of adaptation'.[69]

March and Simon thus note that in this approach:

> (1) Optimizing is replaced by satisfying – the requirement that satisfactory levels of the criterion variables be attained. (2) Alternatives of action and consequences of action are discovered sequentially through search processes. (3) Repertoires of action programs are developed by organizations and individuals, and these serve as the alternatives of choice in recurrent situations. (4) Each specific action program deals with a restricted range of situations and a restricted range of consequences. (5) Each action is capable of being executed in semi-independence of others.[70]

This conception clearly challenges the traditional theory of the firm. The traditional theory assumes the firm 'to be composed of a single, omniscient economic man for whom all problems are given and who, aware of all alternative courses of action and relative consequences, instantly decides on actions to achieve his goal of profit maximization'.[71] No attention is given to the 'inside' of the firm – its social structure and internal processes as well as the psychological characteristics of the individuals within it. The firm,

> faced with a determinate supply schedule for factors of production, a given price for [its] product, and a technologically determined production function, is a predictable animal: profit is maximized when marginal cost is equal to the price that equals marginal revenue; the marginal rate of substitution between products and between factors of production equals their price ratio; equilibrium is achieved at the point of optimal use of inputs and outputs.[72]

Thus, the actions of the firm are rational responses to outside pressures: given its goal and knowledge, the firm behaves in response to economic forces which lie outside of its jurisdiction.

Three main questions arise about this theory.

First, the notion of profit maximization has come under attack. Some have argued that it is not profits which are maximized: Rothschild substitutes survival for profits.[73] Baumol argues that sales are the actual goal subject to a certain profit constraint.[74] Katona argues that a firm does not maximize one objective but a series of objectives: profits, sales, survival, maintenance of a share of the market, liquidity, and managerial comfort.[75] Papandreou sees the firm as having a 'general preference function' which itself is what is maximized.[76] Others argue that the firm really does not maximize. Beyond Simon's 'satisficing' argument, others such as Gordon[77] and Margolis[78] argue that maximization should be replaced by the notion of objectives as constraints which have to be satisfied.

Second, the notion of 'perfect information' has been challenged. As noted above, deciders do not have full information about all alternatives and consequences and are unable to analyse systematically all the options available.

Third, again as discussed earlier, the assumption of monolithism is attacked.

Therefore, a new theory of the firm is needed. This new approach is best represented by *A Behavioral Theory of the Firm* by Cyert and March.[79]

> Proceeding from a careful catalogue of challenges to the classical theory of the firm and a survey of the literature of Organization Theory, Cyert and March make a new departure. In contrast to the traditional theories that explain the firm's behaviour in terms of market factors, Cyert and March focus – as Organization Theory would suggest – on the effect of organizational structure and conventional practice upon the development of goals, the formulation of expectations, and the execution of choice.[80]

Following Barnard,[81] Cyert and March view the organization as an aggregation of participants, not all of which are necessarily on its payroll. An organization is a coalition.

> It is a coalition of individuals, some of them organized into subcoalitions. In a business organization the coalition members include managers, workers, stockholders, suppliers, customers, lawyers, tax collectors, regulatory agencies, etc. . . . Drawing the boundaries in an organizational coalition once and for all is impossible. Instead, we simplify the conception by focusing on the participants in a particular 'region' – either temporal or functional. That is, over a specified (relatively brief) period of time we can identify the major coalition members; or, for a particular decision we can identify the major coalition members.[82] . . . Participants have disparate demands changing foci of attention and limited ability to attend to all organization problems simultaneously.[83]

It is a negotiation process among coalition members which generates the organization's goals: participants bargain among themselves and thus produce a series of actual agreements which impose practical constraints on the organization. 'The list of these more or less independent constraints, imperfectly rationalized in terms of more general purposes, constitute an organization's goals. Organizational expectations arise from inferences drawn from available information'.[84] Thus, organizations have goals but these are not systematically thought out and formally designed to serve as guides to action; rather, they are outgrowths of organizational life which derive from the actual workings of the coalition.

An important feature of organizations is the existence of unresolved conflicts. Participants work within the same organization because they share some minimum goals. But all the goals within the organization are not shared by the whole coalition. Indeed, suborganizations have goals which are particular to them alone. Therefore, organizations live with often considerable latent conflict: 'We assume that an organization factors its decision problems into subproblems and assigns the subproblems to subunits in the organization. From the point of view of organizational conflict, the importance of such local rationality is in the tendency for the individual subunits to deal with a limited set of problems and a limited set of goals'.[85] This 'local rationality' leads to inconsistencies within the organization in that the various choices made are not necessarily coherent with each other. This inconsistency is first bearable due to the adjustment in 'organizational slack' (defined as 'payments to members of the coalition in excess of what is required to maintain the organization together').[86] Further, conflicts are resolved by sequential attention to goals: 'Organizations resolve conflict among goals, in part by attending to different goals at different times . . . The resulting time buffer among goals permits the organization to solve one problem at a time, attending one goal at a time'.[87]

Moreover, organizations seek to avoid uncertainty. Their first rule of operation is to solve pressing problems rather than develop long-run strategies: 'They achieve a reasonably manageable decision situation by avoiding planning where plans depend on predictions of uncertain future events and by emphasizing planning where the plan can be made self-confirming through some control device'.[88] Indeed, organizations use decision-rules that build on short-run feedback. Their second rule is to negotiate with the environment. In order to avoid uncertainty in other parts of their life, organizations work out plans, standard procedures and explicit or implicit arrangements with suppliers, competitors and customers (for example, uncertainty absorbing contracts).

Building on Simon's earlier work, Cyert and March develop a theory of search for solutions to organizational problems: 'Organizations use acceptable-level goals and select the first alternative they see that meets those goals'.[89] This alternative is not compared with others to find the best solution. Specifically, three things are assumed about organizational search.

(1) Search is motivated. Organizational search is problematic search: search is stimulated by a specific problem and motivated to find a solution to that problem.

(2) Search is simpleminded: the sequencing of search is crucial; it follows simpleminded rules that direct it first to the neighbourhood of the 'old' solution to that 'old' problem that most closely resembles the current one, and proceeds in a sequential way along traditional paths:[90] when a problem arises, one looks immediately for the problem that arose in the past closest to the problem at hand, and the first alternative solution which is considered for the current problem is that which was used to solve that old problem; if that is not

satisfactory, one moves to the next old problem most resembling the current one, and so on.

(3) Search is influenced by the particular training and experience of the various parts of the organization, the interaction of hopes and expectations, and the communication distortions reflecting unresolved conflict.[91]

Organizational behaviour is relatively stable. Yet, as dynamic institutions, organizations change gradually and adaptively as a result of experience. Over time, organizations modify their goals, shift their attention and revise their procedures for search. At any point in time organizational goals 'are a function of (1) organizational goals of the previous time period, (2) organizational experience with respect to that goal in the previous period, and (3) experience of comparable organizations with respect to the goal dimension in the previous time period'.[92] Further, with regard to adaptation in search rules,

> when an organization discovers a solution to a problem by searching in a particular way, it will be more likely to search in that way in future problems of the same type; when an organization fails to find a solution by searching in a particular way, it will be less likely to search in that way in future problems of the same type. Thus, the order in which various alternative solutions to a problem are considered will change as the organization experiences success or failure with alternatives.[93]

NOTES

1. Graham Allison, *Essence of Decision*, Little, Brown and Co., Boston, 1971, p. 67.
2. John Harsanyi, 'Some Social Science Implications of a New Approach to Game Theory', in K. Archibald (ed.), *Strategic Interaction and Conflict*, Berkeley, 1966, p. 1.
3. See the Appendix to Chapter II.
4. Graham Allison, *Essence of Decision*, p. 71.
5. James March and Herbert Simon, *Organizations*, John Wiley, New York, 1958.
6. Richard Cyert and James March, *A Behavioral Theory of the Firm*, Prentice Hall, Englewood Cliffs, NJ, 1963.
7. H. Igor Ansoff, *Corporate Strategy*, McGraw-Hill, New York, 1965, p. 20.
8. H. Igor Ansoff, *Corporate Strategy*, p. 9.
9. Herbert Simon, 'The New Science of Management Decision', in *The Shape of Automation for Men and Management*, Harper and Row, New York, 1965.
10. Enid Mumford and Andrew Pettigrew, *Implementing Strategic Decisions*, Longman, London, 1975, p. 60.
11. Enid Mumford and Andrew Pettigrew, *Implementing Strategic Decisions*, p. 61.
12. Enid Mumford and Andrew Pettigrew, *Implementing Strategic Decisions*, p. 37.
13. Richard Cyert and James March, *A Behavioral Theory of the Firm*, p. 43.
14. Yair Aharoni, *The Foreign Investment Decision Process*, Division of Research, Graduate School of Business Administration, Harvard University, Boston, 1966, p. 267.
15. John Dewey, *How We Think*, D. C. Heath, Boston, 1933.
16. Herbert Simon, *The Shape of Automation for Men and Management*.

17. Henry Mintzberg, Duru Raisinghani and André Théorêt, 'The Structure of "Unstructured" Decision Processes', *Administrative Science Quarterly*, Vol. 21, June 1976, pp. 246–275.
18. Graham Allison, *Essence of Decision*, Chapter III.
19. Graham Allison, *Essence of Decision*, p. 301.
20. Henry Mintzberg *et al.*, 'The Structure of "Unstructured" Decision Processes', p. 251.
21. See: William Guth, 'Toward a Social System Theory of Corporate Strategy', *The Journal of Business*, Vol. 49, No. 3, July 1976, pp. 374–388; and Henry Mintzberg, 'Policy as a Field of Management Theory', *The Academy of Mangement Review*, Vol. 2, No. 1, January 1977, pp. 88–103.
22. Yair, Aharoni, *The Foreign Investment Decision Process*.
23. Joseph Bower, *Managing the Resource Allocation Process*, Division of Research, Graduate School of Business Administration, Harvard University, Boston, 1970.
24. Henry Mintzberg *et al.*, 'The Structure of "Unstructured" Decision Processes'.
25. Henry Mintzberg *et al.*, 'The Structure of "Unstructured" Decision Processes', p. 253.
26. Joseph Bower, *Managing the Resource Allocation Process*, p. 50.
27. William Pounds, 'The Process of Problem Finding', *Industrial Management Review*, Fall 1969, pp. 1–19.
28. Richard Cyert and James March, 'Organizational Factors in the Theory of Oligopoly', *Quarterly Journal of Economics*, Vol. 70, 1956, pp. 52ff.
29. Yair Aharoni, *The Foreign Investment Decision Process*, p. 42.
30. Graham Allison, *Essence of Decision*, p.79.
31. Yair Aharoni, *The Foreign Investment Decision Process*, p. 41.
32. Yair Aharoni, *The Foreign Investment Decision Process*, Chapter IV.
33. Joseph Bower, *Managing the Resource Allocation Process*.
34. Yair Aharoni, *The Foreign Investment Decision Process*, p. 124.
35. Yair Aharoni, *The Foreign Investment Decision Process*, p. 132.
36. Joseph Bower, *Managing the Resource Allocation Process*, pp. 64–65.
37. Richard Cyert and James March, *A Behavioral Theory of the Firm*, pp. 123–125.
38. Graham Allison, *Essence of Decision*, pp. 93–94.
39. Graham Allison, *Essence of Decision*, p. 80.
40. Richard Cyert and James March, *A Behavioral Theory of the Firm*, p. 43.
41. Eugene Carter, 'A Behavioral Theory Approach to Firm Investment and Acquisition Decisions', doctoral dissertation, Graduate School of Industrial Administration, Carnegie-Mellon University, 1970.
42. Yair Aharoni, *The Foreign Investment Decision Process*, p. 54.
43. Joseph Bower and Yves Doz, 'Strategy Formulation: A Social and Political Process', working paper, Graduate School of Business Administration, Harvard University, Boston, 1977.
44. Yair Aharoni, *The Foreign Investment Decision Process*, p. 83.
45. Joseph Bower, *Managing the Resource Allocation Process*.
46. Joseph Bower and Yves Doz, 'Strategy Formulation: A Social and Political Process', p. 14.
47. Joseph Bower, *Managing the Resource Allocation Process*, p. 68.
48. Joseph Bower, *Managing the Resource Allocation Process*, pp. 57–58.
49. Graham Allison, *Essence of Decision*, p. 92.
50. Graham Allison, *Essence of Decision*, p. 93.
51. Yair Aharoni, *The Foreign Investment Decision Process*, p. 45.
52. Graham Allison, *Essence of Decision*, p. 88.
53. Richard Cyert and James March, *A Behavioral Theory of the Firm*, p. 119.
54. Graham Allison, *Essence of Decision*, p. 84.
55. See: Richard Cyert and James March, *A Behavioral Theory of the Firm*, pp 121–122.

56. See: Graham Allison, *Essence of Decision*, p. 85.
57. Graham Allison, *Essence of Decision*, pp. 94–95.
58. Graham Allison, *Essence of Decision*, p. 82.
59. M. S. Eccles, *Beckoning Frontiers*, Knopf, New York, 1951, p. 336.
60. Herbert Simon, *Models of Man*, John Wiley, New York, 1957, p. 3.
61. Herbert Simon, *Administrative Behavior*, Macmillan, New York, 1957.
62. Jay W. Forrester, 'The Structure Underlying Management Processes', in *Evolving Concepts in Management*, Academy of Management, New York, 1964. Allison brings a further objection to the requirement that the entire decision tree be generated and analysed. He takes the example of a chess player's problem of rational choice and notes that 'although there are only thirty possible moves in an average chess situation, consideration of all possible countermoves and counters to countermoves and so on leads to a number on the order of 10^{120} paths from the state of the board to the end of the game. A machine examining one of these paths every millionth of a second would require 10^{95} years to decide on its first move' (Graham Allison, *Essence of Decision*, p. 286).
63. James March, *Handbook of Organizations*, Rand McNally, Chicago, 1965, p. IX.
64. Graham Allison, *Essence of Decision*, p. 69.
65. James March, *Handbook of Organizations*, p. IX.
66. James March, *Handbook of Organizations*, p. VI.
67. Graham Allison, *Essence of Decision*, p. 71.
68. Herbert Simon, *Models of Man*, pp. 204–205.
69. Herbert Simon, *Models of Man*, p. 166.
70. James March and Herbert Simon, *Organizations*, p. 169.
71. Yair Aharoni, *The Foreign Investment Decision Process*, p. 246.
72. Graham Allison, *Essence of Decision*, p. 73.
73. K. Rothschild, 'Price Theory and Oligopoly', *Economic Journal*, Vol. LVII, No. 227, September 1947, pp. 299–320.
74. William Baumol, *Business Behavior, Value, and Growth,* Macmillan, New York, 1959.
75. George Katona, *Psychological Analysis of Economic Behavior*, McGraw-Hill, New York, 1951.
76. A. G. Papandreou, 'Some Basic Issues in the Theory of the Firm', in B. F. Haley (editor), *A Survey of Contemporary Economics*, Irwin, Homewood, Ill., 1952.
77. R. Gordon, 'Short-Period Price Determination', *American Economic Review*, Vol. 38, 1948.
78. J. Margolis, 'The Analysis of the Firm: Rationalism, Conventionalism, and Behaviorism', *Journal of Business*, Vol. 31, 1958.
79. Richard Cyert and James March, *A Behavioral Theory of the Firm*.
80. Graham Allison, *Essence of Decision*, p. 75.
81. Chester Barnard, *The Functions of the Executive*, Harvard University Press, Cambridge, 1938.
82. Richard Cyert and James March, *A Behavioral Theory of the Firm*, p. 27.
83. Richard Cyert and James March, *A Behavioral Theory of the Firm*, p. 43.
84. Graham Allison, *Essence of Decision*, p. 76.
85. Richard Cyert and James March, *A Behavioral Theory of the Firm*, p. 117.
86. Richard Cyert and James March, *A Behavioral Theory of the Firm*, p. 36.
87. Richard Cyert and James March, *A Behavioral Theory of the Firm*, p. 118.
88. Richard Cyert and James March, *A Behavioral Theory of the Firm*, p. 119.
89. Richard Cyert and James March, *A Behavioral Theory of the Firm*, p. 120.
90. See: Yair Aharoni, *The Foreign Investment Decision Process*, p. 269.
91. Richard Cyert and James March, *A Behavioral Theory of the Firm*, pp. 121–122.
92. Richard Cyert and James March, *A Behavioral Theory of the Firm*, p. 123.
93. Richard Cyert and James March, *A Behavioral Theory of the Firm*, p. 124.

CHAPTER VI

GCEs with no MN Experience

The basic focus of this chapter is on GCEs' first decision to go MN – why and how GCEs make or do not make such a decision. We will successively deal with problem identification, search for solution, approval and action.

I. PROBLEM IDENTIFICATION

Two types of problems are relevant: actual or threatening performance failures and opportunities.

A. Performance failures (or threat thereof)

There are two ways setbacks in current operations – here domestic operations – can be identified: via procedures and via forces.

1. *Standard procedures*

These can be classified in three sets.

(a) GCEs have sensors for the appraisal of their own economic results – their profitability, their return on investment, their sales growth, the situation of their balance sheet (for example, their liquidity situation) as well as more qualitative variables (for example, the firm's image) and their strategic posture itself. Performance along these criteria is evaluated by accounting and control tools as well as more or less explicit mechanisms to perform a strategic audit of the company. But three intervening factors threaten the effectiveness of this.

First, organizational units often have considerable discretion in their actions. The larger and the more diversified and decentralized the organization, the lesser the ability of headquarters to keep track of their doings. As a result, important decisions about strategy implementation are, at least partially, out of control. Control procedures have to be selective and headquarters tend to have a schematic picture of operating divisions' actual decisions. Thus, errors in the accomplishment of a strategy are often made without top management being aware of them or finding out too late. And many problems are not brought to top management's attention by division management.

Often there is no bad faith involved but merely division management's belief that a problem is not critical or will be resolved in due course. Yet, from top management's point of view, that problem may constitute a threat to the success of the company's overall strategy. Thus, decentralization and imperfect control systems result in problems which develop with current operations and remain uncovered because division management does not see the urgency or the gravity involved.

Second, certain control procedures – and particularly accounting procedures – are distorted. This is of course no place to engage in a detailed discussion of GCEs' accounting methods. It should be enough to say that not infrequently GCEs' financial data do not give a true picture of the company's situation – as reported by an Italian interviewee: 'Neither the public – to whom these companies are in fact accountable – nor the government, nor even management generally know what is going on on the financial front. Financial statements are available in but incomplete form and where data are available they are not worthy of much faith because they are distorted'. This is well documented in the literature and in the press (a good illustration is the recent scandal about IRI's accounts which called for a public audit by Arthur Andersen).[1]

The causes for such distortions are manifold and complex. The practice of distortions has evolved over time and has been possible thanks to an overall laxness *vis-à-vis* economic efficiency. Several interviewees with long tenure in GCEs have stated that as GCEs were increasingly called upon to perform tasks not directly related to their own economic development, less attention was given to rigorous financial reporting. Another Italian executive argued:

> When a company is called upon to bail out ailing firms, when it is asked to retain redundant employees (and even to hire new ones when it already has too many), when it is asked to locate plants in the worst sites for it, then it is inevitable that management cannot be held accountable for financial performance. This is pushed into the shade. And thus rather little attention is given to accounting data. Yet, for reporting purposes, there is some window-dressing. These distortions further decrease the faith given to information concerning economic efficiency.

Third, analysis of financial statements is often overshadowed by other concerns. A French executive said: 'Of course we are theoretically expected to operate as commercial businesses. But in fact we have to worry about so many other tasks – socioeconomic aims of a macro character – that everybody feels that our profitability is not that important . . . In fact, as long as we rock along, financial data do not receive much attention'.

These factors reduce an organization's aptitude for being readily sensitive to a threat in its economic health. Deterioration in economic performance remains uncovered either because accounting indicators are misleading or because indicators are simply not read with the appropriate attention, and problems which appear *a priori* straightforward as to their identification are in reality not detected.

(b) GCEs also have procedures to evaluate their performance other than their financial performance – notably their contribution to macro socioeconomic issues. GCEs which have a history of strong pressures to pursue macroeconomic and social ends, develop a set of idiosyncrasies which cause them to be sensitive to such issues on their own, that is, a set of sensors which enable them to decide for themselves whether they are behaving appropriately *vis-à-vis* macro types of issues. One interviewee said: 'Continued practice in being responsive to such macro issues and repeated reinforcement in the pursuit of such behavior has resulted in many GCEs developing a series of reflexes for social questions. Even when nobody pressures them to, they instinctively focus on these variables. And they themselves monitor their performance along such criteria'. These idiosyncrasies result in things such as a division investing in one project and not another in view of employment considerations or the purchase of domestic equipment, even when no government pressure is exerted in this connection.

This is related to the familiar argument that governments, do not really intervene that often in GCEs' decisions. A traditional analyst limits himself to counting the number of such interventions and weighing their importance in terms of their immediate impact. This leads one to the conclusion that most GCEs, really operate with high autonomy. The fact of the matter is, however, that the true impact of such interventions goes far beyond the object of an intervention *per se*. Such interventions condition the overall decision-making process of the organization – beyond our present concern with problem identification as such.

Over time, interventions geared to macro types of issues, though in themselves isolated events, have a continuing bearing on the problem-detection process. A French interviewee said: 'When you see that your owner steps in primarily to raise problems of a macro nature, you end up concluding he is interested in those questions only. You soon begin to second-guess him and to focus primarily on those types of questions'. We found that in many cases the government does not need to intervene and that GCEs focus on macro questions on their own. Thus, a concern of the government is transmitted to GCEs in the form of concrete expectations for action; even when that concern has passed, GCEs tend to continue to pursue that type of action until explicit corrective action is taken either from within the company or from the government.

This is all the more so when the GCE involved is large, diversified and decentralized. A goal coming from government and concerning all or most divisions of the company is particularly difficult to extirpate. A steel executive said: 'It is difficult to stop them [the operating companies] at the right point because when you reach this point, it first of all takes time for you (and even more so for the government) to realize it; secondly, it takes time to take action to stop them; and thirdly, it takes even more time for them to stop doing what you had asked them to do'.

Therefore, GCEs tend to be even more sensitive to other issues than their profit performance as one might expect. A good illustration is that of a GCE which for some time had been under pressure to invest in a depressed area of the country. With the change in government, the GCE was suddenly not required any more to worry about anything more than its own economic results. Yet, it clearly continued to invest in that area for a considerable period of time.

(c) Problems are also raised about GCEs' performance by outsiders. Thus, state organizations can find fault in GCEs' performance. These include ministries – a GCE's sponsoring ministry, the ministries for economic or financial affairs as well as for labour, industry or commerce. They also include key agencies (regional development agencies, for example). Further, beyond state bodies, other organizations can have considerable weight – such as unions.

Among these organizations there are 'specialized' and 'general purpose' units. By the former we mean an organization whose field of interest is a relatively narrow one which will lead it to have specific expectations from a GCE. For example, a regional development agency is interested, say, in the growth of employment in depressed areas. It focuses on GCEs in labour-intensive sectors and typically on growth sectors which are most likely to build new plants. Its own processes for problem detection are relatively straight-forward – they are geared to the actual amount of such investments made by the relevant GCEs.

By the latter we mean organizations responsible for a broader spectrum of issues related to GCEs. A good example is the ministry for state holdings, whose mission is to monitor and co-ordinate the behaviour of GCEs. Need-less to say, this is a broad task and certain issues will receive more attention than others; which issues depends on routines which in turn evolve over time. A new interest concerning GCEs' behaviour first emerges thanks to a force which causes a procedure to develop focusing on that aspect of behaviour. For instance, this is the case when a new organization is created whose task is to monitor behaviour according to a particular parameter (for example, regional development). This is also the case when an existing organization is asked to pursue a new focus that is monitor the behaviour of GCEs along a new dimension. Once the force has given the impetus for the birth of the new activity, processes gradually develop which standardize the accomplishment of the activity. At the beginning the force often intervenes to shape the new activity and thus has a direct bearing on the development of the processes. But then this development becomes the product of self-reinforcement: habits are taken to carry out the activity in a particular way which progressively becomes the standard, accepted and 'right' way of doing things. Thus, organizations grow into the habit of focusing on certain problems and not others as a result of a choice made at the outset. How this initial choice is made depends on the particular concern of the force which is at the origin of the activity, at the particular point in time in which it intervenes.

Moreover, outside organizations must be able to communicate a problem they perceive to the relevant GCE. The effectiveness of this communication stems from repeated relationships between the organization and the GCE. At the beginning, procedures are imperfect and communication is poor. With experience, procedures are improved and the outside organization can convey information to the GCE with relative precision.

2. *Initiating forces*

These are instrumental in raising new types of problems about existing activities – to appraise current operations with new parameters.

As far as evaluation of the firm's economic performance is concerned, this can first regard correction of existing parameters. As we say, GCEs' standard procedures are often distorted. An intervening force can step in and be instrumental in correcting these distortions. Thus, we found that a determined new minister for state holdings can actively seek to stop or at least limit misleading manipulations of accounting data. By throwing in all his weight and by thorough investigation, he can try and modify the routines and introduce more rigour in the procedures. We must, however, point out this is arduous. Thus in Italy, where the problem is most acute, several successive ministries have attempted to tackle the problem. But, partly due to their own weakness and partly due to the entrenchment of the accounting practices, they have all failed to date. (This is indeed a superb illustration of the strength of organizational routines.)

A force can also introduce new criteria. A new top management can promote attention to new kinds of concerns. The firm's behaviour is then evaluated bearing in mind such criteria. If top management's attention to this criteria is kept up for long enough, it will become part of the normal decision process and procedures will be developed to monitor these concerns on a regular basis.

We should note that when a force steps in at the problem-identification level, it rarely stops there: it usually also proposes a solution, that is, acts also on the search process. As a German executive said: 'When, say, a chief executive becomes aware of a new type of problem and manifests his concern, he usually also has an idea on what to do about it and he in fact pushes his solution as much, if not more, than he manifests concern for the problem'.

The bulk of new performance criteria created by initiating forces is really related to GCEs' action *vis-à-vis* macro socioeconomic aims. This can stem from a company itself. Especially where government planning is inefficient, management can take steps to foster concern about a new kind of problem either because it feels that problem is simply important or because it feels the government will eventually raise it anyway. Here too the force generally proposes a solution together with the problem it raises.

New performance criteria related to GCEs' behaviour *vis-à-vis* macro aims can also – and in fact mostly do – stem from government organizations. An initiating force may be related to the creation of a new governmental organization. The recently created energy-conservation agencies are good illustrations. Such newly created units are the most likely ones to merely raise a problem without becoming involved in the search process because on one hand, their newness results in novel issues being raised, and on the other, their inexperience conduces them to posing problems and not imposing solutions. As an interviewee of a regional development agency put it:

> At the outset we didn't know much more than what our concern should be – help stimulate industrial developments in certain areas of the country. We were in no position to suggest to any enterprise what type of specific investment might be done and how. We were content to raise the question with them and let them figure out an appropriate course of action which brought a positive answer to the issue. Now, with experience, we have the capability of working with the companies to help them find a course of action both attractive to them and contributing to regional development. And we have the contacts and the know-how for dealing with management on such issues.

An initiating force may also come from an existing government organization concerned with a new type of issue or with GCEs in which it did not take any interest before. In this case, given that the organization from which the force originates has a certain experience, chances are greater that a new problem be raised together with a solution.

3. *Implications for MN activities*

Given these mechanisms, what kind of problems can be identified and what is their impact on potential MN expansion?

A first point is obvious: since we are considering GCEs with little or no MN activities, problems related to existing activities do not in themselves contain an *a priori* element of multinationalism; focusing on current operations will not in itself point to foreign activities. For the MN dimension to be introduced at this point implies that a problem be identified which is apt to lead to an MN solution.

Let us first consider problems uncovered by procedures. These are known types of problems; while in the context of strategic decisions every other problem tends to be a new problem, procedures uncover *kinds* of problems which are familiar.

Specialized outside organizations tend to have a relatively limited scope in terms of their concerns. They tend to push for an intensification of companies' contribution to their own mission and the problems they raise are normally related to their own parochial preoccupations. It is improbable that such organizations come up with any problem which might find an MN solution. This is also the case of organizations other than state organizations. Thus, unions have relatively narrow foci and are for the most not geared to problems which are not domestic.

General purpose organizations should, at least in principle, have less limited types of concerns. In fact, the state sponsoring bodies should be responsible for the overall strategy and performance of GCEs – both their results in terms of contributing to macro socioeconomic endeavours and their own microeconomic results. Therefore, they should be sensitive to more general kinds of problems which are more likely to lend themselves to MN solutions. Yet, in practice, they too have their parochial perceptions which limit the scope of their concerns. Because they typically must deal with other government units which have their own goals of a macro nature, they become more sensitive to these types of issues and less to GCEs' micro performance as such. For example, a ministry for state holdings has to deal with various agencies (such as for regional development), with Parliamentary commissions (such as for economic planning), with other departments (such as for labour). Its concerns will be tinted by these issues and the problems for which it will have developed procedures will be related to these issues and little else. And these issues are generally national ones precisely because they derive from other organizations whose scope is primarily domestic. Of course there are exceptions: in certain sectors the dominant concerns of government are international. But these usually then involve GCEs which are already MN.

As for issues raised by GCEs themselves, macro concerns rarely lead to problems which can receive more of an MN solution than those uncovered by government organizations. The same is not true for micro issues. If procedures function in an unbiased fashion, the same problems should be detected about micro performance as in private companies. Thus, a number of problems should arise which could receive an MN solution. Yet, given the distortions we discussed, relatively less attention is given to micro issues; therefore, the chances are less that the kind of problem will be identified which might lead the firm to seek to go multinational.

Turning to the problems uncovered by initiating forces, it is clear that when the distortions in firms' procedures are corrected, sensitivity to micro issues can be restored. This then gives firms the ability to identify problems which in turn may result in MN decisions. (Yet, we should be reminded of the difficulty of this task in many cases.) Further, the new parameters introduced by forces may raise problems which might find an MN solution. Still, one must be reminded that usually an initiating force comes with a proposal for action. Thus, one can rarely say that new problems are raised which might induce MN solutions *per se*. More often than not the force acts on the search process also and the MN dimension is introduced – if at all – at that point. We will return to this.

Regarding socioeconomic performance, the new issues raised by forces can pose problems which might receive MN solutions. For example, a new agency responsible for monitoring the safety of national oil supplies may ask that oil GCEs be directly involved in the drilling of crude. If no crude is available at home, the relevant GCEs will be pressured to go abroad.

In conclusion, we should repeat that the number of problems to which GCEs are sensitive is limited. Limitations stem from the finite scope of procedures and the fact that forces are triggered by certain events or sources only. In terms of procedures, and at least for those GCEs which have been strongly affected by government interventions, chances are slimmer than in comparable private firms that problems be identified which might receive an MN solution: the macro issues identified by procedures naturally tend to call for national solutions. Certain microeconomic problems can in themselves receive MN solutions; yet, given intervening factors which distort the clarity with which they are seen, these problems often remain in the shade. As to the problems uncovered by forces, they indeed may at times receive an MN solution. But here too there are limitations– the limited range of issues which can trigger a force.

B. Opportunities

Here too there are procedures and initiating forces both at the company level and at the government level.

1. *At the GCE level*

a. Procedures Organizational routines are heavily influenced by past experience. They scan the environment for familiar types of problems. Therefore, if an enterprise has no MN activities and has had none in the past, it normally has no sensors to detect MN opportunities. Companies with no MN experience

> never both to look at the possibility of investing [abroad]. In particular, they do not even consider the possibility of launching manufacturing operations in the less developed countries of the world. Companies do not in practice reject such investment opportunities because the expected profits are not sufficient to compensate for the risks involved; they simply do not bother to devote the time and effort necessary to calculate the rate of return on such investments.[2]

Problem-identification procedures are built up gradually through the repeated practice of identifying problems of a particular kind. A firm which has never operated outside of national frontiers thus cannot have standard procedures to look for investment propositions outside of its country. This is consistent with Aharoni's findings about US firms' foreign investment decisions:

> Investments in foreign countries are not within the sphere of interest of the overwhelming majority of businessmen in the United States. The possibility of looking for investment opportunities outside the United States (and Canada) simply does not occur to them. This way of thinking manifests itself in such expressions as, 'There are enough profitable opportunities in the United States. Why bother to go abroad?' When a foreign investment opportunity is brought before management [by a proposer outside of the normal decision process], the burden of proof that such an opportunity should be considered (let alone decided upon) is on the proposer. It is not enough to show that the expected value of profits is high. It must be proved that 'it is worthwhile to go abroad'.[3]

b. Forces   For an MN opportunity to be identified in a GCE with no existing MN experience, an initiating force must intervene. The initiating force can be either corporate top management or the management of a unit – say, a division. The opportunities thus identified can either involve a potential course of action for the entire organization or for parts thereof. In large diversified companies it typically happens that top management spots interesting prospects for certain parts of the enterprise only. Thus, the head of the planning staff of a holding type of GCE reports that some years ago

> top management 'opened up' to foreign markets and realized there was room for us abroad. In principle, the interest in MN expansion was related to all of our areas of activities. In fact, it became obvious quite soon that only certain .areas were truly thought about, and encouragement to look abroad was really addressed to certain of our operating companies alone. This is in fact inevitable, given the size, diversity and complexity of our operations; the attention of top management has to be focused more precisely on certain parts. And then one has to start somewhere; you can't do everything at once.

When it is a unit's management which is the initiating force, this specialization is all the more acute. This is especially the case when a suborganization's management focuses on opportunities directly relevant to the suborganization itself. One then finds a clearly parochial point of view reflecting the desire to improve one's performance and territory. It can also happen that a unit's management promotes interest in opportunities for the total organization. This happens in particular in functionally structured companies. Here, say, the marketing vice-president may push for a broadening of the organization's action-range to MN dimensions. Yet, in such cases too, parochial priorities and perceptions and suborganizational imperialism limit the initiating force's scope. A marketing vice-president will inevitably have a marketing point of view and be more sensitive to, say, demand potential than, say, financial or production variables. And he will most usually have a more or less explicit desire to broaden his department's territory and extend its frontiers. For example, we found that marketing vice-presidents tend to give special attention to extending sales, say, by looking at opportunities for setting up foreign sales subsidiaries as opposed to manufacturing operations.

Specialization is accentuated by the fact that the first 'look abroad' is a specific one: it rarely occurs that a force pushes for a global look at MN opportunities in general. Rather, it usually focuses on a particular kind of opportunity. This is a look

> at the possibilities of a specific investment in a specific country, not a general resolution to look around the globe for investment opportunities. The most crucial decision is taken when the first venture abroad is considered. At this stage, the organization has had no experience whatsoever in the complicated field of foreign investment, although it often has had export experience. No standard operating procedure exists to give some guidelines in dealing with the problem. No one in the organization is explicitly responsible for dealing with this type of problem. In all these cases, quite a strong push is needed for making the decision to look abroad.[4]

The fact that the first look abroad is a specific one encourages specialism in terms of what opportunities are considered in view of particular organizational units' goals.

A force can be triggered in three basic ways.

(1) A given event can call attention to an opportunity. The event must be visible enough to impose itself to the attention of the one who will be the initiating force. To take an extreme case, the oil crisis called the attention of many upon the opportunities in the newly rich oil-producing countries; or a division manager witnessing that his major competitors are going MN may in turn be induced to look abroad himself.

(2) Management's attention may be drawn to foreign opportunities by active solicitation from outside sources – for example, distributors, representatives of foreign governments, major clients or vendors, the company's banks, managers from other companies (such as suppliers or customers).

(3) An individual's own experience can play an important part. A trip abroad, a professional conference or golf-course conversation may trigger awareness of potential avenues abroad. Also, the recruitment of an executive with personal international experience can result in an initiating force.

Moreover, a special case is represented by the takeover of an enterprise with MN experience. This has been the case notably with state holding companies which have acquired a variety of companies with foreign activities. The MN experience of the acquired firm then percolates into the buyer and thus generates awareness of MN opportunities. For example, if the acquired company continues to formulate plans for foreign investments which it submits for approval to the parent, the parent will have to appraise such proposals and thus be forced to look abroad were it only to appraise the setting in which the investments are to take place. This will foster awareness of foreign environments and attract the attention of the parent's management to foreign investment avenues for the company in general.

Here too a force does not usually stop at the problem identification level and gets involved, in particular, in the process of action planning. Besides, a strong force calling attention to an opportunity more or less deliberately causes it to receive special attention when it comes to finding ways of exploiting it. A German executive said: 'If the President asks that a particular opportunity be appraised, not only will it be looked at with particular care but also will avenues be investigated immediately as to how to capitalize on it, and this even before any decision has been made that the opportunity in itself is worthwhile'.

2. At the government level

a. Procedures Sensors for the detection of MN opportunities exist only in those organizations which are used to scanning the international environment. The ministry of foreign affairs is an obvious instance. Yet, to spot opportunities for GCEs, an organization has to be sensitive to issues which are of relevance to commercial undertakings. As one interviewee argued: 'The people in the Ministry of Foreign Affairs are in contact with what goes on abroad. But they are so far away from the concerns of business enterprises that they can rarely be counted upon to make a sensible industrial proposal'. Of course there are certain organizations which are attuned to commercial propositions abroad. They include general purpose organizations (for example, a ministry of international commerce, a ministry of economic or financial affairs) as well as specialized organizations (for example, any energy commission which is by necessity in contact with oil-producing countries.) Still, we should note that such organizations are often closer to GCEs which already have MN activities. Their field of interest leads them to entertain ongoing relations with GCEs whose sphere of action corresponds to these organizations' own preoccupations.

b. Forces Initiating forces play a major role in those government organizations which do not commonly scan the MN environment for opportunities which might be relevant for GCEs. And they also are instrumental in causing organizations which are used to focusing on foreign countries to do so in terms of new types of issues.

But we need to be more specific. An initiating force is someone in a government organization proposing a new type of opportunity which normal procedures do not pick up. This can be a high-ranking government official such as a minister, or somebody holding a responsibility in a suborganization. As was the case in GCEs themselves, a certain specialism is inevitable. He who is responsible for a suborganization will inevitably be sensitive to the opportunities close to his unit's aims. For example, if a unit focuses on the industrial relations with OPEC countries, a force originating from it will most likely be responsive to a problem related to its own area of responsiblility. And more general purpose organizations also tend to have limited foci of attention. Even when, say, a sponsoring ministry looks abroad for opportunities for the GCEs for which he is responsible, he necessarily focuses on certain countries, certain sectors, certain GCEs.

Someone in an organization can become an initiating force when an event 'imposes' a foreign opportunity to his attention. For example, a radical political change in a foreign country may constitute an opportunity which is very obvious for the one who is attentive to political developments in the area. Alternatively, attention can be awakened by outside sources. These include people in other parts of government, in other GCEs, in potential host country governments . . . For example, somebody in the ministry of foreign affairs may suggest that a given GCE become involved in such and such a country for political reasons. While he may have neither the motivation, the authority, nor the expertise to articulate a real proposal in this connection, he may suggest it, say, to the ministry of state holdings. The minister himself may seize the idea and present it as an attractive investment prospect.

One also finds a special instance similar to one discussed for GCEs themselves. It happens that a government takes over a GCE which has existing MN activities. For example, as Mr Driscoll, Managing Director, Corporate Strategy of British Steel, said: 'When we were nationalized in 1967 the British Government also picked up about 125 million pounds of assets overseas'. In such instances, the company's management continues to operate the MN activities and periodically consults with the relevant government organizations about its doings here. In particular, the sponsoring ministry has to evaluate the plans and actions of the company in this connection. In this process, 'if the ministry has little or no experience with thinking about foreign environments, he learns fast' – as an interviewee put it. Indeed, the experience of the company is at least partially transferred to the government. The government then becomes sensitive to the MN environment and can begin to spot opportunities for other GCEs.

3. *Implications for MN activities*

The opportunities identified by procedures are heavily tinted by the goals of the organization in which they arise. Thus, an organization responsible for energy supply will have sensors to detect opportunities to secure raw materials. These will not merely focus on securing raw materials at the best possible economic conditions. Other considerations will be important. For instance, procedures will be geared in particular to those countries with which the government has good political ties. Further, if an organization is reaching its aims in the context of the activities of its existing procedures, it will not seek to go beyond the opportunities detected by these procedures.

Initiating forces are also influenced by the organization in which they originate. To illustrate, a major French GCE reported that some years ago it invested in a particular country not because of microeconomic or macroeconomic reasons, but because of political reasons: 'Our country had poor relations with the host country and France had no embassy there. So we were encouraged to invest there because this was an opportunity to establish semi-official, yet unobtrusive ties with the foreign country, which might be useful to develop new relations with local authorities'. Reportedly, this possibility was first imagined by the ministry of foreign affairs. But the ministry did not have either the competence or the authority to directly act upon the relevant GCE. So it suggested the possibility to the cabinet of the prime minister which then acted as an initiating force and formalized the project. In this case, the characteristics of the source – the ministry of foreign affairs – and the actual initiating force were determining in terms of what issues either one was receptive to – the source being sensitive to the desirability of some kind of state-business representation and the force being receptive to that source and being able to formulate and promote the proposal as an actual opportunity.

This suggests that the opportunities raised by government concern were but a limited number of issues vitally dependent on the organizational mechanisms responsible for their identification. These opportunities are closely related to the aims of the organization in which they are raised; they are heavily tinted with parochialism. Therefore they concern certain aspects of GCEs' actions only; the company's overall strategic posture is rarely considered and opportunities are really looked for in connection with parts of the company's activity.

Further, the opportunities raised by government usually concern macro ends. A government unit is really concerned with how much a GCE can contribute to the accomplishment of its own goals. These have little to do with GCEs' microeconomic performance. Indeed, government organizations rarely bring up profit-related opportunities because they do not *see* such opportunities. Even those general purpose units which are responsible for the overall behaviour of GCEs – that is, the sponsoring department – are mostly concerned with the attainment of macro aims precisely because, being part of the state, they are primarily concerned with general interest types of issues. Beyond a certain financial performance level sufficient to guarantee the overall company's health, government organizations do not really worry much about GCEs' economic results: 'If a certain minimum level of profitability is attained', said one GCE's chief executive, 'we are not asked much in terms of financial results; government's concerns are then much more in the realm of our behavior relative to macro kinds of parameters'.

In our discussion we have deliberately focused on MN opportunities. In this study we only deal with domestic issues when they have a bearing on MN decisions. This is not the case here. Yet, it should be clear that, given the overall relative paucity of ways of detecting foreign opportunities, it must follow that the majority of the opportunities detected by GCEs are domestic. Indeed, organizational processes push GCEs to do more of what they are doing already – for GCEs with no MN experience, more domestic operations. In government, except for certain organizations which do have international responsibilities, the bulk of the procedures are also critically influenced by the prevalently national activity of the government. While initiating forces represent the best chances for MN opportunities to be identified, they too are frequently tied to national issues: initiating forces are generally triggered by an event or a source; in GCEs as well as in government the sources and events to which forces are mostly exposed are often domestic.

II. SEARCH

The nature of search depends on the type of problem for which a solution is to be found. Accordingly, our discussion will have three parts. (1) In the case of (or threat of) performance failure, search focuses on trying to find a solution which can or can not be MN. (2) In the case of opportunities, the problem may on the one hand start with the need to narrow down a variety of alternatives and specify a particular project to pursue. (3) On the other hand, and more frequently, a particular opportunity has already been identified when search as such begins. Search then has to find specific ways of exploiting that opportunity.

A. Search for solution to performance failure (or threat thereof)

The question is, how and when can the problem receive an MN solution? A solution can either come from the company or from government.

1. *Company search*

When a problem arises, search focuses on courses of action which are known to the firm. Even if the problem is an entirely new one, the solutions which are investigated are drawn from past solutions already familiar to the firm. In the context of GCEs with no MN experience, the solutions which are considered tend to be domestic ones. Thus, we found a variety of instances in which a GCE was confronted with a problem in its domestic operations which clearly could lend itself to an MN solution (that is, for which an MN solution was at least a clear alternative); when asked about the possibility of following an MN course of action management recognized that such a solution had not even been truly considered.

A new solution can only be found when a force intervenes. Either a chief executive or a man responsible for a particular organizational unit can suggest that a new type of solution be investigated. How he comes to this is comparable to the way an executive is led to uncover a new kind of problem: solicitation by an outside source (for example, a union), exposure to factors suggesting to him the possibility of the alternative in question (for example attending a professional conference), the example of competitors, his personal experience in another company, etc. Furthermore, in holding types of GCEs, the solution to a problem of an operating company may come from or be suggested by a member of management of the partent holding. In such multi-industry-type organizations, the experience of a company which has recently been taken over can be quite valuable in terms of introducing new types of solutions: a particular working company can benefit from the experience of a company recently taken over with types of actions the working company is not familiar with.

Thus, several GCEs reported that they detected problems stemming from raising labour costs which made their products uncompetitive against foreign competition. At first, problems were acknowledged but little innovative solutions were put forward to solve them. Then, because of an initiating force, the possibility of foreign production was investigated. One company reported:

> At first we tried the usual actions which are taken when your costs rise unduly: we tried to increase productivity by rationalizing production, by accelerating the assembly process, by trying to save on raw materials. But this really only delayed tackling the real problem. Then one of our higher-ranking executives somehow came to the idea of transferring at least part of the production process to lower-cost countries. It was a simple concept and in fact an obvious thing to do, but nobody had really thought of it before.

When the executive in question was asked how he had arrived at the idea in the first place, he simply acknowledged that it was 'by watching other companies go abroad when they had the same kind of problem.'

And an Italian company which had been taken over by a state holding company reported an interesting case.

> After a while we had come under [a state holding company's] control, things began to turn sour in this country on the national socio-economic front. Companies were seeing mounting threats to their health in terms of rising costs, rising social unrest and deteriorating domestic sales. After a while we, as many others, came to consider the possibility of investing abroad to at least partially escape the domestic crisis. This would have been a radical departure from our existing strategy, since we never had had foreign investments. It was

our president who, coming back from a trip abroad, made concrete the idea in terms of a specific alternative for action. It took his weight to force the company to seriously look at such a radically new solution. But the interesting part is that while it took his weight to promote attention to such a possibility, this didn't take into account the new obligation of the company as a GCE: the reasons which justified considering foreign investment from the company's point of view were precisely the reasons which made the government anxious to retain at least its companies' production at home. The national crisis called for continuous and sustained domestic production and investments. What this shows is that belonging to the state impedes you from being responsive to environmental stimuli which otherwise would push you towards MN expansion.

This instance is an illustration of how a force – the president – can make a company look abroad even when it has a particularly domestic scope. Besides, it shows that a force in a GCE can be responsive to certain sources or events only. It would have been interesting to know how, procedurally, the alternative of investing abroad was rejected. The interviewee chose to pass this under silence. Yet, one may speculate that the company's idea was not really rejected. But as the alternative was not being contemplated as a realistic prospect from the government's point of view, the review procedures were not fitted to appraise it. The alternative was thus lost in the reviews and negotiations between the company and the government or the holding to which it belonged. This should become clearer when we discuss the process of approval.

2. *Government search*

An interviewee said: 'You just can't wait for [government units] to help you solve your business problems'. Government organizations are only interested in those types of problems which are relevant to them given their preoccupations; their interventions in terms of solutions revolve mostly around macro problems. Special purpose government organizations tend to focus on the problems they themselves were instrumental in raising. For example, a regional development agency having raised the problem that a GCE invests insufficiently in depressed areas tends to also assist the company in devising plans for such investments. And general purpose organizations also provide solutions mostly to problems they raise themselves.

In government, too, search is simpleminded. Solutions are usually drawn from a finite range of actions which are known to an organization. Innovative solutions are considered only when a force intervenes.

Government organizations which customarily deal in an international environment can come up, given their existing processes, with an MN course of action. Yet, these organizations tend to be closest to CGEs which already are MN in scope.

Further, in a government organization whose sphere of responsibility involves little or no contact with international issues, a force can step in and propose an MN solution for a GCE. For example, the advent of a new minister for state holdings may, given his experience, result in the ministry suggesting to GCEs to seek to exploit MN opportunities. Or a minister of foreign affairs may suggest to his colleague in the finance ministry – which is often the sponsoring department of GCEs – the possibility of an MN solution for a given company's problems; the sponsoring ministry can adopt the suggestion and become a force actively promoting its adoption by the company. Moreover, here too the experience of companies recently taken over by the government can be important: when this experience is conveyed to the government it can serve as a vital source of inspiration for new action ideas for other companies to be promoted by the government.

Several GCEs reported that an MN solution had been suggested by government. For example, a company which was considered to furnish a vital product for the country and which used a particular raw material in its manufacturing process was asked by a government agency to become directly involved in the procurement of the raw material as opposed to buying it from whatever vendor appeared most attractive at those points in time where the company needed to buy it. As a manager reported:

> We were buying the raw material on the open market and often from foreign sellers. Given the recent crisis in raw materials, the government developed a general concern about the supply of such materials. It became clear that it wanted companies which were heavy users of key raw materials, to secure as much as possible direct access to sources of supply of their own. We thus faced the problem of finding a satisfactory way of doing this. At first we looked at possible domestic sources. This was natural since we had no experience in international investments. Then the government agency stepped back in and itself proposed the foreign alternative. Frankly, though this was financially more attractive, we would not have considered it on our own.

B. Search for a specific MN project

Here the MN dimension is a given: the starting point is either that the company has realized that it has an opportunity in MN expansion in general or that, given an actual or potential deterioration in current operations, MN expansion appears the most promising solution. In either case, when search begins, it is already clear that MN action is to follow. In either case, search is to focus on identifying a precise resource allocation proposition abroad.

To reach this stage, most often an initiating force has to have intervened at one point or another. And, as noted earlier, in most cases a force does not stop at one element of the decision process. Thus, when a key executive detects the possibility that there might be attractive MN opportunities or that the best solution to a company's problem may lie abroad, he more often than not already has a specific project in mind. And the same, though perhaps less distinct, phenomenon occurs in government – as explained by one executive: 'When somebody in government develops the idea that a GCE should pursue international expansion, he rarely stops short from actually at least hinting to a particular action. And for a company with no foreign operations such a hint usually becomes mandatory; it focuses exclusively on that project because it doesn't know better.' What this means is that often, once the MN dimension is introduced in the decision process, there is no need for incremental efforts to look for a specific MN project: the particular project comes together with the look abroad itself. Indeed, in many cases there is no need for a special search for a particular MN opportunity.

Yet, there are cases where search for a specific project does occur – in three kinds of instances.

1. *An in-company force advocating a particular project*

A key executive can become the champion of a given investment for a variety of reasons. His attention may be drawn to it by an outside source and closer analysis may persuade him of its economic attractiveness. Or he may have purely personal motives for the investment (for example, a personal attraction to the country). We should repeat that this presupposes that foreign investments in general have been already considered and that the force presently under consideration has had no role in this. This is unusual for a high-ranking executive: normally, if he is to intervene at all he will do so earlier in the decision process. In fact, the only instances we encountered where the chief executive intervened only at the level of finding a specific MN project were cases in which the general look abroad had stemmed from outside the company – typically from the government. Thus, several GCEs reported that for one reason or another, the government decided at a certain point that the company should be involved in foreign operations: 'At that point, one is stuck with the problem with no further guidance from government', said one president, 'the chief executive must then himself decide where the company should start its foreign operations.' Also, it may occasionally happen that the head of an operating company in a holding-type GCE has to intervene in this fashion, if the parent company asks the operating company to invest abroad with no further specification as to what kind of investment it should make.

What is somewhat more common is for an individual who is not a top manager to become a force promoting a particular MN project once the overall notion of MN investment has been accepted. A man may be in a position where he does not perceive the possibility of MN investment in the first place. Yet, once he realizes that there is room for MN expansion, he may attempt to put forward his own ideas. We encountered instances in which a company had engaged in a given project as a result of, say, a division head (and even in one case a product manager) having actively pushed for it.

Again, the motivations can be quite varied. A man can be familiar with the country and be convinced that it offers particular opportunities for the company; or he may entertain hopes of fostering the development of his own unit: he may reason that a particular country offers particular opportunities, say, for his division.

2. *In-government search*

A government unit familiar with international problems and with business can identify a particular opportunity. Still, this is relatively rare: a government organization having this kind of experience is usually close to GCEs which themselves operate multinationally. What may happen is that a general purpose government unit which first raised the problem, resulting in a look abroad, refers to such a special purpose organization in its own search for a specific action plan. On a few occasions we found that the sponsoring ministry, for instance, caused a look abroad, while it had itself limited experience with international business questions. It then sought assistance in another government unit. Search is then inevitably biased by the aims of such a unit, opportunities being sought in those areas where the unit has experience and where it can – more or less explicitly – hope to see its own goals fostered.

Alternatively, search can take place as a result of an intervening force. Again, in most cases, this occurs as part of an earlier intervention. Yet, we did find a few exceptions. A government unit not involved in the early parts of the decision process may intervene at this point to try and push the selection of one alternative rather than another. This is the case in particular of a government organization which is relatively far away – in terms of its own preoccupations – from GCEs and does not keep abreast of their activities. A key individual in the organization may learn of a given potential expansion plan; at that point, it may occur to him that if the expansion materializes in a particular way, his own organization's aims may be fostered. He may then actively promote the selection of a particular course. And if there are no other pressures for other kinds of action, this course may indeed be pursued. An interviewee commented: 'In such cases a GCE may end up not pursuing a course of action designed to foster its own aims but an opportunity whose primary merit is to help a given state agency or department in its own endeavours'.

3. *Search via in-company routines*

What happens if search neither occurs in government nor through an in-company force? In GCEs with no MN experience there is no precedent and the organization is, so to speak, left on its own without any proven procedures or experience to guide its search. Two basic factors characterize this search.

(a) Search for an MN opportunity starts by looking at that which resembles most the current predicament: search for an opportunity in the context which is familar to the company, that is, search for a domestic opportunity. Indeed, we found considerable evidence that the search for an opportunity abroad by a company with no previous MN experience takes as a base of reference search for opportunities at home. As one among many interviewees reported: 'The first time we looked for investment projects overseas we did it according to the same patterns we followed when looking for domestic projects'.

It follows that search has certain characteristics which are not adapted to the quest for MN opportunities. A number of problems result. Of course, each case is *sui generis*, but some generalizations are possible. First, variables which are pertinent to the search for a foreign opportunity are not appropriately taken into account. These variables may be related to international business transactions at large and concern the transfer of resources in general (for example, exchange rate problems for capital transfers or behavioural problems for the transfer of people). Yet, a company having, say, some import/export activities may be aware of such problems. More importantly, variables specifically concerned with the country in which the opportunity arises may create more serious difficulties. These variables concern the special economic, legal, political and social characteristics of the country. A partial list of such variables would include the following:

(1) The general economic environment.
(2) The general political environment.
(3) The general social climate.
(4) The policy and attitude of the government towards foreign investment and towards investment by foreign GCEs in particular.
(5) The legal system of the country.
(6) Regulatory and administrative practices affecting a foreign investment (for example, tariffs, import or export quotas, taxations, customs protection and procedures, availability of patent, copyright, trademark, and other protection).
(7) Existence of an investment guarantee agreement with the home country.
(8) Trade agreements with other countries.
(9) Governmental assurance as to the remission of profits and repatriation of capital.
(10) The tax structure and the existence of double taxation agreements.
(11) Availability of auxiliary industries.
(12) Availability and efficiency of services such as telephone and telegraph facilities.
(13) Sea, road, air and rail transportation.
(14) Banking facilities available and nature of credit offered.
(15) Social policy, labour laws, regulations and organization.
(16) Accounting conventions and requirements.
(17) Social customs and formalities.
(18) Cost of living and availability of housing, food, medical and educational facilities for personnel.[5]

A company with no MN experience can rarely perform a proper analysis of such variables. As an interviewee reported: 'When we made our first foreign investment we didn't look at half of the relevant issues and we blew our analysis of half of the other half! Particularly, qualitative variables which are often both the less obvious ones and the ones which are the most difficult to appraise, are the cause of many errors indeed'.

Moreover, search frequently overemphasizes certain variables which are important for national projects but which are negligible for MN ventures. In particular, GCEs lay considerable weight on the consistency of a domestic project with national macro socioeconomic aims. In the search for foreign opportunities, this is often not warranted, since there is just no particular expectation on the part of the local government. Yet, the company may still try hard to resolve what the government's own aims are and how an investment by the company would fit such aims. A French chief executive reported:

> Not infrequently in domestic projects many questions as to the location, size, timing, etc. are in practice answered by the government so that the company doesn't need to worry much about sucn broad questions. They [the government] resolve such problems for us. Now, a few years ago one of our divisions was considering the possibility of our first foreign investment. In their effort to identify the most suitable project, I found the planning staff was at a loss because in one of the countries they were considering, there was no national plan: they felt they lacked the proper guidance because nobody was telling them as clearly as at home what kind of investment was considered suitable and what locations were acceptable and which not.

(b) For those issues which are not addressed in the context of a domestic search but cannot help being addressed, reference is made to what we term – using the French expression – *points de chute*. By this we mean certain fixed reference points which are visible enough to serve as benchmarks to guide the search process: they are landmarks which are instrumental to direct search towards selecting particular avenues of investigation. The issues involved pertain to the most basic questions related to a foreign investment: where, when, how, that is, in which country to look for an opportunity, at what point in time, what type of opportunity to seek, etc.

While there is no precedent to guide answers to such questions in terms of existing procedures, reference is made to whatever benchmarks come up to guide search – to help bring down the range of all theoretically possible alternatives to a manageable set. Given that all possible opportunities all over the globe can obviously not be considered, a selection has to be made. Such *points de chute* are represented by certain poles of attraction related to certain potential opportunities. For instance, an importer of the firm's products in a foreign country with which the company has entertained long relations can attract the attention of search to that particular country. Similarly, attention can be focused to a given country if the firm has certain contacts there, say, because a deal has been done in that country or because of personal relationships there of key executives involved in the search process. The attractive power of such poles does not need to be all that strong. As one interviewee put it: 'When you have nothing else to hold on to, you start by looking at those prospects where you have a point of departure for your investigation'. A *point de chute* in a country not only entails by its very existence a natural attraction for search to focus upon that country, but also constitutes a concrete base for an investigation; it can assist management in putting some of the basic questions concerning the local situation.

A *point de chute* is not necessarily contacted overseas. Given the inexperience of the firm with MN investments, organizations which can be of assistance are referred to early on. These include banks, consultants or lawyers. And a GCE may refer to government organizations. For example, one company reported that its first MN investment was made in a particular country because of the personal relationships between a key executive and a high-ranking civil servant in the ministry for foreign affairs who was particularly familiar with that country. For GCEs which are part of a state holding company, it is clear that a natural source of *points de chute* is the parent company. And other GCEs, particularly when part of the same holding, can also provide useful *points de chute*.

The visibility of *points de chute* is important: it is that *point de chute* which most stands out which will attract search. Further, their characteristics are important. If a company first perceives the *point de chute* related to a particular opportunity it will most likely pursue that opportunity – if at all feasible. If a company refers to an organization for a *point de chute* it will first look at the opportunities raised by that organization. Such opportunities. will clearly be a direct product of the organization's own experience and aims. Thus, GCEs referring to government organizations in this context are inevitably affected by these organizations' own goals and interests.

But how is a specific opportunity actually selected? The order in which various possible courses of action are examined is essential. It follows that the determinants of this order are critical. When search occurs via an in-company force, we must ask what opportunity this force is most likely to come up with. When search occurs in government, we must ask how this takes place. If an alternative stems from a special purpose organization it will reflect the experience and goals of that organization. And similarly, when search occurs via standard company procedures, the key role belongs to the *points de chute*: it is that *point de chute* which most attracts search which imposes consideration of the first alternative. It is then trivial to know whether that alternative is the best one available. As long as it meets certain minimum criteria, it will be pursued.

Further, we saw that the investigation of MN opportunities is most often lacking. It is thus more difficult to make a conclusive appraisal of an alternative. Also, given the lack of precedents, there are no points of comparison, which puts further limitations on the evolution process. Therefore, for companies' first investment decisions, it is often difficult to ascertain whether an opportunity satisfies a certain level of expectations or not: the evaluation procedure is often unadapted and the parameters used frequently shaky. Consequently, the order in which opportunities are looked at is all the more important. Given the uncertainty attached to their appraisal, the first project considered may well be adopted even if it appears but an approximation of a satisfactory proposition. Indeed, if at all 'half decent', as a British interviewee put it, chances are that the alternative which comes up first will be pursued – either one that is brought forward by a government organization or an in-company force, or one that is considered thanks to a *point de chute*.

C. Search for a specific strategy to exploit an MN opportunity

At this stage the foreign project which is to be pursued is defined: an opportunity has been identified and specified in relatively broad terms (for example, the location of the project and its overall nature – whether it is to be, say, an assembly plant or a plant manufacturing components). It then remains to devise a specific action plan to draw the most out of the project. Relevant issues include specification of precise characteristics of the project (for example, size of investment, specific timing, expected returns). They include the definition of the method of entry: will the company set up a fully owned subsidiary, enter a joint venture (and then with what kind of partners – a local firm taking an active part in the management of the venture, private stockholders whose contribution will be but financial, another foreign company...?), take over a local enterprise ...? And they include questions regarding the resources to be mobilized – people, financial resources, knowhow etc.

Before going on we should point out that, of course, search for a specific action plan and search for the particular opportunity itself are closely interrelated. In fact, the distinction is often more of a conceptual one, since in practice they frequently overlap considerably. When an alternative is generated, investigation tends to follow closely. Analysis of the alternative stops when it appears that the alternative is inadequate. Until then, however, no other alternative is really considered seriously at all. Normally, investigation of an alternative takes place effectively in the context of search for a specific plan for action related to the alternative under consideration.

Search for a specific action plan can follow two basic routes.

1. *Via established procedures*

Many GCEs reported that while consideration of the first MN investment (and most often also definition of a particular opportunity) had indeed been the

product of a force actively promoting that alternative, actual formulation of a
plan to follow that alternative had been left to the companies' processes alone.
This appears to be the case in particular when the force is an outside one – a
force stemming from the government. One interviewee said: 'The government
spotted the opportunity of a foreign investment and even defined it in broad
terms. But we were left on our own to actually find the appropriate way to go
after it in practical terms'. Yet, this can also occur when the force is an
in-company force. This is less frequent since an in-company force tends to feel
close to the actual pursuit of an alternative and to get involved in the formulation of an action plan to exploit a prospect it was instrumental in identifying.
Still, there are cases in which a force steps out of the decision process once a
given alternative has been selected. This occurs most in large diversified
companies in which top management acts as a force to identify such an alternative and then leaves the task of actually pursuing it to an organizational unit.
Thus, an operating company of a state holding company reported that it has
been asked by its parent company to proceed with a particular MN course of
action, 'but received very little guidance in terms of defining such an alternative
specifically and formulating a plan to pursue it'.

When search for a specific action plan occurs according to set procedures in
a company with no MN experience, it takes as a starting point the formulation
of an action plan for the exploitation of a domestic opportunity. This has two
basic sets of implications.

a. Kinds of actions considered   As far as possible they are similar to those
pursued in the context of domestic projects. While each case is *sui generis*, a
few generalizations are possible.[6]

There tends to be a correlation between mixed enterprises at home and
joint ventures abroad: a GCE which is used to having private stockholders in
its capital is more likely to enter co-operative agreements with private partners when it goes abroad. Thus, Italian GCEs which are part of state holding
companies and whose shares are partly in the private sector are inclined to
work with private firms in their foreign operations. And depending on
whether the private partners at home are mere investors or also take an active
role in management, the foreign joint ventures tend to have 'passive' partners
or 'active' partners in terms of the role played in the administration of the
venture.

GCEs tend to enter a joint venture with foreign governments more easily
than private firms do. Because they are used to working with the government
at home they find it normal to operate in a similar fashion at home. To cite
ENI's Marcello Colitti:

> From the first days of our MN expansion we have been pioneers
> in co-operation with foreign governments. We have asked host
> countries to work with us. While most large multinationals were
> full of preconceptions against this form of collaboration, we have

shown the way in this direction to everybody – including the largest and most experienced companies. We have taught how to do business on a joint-venture basis even with minority holdings (as low as 10 per cent). This is so because we find it easier to work with governments. This helped us a great deal particularly in LDCs where the government is everything.

The inclination of GCEs for joint ventures can have a bearing on the resources employed in foreign investments. Of course, a joint venture reduces the financial requirements for the firm. But, besides, GCEs tend to have relatively high expectations from their partners beyond capital (for example in terms of know-how, administrative facilitations or dealings with local suppliers, authorities or customers).

GCEs appear to be less inclined than private companies to pursue a strategy of foreign acquistions. One executive argued:

Particularly in the last years which have been recession years with high unemployment, we have been conditioned in our national activities to make new incremental investments which make a contribution in terms of creating new jobs. We tend to buy out companies only when they are ailing enterprises which would fail otherwise. And we tend to operate in the same way abroad: we just don't consider the possibility of taking over going concerns as a way entering a foreign market.

b. *The investigation process*   When a GCE has no MN experience, the investigation of a specific foreign prospect follows similar paths as an investigation for a domestic project. Errors and wrong evaluations thus tend to be inevitable.

First, certain aspects of a plan are not considered or wrongly taken for granted. A GCE having always followed certain types of actions at home will be led to assume that it will be able to operate effectively abroad in the same fashion. A number of instances were cited in our interviews. One company was used to subcontracting a great deal in order to avoid the risk of being struck with overcapacity in recession times; it invested in a foreign country with a capacity geared to a very conservative market estimate with a tacit contingency plan of subcontracting in the case demand turned out to be greater than expected. Demand indeed proved to be far greater than the company's capacity but the additional demand could not be satisfied due to a lack of competent firms to subcontract. As an executive reported: 'We lost considerable sales to our competitors and we still haven't been able to recoup market share. What happened is that we were so used to subcontracting that we took it for granted that such possibilities would exist abroad as well.

Nobody in the planning process thought of checking this out'. Another company reported that its first manufacturing foreign investment was in an LDC and that it ran into trouble because it did not check the availability and cost of local machine shops, spare parts and maintenance services for its machine tools. As an executive said:

> We were used to having all the outside service we needed for our machine tools and it really never occurred to us that abroad things might be different. We did our first investment using relatively old machinery we had in one of our plants at home which were obsolete in our domestic market but which would be quite appropriate in an LDC. When we had installed the equipment and once we started operating we found out that there was nobody around to help us keep the machines in shape.

Furthermore, here too certain variables are overemphasized. A GCE's strategic search process is conditioned to take certain issues into account which are related to macro concerns of the government. It frequently occurs that such issues are given similar weight in an MN context where this is unwarranted or at least not as vital. An Italian executive made this point very clear:

> Especially in the early days of our MN expansion there was no national planning to speak of in Italy. We had thus grown into the habit of autodisciplining our actions and divising strategies consistent with what we thought was the collective interest. When we first went abroad we instinctively did the same *vis-à-vis* the host country. Our plans were taking into account what we felt was good for the local society. But we then came to realize that we were in fact exporting our values – we were making choices in the name of the collective good using parameters which were quite subjective and not necessarily tailored to the local society. For example, in one case where we were building a major new plant, we were in addition building houses for our future workers and we were also getting involved in projects such as the construction of a school and a supermarket. This seemed natural to us given the area was relatively depressed and no suitable facilities appeared to be available. But this turned out to be for the most a superfluous effort: people didn't like the houses and felt even hurt in their pride that we got involved in building a school for them – they felt they shouldn't need us for that. In fact, when you try to go for profits alone, it is clear to everybody what you are doing and if the host country agrees with this end of yours it can understand your behaviour and adapt to it. But when you pursue other aims your behaviour is more ambiguous. We often found – but only later – that we were not seen as doing what was expected from us.

Here too a search process borrowed from domestic operations can be supplemented by certain *points de chute* giving it a certain more specific direction. For example, co-operation experience with a given MNC in connection with domestic joint ventures can have an important impact on an MN strategy. In one case we found that a GCE intending to invest abroad sought to do so in partnership with an MNC with which it had worked at home. In another instance the MNC was consulted on an informal basis: 'Not only did we end up investing in their home country', said a company executive, 'but also did we decide to use some of their idle plant capacity and drew on their marketing organization. Besides, we ended up using their bankers and their lawyers'. Another kind of instance is to be be found in IRI type of GCEs where the parent company often serves as a guide for an operating company's initial overseas expansion.

2. *Via a force*

Here a force cannot be responsible for the entire search process: since search involves a whole variety of tasks connected with the investigation and since the output of search does not merely involve defining an opportunity in broad terms but the formulation of an actual specific plan, an individual force cannot accomplish the process on its own. Rather, its role is to monitor the workings of organizational procedures which remain the basic mechanisms by which search takes place; a force then intervenes in a punctual – though often determining – fashion to modify the process here or there.

A force here may be the same as that having had a key role in previous phases of the decision process. This happens infrequently with government forces: the government in fact, quite rarely gets involved in this phase of search. As one interviewee put it:

> When it comes to being specific about what to do in concrete terms, the government loses interest. A bit because this is not their actual responsibility, a bit because of sheer incompetence, they stay away from the development of the action plan *per se*. On the contrary, this is often the case with in-company forces. Thus, an executive frequently identifies an opportunity abroad and then himself is the key element in the formulation of a plan of action to exploit it.

Alternatively, the force intervening in this phase of search may be one which had no role before in the decision process. This is most frequent when of course no previous force was involved (but, as we saw, this is a rare case), or when the previous force steps out of the process when it comes to devising a specific action plan. This occurs mostly when the previous force stemmed from the government. Yet, this can also be the case when this force was an in-company one. Especially in multi-industry enterprises, the earlier force may stem from corporate management but concern only part of the company. When it comes to actually formulating a plan of action, corporate management often does not get involved.

A force intervening at this stage is clearly close to the accomplishment of the strategy. It may be somebody with a direct stake in the results of the operation (such as a division head or a member of top management), or an individual who will end up being responsible for the implementation of the project (if such a person's identity is not known at this point, the stepping in of an individual here may result in a self-fulfilling prophecy: a person taking the role of a force at this stage puts him or herself in a position of being selected to become responsible for the plan's implementation).

When a force is involved, search tends to be more effective. When a force intervenes it usually (though certainly not always) means that it has a certain competence in the matter involved. Several examples were cited in our interviews. Thus, one executive reported: 'Planners were going to use the standard production process employed by the company at home in a foreign plant without taking into consideration that while the process was a high water user, water was scarce in the area they were thinking of'. The executive stepped in and was instrumental in changing both the process to be used and the location of the plant. And a marketing executive reported that his company was going to invest in a foreign country 'Without challenging any of the tacit assumptions about the product-mix and the distribution system, and in fact just believing that what was going at home had to go abroad'. The executive added: 'I honestly think that hadn't I stepped in with my international experience [he had worked for many years in a multinational food company], we would have blown it completely. We had to change our product-mix totally and adapt to a radically different kind of distribution system'.

III. APPROVAL

Approval is an outgrowth of two elements: commitments in favour of, as well as opposed to, a given course of action and formal review procedures which indirectly condition approval.

A. Commitments

'It is . . . not so important to learn when exactly – if at all – and by whom the "official" decision to invest or reject an investment opportunity was made. Rather, the cumulative process of individual and organizational commitments causing this decision to come into being should be studied.'[7]

When a particular investment proposal is brought forth for approval, a host of commitments are aroused in connection with the decision. Each case is different and it is impossible to enumerate all the commitments which can come into play. What is important here is to indicate the major types of commitments which exist, and their origin; and we should explain how they interplay with each other and shape decisions. We must distinguish between prior commitments and commitments made in the course of the decision process itself.

1. *Prior commitments*

These are commitments existing over and beyond the decision process of a particular strategy. There are three types of such commitments.

First, those related to the firm's own economic performance. A good illustration is the first foreign direct investment decision by a company with significant though maturing export markets. The existence of these markets more often than not creates a commitment to defend such sales. As noted about one such case, 'This commitment was part of the general value structure of the executives . . . who were trying to keep, preferably to increase, the company's market share in each one of its markets'.[8] If exports are declining because they are no more competitive costwise, foreign production may enable the firm to produce more cheaply and thus retain its market position. In such conditions, therefore, commitments to hold foreign markets call for foreign direct investment. At the same time there may be counter-commitments hindering foreign investment – general attitudes, policies and beliefs challenging the desirability of going MN in general or of investing in the particular country or countries under consideration. Examples include a policy of not investing in certain countries where political risk is seen as too high, an *a priori* attitude against LDCs, or a feeling 'that we should not invest in country X because the culture is too distant from ours'.

Second, are the commitments relating to macro issues, that is, pertaining to concerns lying beyond the company's own performance. Examples include commitments to the national labour force (in other words, 'a global attitude towards all the workers of this country to contribute to their employment opportunities and the improvement of their standard of living', as a French interviewee put it), to regional development, to national independence (or 'to contribute to the country's autonomy in a political, economic and military sense', as another French interviewee put it).

Third, are commitments that government organizations have concerning the behaviour of GCEs'. Thus, a regional development agency will be committed to making sure that at least some new plant investments be made in certain backward regions; a ministry for foreign commerce may feel obliged to strive for a minimum rate of annual increase of GCEs' exports; and a labour ministry may be committed to a periodic increase of the jobs provided by GCEs. Government organizations' commitments may be conducive to MN decisions. A case in point is the commitments of certain governments to maintain and develop good relations with certain developing countries – notably former colonies – which may result in pressure on GCEs to invest in those areas.

It should be clear that there is considerable room for conflict among commitments. A typical instance is the commitment to hold market shares abroad (which may call for foreign direct investment) and a policy precluding expansion into certain countries. Or the commitments of a government unit calling for MN expansion and those of another unit pushing for domestic growth. In general terms, such conflicts among commitments are resolved by the strongest one being followed to the detriment of the others. Sometimes steps ·are taken to meet the requirements of these other commitments as well. For example, we found that one company made a direct investment in a country despite the *a priori* feeling that it was a risky country in which to become involved; yet, steps were taken geared to reduce the risks involved: insurance against expropriation was secured, higher customs protection was negotiated with local authorities and a guarantee was arranged with the host country's government that the exchange rate at which profits were to be repatriated was to remain unaltered etc.

In this connection, the findings of Anastassopoulos – though in the domestic context – are illustrative of how conflicts can be, at least partially, resolved:

> In 1963—1964 the DATAR wanted Renault to invest in Lorient, Brittany, because an old local company called for public intervention and seemed to be condemned to close down. Renault refused to buy it, arguing that the production facilities (forges) were completely obsolete and that it had no need for them anyway. But the DATAR insisted that Renault should create new jobs in the area, by building something entirely new if not by using the old plant. A compromise was finally arrived at when Renault agreed to build a modern electrical foundry (the SFBM), which it needed but which it would have located near Paris otherwise. A low-interest loan was accorded which could theoretically offset the supplementary cost of transportation due to the remote location. The new plant began producing in 1967, employing 800 people at that time (over 1000 since 1971).
>
> Still in 1963—1964, the area of Nantes, Loire Atlantique, suffered considerable unemployment due to a recession in the shipbuilding activities, and the DATAR asked Renault to invest there. At that time, Renault needed an assembly plant which had to be located near the plants producing the parts to be assembled, which were costly to transport (body parts). Projected location was the already existing complex of Flins, Normandy. The DATAR opposed that project categorically, and exerted strong pressures, through the Minister of Finance and the Prime Minister, to make Nantes be chosen. It took a long time and endless technical discussions for Renault to convince the Prime Minister that Nantes was

really a bad location which would prove very costly. But as they accepted that the plant be built in Le Havre – which was all right for Renault, although not the location originally projected – the DATAR and its supporters demanded that Renault do 'something' in Nantes. Renault had to build there a small plant producing rubber parts (CPIO) employing 700 people in 1968, and over 1220 in 1971'.

2. Commitments built up during the decision process

Three types of commitment are relevant.

a. Commitments made by a GCE per se   The more resources spent on the development of a proposal the more difficult it is to reject it. A few examples will illustrate this.

Commitments can result from investments in the investigation process itself. One company reported that initial investigations for a prospective foreign investment had cost a lot of money and taken considerable time 'due to the complexity of the project and the company's inexperience with foreign investments'. At a certain point, the company 'discovered new factors (mainly the unavailability of necessary natural resources and the inadequacy of local infrastructures) making the project far less attractive'. Still, as the executive commented, 'we had spent so much money and efforts on prior research that we felt we had to go on. We just didn't have the nerve to write our investments off'.

Commitments can also come from in-company investments in the form. primarily of time spent to get proposals through. Thus a company reported that one of its executives felt strongly about the desirability of the company investing in a given foreign country. The executive was not a high-ranking one and he thus had had to work hard to receive permission and funds to actively investigate the possibility of such a project. As he himself acknowledged: 'I went off with a bias in favour of the investment, given all the efforts I had put into convincing people that this looked like a potentially attractive prospect. More than actually trying to find out whether or not such an investment was attractive in the first place, I guess I really set out to develop a plan which would make the proposal attractive to top management'.

An IRI company reported that it often finds itself having made commitments to actually *make* a particular investment by virtue of the time and effort it spent to convince its parent holding that a particular strategy is worth *considering*. As the president said: 'By the time we get approval for making a feasibility study (which in our field involves major outlays of human and financial resources) we have spent so much effort in in-company arguments with our parent trying to show the project's potential benefits, that we have become convinced that these benefits are not potential but actual, real'.

Conversely, top management can develop commitments via periodic consultations with lower echelons in the course of the elaboration of a proposal. Frequently, lower echelons refer to top management in an informal fashion to inform it of their progress and to make sure they are conforming to its expectations. By giving feedback to lower echelons, top management provides reinforcement of their work. Ultimately, when the proposal is completed its acceptance is virtually inevitable. One company reported that top management had asked its planning staff to analyse the possibilities of investments in a given foreign country; the assignment was *not* to develop a plan for a specific project nor to investigate the feasibility of a given investment; rather, it was to find out whether, on the whole, it might be worthwhile to look for a specific opportunity in a second stage. Because of the company's lack of MN experience, top management got involved in the staff's work. Soon the staff found itself focusing on a specific opportunity that one of its members had come across during his fieldwork.

Since the opportunity appeared attractive, it was investigated further, with top management's tacit assent. As the chief executive said: 'We suddenly found we were committed to do far more than we originally intended when we first asked for the general investigation; not only did we have commitments to actually pursue investment possibilities in the country, but also did we have commitments *vis-à-vis* a specific project'.

Still, commitments can take other forms. A GCE reported it had invested in a South American country as a result of a succession of small acts:

> 'In particular, negotiations with third parties – principally local government authorities and financial institutions – were complex and took considerable time and effort. By the time we got through with these negotiations, the economic conditions had changed and the project appeared far less attractive than at the time we began negotiating. Yet, we had invested so much energy in it that we felt pledged to its pursuit. We went ahead with it and it turned out to be a failure. Had we been objective about it, we would have avoided this mistake . . .'

b. Commitments made by government This constitutes government's involvement in one or several of the key components of the process underlying a MN proposal – the identification of a potential opportunity, its analysis, the development of a plan to exploit it, the negotiations necessary for its pursuit with all parties concerned . . . In such instances, the government 'sticks its neck out' and itself actively develops a proposal for action for a GCE, or at least, makes a sizeable contribution to such a development. By so doing, it makes certain investments which in turn result in commitments for it to use its best efforts to foster the accomplishment by the relevant GCE of the proposal in question.

For example, a subsidiary of a diversified GCE reported that it got involved in an Eastern European country as the result of commitments taken by its government with the host country's government:

> In the context of its overall policy of increasing and improving relations with that country, our government identified an opportunity which it felt would be both beneficial for its political relations with that country and attractive for us. It then proceeded to negotiate a proposal with local authorities. In the process it only briefly consulted with our parent company and not at all with us. When we were actually brought into the picture the real question was less 'are you interested in pursuing this opportunity?' as 'what is the best way you can think of to exploit this opportunity?' The government had gone so far in the negotiations that it appeared difficult indeed not to go forth with the project.

The government can also make commitments *vis-à-vis* GCEs themselves. We found more than one case where the government had asked a GCE to pursue a particular avenue, providing the required financial backing. Whereas the company indeed gets involved in this path, the government may lose interest or find the project really to be unattractive. Yet, given the resources already spent on it, the government finds it hard to write them off and back out from the project. It then ends up putting new resources in to allow the completion of the project. A prime example is the Concorde. As the project advanced, it appeared that it was increasingly difficult to halt its further progress. As one executive said: 'After the fact, we have learnt that one should better think twice and do as thorough an analysis as possible *before* embarking on this kind of venture, since once it is launched it becomes truly very hard to stop'.

c. Commitments stemming from relations between government and GCEs
Commitments emerge from negotiations between a GCE and the government about a particular project. As we will see below when discussing review procedures, when a GCE wishes to pursue a particular project which constitutes a departure from its existing field of activity, it usually needs to negotiate approval from government. This is the case in particular for the first MN investments. The obtaining of such an approval is often cumbersome and requires considerable time and effort which in turn results in commitments in favour of MN expansion. As reported by an interviewee:

> We wanted to invest in South America in a manufacturing plant. Approval of the project by government took very long and we fought hard to get it through. Yet, by the time we got the approval we felt much less strongly about the venture due to the changed economic conditions locally. But we had gone through so much

pain to get the project through with the government that we still went ahead with it once we got their OK.

Further, the government frequently makes commitments *vis-à-vis* a plan of a GCE during the very process of elaboration of this plan. A GCE's management tends to consult periodically with government to seek endorsement of its plan: though usually implicitly, the government reinforces the doings of management and thereby often makes a commitment to go along with the plans once they are completed.

It can also happen that a GCE makes commitments to pursue a proposal originally made by government but then forgotten or neglected by it. Thus, one GCE was approached by a ministry and asked to consider an investment in a particular country. The company complied with the request and investigated the possibility thoroughly. In the meantime there was a change in government and the new misister showed little interest in the project. Yet, the company had undertaken substantial work to investigate the project and thus ended up continuing with further analysis on its own which ultimately led to a decision to invest.

B. Formal review procedures

These are the established organizational mechanisms by which decisions are taken 'officially'. While approval does not really occur via these formal procedures, they do have an indirect impact on decisions.

1. *Company procedures*

For major decisions, five reviewing units may generally be distinguished.

(1) The first screening body – those executives who evaluate the general indicators.

(2) The investigators – those collecting the data and evaluating them in the field.

(3) The co-ordinating unit – the executives who receive the investigators' report, evaluate it, and perhaps present it to the higher echelons for approval.

(4) The finance staff – the group assigned to analyse the need for appropriations and to maintain control of the company's funds.

(5) The final authority – the highest management echelon to which a project is presented for approval.[10]

In fact, there are variations according to the size, structure and type of company involved and the kind of decision involved. Still, what is more important than reviewing units' formal position is their attributions or duties – what a unit's scope is in terms of its responsibility and authority. These attributions determine when and how units get involved in the decision process and thus affect their influence on approval. Three aspects are noteworthy.

a. The relationships among the different units are critical   Notwithstanding the exact organizational arrangements, the important factor is that there are several organizational units involved in the decision process. Before a final decision is reached, a proposed project is reviewed not once but several times, not by one person but by different management echelons, with different objectives and motivations and on the basis of different information . . . Three features of these relationships [among units] should be explicitly [pointed out]. First, the perception by lower echelons of the factors important to higher echelons influences the way in which they evaluate a project. Second, the higher echelons are generally not actively involved in the earlier phases of the investigation and, therefore, they have less at stake. They may approve a project, however, because they feel the organization has been bound by commitments made by lower echelons. Finally, lower echelons generally become committed to a project before they submit it for approval; otherwise, it will not be submitted. Virtually never is the analysis presented to higher echelons in a form that is intended to offer a real choice. In practice, one of two things happens. Either the lower echelon becomes sufficiently committed and therefore presents top management with arguments for accepting the project, or when the lower echelon is not committed, a project will be presented only if absolutely certain of acceptance.[11]

Various units have distinct roles. Lower echelons responsible for the field-work and the drafting of a first report are both influenced by the higher echelon to which they are to report and themselves influence acceptance of the project. They can influence acceptance by presenting the project under a favourable light to higher echelons and by building commitments in favour of it. And they are influenced by higher echelons:

> In performing their evaluation, the investigators must take into account not only what they perceive to be correct but also the point of view of higher management echelons as they see it. Sometimes [they] may try to verify [their] perceptions by clearing the project with a higher echelon on a provisional basis prior to proceeding with the investigation. If for some reason [they] feel committed to the investment proposal [they] will modify it in a way [they] think will make it acceptable to others.[12]

Staff people tend to focus on special aspects of a project only. A case in point are the finance people. While their official attributions should often give them authority to block a proposal, they rarely do so and they confine their role to bringing amendments to the financial aspects of a project. As argued by Zwick, proposals are 'implemented regardless of the finance department's initial recommendation. Typically, division personnel will eventually arrange a financial plan which is suitable to the finance department'.[13] Discussing a specific case, Zwick notes that 'the finance department appears to have been more interested in determining what preventive actions could be taken to eliminate foreign risks . . . attention has been shifted from the undesirable event – that is, the foreign risks . . . to the preventive action'.[14]

The role of top management varies according to whether a project was initiated by it or not. When the project was not initiated by top management, its role is essentially of implicit influence during the investigation process – providing guidance and reinforcement to lower echelons in the development of their projects. When the project is initiated by top management, commitment to the project comes from the top and is thus all the more powerful. As one middle manager put it, who was in charge of the investigation of a project initiated by top management:

> While we were told to look into the possibility of making the investment (i.e. see whether an investment in general was attractive in that country), we knew that, given it was the boss's idea and one he obviously was emotionally involved in, chances were that it would be accepted anyhow, regardless of our recommendation. We thus endeavoured to find arguments really justifying it and worked hard to develop the best action plan to draw the most out of it.

b. The impact of a strong force on, and its role in approval   We saw that for a new kind of course of action to be considered and analysed, a strong force has usually to intervene. Similarly, a force is often needed to back a new idea up in terms of obtaining approval for it: unless the new idea enjoys a virtual *a priori* commitment by the final authority responsible for approving it, a force is needed to secure approval for a new type of strategic action. And, as we will see, a force is also needed to seek approval of sponsoring government authorities. Thus, even if top management is committed to the project, a force is still necessary to obtain approval from government.

Existence of a force often has the consequence of creating even stronger commitments. While for a familiar type of investment decision where a strong force is not involved commitments are built up gradually, here they are developed rapidly. The first stages of an investigation process may then be sketchy or even omitted completely and the organization may find itself pledged to pursuing a given route before much analysis has been performed. As an interviewee put it: 'Our first foreign investment decision was taken when our Chairman had the idea and fell in love with it. Though he asked us to "look into the potential" opportunities in America, we soon found out that all which was sought in fact were *ex post* rationalizations for a decision which had really been made long ago'.

c. Consequences of lack of procedures to review MN decisions   When a new type of action such as the first MN investment is considered, there are no procedures tailored to appraise it. It is existing procedures which have to appraise the proposal. This can result in one of two situations.

On the one hand, a reviewing body which would normally be involved in the appraisal process may simply not get involved on the grounds that this falls outside of its normal attributions. While this is not frequent, we did encounter such cases – as reported by one interviewee: 'We are so diversified and tasks are so specifically assigned to particular groups of people that it can happen that when a situation arises, nobody feels concerned by it because it falls outside of the scope of everybody's normal responsibilities'. In such cases, the step of the process normally performed by the unit in question can even be omitted altogether.

On the other hand, the more common situation is that a reviewing unit gets involved in the investigation despite its relative unfitness for appraising the particular problems of MN investments. Two things then usually happen. First, the reviews and analyses made by the unit are of doubtful quality. Second, the investigation is necessarily cumbersome; given the unit's unfamiliarity with the problems involved, a learning process has to take place and hesitations are inevitable. This results in a tendency towards immobilism, a unit's natural inclination being that of 'doing nothing'. This then calls for a force to intervene, which in turn creates further commitments around the proposal. Thus, additional steps are taken towards its acceptance.

2. *Government procedures*

Government units having a formal role in the approval process differ from country to country and from company to company. At one end, a GCE belonging to a state holding may be able to invest abroad without needing to formally consult with the government, approval from the parent company being enough. At the other end, certain GCEs need not only a formal approval by government (the sponsoring ministry) but also that of Parliament: many GCEs have their field of activity precisely defined and need a formal permission from Parliament to depart from it. Further, many GCEs undergo the control of a host of what the French call *contrôles à priori* – supervision of their decisions before these decisions have been implemented – as opposed to *contrôles à posteriori* – evaluation of decisions based on the company's results. The French Socialist Party is quite articulate about this – as one of its high-ranking officials put it:

> While we do want to expand the public sector, we are for GCEs' freedom of management. We want to specify their objectives and indicate to them what the main axes of their behavior should be, but then we want to let their management act as it sees fit. We will only look at results. Today, it is the opposite which takes place. *Ex*

ante controls are innumerable. Government wants to check all the decisions management takes from all kinds of points of view – financial, technical, supply policies, etc. This of course has debilitating effects for innovation: it is hard indeed to get any new type of action decided upon, given the existence of all the controls which come into play when a new path is considered.

Leaving aside ideological and partisan overtones, it is true that the many *contrôles à priori* to which certain GCEs are subject constitute a hindrance to their taking new paths.

For their first MN investment, most GCEs have to secure some kind of government approval (for example from the ministry of state holdings). In addition, approval may have to be secured from specialized government units. To illustrate, consider the typical IRI company case. Plans of the company are integrated in the overall plan of its *Finanziaria di Settore*, which is itself integrated in an overall IRI plan. This plan, which can be quite detailed for certain investments (including a particular foreign investment) is then submitted to the *Ministero delle Partecipazioni Statali*. The ministry in turn presents a *relazione* (a report) to Parliament, which is to approve it. In addition, certain special organizations get involved. A case in point is CIPE – an interministerial committee for economic planning. Thus, from the GCE's point of view, it does not directly get involved with government, but it has to obtain its approval via its parent and its sponsoring ministry. This is particularly the case for typical projects which receive special mention in all the successive plans, including the *relazione* presented to government and that examined by CIPE.

Again, what is more important than the official role of each unit is what impact these units have in practice. While the official function of each tells us little about their real role, this function does have a major bearing on their *de facto* influence on decisions, since it affects how, when and for what a unit is brought into the decision process. Here too, three aspects are noteworthy.

a. The role of government This is comparable to that of top management within a company. If a project of MN investment stems from government, it will come with considerable commitment on the part of government as to its pursuit. As one chief executive said: 'Our first foreign investment originated from an idea of the prime minister himself. While he was the one to formulate the general concept of the investment, we of course were responsible for analysing it concretely and to develop a specific action plan. We did formulate such a proposal. Needless to say, it was readily accepted'.

If the project does not stem from government, the government's role varies according to the extent to which the project was elaborated in close consultation with it or not. If consultation was close, the government is rarely in a position to actually approve a project or not. Rather, its inclinations are then taken into account and commitments in favour of the plan secured. If there was little consultation, the proposal may not only not meet with government's expectations but also have no back-up in government. We will return to this.

b. Impact of a force   As we saw, in the majority of cases where a project's original idea comes from the government, a force is involved. Such a force entails commitment to the project before much analysis is made about its real potential. Thus, one government official reported:

> A few years ago, the finance ministry came out with an idea that one of our GCEs should invest in South America. By the time preliminary investigations had been made and a few contacts established, the decision to invest had been made. It was only possible for the company to back out from what would have been a bad mistake, because it waited long enough to start investing sizeably in the project until there was a change in government.

c. Inertia of reviewing units   A proposed change in a GCE's strategic posture towards MN expansion may not receive appropriate analysis from a reviewing unit either because the contemplated change raises questions existing procedures are not fit to address or simply because the unit does not feel concerned by the change.

On one hand, a reviewing unit may do nothing but the project still *de facto* be approved. If the unit is not critical to the project's approval, it may be skipped altogether. For instance, there are certain government departments which have a right to intervene in a GCE's investment plans. Yet, if they do not exercise the right promptly when a plan is in government's hands for approval, they in practice forfeit any prerogative of hindering adoption of the plan. Alternatively, when a plan comes before a unit, it may actually for all practical purposes approve it, though indirectly. A good illustration is that of a company's plan to invest abroad passing the test of parliamentary approval without there being any discussion of the issue. When the procedure is such that a given company's plan comes before Parliament as part of a broader plan including the proposed activities and investments of several GCEs, the broader plan may be discussed in its totality and approved as a package without there being any discussion of the particular company's project.

On the other hand, a reviewing unit may have to give its explicit approval for the project to go through. This is the case of many government organizations whose formal endorsement is necessary. In such cases and when the unit either feels undecided about the plan or not responsible for the kind of issue involved, there may be considerable footdragging and delay in approval. As a GCE executive put it:

> At the time of our first foreign investment we submitted a plan to government and gave them all the necessary data to make a decision. But then nothing happened. We later found out that nobody

felt concerned by the proposal and that there was just no built-in procedure in the bureaucracy to cause action to be taken on the proposal. As long as we kept on doing what we had been doing in the past, our plans were approved. Even if our results were not too good, nothing much happened and we continued to get OKs on our proposals. But when a change was considered, everything seemed to be paralysed.

Beyond the obvious tendency of perpetuating the *status quo* and thus hindering MN expansion, this engenders the need for a strong force to push a proposal through. While such a force can come from within the government, it more often comes from the GCE involved. Further, such a force is necessary to build commitment in favour of the proposal during its elaboration itself. As we saw, rather than waiting until a plan is completed to submit it to the government, it is desirable that government be consulted during its very development. Reportedly, the government often does not have specific expectations as to what precise form an MN investment should take; yet, if no commitment is built around a project, the project will frequently have a hard time going through because of organizational inertia: more than rejecting it, government may just not act on it.

IV. ACTION

Decision and action do not necessarily match each other perfectly; a project is far from always being pursued as planned. Risks of distortions are particularly serious when a new kind of activity is involved. While it is difficult enough to take the decision of going MN, additional problems arise when it comes to implementing such decisions. Further, a strategic plan is virtually by definition a plan for the total enterprise or at least a plan affecting the posture of the firm as a whole. A project of strategic importance calls into play various parts of the company, all having a substantial degree of independence *vis-à-vis* each other. This means that risks of distortion are even higher: the more numerous the organizational units which are involved in the accomplishment of a project, the lesser the chances that the project will be pursued as intended. And with GCEs, government is also involved, which brings into the picture another host of units. While government is not concerned with a plan's implementation *per se* – in the sense that its component organizations are not themselves to accomplish the actual moves constituting the realization of the plan – they *are* concerned with what happens in practice to the plan.

Specifically, difficulties arise in three main areas.

1. *Different deciders and implementers*

A gap can separate plan from action because those responsible for planning are frequently not the same people responsible for doing. Distortions may occur because various moves are ill-fitted to the overall plan.

For example, an Italian *finanziaria di settore* reported that a few years ago it was decided that one of its operating companies should make a particular investment in a given country. The plan specified the location of the facilities, their size and capacity, the timing of their construction, the human, technical and financial resources to be used; it also specified time-phased objectives in terms of sales and profits. Yet, beyond this, the operating company was to decide and act as it saw fit. As an interviewee from the *finanziaria* put it: 'While they did stick to the directives of the plan, within the plan they did everything wrong. Basically, they went about doing the investment by applying the procedures they were used to applying in domestic investments'. What happened in practice was that a succession of relatively minor acts were misguided. 'Thus the feasibility study for the construction of the plant did not take into account local variables such as labour relations. In the actual construction of the plant each unit did what it knew how to do without much concern for whether its actions were appropriate, given local conditions. (For example, given the country was an LDC, the company had to build certain infrastructures itself; it did so without paying attention to the local climatic conditions and to the geological characteristics of the soil; the infrastructures thus turned out to be inadequate under many aspects). 'The result is that so many components of their actions were ill-focused that the entire venture was impaired,' said our interviewee.

Another case is that of a government asking a GCE to make a particular investment abroad. Usually, the government specifies the broad lines of the project. But the company is then normally left on its own in carrying out the plan in practice. Again, the inexperienced company goes about implementation in a way unadapted to an MN investment. For example, all sources of financing may not be investigated (in one instance a company reportedly was importing most of the capital required while its finance staff had not investigated the possibility of trapping cheaper local funds); local sources of supply may not be studied thoroughly and the location of the plant may be chosen hastily (in another case a company put up a plant abroad next to the sea because this was what it had successfully done over the years at home, while locally the obvious location was inland, next to the capital which was the main industrial centre of the country).

2. *Lack of co-ordination between units*

Distortions occur because action is carried out by a variety of units which are but imperfectly tied to each other. For instance, a functionally organized company reported that when it had decided to make its first foreign investment, it had assumed that the various departments would co-operate and communicate among each other in view of co-ordinating their actions. In fact, this did not happen and considerable discrepancies occurred between the actions of various departments. In particular there was a lack of co-ordination between the production and the marketing departments. Exchange of information was scanty. Besides, each had a different set of ends: the production department wanted to unload old machinery while the marketing people wanted modern equipment to be able to sell the best product possible at the lowest price. As the President said:

> Using different sources and types of information and different perceptions, each acted on the basis of different presumptions; therefore, the moves of each were not complementary and the expectations of marketing were in many ways not met by production. For example, the technology employed by production wasn't that which marketing expected and the characteristics of the product supplied to the marketing people were not those which they were counting upon... The explanation of the lack of co-ordination is that each acted on its own. This was consistent to what usually happens at home. Except that in the context of domestic investments, the moves and procedures tend to be constant from one project to the other, which results in units *de facto* operating in a more or less co-ordinated fashion even without much exchange of information between them: repetition of certain patterns of behaviour doesn't make consultation as necessary for co-ordination. But this lack of information in a new setting was fatal to any hope of co-ordinated action.

Another example was given by a government official:

> After the outbreak of the oil crisis, the government decided that it would be desirable for various GCEs to co-ordinate their actions and thus present a common integrated front to the OPEC countries. The idea was that in order to pay at least part of the oil bill, GCEs could offer industrial investments to oil-exporting nations which typically badly need such investments. The idea was further that by co-ordinating the efforts of the various GCEs, we could achieve greater effectiveness than if each acted on its own. And, given this country had GCEs both at the demand end (i.e. oil companies) and at the potential supply end (i.e. companies capable of making investments attractive to OPEC countries), this route appeared a promising one. So, we devised plans towards this end. These were based on broad consultations between government economic experts and the managements of the relevant GCEs. Yet, once the plans were completed, not much happened. The oil companies continued to 'go it alone' and the few projects of GCEs in OPEC countries which came off the ground were the product of individual companies. What happened? Once plans had been made, nobody took the responsibility of following through. Top managers who had participated in the development of the

plan indeed asked their staff people and sometimes their division heads to devise means to co-ordinate their company's doings with those of other GCEs. But taken in the bustle of other concerns they didn't devote much further attention to the matter. The subordinates didn't do much for co-ordination either: from their vantage point, they didn't perceive the importance of co-ordination and couldn't quite see what to do with the whole concept. And, you might ask, how about the government? Well, it was overthrown and replaced by a new government who didn't find the issue one worth worrying about . . . .

3. Lack of action

As the above example begins to suggest, certain decisions are simply ignored altogether. A government official thus reported that in a similar context as above, the government had asked a number of GCEs to look into the possibilities of investing in OPEC countries. About one third of the GCEs had no previous MN·experience: 'None of them really seriously investigated that possibility at all'. The official concluded: 'Nobody in the companies was really committed to such a type of venture and nobody charged himself to make sure a real effort was made in this direction'.

Of course, major strategic decisions are rarely totally ignored. When a strategic plan is clearly formulated, its major features usually do occur. However, certain components or certain moves of the plan may be omitted or accomplished differently than originally decided. Such omissions or amendments may have a determining effect on the plan's success. In particular, certain decisions regarding procedures are often ignored. Thus, one executive reported that some years ago, at the time the company was making its first foreign investment, an instruction of his had been ignored which had important consequences on the project's outcome.

Once the decision had finally been made to go ahead with the investment, the [ABC] division started to take the first step to build the new facilities and mobilized the human and financial resources necessary for the project. I soon found out that they were using a construction process which, while OK for our usual domestic operations, was unadapted to the local conditions. I then asked that a different process be employed and assumed this would be done. A few months later, during a trip to the country to check the progress of the construction of our new facilities, I found they had continued to use the old standard process and not the new one I had asked for.

What had happened? The executive in question was a project manager officially responsible for monitoring the development of the foreign investment. In this capacity, he was in a position to ask that a particular process be used and not another. Yet, the construction of the facilities and the installation of the production equipment was the direct responsibility of the engineering department which usually took charge of the construction of all such facilities. The existence of the project manager was only justified by the fact that this was the first foreign investment of the company, one presumably requiring special attention. The usual absence of a project engineer made the unit responsible for the construction of the foreign facilities insensitive to his instructions: had the instructions come from the engineering department, chances are that they would have received greater attention. But the engineering department, because of its own organizational idiosyncrasies, was not in a good position to develop such instructions. Presumably, this is precisely the reason for which the project engineer was brought into the picture in the first place. It thus appears that the very reasons calling for the existence of the project engineer made him powerless to act effectively.

V. CONCLUSION

In this chapter we analysed the organizational procedures which govern GCEs' decisions to go or not to go MN – GCEs with no prior MN activities. We identified four key elements in the decision process and our focus was to understand the routines on which these elements rest. Our basic conclusion is that there is a built in tendency in companies on the one hand to stay home and on the other to go abroad – when this does occur – in an awkward fashion. In particular, we should re-emphasize three points:

(1) The decision to invest abroad in the first place is not made easily. Because of their organizational features, as major a change as that entailed by an internationalization of their field of activity is not undertaken lightly in GCEs: the mechanisms designed to identify problems in or threats to current operations tend not to be geared towards problems which might receive MN solutions; those which are to find new opportunities are not international in scope; search routines are neither tailored to seek out attractive MN projects nor able to devise ways to draw the most from MN opportunities; the approval procedures are not fit to take action on proposed courses which constitute as radical a departure from existing activities as that implied by the first MN investment.

(2) The plan for the first foreign investment is usually suboptimal when it is not plainly inadequate: the underlying procedures tend to be borrowed from domestic operations with little adaptation to the MN environment; this hinders the formulation of a truly effective strategy.

(3) The accomplishment of a strategy puts further limits on the results which a first MN investment can yield: given they rarely follow new kinds of plans faithfully, GCEs' actual behaviour and moves are often further unadapted to the MN undertakings they pursue.

For a more effective exploitation of MN investment propositions, it is normally critical for a force to intervene. Only a force can really raise a problem liable to receive an MN solution, cause consideration of an MN alternative, identify an MN opportunity. Only a force can mitigate the ineptnesses of the means by which MN projects are actually pursued. And a force is instrumental in causing key organizational units to take action on a novel kind of proposal.

When a force steps in early in the decision process, it often continues to play a role later as well. Thus, when it intervenes in problem identification, chances are it will also be involved in search. It then is in fact often difficult to distinguish between problem identification and search in terms of sequential phases: they tend to occur simultaneously[15] (though a government force normally tends not to go beyond the point where an opportunity has been found, stopping short from getting involved in the development of a specific action plan). And not infrequently will a force having stepped in early also play a role in approval.

Yet, the reach of a force is limited: while a force can give an impulse in a particular direction, actual corporate behaviour is the product of standard procedures. In particular, the investigation underlying the development of a strategic plan and the implementation of a plan are primarily the result of existing routines. A force can step in occasionally to correct the workings of these routines, but this can happen only on an *ad hoc* basis: the core of organizational action is the output of standard procedures and the impact of a force is necessarily limited to certain spot interventions in a pre-established process.

This means that the fundamental organizational propensities are a constant of these GCEs' attitude *vis-a-vis* MN expansion: to repeat, notwithstanding the mostly sporadic interferences of forces, (1) to preserve the strategic posture's *status quo* (that is, remain an essentially domestic enterprise), and (2) where this does occur, to go abroad via imperfect means.

This analysis, then, begins to answer some of the questions raised by the traditional view:

(1) Most significantly, the traditional approach left us with the puzzle of why several GCEs, which on the one hand clearly face attractive prospects abroad and on the other are under little or no pressure by the government to stay home, just do not take advantage of MN opportunities. This discussion explains this in organizational terms: those GCEs which do not have prior MN experience generally do not have the decision-making procedures to consider foreign prospects in the first place. And they do not have the bureaucratic processes to allow action to be taken properly on MN proposals.

(2) The traditional approach was unable to account for obvious errors in the timing of certain actions. For example, the case where an opportunity

recognized in time to constitute an attractive prospect is actually exploited with so much delay as to lose most of its appeal (for example, the Alfa Romeo example reported in Chapter IV). The explanation here is clear. Decisions constituting major shifts in the organization's strategy are slow to be taken – when they are taken at all. This is true because of in-company decision-making routines as well as approval procedures in the state apparatus. Indeed, the first steps in a company's multinationalization can constitute such a radical shift that decisions can be retarded in a dramatic fashion simply for lack of administrative mechanisms tailored to collect, process, analyse and draw action conclusions from the relevant data. This is particularly so at the government level.

(3) Given the postulated unitary character of GCEs and government, it was also unclear why co-ordination between GCEs is so often imperfect. And why especially what was referred to as 'conglomerate strategy' is pursued with so little consistency. This should be understood now: particularly for novel kinds of actions, it is difficult to achieve much harmonization between different organizations. It is hard to cause a GCE to pursue a new strategy for motives other than its own self-interest (for example, to pursuade a GCE to invest in an OPEC country for macro reasons or for the sake of helping another GCE in its efforts to secure crude oil). And at the implementation level it is hard to co-ordinate the actual moves of two enterprises – to cause two GCEs making their first steps in the international arena to do so in concert 'in the field'.

(4) We were unable to explain the frequent imperfections or inefficiencies with which certain governmental policies are pursued. A case in point is the location of certain capital-intensive projects in depressed high-unemployment areas, and this in the context of regional development efforts. Thus, we asked why many of the state-sponsored investments in the Mezzogiorno in reality do relatively little to use local labour. The fact of the matter is that many GCEs which are pushed to invest in the South are also pursuing a policy of shifting to less labour and more capital intensive production processes; for lack of any force prompting them to do differently, they go to the Mezzogiorno with the same policy. Thus one interviewee reported: 'To comply with the state's requirements we invested in the Mezzogiorno. But since nobody in the government provided us with specific guidance as to what type of investment was appropriate, we instinctively put up the kind of plant which we would have built otherwise – a high technology process which didn't do much to alleviate local unemployment problems'. The inadequacies of government planning processes and the inefficiency of the communication procedures between the various government units concerned and GCEs do not permit to check this organizational propensity to transfer a way of doing things from one context to another with little adaptation. The deficient control mechanisms of the government further prevent the effective monitoring of the appropriateness of GCEs' actions.

(5) The traditional approach suggests that when free of any encumbrances from the tool goal a GCE virtually automatically strives for the highest possible returns. As we saw, this is not always the case in fact. The process approach suggests that, at least initially, a GCE behaves abroad in a similar fashion as it does at home. If domestically its search process makes considerable room for the taking into account of governmental preoccupations, it will tend to also be quite attentive to make its MN actions consistent with macro concerns. Thus, the traditional view leads one to expect, for example, that if this appears to be the best way of doing it, GCEs do not hesitate to go abroad via takeovers of a healthy local concern; but because this is often not the way GCEs behave at home, they rarely do so in their early MN expansion. To repeat, patterns of MN decision-making, at least initially, reflect domestic patterns regardless of whether or not companies are under the same macro type of pressures and even if this entails self-imposed constraints which are not warranted in an MN context.

Yet, this analysis too leaves certain questions unanswered.

First, several of the puzzles raised by the traditional approach do not appear to be resolved. Thus, certain rather incomprehensible myopic attitudes identified in Chapter IV are still not clear. For example, how can governments' resistance to high-technology transnational linkups be accounted for? Or how can one explain a government's insistence that foreign markets be served by exports (as opposed to foreign direct investment) when the only real way for a company to be competitive abroad is through local production (thus threatening the very employment and balance-of-payments aims sought by the state)? And this account does not allow us to fully understand certain decisions about investment locations. For instance, why are certain GCEs not consistent in pursuing regionalization policy aims? Or how are certain choices made between one spot or another *within* a country's depressed areas (a process view suggests that a company will tend to go where it already has operations or where there are certain *points de chute*; yet, the evidence suggests that they not infrequently go to totally different locations)?

Second, we also find a number of anomalies in GCEs' strategies – actual behaviour different from what one might expect. Thus, there are a number of cases in which a GCE stopped abiding by government pressures without there being a clear force which might be held accountable for this. For example, we found an Italian company which for many years had complied with government directives in particular in the context of regionalization efforts. Then it apparently suddenly changed its attitude and practically ceased to invest in the Mezzogiorno. In a company executive's words:

> We had grown into the habit of seeking to favour the South in our new plant location. Then one day this stopped. It happened rather quickly, yet, no one event can be said to have caused it . . . What happened is that for a particular project which *a priori* was to be a natural for an investment in the South, somebody in government

intervened to try and cause us to put it elsewhere. In fact, we didn't do so. Still, we didn't even put it in the South. Rather, a long debate developed between various top management people and government representatives as to where to locate the new plant. Finally, we somehow put it in [a given location]. But, frankly, I am not sure how that choice rather than another emerged.

Similarly, in another instance we found that a GCE took its first look abroad thanks to a force trying to cause the company to invest in a particular country; yet, while the company did end up investing abroad, it did not go to that particular country.

The intervention of [the force] served to cause us to become aware of foreign opportunities [said the executive vice president]. Yet, once the principle of foreign investment was admitted, a struggle developed between top management and the sponsoring ministry (as well as other key political men) as to where we should go first and for what. We ended up in a place nobody really had wanted in the first place. I guess this was the only acceptable compromise.

In both these cases a force was indeed instrumental in causing a departure from organizational routine. Yet, what happened once the *status quo* was no more taken as a given, once the notion of a strategic shift *per se* was accepted? How was a particular alternative chosen? The force was neither strong enough to impose a solution of its own nor seemingly was action taken via standard processes.

Third, and related to the above, the specifics of how forces function are unclear. As we saw, the role of initiating forces is a central one in the process approach. Yet, one does not truly understand why when they intervene they push for one kind of action rather than another and how they actually can exert influence and the limits of such influence. More significantly still, the question of what happens when several forces play a role in the context of the same issue is not answered. In other words, the process approach conceives of forces as a black box, the internal dynamics of which it does not attempt to uncover. Thus, one is left with several basic questions:

(1) In the context of a given issue or event, a force can trigger certain routines. But when precisely are certain routines set in motion as opposed to others?

(2) How can one predict the relative role in a decision of an intervening force and of standard procedures? In certain cases a decision is manifestly taken essentially via routines, while in others the role of a force appears predominant for the same kind of decision in a seemingly equivalent kind of organizational setting. Why? What determines the point at which forces stop and routines take over?

206

(3) How does it happen exactly that certain initiating forces, while giving an initial impulse in a given direction (for example, introducing the concept of foreign investment), are then unable to impose the particular course of action they advocate? Why does their influence stop at a given point? And what happens thereafter in terms of decisions about what course to pursue?

(4) Often it must be that more than one force intervenes and tries to have a bearing on what is done. How do forces relate to each other? What happens if different forces push for different decisions and actions? How is conflict resolved between them? Who wins, when and why? What determines the relative influence of forces in given circumstances?

NOTES

1. See M. V. Posner and S. J. Woolf, *Italian Public Enterprise*, Gerald Duckworth, London, 1967; *Corriere della Sera*, 10 June 1977, p. 29; *Corriere della Serra*, 11 June 1977, p. 21.
2. Yair Aharoni, *The Foreign Investment Decision Process*, Division of Research, Graduate School of Business Administration, Harvard University, Boston, 1966, p. 50.
3. Yair Aharoni, *The Foreign Investment Decision Process*, p. 42.
4. Yair Aharoni, *The Foreign Investment Decision Process*, p. 54.
5. These are a partial listing from 'Foreign investments checklist – some factors for consideration by US businessmen in exploring investment abroad', published by the US Bureau of Foreign Commerce. See: American Management Association Seminar, 'Going Abroad: The Profit Opportunities of International Business for the Smaller Company', New York 1961 – Washington: Government Printing Office, 1961, pp. 215–219.
6. The following should be taken with care. The supporting data is partial and impressionistic. In fact, these observations should primarily be considered as illustrations of the influence of domestic operations on MN activities.
7. Yair Aharoni, *The Foreign Investment Decision Process*, p. 123.
8. Yair Aharoni, *The Foreign Investment Decision Process*, p. 125.
9. Jean-Pierre Anastassopoulos, 'The Strategic Autonomy of Government-Controlled Enterprises Operating in a Competitive Economy', PhD dissertation, Graduate School of Business, Columbia University, New York, 1973, pp. 272–273.
10. Yair Aharoni, *The Foreign Investment Decision Process*, pp. 142–143.
11. Yair Aharoni, *The Foreign Investment Decision Process*, p. 143.
12. Yair Aharoni, *The Foreign Investment Decision Process*, pp. 143–145.
13. Jack Zwick, 'Aspects of the Foreign Capital Rationing Procedures of Certain American Manufacturing Corporations', DBA dissertation, Graduate School of Business Administration, Harvard University, Boston, August 1964, pp. 35ff.
14. Jack Zwick, 'Aspects of the Foreign Capital Rationing Procedures of Certain American Manufacturing Corporations', pp. 35ff.
15. It sometimes even seems that a force proposes an action and finds a problem justifying it afterwards; the force promotes an action for reasons of its own and rationalizes it *ex post* by looking for a reason warranting it from a corporate point of view.

CHAPTER VII

GCEs with MN Experience

This chapter has two parts. In the first we look at how GCEs with MN activities make their MN strategy decisions – principally how they decide to make new foreign investments. In the second we look at their policy decisions – their modus operandi on an MN scale.

I. STRATEGIC DECISIONS

GCEs with MN experience exhibit relatively fewer particularities than those with no such experience. Besides, a number of features of the decision process are similar to those of GCEs discussed in Chapter VI. Therefore, we will essentially limit ourselves to highlighting the differences between GCEs with and without MN experience.

A. Problem identification

1. *Performance failures (or threat thereof)*

Here there are two kinds of problems: problems in current domestic operations and problems in current MN operations.

a. Actual or potential performance failures In domestic operations these are detected by similar kinds of procedures and forces as in GCEs with no MN experience. Yet, a few important differences are worth noting.

There often appears to be, so to speak, an arbitrage phenomenon between procedures governing domestic and international operations. As we will see, on the whole, international operations tend to be freer of macro types of pressures. There are thus fewer distortions in the procedures designed to monitor performance. This then is conducive to lesser distortions in domestic-oriented procedures as well – as argued by one interviewee: 'When we went MN, after a while, when our foreign operations became established and reached a certain importance, a change was noticeable in our domestic way of doing things. Methods we were using abroad percolated into our domestic operations. We became more financial performance conscious'.

A comparable phenomenon is even more true for forces. MN operations can be a source of inspiration for a force – particularly for in-company forces.

This can occur in terms of a force correcting existing parameters or a force introducing a new kind of parameter. For example, in one GCE a force stemming from MN operations was instrumental in correcting the distortions affecting performance-control procedures – notably the macro types of distortions. In another instance, the head of a GCE's international division was promoted to a high-ranking general management position at the corporate level. When he came to this post he was reportedly shocked by the distortions and manipulations which were going on in the internal accounting practices of domestic operations. He commented:

> In our MN operations we had relatively good internal accounting methods. But at home there was little which was reliable and precise enough to be of any help in management. When I came to this job the first thing I tried to apply my efforts to was to clean up our internal accounting. I can't say I have succeeded completely but we are certainly making progress.

And a controller reported somewhat along the same lines that in his company a force stemming from the MN side of the enterprise was responsible for having introduced *ex novo* a true internal control system whereas before 'we had nothing but our hunches'. He added:

> We owe our entire capital budgeting system to our MN activities. In the MN side of the company we have always functioned internally pretty much as private companies. Given we are active primarily in advanced industrial countries such as the U.S., we learned from competitors. At home we had nothing comparable. Then the man responsible for finance in our international division became VP for finance for the whole company. He soon endeavoured to install a capital budgeting system for the whole company similar to that used in the international side of the organization.

b. Negative results in current MN operations   These can be detected via standard procedures or via forces. Here too, procedures can be classified in three sets.

First, GCEs' procedures geared to their microeconomic performance. They are similar to those found in the domestic context. Yet, they are more complex and in many ways more vulnerable. Their complexity stems from the intricacies and the many variables and uncertainties involved in controlling an MNC (for example, the need to work with many currencies, the need to take into account exchange-rate fluctuations and the consequent leads and lags in intracompany payments, the need to work in the context of often complex legal and financial structures designed to limit the overall corporate tax liability . . .); as one interviewee put it, 'Things are so complex in an MN context and you have to manipulate figures so much in view of so many exogenous considerations (e.g. tax purposes) that your internal auditing often becomes very intricate and ineffective'. This complexity makes procedures vulnerable. A chief executive said: 'Compared to our domestic operations, MN operations are under lesser control by headquarters. Thus, problems are less evident to us or become apparent with undue delay'.

Moreover, just as MN procedures affect domestic procedures, domestic procedures affect MN procedures: intervening factors biasing domestic routines percolate into MN operations and reduce the effectiveness of routines. Thus, a company which had been taken over by the government about ten years ago reported that its MN operations gradually were 'infested by the bureaucratic diseases of GCEs' domestic way of operating'. In an executive's words:

> Our domestic operations became subjected to a whole lot of outside intervention in terms of things we were to do which had little to do with any commercial rationale. This had the effect of soon jeopardizing the effectiveness of our internal procedures at home and especially our accounting system. But then the problems spread to our MN operations: while our MN operations were not directly subjected to interferences, the distortions in the domestic side of the enterprise came to affect the international side as well. Imperceptibly, our MN control system became poisoned by the same distortions as those plaguing our domestic system.

In a GCE under pressure to pursue marcro aims at home but whose MN operations have limited relevance in terms of such macro aims, headquarters rarely tend to have a very exacting attitude *vis-à-vis* foreign subsidiaries. In the words of an interviewee: 'From the point of view of the subsidiary, one has the impression that the attitude at headquarters is "give us certain minimum results and don't give us any trouble". And this minimum is often well below the real potential of the subsidiary. As long as the subsidiary achieves these results, its management is rarely bothered for much more'.

At the subsidiary level, the fact that the subsidiary's activities are not prone to macro types of interventions, coupled with the frequently greater decentralization of MN operations, often results in foreign subsidiaries having control processes of their own more closely focused on their own financial performance. Still, as we saw, subsidiaries' procedures may be influenced by the distortions of procedures in the parent company. In fact, it is not enough that their activities have no relevance for macro aims to allow subsidiaries' procedures to remain unbiased; there must also be a true decentralization of foreign activities: when domestic routines are overshadowed by macro issues, for foreign routines not to be equally overshadowed, foreign subsidiaries have to enjoy considerable autonomy of their own.

In the case where MN activities do have relevance for macro aims, procedures to monitor performance of international activities tend to be overshadowed by macro concerns both at the subsidiary and at the headquarters level. Besides, GCEs which have only been for a relatively short period of time are generally still influenced by their domestic operations and are more likely to be distorted by intervening factors.

Second, GCEs' procedures geared to their macro performance – how a GCE perceives the effectiveness with which it is pursuing collective socioeconomic ends in its MN activities. A GCE can develop such procedures when its first MN activities are themselves the object of macro concerns: when an outside organization with influence – notably the government – intervenes repeatedly in a GCEs' MN operations to push it to pursue macro aims, the company will gradually develop idiosyncrasies of its own and a sensitivity for such concerns over and beyond the interventions *per se*. These idiosyncrasies can in fact go too far. For example, a GCE reported that some years ago its government asked it to do all it could to maintain or even increase its operations in a country in view of contributing to its economic development. The government wanted to improve its relations with that country and it knew that the local government would be especially sensitive to whatever was done to help its industrialization. As years went by, the local economy developed quickly and the need decreased for the types of investments the GCEs could make. On the other hand, a change in government in the company's home country resulted in a new foreign policy which laid far less stress on relations with the foreign country in question. This then decreased the importance of operations there. Yet, for an extended period of time the company continued to treat its operations in that country with particular attention – as reported by the executive vice-president:

> We were constantly on the watch for potential problems which might lead us to decrease our industrial commitment in that country; and our concern was not so much our own financial interests as the feeling that we should not let the local economy down and particularly avoid compressing our work force. We did this even while nobody obliged us to. It had become part of our local policy to be sensitive to such problems.

Alternatively, a GCE can develop such procedures by a transfer from domestic operations: for GCEs with recent MN experience in particular, procedures are often borrowed from domestic activities. Since domestic procedures are heavily tinted by macro concerns having their origin in the national context, they are rarely very effective. They frequently result in GCEs being overly sensitive to aims which have little relevance in an international context. For instance, a GCE reported that in its first years of MN operations, reviews of foreign activities repeatedly focused on the problems of whether the company was abiding by local sectorial policies while there were few such policies in the first place.

Third, procedures of outside units – notably government units – geared to appraising GCEs' performance. In an MN context there are not very many special purpose organizations involved. On the whole, these tend to concern the behaviour of companies in particular sectors. The best example is the energy sector, where countries increasingly have specialized agencies monitoring the actions of enterprises in view of safeguarding the national interests in the field.

Moreover, general purpose organizations get involved. On the whole, in the context of MN strategic decisions, they tend to have relatively loose routines to monitor GCEs' behaviour. As long as a GCE remains within reasonable bounds in terms of performance, government will rarely intervene. This is true for its micro results; in the case of MN operations in particular, it often occurs that results do not receive much special attention from the government: as long as the overall company performance is satisfactory there is generally little concern for MN operations as such. This is also true for macro concerns. The main centres of interest of most government organizations are domestic. 'Once MN activities exist, GCEs are relatively free to operate as they see fit', said a German executive. The government in fact generally steps in only in the case of major problems, for instance, a GCE developing its MN activities in a way which is detrimental to the national interests. For example, the government would intervene if a GCE were to invest in a country which is considered inappropriate, given national foreign policy (Chile or Rhodesia might be a case in point). Further, a GCE developing its foreign operations in a way which is seen as detrimental to certain national aims at home can also create problems. For example, in a country such as Italy where the recession is quite severe and where social unrest is threatening for a firm's long-term competitiveness, management might be tempted to give precedence to foreign expansion to the detriment of domestic operations. Clearly, the government would then step in.

Yet, these are rather extreme cases which occur rarely. In fact, GCEs themselves tend to refrain from engaging in such behaviour. As an interviewee said: 'Of course a government would stop a GCE, say, from expanding its MN operations into a country the regime of which it disapproved; but the government doesn't really need to intervene in such a context: GCEs stay away from doing so on their own'.

With forces we turn to situations in which existing activites are evaluated via new parameters.

With regard to micro performance, a force can step in and intervene to correct existing parameters. In particular, in GCEs with recent MN experience, a force often has to step in to adapt procedures borrowed from domestic operations to MN activities. And a force can be instrumental in introducing new criteria altogether.

With regard to macro performance, new parameters can be introduced by an in-company force. When management believes that a particular problem is important from the point of view of the collective interest, it may actively draw attention to it, over and beyond any intervention by government. Thus, during the autumn of 1973 and the winter of 1974, a particular oil GCE took certain initiatives in view of protecting the country's interests in terms of oil supply even before the government had a chance to issue directives in this connection. As a company executive recalled: 'Our top management decided very quickly that we should give precedence to focusing on a new question we hadn't had to think about before: given scarcity of oil, what should we do to safeguard national interests?'

Here, too, it is most often difficult to separate clearly the definition of a problem and the development of a solution. When management introduces a new parameter, it usually does so in the context of a particular problem, and in the process of actually posing certain questions it more or less explicitly suggests answers.

New parameters can also be introduced by forces outside the company – notably government. In one case, in the context of its policy of *rapprochement* with a particular country, a government asked that GCEs' MN expansion take into account the desirability of an increased commitment in that country. At that point, a new variable was introduced posing a new kind of problem to GCEs: to what extent is the corporate strategy responsive to the new foreign policy demands?

Given such procedures and forces, what are the characteristics of the problems uncovered by GCEs with MN experience?

First, and quite clearly, the problems related to MN activities themselves contain the element of multinationalism. There is no need to wait for search for the MN dimension to be introduced.

Further, GCEs with MN activities tend to be more sensitive to micro problems, that is, to problems related to their own financial performance. MN activities being generally less amenable to macro concerns and foreign operations tending to be more decentralized than domestic operations, there are fewer interferences stemming from macro aims. There are thus fewer distortions of procedures which are more attuned to micro types of concerns. This greater sensitivity to micro problems tends to be conducive to greater potential overtures to MN courses of action: as discussed earlier, micro problems usually lend themselves more to MN types of solutions than macro problems; being more sensitive to micro issues thus tends to lead GCEs to focus on types of problems which are more readily amenable to MN solutions.

Besides, especially as far as macro issues are concerned, forces often tend to pose new kinds of domestic problems to GCEs with no MN activities, saving MN problems for GCEs which already have MN activities. As mentioned earlier, if, say, somebody in government is confronted with the need for greater investments by GCEs in a given country, it is typically GCEs with existing MN operations which will be solicited.

2. *Opportunities*

(a) Within GCEs, opportunities are detected either via procedures or via forces.

A fundamental difference with GCEs with no MN experience is that here GCEs have sensors to scan the MN environment: as a result of their MN activities, these companies have developed standard mechanisms to identify opportunities abroad. Of course this is really true for GCEs whose MN experience is extensive enough. And the extent to which the MN experience has been positive or not is important: if the company has suffered failures in its MN ventures, sensors are far less likely to have developed as much than if the company has been successful. One author noted:

> The accumulation of experience by executives in various echelons regarding foreign investments creates profound changes in the organization itself. These organizational changes have important implications when subsequent opportunities are analyzed. Thus, the failure of a first venture abroad may be an obstacle to consideration of subsequent opportunities while its success often results in an expansion of foreign operations. Gradually, organizations may evolve into multinational corporations, vigorously looking for opportunities abroad. Thus, the repetition of the decision process gradually causes profound changes in the policies of the organization and in the roles of its members. These changes, as well as the expertise gained in foreign operations, bring new outlooks to the organization.[1]

As a GCE successfully acquires experience in the international field, it develops routine mechanisms to cope with such activities on an ongoing basis. Such mechanisms are gradually grouped in a standardized organizational pattern. A case in point is the creation of an international division whose purpose is to co-ordinate and monitor the whole of the company's international activities.* This division in particular develops sensors to keep abreast about the dynamics of the environment in which it operates. Such sensors are instrumental in the development of new MN opportunities: 'The international division usually has people "in the field", that is, in foreign countries. These people not only are important suppliers of information on the existence of foreign opportunities but also are trying to expand their range of activities, thus using whatever influence they have to "sell" additional projects and expand existing

---

*Another form of organizational adaptation is the adoption of a global structure: as the scope of MN operations increases, the company adopts a global strategy and structure. Foreign activities are no longer a separate part of the firm's operations. Rather, operations are organized so that the entire company is structured on an MN basis, every unit being involved (or potentially involved) in worldwide operations.[2] Yet, there are still a few GCEs organized in this fashion (BP, for example).

ones'.[3] Indeed, the international division actively seeks new foreign prospects: like any organizational unit, it is imperialistic and seeks to broaden its scope. Soon

> the international division begins an active search for foreign opportunities. The very existence of the division gives a momentum to international operations . . . [The management of the division] feels obliged to enlarge and expand international activities of the firm. Such expansion gives [it] a sense of achievement, or fulfilment of [its] duties and mission, and esteem in the corporation. It also helps to give [it] a sense of power in the building of an empire. Executives in the international division, like other executives, ever strive to make a success of their jobs, and they will press the higher echelons of management for more funds for the type of activities for which they are responsible.[4]

There are two main classes of sensors. First, those developed by the operating units which actually operate abroad. A foreign subsidiary, for instance, elaborates routines to analyse the local environment. In so doing it develops procedures which in time call attention to other prospects in the local economy. For example, a company reported that a few years ago one of its foreign subsidiaries was analysing the local environment for the purpose of launching a new product. In this connection, it focused on potential competitors; in the process it looked at one company in particular: 'The more we looked at it, the less we were concerned by it as a potential competitor; yet, the more we saw in it an attractive company to take over'. Indeed, even when there is no conscious effort to seek out new opportunities, the analysis which a subsidiary inevitably makes of the local environment often results in new opportunities being identified. This, in turn, is frequently conducive to the elaboration of more systematic approaches to opportunity identification. As this company's executive concluded: 'We ended up not buying that company because the price wasn't right; but the exercise certainly got us into looking carefully at others; indeed, we ended up with the habit of periodically looking at such local opportunities in a rather systematic fashion'.

Second, sensors developed at headquarters. As experience is accumulated and as the head office elaborates procedures to monitor MN operations, sensors are developed to detect MN opportunities. The management of the international division at headquarters has a number of sensors to appraise new prospects abroad. And in those companies with the most extensive MN experience, central management itself typically is involved in the appraisal of foreign environments. The corporate planning staff is then actively involved in the definition of opportunities. And so is top management: 'These companies try to devise more sophisticated procedures to cope with problems of foreign operations, and top management takes a much more active part and devotes a larger portion of its time and attention to these operations'.[5]

Forces are instrumental in detecting opportunities which normal sensors miss. These include new industries or new markets. Thus, one company reported that it had long been active in LDCs but that 'it took our international VP's initiative to prompt us to consider investing in the U.S.'. These also include opportunities for parts of a GCE not yet MN; even if certain activities of a company are international in scope, a unit with a sizeable degree of autonomy and no MN operations of its own may well have no procedures to scan the international environment. For it to look abroad a force is necessary.

The triggers causing a force to develop in a GCE with MN experience exhibit three main particularities. First, a GCE with MN activities is more likely to be exposed to outside sources which may trigger the development of a force. In particular, an international division is often a very effective catalyst of outside proposals for new MN activities: 'An international division receives a large number of inquiries and suggestions from abroad: this may be due to the fact that these divisions exist mainly in large, universally known corporations, or because word about the activities and successes of the company in other countries has spread'.[6]

Second, there can be cross-fertilization: a force may be triggered by exposure to the international activities of one division and cause a purely domestic division in turn to go MN. For example, one company reported that one of its divisions had invested in a country as a result of an executive actively promoting the idea: 'The man had come to the idea by being in contact with another one of our divisions which was already active in that country'. It may also happen that the origin of a new foreign investment proposal by a given unit be outside the unit. For example, in a company which domestically is vertically integrated, a division active in a given country solicited the involvement in that country by another division in view of integrating its foreign operations with those of this other division. And the executive of a state holding company said:

> Some years ago [an operating company] invested in [a South American country] in manufacturing facilities. Given the relatively backward stage the country was in in terms of industrialization, the company found that there was a lack of related industries such as component manufacturers. Since we in our group have such a manufacturer, it went to it and suggested it consider investing in [the country]. And for this enterprise this was an opportunity: while it couldn't think of investing there before because of the thinness of the local demand for its products, now it saw there was a captive market for it.

Third, an executive of a GCE with MN experience tends to be knowledgeable in the international field: 'He follows world trends, reads specialized literature, goes to conventions, and learns from the experience of others. All these make him more aware of world problems and give him possession of more information'.[7] This makes him a more likely candidate to become a force for new kinds of investments. As one interviewee put it: 'Our executives' familiarity with the international environment leads them to constantly think of new markets we might enter or new sectors we might become involved in abroad'.

In sum, the processes of GCEs with MN experience are much more likely to detect MN opportunities than in GCEs with no such experience. Further, sensors play a more important role. Because sensors scan the environment in a more global and less subjective fashion, specialization tends to be less acute. In addition, because potential forces are more numerous and exposed to a greater range of possible triggers, they tend to be broader in the kinds of opportunities they can identify. This, coupled with the sheer experience MN GCEs have accumulated, results in the foreign investment decision process tending to be less partial and less frequently tied to one particular project.

(b) Within government organizations, processes are similar to those discussed in Chapter VI. Still, we should note that government organizations which are oriented towards international questions tend to be closer to GCEs which themselves have MN activities: government units whose aims lead them to focus on international issues are naturally closer to GCEs which themselves are active abroad and are thus prone to engage in actions which satisfy the expectations of such units. Thus, an agency responsible for monitoring industrial undertakings in a country's ex-colonies will naturally seek ties with GCEs which are most likely to be involved in such nations. One interviewee said: 'Such an agency instinctively tries to develop good relations with those government enterprises which can help it fulfil its aims; and these are first of all GCEs which have already operated abroad'.

This means that government organizations which mostly have sensors geared to MN problems are close to MN GCEs which, as we saw, themselves have sensors focused on foreign problems.

The same is true for forces. When a new type of prospect arises in government raising the possibility for a GCE to engage in a project abroad, it is MN GCEs which are typically contacted. An interviewee said: 'A few years ago, the government wanted to promote more investments by GCEs in Eastern countries. This was a new concept in the framework of a new foreign policy. And while no GCE had much direct experience in such countries, those with the greatest MN experience in general were referred to in priority'.

In sum, GCEs with existing MN operations are far more sensitive to MN opportunities than GCEs with no such experience. Company procedures and forces are clearly geared to looking for new prospects abroad. And government units which are most likely to identify opportunities abroad are closest to such GCEs.

B. Search

Again, three phases can be identified.

1. *Search for solution to performance failure (or threat thereof)*

(a) In the context of a problem in domestic operations, how and when can an MN solution be developed? When the solution comes from the firm there is a major difference with GCEs with no MN experience: the normal decision process may come up with an MN solution – normal in the sense that no force is necessary for such a solution to be considered. As a chief executive said: 'Our first foreign investment required a lot of personal fighting to get the idea accepted. Now investing abroad is normal. We think of this alternative just as easily as we think of domestic alternatives'.

As far as forces are concerned, they are comparable to those in a GCE with no MN experience. Still, we should note that here too, potential forces are often exposed to more numerous and stronger factors which might cause their development than in purely domestic enterprises. Solicitation by an outside force, the example of competitors, the personal experience of executives . . . are all likely to be more tinted with internationalism. Besides, cross-fertilization is also often conducive to the development of a force; executives of the international side of the organization not infrequently take the starting point of a problem in domestic operations to introduce a proposal for an international project as a solution.

A solution can also come from a government organization, either via standard procedures or via a force. Particularly as far as the former is concerned, we must be reminded that a unit is concerned by those issues which have a bearing on its own aims. This means that a government organization is most likely to come up with an MN solution when its own aims are MN in scope. Such organizations are closest to the GCEs which have existing MN operations. Indeed, those government units which are most likely to develop MN solutions tend to be close to GCEs which are already involved in the international field.

(b) When a problem arises in current MN operations, the question is whether the solution will be MN or domestic. For it is conceivable that an MN problem receive a domestic solution.

Within GCEs, standard search procedures usually develop an MN solution: when a problem arises solutions are searched in the neighbourhood of analogous problem symptoms; and generally, past MN problems will have resulted in MN actions. This is particularly so in companies that have had extensive MN operations for a long period of time, which have a standardized set of MN courses of action from which they can draw.

A domestic solution is somewhat more likely to be considered when a force is involved. When a problem arises with foreign operations, a force may take the initiative within a company to propose that it be solved by a domestic alternative. This in fact may be the beginning of a contraction strategy of MN activities. Thus one interviewee reported: 'A few years ago a new management team took over. It was clearly committed to push domestic expansion to the detriment of MN operations. To get the point across, top management itself got involved in the closure of several foreign plants which were experiencing problems'. Such cases, however, are relatively exceptional.

It is in fact within government that a domestic solution is most likely to be elaborated. While a GCE having gone MN has different processes which do scan the international environment, the processes of the government units are essentially the same and are not particularly geared to international courses of action. True, government organizations which have international kinds of aims are generally close to MN GCEs. Yet, even MN GCEs are in contact with organizations which have a domestic scope. Such organizations are often directly involved in search; and these are likely to come up with domestic solutions. Thus a GCE reported that for a few years it was under pressure by the government to increase its domestic investment rate in view of creating employment at home: 'Each time we have a problem abroad they [the government] step in to pressure us to close down and transfer production home'.

A government force can cause an MN GCE to look at a domestic solution. For instance, a new minister for economic affairs wanting to use a GCE for regional development purposes may take as a starting point the deterioration in international operations to foster domestic investments to the detriment of international ones. If the standard decision procedures of the ministry are not normally such that the ministry would get involved in the search for a solution to a foreign problem, then the minister will have to step in and actively promote attention to a domestic solution himself.

The main conclusion is that in an MN GCE search for a solution to a problem in existing activities is clearly more likely to result in an MN course of action than in a purely domestic GCE. The chances that a problem in domestic operations find an MN solution are relatively good. And for problems in MN operations, the normal in-company processes call for MN solutions, particularly where the GCE involved has extensive MN experience. It is really only in government that search may result in a domestic solution.

2. *Search for a specific MN project*

Given that the solution to be pursued is to be MN, how is a particular project selected – a particular opportunity in a particular country?

GCEs with MN activities have organizational processes to consider MN solutions to problems in current activities and to identify MN opportunities. They therefore do not need to rely on a force to look abroad. As a result, this phase of search is more meaningful: as we saw, when a force is involved, it tends to intervene in terms of a specific project; therefore, this phase of search *per se* – looking for a specific project – is often omitted; but when no force is involved, it is indeed necessary to identify a particular prospect to pursue; here then, when no given project is introduced *a priori* in earlier phases of the decision process, search for an MN solution in precise terms is an essential activity in its own right.

Multinational GCEs have developed procedures which are tailored to this phase of search in an MN context. Thus, the variables discussed in Chapter VI relevant to international kinds of investigations are more appropriately taken into account. And there is less of an overemphasis on certain variables which are of lesser importance in a foreign context, while other critical issues are not omitted from the analysis. Yet, it is noteworthy that GCEs with relatively limited MN experience do at times still misjudge certain variables. In particular, we found that a number of GCEs continued to focus on certain issues which, while important at home, appeared relatively trivial abroad. For instance, one company which had gone MN four years ago, still appeared quite sensitive to local socioeconomic ends, even though the government appeared to have no such aims to speak of. The new international vice-president said: 'Our foreign subsidiaries are often still abiding by local macroeconomic policies which are more imaginary than real'.

There can also be the transfer of domestic concerns to MN operations. Thus one company reported that, given current recessionary times, top management had requested that every new capital outlay at home be evaluated in light of its contribution to new jobs creation. The interviewee said:

> Obviously, this was relevant for domestic projects. But top management put the message across so forcefully that everybody in the organization felt concerned. In addition, a few months after the policy was issued, the international division received a new planning head coming right out of the staff reporting to top management. The man was so influenced by the policy that he couldn't think of questioning it. Thus, for a long while, our foreign investment projects were developed taking into account employment considerations even where, objectively, we had no reason to worry about this type of problem.

But obviously, this is a rather extreme case. In the majority of cases, the greater a GCE's MN experience, the more procedures tend to be well suited to foreign projects and the more they are routinized. Then 'an investigation is carried out in successive phases with built-in check-points . . . A very distinct pattern exists in the way information is collected, scrutinized, communicated and evaluated'.[8] The first phase is carried out at the company's office; then the investigation goes into the field for an on-the-spot investigation; various organizational units get involved in the investigation and evaluation; with standardization, the results of an investigation are presented increasingly in written form.[9]

The emphasis in this phase is first on narrowing down alternatives, eliminating opportunities which are clearly unacceptable, then singling out one particular project which will further be searched in terms of the development of a precise strategy.

> In the first phase of the investigation, several generally available crude indicators are consulted to form some opinion of the feasibility of the opportunity considered . . . The specific crude indicators to be used depend on the nature of the project. They are designed to check three major crucial areas: first, an opinion is formed on the risk and uncertainties involved; second, the market size is gauged; and third, possible conflicts of the suggested project with existing company policies and resources are checked.[10]

As far as risk is concerned, political and economic stability are critical. Common areas of worry include risk of war, expropriation, inconvertibility of currency, exchange controls . . . The size of the market is important because of the fixed investment in time required in any project: given that a certain amount of management time has to be devoted to the investigation (and later to the approval and implementation) of a project regardless of its size, a project has to be large enough to justify such a fixed investment. The conflicts refer to the congruence of an opportunity with the overall company's strategy and its compatibility in terms of financial, human and technical capabilities.

Search may also occur in government. Government units with MN experience of their own have a standardized search process tailored to MN projects. The only real difference with GCEs with no MN experience is again that such organizations tend to be closer to MN GCEs.

Search can also be influenced by a force. A force can modify the course standard procedures would otherwise give to search. It can be instrumental in forcing attention of search on new types of variables or issues. Thus, if a company never invested in a particular country, chances are that a force will be required for investment possibilities to be considered there.

Here too a force rarely intervenes in this phase of the decision process alone: given the existence of set procedures for search, there is less of a need for a force to intervene; thus, if it does intervene it is usually to get a specific project through. In such cases, it will not wait for this phase of the decision process to step in; it will do so earlier. Yet, some cases do exist when a force intervenes at this stage only.

As far as an in-company force is concerned, an executive may step in in this phase once he has become aware of the existence of a foreign investment possibility in general: while he did not think of the possibility *a priori*, he may step in once he realizes there is such an option, and thus try and give the venture a particular twist. Further, the intervention of a top management member is often more likely than in GCEs with no MN experience. Once MN operations reach a certain importance, they often are grouped in a division by themselves. This division is responsible for the company's activities abroad and decisions about MN projects are primarily made here. Yet, top management can intervene and modify the division's decisions. Thus, one interviewee reported that

> the international division had come to the decision that it needed to expand the scope of the business in a given product line abroad. This

would have entailed greater foreign investments – in particular, greater assembly operations in South America and a greater direct sales organization, including the servicing of products once sold. The division was going to invest in Argentina. At that point, the President himself stepped in and caused the company to increase its industrial and financial involvement in Brazil instead.

A force can also stem from government. Here too, a force intervenes at this stage mostly when it is to correct a decision of either a GCE or of another government organization. For example, in one case the sponsoring ministry had decided that a GCE would make an investment in a particular country. At that point the ministry for foreign affairs stepped in and exerted pressure via the prime minister himself for the investment to be made in another country 'in view of the nation's foreign policy interests'.

3. *Search for a specific strategy to exploit an MN opportunity*

In Chapter VI we saw that this phase of search is often left to standard procedures with no intervention of a force. This is all the more so in GCEs with MN experience.

Procedures here yield smoother and more effective results than in purely domestic GCEs. They are adapted to MN issues. Over time, the company has developed special routines to formulate an MN plan as such. It benefits from its experience in previous investigations abroad and has standardized mechanisms specifically tailored to search in foreign environments.

The investigation focuses more on the key issues. The relevant aspects pertinent to MN situations are more appropriately taken into account and there is less of a chance that certain typically domestic variables be over-emphasized.

> Information is gathered on those product characteristics that are deemed most important according to the way the problem was initially defined or those regarded as most crucial for success or failure. For instance, economic data are collected in order to esti-mate the size of the market; and inquiries are made into the charac-ter and financial standing of proposed partners. If raw materials are to be imported, a check is made into the problem of imports, regulations governing them, and transportation facilities. If crucial materials or components are to be acquired locally, an inquiry is made into the likelihood of securing them. Where water is a crucial factor for production, its availability and costs are thoroughly checked.[11]

Some companies have developed elaborate checklists for investigators.

> For example, one questionnaire includes nearly 300 questions, some further broken down into subquestions, on governmental

policies and regulations, marketing, competition, production, financial conditions, engineering, affiliations, and 'general data, condition of an establishment of an enterprise, etc., in a foreign country'. Additional questionnaires have been prepared by this company for participation projects and for licensing agreements.[12]

Other companies equally experienced in the MN field, do not have explicit guidelines. Yet, 'the presentation as well as the investigation does not differ significantly between companies with and without written guidelines to investigators. It seems that although written guidelines do not always exist, the investigators learn from experience what information should be included in their presentation'.[13]

While investigation is more effective, its costs tend to be lower.

The cost of investigation in an international division is generally lower the larger and more diversified the foreign activities are. Knowledge has been accumulated from previous investigations; executives travel a great deal and can make preliminary investigation 'on their way'; and, mainly, the people in the field can carry out a large part of the investigation.[14]

This means that the problems encountered in the first foreign investment are for the most part avoided. As a French interviewee said:

In our early days of international operations, we were making our decisions under the influence of our national operations. Now that we have built up extensive and long experience in the international field, foreign decisions are made with a rationale specifically adapted to them. For example, while at home we could hardly buy out a healthy company simply because it fitted our own economic interests, abroad we feel quite free to do so.

Having said this, a force can at times intervene to modify the standard organizational processes – particularly in terms of new issues or new kinds of plans. For example, when a GCE is considering investing in a new country, a force may be instrumental in adapting search to the new types of variables which might be confronted. Thus, a major German company reported that a few years ago, while it had considerable foreign activities, it was in the process of making its first investment in a communist country:

We were confronted with a whole set of new problems we knew little about. We thought we knew everything in international business and here we were confronted with a new universe we actually were quite ignorant about. Fortunately, we hired a man who had worked with the USSR for several years with another company. He was extremely helpful and saved us many mistakes by pointing out what we were going to do wrong by following our habits, by doing what we were used to doing elsewhere.

The role of the government is generally limited in this phase of search. As we saw with GCEs with no MN experience, government organizations usually have neither the expertise nor the motivation to get involved in the specifics of a plan. The role of the government tends to be limited to that of a *point de chute* – the company in its own search referring to a government unit for assistance on certain issues. Or it can occasionally happen that somebody in government steps in as a force to modify a company's decision on some particular aspect of special concern to him. But on the whole, this is exceptional for GCEs with extensive MN experience.

C. Approval

1. *Commitments*

Four points should be noted about the distinctiveness of MN GCEs' prior commitments.

(a) The results of prior MN operations have a major bearing on new foreign investment decisions. If a company has a history of successful foreign operations, there will be a positive disposition towards such activities, and proposals for incremental MN projects will be looked at in a favourable light. This translates itself in commitments to hold on to and/or improve foreign positions – both in micro and macro terms. Thus, a financially successful set of foreign investments will engender commitments to defend foreign markets and attempt to capture new ones. If a GCE has been successful in achieving macro aims abroad, there will be a commitment to repeat endeavours geared to macro ends. On the other hand, if a company has failed in its MN ventures, there will be commitments opposing new similar ventures. Thus, an Italian executive said:

> A few years ago we made an important co-operative agreement with a large British firm. This agreement was to be followed by others of a comparable nature, the various agreements being intended to be part of an overall plan which was to link the two companies together. Yet, after the first arrangement had been signed, our Italian operations entered into a deep crisis due to dramatically deteriorating national conditions. The English company's results being affected by our misfortunes, the result was that they became very wary about such arrangements.

In fact, these set-backs for a long time appeared to have jeopardized the whole idea of a link-up between the two companies.

(b) Given the frequent establishment of an international division, MN activities are often decentralized: given there is a general management responsible for them, they can be kept somewhat separate from the rest of the company's activities. In consequence, MN decisions tend to be under less influence of macro domestic commitments than in GCEs with no MN experience. One interviewee reported: 'A few years ago we set up our international division grouping our activities abroad. Rather quickly we could notice a change in attitude regarding new foreign investments. It was as if the idiosyncrasies of the organization *vis-à-vis* national macroeconomic and social types of problems were if not vanishing, at least shrinking'. This is not to say there are no longer pressures for a GCE to pursue domestic macro endeavours but that management's own commitments to such ends are distinctly reduced.

(c) Commitments of government organizations relating to MN GCEs tend to be more international in scope; a GCE having international interests of its own is naturally closer to MN GCEs. Consequently, such companies bear the commitments of organizations *vis-à-vis* foreign countries, which not infrequently result in their being stimulated towards a further intensification of their foreign activities.

The above three factors further add to the tendency of MN GCEs to do more of what they are doing already: it is those GCEs which have existing MN operations which are most likely to engage in new foreign ventures.

(d) As a company acquires MN experience, it increasingly develops commitments about the way foreign projects are undertaken – commitments pertaining to the formulation of a specific MN strategy. A company develops commitments to norms and guidelines specifying what characteristics its MN projects are to have. For example, an interviewee said: 'Our first international investments were all on a joint-venture basis with local partners. Now it seems that we systematically seek this type of agreement in all our MN operations'.

Two points should also be made about the particularities of commitments built up in the course of the decision process.

(a) Given that MN projects are more routine, they require fewer investments to be approved. The monetary cost of the investigation tends to be lower. And the time required to obtain approval is lesser for the investigation and especially for in-company negotiations. Since a foreign investment is not a departure from the usual kinds of activities the company pursues, no radical change of processes is involved. Particularly when an investment is one which is of a familiar type for the company (that is, it is comparable in its broad lines to other previous investments – say, in terms of the country, of its location or the type of sector involved), there are set procedures to investigate and appraise it. As a French executive put it: 'There is no philosophical battle to be fought to get approval for looking abroad'. This is especially true when there is an international division with sizeable independence of its own. Here – as a German executive put it – 'decisions are made in a context where everything is made for them and little consultation needs to take place with headquarters'. The same may be said about government: GCEs with MN activities tend to have less of a need to secure government permission to consider foreign ventures. And approval is usually obtained relatively rapidly.

Lower investments imply lower commitments. More precisely, since in GCEs with no MN experience many of the commitments related to an MN project are really made in connection with the question of whether to consider the possibility of foreign investment in general, we should talk of lower *a priori* commitments: in a purely domestic GCE the greatest commitments are not made *vis-à-vis* a well-documented proposal for a specific foreign investment but *vis-à-vis*, so-to-speak, the general principle of MN expansion. As a result, when the principle is adopted, so many commitments have already been made that one MN project or another *has* to be made. It is this kind of commitment which there is less of in MN GCEs. Therefore, an international proposal is easier to reject: given lesser *a priori* commitments, a specific project is evaluated more objectively. This, together with the lesser biases affecting appraisal criteria, makes the foreign investment decision process distinctly more effective than in GCEs with no MN experience.

(b) MN GCEs are more likely to be involved in the fulfilment of commitments created by the government in terms of foreign investments. As mentioned in Chapter VI, the government itself not infrequently engages in discussions with foreign countries about investments by national enterprises; and thereby it builds up commitments for such investments. What exact investments actually take place and by whom is often of secondary importance. What is important is that investments *take* place – one way or another. In such instances, it is GCEs with existing MN activities which most frequently get involved – as noted by a government official: 'Where government engagements abroad can be met by GCEs, it is those GCEs which have international experience that the state solicits'.

A French interviewee from a GCE with a history of extensive MN operations made revealing comments in this connection:

> Over the years, we have found ourselves more than once obliged, or at least on the verge of being obliged, to 'do something' (in terms of a direct involvement) in a particular country or another as a result of our government finding itself committed to make sure that some degree of investment be made by national companies in the country in question. The process is always relatively similar. In connection with a policy of re-establishment of good relations with a particular country, the government engages first in informal talks with local authorities about the possibility of certain investments. In this process, it tries to show the potential benefits for the prospective host country of such investments thereby hoping to foster its aims of establishing better relations. Gradually, talks become more focused, and the government's arguments to negotiate with local authorities more specific; until the point is reached where actual

226

commitments are made that certain investments be undertaken by national companies. At this stage, it may well be that several companies – private or public – will want to take advantage of the 'opportunity'. But it may also happen that nobody wants to do so. In that case, the government can refer to GCEs and ask them to invest in the country in question. Even if there is usually room for bargaining between the company and the government, the final argument is often of the kind, 'it is a question of national interest; somebody has to do it'. What can one do in these cases? One GCE or the other ends up doing some kind of investment in that country. And it is only natural that it is usually a GCE with existing international activities.

2. *Formal review procedures*

(a) As far as in-company procedures are concerned, the main distinctive feature of MN GCEs is that there are fewer problems in the approval process. As a company develops experience in the international field it adapts its formal procedures to such activities. This is most evident in the adoption of an organizational structure in which MN operations have a place of their own – as with an international division – and where international projects are evaluated by special routines. Besides, such a structure often entails that less organizational units get involved in the decision process that are unfit to take action on international proposals. Thus, given the decentralization of MN decisions which comes with the setting up of an international division, other reviewing bodies either do not get involved or get involved formally, but *de facto* leave the division free to act as it sees fit. For example, an international division more often than not cannot decide on a major capital expenditure without consulting other units of the company. Yet, the number of these units is generally lower. And those units which are consulted either have developed procedures of their own to appraise an MN proposal or limit their role in the decision process to a formal function: while they do need to give their official approval, in practice they do not form much of a judgement of their own on the proposal and rely on the division's recommendations. A case in point is top management. Over time, it usually has developed ideas about the company's MN strategy, which are usually formalized in certain procedures or guidelines. Confronted with the need to approve a major investment abroad, it will refer to these guidelines. Beyond these procedures (which are often rather broad), it really leaves the international division free to decide as it sees fit.

This entails three consequences. First, the analysis underlying foreign investment decisions is more reliable. Since the units involved have procedures specially tailored to MN projects, their appraisals are sounder. Yet, this in itself does not make a substantial difference. 'They write better reports', said a British executive. But the real impact on the actual decision process is not very great. To repeat, a decision is not truly made via formal processes and the quality of their output does not *per se* substantially affect approval.

Second, and far more importantly, the decision process is swifter and less cumbersome. There is less hesitation and less immobility on the part of those organizational units whose approval must be secured.

Third, there is less of a need for a strong force to push a proposal through: given procedures exist to appraise and secure approval of a foreign project, it is not necessary for somebody to fight for the attention and endorsement of key organizational units. This, together with the generally lesser role of forces in earlier phases of the decision process, results in lesser commitments being built up on an *a priori* basis. This too contributes to the objectivity of investment decisions.

(b) Things are also different for procedures in government. Given a GCE has existing MN activities, a new foreign investment project does not constitute an abnormal proposal – one requiring a redefinition of the company's scope. Thus, in most cases, a GCE is required to obtain less formal authorizations to proceed with a foreign investment. As one interviewee argued:

> The big difficulty for a GCE is always to depart from its existing line of business. Thus, the first foreign investment generally encounters resistance in government. But once you have been operating internationally for a while, foreign investments are normal business. It is therefore much easier to go ahead with them.

Furthermore, MN GCEs tend to suffer from less inertia on the part of government reviewing units. On the one hand, a government organization to which a GCE is answerable can itself be endowed with more effective procedures to appraise foreign investment proposals. This implies that the government organization has itself learned from experience with monitoring GCEs' foreign activities. On the other hand, a government organization may stay out of approval altogether. As one Italian executive said: 'Given a company is already MN and given it doesn't do anything outrageous in its MN operations, a government organization may choose to give up its right to review decisions because they fall outside of its own true concerns'.

Consequently, an MN GCE can more readily obtain approval from the government for other foreign investments. In particular, when a company presents sound projects which are similar in nature to existing foreign activities, they are often fairly straightforward to get through the government's reviewing units. Further, here too there is a lesser need for a force to secure formal approval. Since existing procedures are tailored to MN proposals or, at least 'neutral' (that is, not clearly forbidding), it is usually not necessary for an individual to actively fight for reviewing units' assent. Once more this results in lesser commitments on an *a priori* basis. And this in turn enhances the objectivity of the evaluation process.

Thus, we see that with MN experience, there are fewer bureaucratic encumbrances. The decision process is therefore swifter and more effective. A French interviewee said:

> The more international experience we build up the more our MN decisions are easy to take in an efficient way . . . Yet, of course, this is relative to the days in which we had no MN experience. The fact still remains that our decision-making processes are slower than for private MNCs. There always remains a bureaucratic atavism in GCEs. The need to respond at one point or another to the state inevitably threatens to reduce our flexibility.

Indeed, as this interviewee points out, this discussion is relative to GCEs with no MN experience. This should not allow us to forget that relative to private sector enterprises, GCEs in general still appear to have to go through more elaborate and therefore more cumbersome decision processes than private enterprises.

D. Action

Generally speaking, distortions between plan and action occur principally when new types of moves are pursued. In MN GCEs, foreign investment clearly involves fewer new kinds of moves than in a company with no MN experience. Thus, the company's units which are actually to implement a plan in the field learn how to act more effectively. They learn how to interpret a plan's directions and carry them out appropriately. In particular, they devise patterns of action better adapted to foreign undertakings. And they develop ways to better work with each other.

Having said this, one qualification must be added: learning occurs more quickly for planning than for implementation. Both those units which are responsible for the formulation of a plan and those responsible for implementation have to learn to adapt to the particular conditions represented by foreign investment. Yet, the former tend to acquire an experience in the first foreign projects, which is relatively transferable to other foreign projects; this is often not the case for the latter. Formulation focuses on relatively broad kinds of issues. Within limits, issues are often found again from one investment to another. In particular, within the same broad category of investments, the problems encountered have a clear element of repetitiveness attached to them: within a group of countries with common characteristics, within the same sector, activity (for example, assembly operations) and format (for example, kind of entry strategy) . . . the issues confronting planners are frequently relatively common from one project to another. Therefore, deciders can learn relatively quickly to function effectively in the context of MN activities. Implementation, on the other hand, often raises new problems. Each new project tends to confront the organization with new kinds of issues. A German executive said, 'In the field, the problems are more specific. Each new country tends to raise new types of problems. The variables you have to worry about are unexpected and particular to each situation'. Thus, the experience of the organizational units which are responsible for the accomplishment of a plan in the field is not as readily transferable. Given a certain MN experience, a particular foreign project may be regarded as a familiar project in the context of planning, but one containing a sizeable degree of novelty in terms of action.

The same German executive concluded:

> To perform effectively at the implementation level takes often more experience than at the formulation level. It took us a long time to have the feeling that we knew what we doing in terms of concrete action. For a long time we had the impression that in the actual practice of carrying our foreign projects, past experience in other such investments didn't help much, so dissimilar were the difficulties we were confronted with each time around.

Thus, while it is true that in general the problems of implementation are distinctly less serious in GCEs with MN experience, it not infrequently happens that decision-making *per se* is ahead of action in terms of having become adapted to foreign projects.

II. POLICY DECISIONS

The MN policy decisions of GCEs are distinctive in three main areas: their behaviour in host countries, their attitude *vis-à-vis* norms and regulations governing international corporate behaviour in general, and their conduct in the area of finance. Our analysis of these areas will uncover and explain new facts about GCEs' behaviour as well as provide different explanations to facts dealt with in the traditional approach. While we are dealing with GCEs which have foreign activities, a useful distinction will be made between GCEs with extensive and long MN experience and GCEs whose MN experience is limited and recent.

A. GCEs' behaviour in host countries

1. *GCEs with limited NM experience*

In their early MN activities, GCEs' foreign operations exhibit striking similarities with their domestic operations; a foreign subsidiary tends to adopt policies borrowed from its national activities. Each case is rather *sui generis* since a lot of the operating policies depend on the special internal culture of an organization. Organizational biases in particular are determining here: '(1) Bias reflecting special training or experience of various parts of the organization, (2) bias reflecting the interaction of hopes and expectations, and (3) communication biases reflecting unresolved conflict within the organization'.[15] It should be clear that such factors have distinct configurations in each case and that generalizations are difficult to make. Still, we found three characteristic features which can be encountered in most GCEs.

(a) A foreign subsidiary of a GCE tends to be sensitive to issues the parent company is sensitive to at home. This is especially noticeable in the case of social policies. Three cases are most significant.

The first concerns GCEs' policy *vis-à-vis* ecology. A GCE with limited MN experience tends to use the same standards as at home, even where such standards are stricter than what is required locally. Thus, a German company reported that for several years one of its subsidiaries was imposing on itself strict antipollution controls which exceeded local demands, while competing firms were far more casual about the problem. The interviewee said: 'What happened was that when we started our local operation we instinctively applied the same standards as at home. And nobody thought of changing the policy for a long time. One factor was certainly the fact that in this organization we were conditioned to operate in a way to show the example to others'. Search for a *modus operandi* abroad had led the company to adopt a policy borrowed from domestic operations in the first place; and the internal culture contributed to perpetuate these standards longer than would otherwise have been the case.

The second concerns employment. Several GCEs reported that in their early foreign investments they had a tendency to overhire: given their policy of contributing to the solution of domestic employment problems, these companies frequently found themselves overly liberal in their hiring practices abroad. This, of course, was found mostly among companies from countries which had severe national unemployment, such as Italy. Beyond hiring policies, a similar phenomenon is found for firing; when a GCE at home is careful to minimize what the French call 'collective layoffs' (that is, bulk firing of employees as opposed to individual employees being fired), it behaves similarly abroad. As an Italian executive noted: 'After a while we found we had too many people. Yet, we were reluctant to get rid of them. Then, with time, as we got used to different norms from those back home, we did indeed proceed with lay-offs'. Firing is in fact often somewhat less of an issue since the problem arises some time after foreign operations have come into being – at that point a GCE generally has more MN experience.

The third concerns labour policies – the way workers are dealt with and treated. At home GCEs are often at the forefront of labour policies. Their foreign subsidiaries then, at least initially, show similar kinds of concerns. One company thus reported that its first foreign investment

> was in an advanced industrial country where there was no legislation or even expectations in terms of labor policies comparable to those we had at home. Yet, for a while, we gave our workers abroad the same social benefits as we did to our domestic workers and this in addition to the fact that we had to pay them local salaries which were distinctly higher than those at home.

We should point out that, contrary to what this discussion might imply, the transposition of policies from national to foreign operations does not always result in positive effects. Beyond the obvious financial costs for the company, such patterns of behaviour are not necessarily efficient from the point of view of the host country. By transferring policies from national to foreign operations with little adaptation to local conditions, the company may do less than it thinks in terms of contributing to the progress of the local society. For example, if a company imports worker-participation practices into a country where such practices are non-existent, the disruption may not be negligible. Thus, an Irish government official stated flatly that from a host country's point of view, 'beyond the normal rules of good corporate citizenship (for example, no shut-downs overnight), a foreign company should really worry about performing efficiently from an economic standpoint'. Indeed, a German interviewee commented: 'Not only do these policies cost the company money but also they can displease the host country. You even may generate some ill-will for the firm'.

(b) GCEs' attitude *vis-à-vis* local norms and regulations. Norms and regulations refer to the host country's laws and government policies as well as more tacit expectations as to what constitutes proper business behaviour (that is, implicit standards of good corporate citizenship). GCEs that are conditioned to be particularly responsive to norms and regulations at home tend to be similarly responsive to norms and regulations abroad.

This is clear in their attitude *vis-à-vis* local laws. Thus, in the area of taxation, they have a lesser propensity to try and circumvent the law, let alone cheat. This is even more noticeable in their responsiveness to government policies. Given at home they are frequently under pressure to operate as vehicles to implement government plans, abroad they tend to be equally responsive to government directives. And – in the words of a government official – 'They are less likely to do things like engaging in misleading advertising, unduly squeezing the margins of small subcontractors (perhaps with a view to buying them out when they are not profitable any more), or indulging in any sort of mistreatment of customers, employees, suppliers, etc.'.

Still, this requires a qualification. A foreign subsidiary of a GCE tends to be truly responsive to local norms and regulations if they are similar to the norms and regulations of the home country. A GCE which at home is geared to be responsive to norms and regulations is often really responsive to concrete issues: the commitment which originally is to norms and regulations *per se*, *de facto* becomes a commitment to tangible issues. A GCE's processes may be focused at the outset on abiding by government directives, whatever they might be. But then in practice the company ends up focusing on certain particular desiderata (for example, contribute to employment or the state's ecology policy). At that point, the company's processes really become focused on these specific desiderata and less on the principle of abiding by state directives as such. A subsidiary's processes tend to be influenced by such a development in the parent company's processes. Where the parent's commitment to abide by

232

norms and regulations as such is overshadowed by the commitment to concrete issues norms and regulations call for, a subsidiary will tend to be sensitive only to local norms and regulations which call for issues comparable to those called for at home. When local expectations differ from the home country's expectations, the subsidiary will show a limited propensity to be responsive to such local desiderata.

Thus, GCEs can end up exporting national values and priorities to countries with different values and priorities. A case in point was reported by an Italian GCE *à propos* its first foreign investment:

> In Italy there is a historical deficiency in government policy in connection with issuing directives for industry. Yet, GCEs are expected to act in the national interest. Therefore, they are in a position at home of acting in the national interest without anybody in government telling them what specific behavior this implies. Many GCEs then act on their own initiative and decide for themselves what is good for the collectivity. This is possible at home because over time a company develops a pretty good feel for what the country and the government want. In our first foreign investment we found ourselves acting similarly abroad. This was in an LDC where the national interest badly needed responsible business undertakings and yet was not under any effective tutelage in terms of governmental industrial planning. Our subsidiary thus adopted certain policies which it felt were desirable from the macro viewpoint. We, in fact, found that it was not acting in accordance with local aspirations; the form of economic development it was fostering did not correspond to the expectations of the host country.

(c) The internal administrative policies of GCEs' subsidiaries bear the mark of the policies of the parent company. While here more than anywhere else each GCE has peculiarities of its own, the following two cases appear quite typical.

The first is in the area of control. As we saw earlier, GCEs' administrative processes are often influenced by a number of intervening factors which reduce their effectiveness. Such distortions tend to be transferred to foreign subsidiaries, and generate byproducts which can have a bearing on behaviour at the operating policy level. Thus, an Italian executive said: 'When [a particular GCE] first went abroad it brought with it all the biases it developed at home. As a result, its commitment to financial results was far from absolute. In particular, its internal accounting system was inefficient. It just didn't know how well or how poorly it was doing and as a consequence, people didn't really concentrate on performance'.

The second is in the area of purchasing policy. When a foreign subsidiary begins its operations it faces a number of problems which call into play outside companies – suppliers of raw materials or equipment as well as subcontractors. This also includes service industries – banking, for example – as well as companies providing things like transportation or sheer know-how (like engineering). In domestic operations, GCEs tend to refer to other GCEs in such instances (particularly in a country where the public sector is especially diversified). When this is the case, foreign subsidiaries tend to act likewise. As an IRI company executive said: 'Abroad we still tend to buy preferentially from the same suppliers we use at home. We do this not because anybody forces us to, but merely by habit. The government never told us to do so nor did our parent holding company; it is a perpetuation of a *de facto* osmosis developed in our domestic operations'.

There are several other cases where internal administrative policies are transferred from domestic to foreign operations. Many of these in fact tend to be common to GCEs and private companies. (For example, marketing or production policies of foreign subsidiaries are borrowed from domestic operations; given this is often done with little adaptation to foreign situations, such policies are often ill-suited to local conditions). An exception is finance. This is a special case which we will discuss below.

2. *GCEs with extensive MN experience*

Firms change adaptively as a result of experience. Over time, organizational learning produces changes in GCEs' processes. As a company builds up MN experience, its foreign subsidiaries develop policies of their own, more suited to local conditions.

Over time, a foreign subsidiary's processes gradually break away from domestic processes. Experience with working in a different environment shows that domestic processes are often ill-suited to local conditions. Gradually, operating policies evolve and acquire their own physiognomy. Given the greater autonomy of the subsidiary and the general lesser interest government organizations have for foreign subsidiaries' operating policies, processes tend to be relatively free to develop unencumbered from other preoccupations than those of the organization's own welfare.

Thus, a subsidiary of a GCE with high MN experience usually is less sensitive to the same issues to which its parent company is sensitive. Again, this is most notable in social policies. Thus, such companies have proceeded with massive layoffs. While our data does not enable us to test this, there appears to be a correlation between discrepancies between domestic and foreign operations and the degree of MN experience. For instance, we encountered several companies which reported they had proceeded with massive layoffs abroad and which responded negatively when asked whether they had done the same at home or whether they could conceive of doing the same; and these companies all acknowledged that they considered such practices to be feasible abroad only once they 'had been around for some time on the international scene and had watched the others doing it', as a British executive said. And an Italian executive said: 'Now we have learned the lesson; we try to be as hard-nosed as possible; we don't run around offering our prospective workers higher than normal benefits or trying to meet the host country's wants and needs more than what is generally considered normal decent corporate behavior'. And the same tends to be true for GCEs' attitude *vis-à-vis* local norms and regulations. As an official of a foreign affairs ministry said: 'The more a GCE lives and works abroad the more it loses some of its rigor in terms of sticking to the law and its spirit and government policies and their spirit'. Several companies reported they had had disputes with foreign countries' authorities. All such companies had sizeable experience in foreign operations for an extended period of time. Here, too, our data is not significant in a statistical sense, but it is symptomatic that no such event was found in the early MN expansion stages of any GCE.

B. GCEs' behaviour on the international scene

Here we turn to distinctive features of GCEs' attitude in the international environment in general, which may include countries in which they do not have direct investments (for example, their policies in terms of currency transactions regardless of whether they are involved in the country to which a particular currency belongs). Our focus is on GCEs' policies *vis-à-vis* norms and regulations which govern corporate behaviour. An important distinction is between norms and regulations which are permanent in character and those which are transient (in other words, which apply in a given situation at a particular point in time).

1. *GCEs' attitudes* vis-à-vis *permanent norms and regulations*

Two types of issues are critical.

(a) GCEs' attitude with regard to international taxation – for example, the use of tax havens or transfer price manipulation. This involves less outright violations of fiscal laws as breaches in the spirit of the legislation. A GCE with limited MN experience generally does not take liberties with norms and regulations: when a company goes abroad it tends to borrow heavily from domestic policies; given companies with purely domestic activities usually do not make much use of such techniques, a GCE will tend not to infringe norms and regulations in its early MN operations. As a British interviewee said: 'It takes time to pick up such practices'. Besides, organizational biases reinforce this; when a GCE first begins to operate on an MN scale, it will transpose its cultural patterns from its domestic to its MN activities. If domestically the company has traditionally operated rather strictly in respect to norms and regulations, the same will be true on an international scale.

On the other hand, a GCE with high MN experience tends to behave quite differently. Over time, its processes evolve and it learns to adapt to MN situations. Its policies are more tailored to the needs created by the MN environment as well as to the opportunities. Competition with privately owned MNCs exposes the company to such companies' practices; this further contributes to their policies' evolution. Also, foreign operations' lesser dependence from headquarters and their greater autonomy *vis-à-vis* domestic operations reduce organizational biases stemming from national activities. Gradually, organizational propensities develop in a way which is distinctive for MN operations. In this context, it is not infrequent that tax norms and regulations be treated with less rigour. As a private sector executive said: 'Look at the state-owned oil companies. The more time goes by the more they tend, at least abroad, to behave *vis-à-vis* taxes as private MNCs'.

(b) Currency questions – GCEs' policies *vis-à-vis* exchange controls, hedging against evaluations or revaluations, currency speculation, etc. Again, GCEs with limited MN experience usually stay away from violating the law and the spirit of the law concerning these issues. But they do so not because of an explicit choice, but because they do not know any better. In their early MN operations GCEs do not master the techniques required for the exploitation of the opportunities offered by currency transactions. Yet, with time, they both become sensitive to the potential advantages of such practices and develop the necessary know-how. Their processes gradually become adapted to a looser interpretation of norms and regulations.

A widely cited example is Renault's finance subsidiary in Geneva, which centralizes the company's international financial management.[16] As a banker said: 'We have worked with them and I can tell you they hedge and speculate like everybody else. Maybe they just are better than the others at it! Indeed, they are quite sophisticated at this point. And more and more they even act against the French franc'. The more experience Renault builds up the more independently its finance subsidiary grows and the more it loses – in another executive's words – 'any inferiority complex *vis-à-vis* the currency of its own country'.

Having said this, it happens that a force steps in and tries to correct the policies of a GCE in a given area. Thus we found instances in which an influential member of the government tried to modify the behaviour of a GCE with high MN experience either in the tax or currency area. Yet, his success reportedly was limited. As an Italian interviewee said:

When a minister steps in and tries to modify the *modus operandi* of GCEs, his impact is modest, especially over time. For instance, our former minister of the Treasury wanted to stop certain GCEs' practices in terms of speculation. He tried hard and the companies listened for a while; for a few months they behaved a bit better. Then there was a change of government and they soon reverted to their old practices. In fact, in such things the government's power can really be quite limited.

2. *GCEs' attitude* vis-à-vis *transient norms and regulations*

These are essentially government policies calling for short or medium-term patterns of behaviour. Facing certain particular conditions – economic as well as sociopolitical – the government may want companies to adopt certain behaviours as opposed to others. These wishes normally take the form of policy directives. They range from, say, a five-year plan to conjunctural measures extending, say, over a few months. In fact, the time can even be shorter: for instance, facing a crisis of the national currency, the government may want companies to adopt a certain attitude for a few weeks or even, in some cases, a few days. Specificially, these policies can be classified in two sets.

a. Vis-à-vis *international monetary questions* When a country's currency is under strain, the government may want companies to adopt certain patterns of action and not others (for example, accelerate dividend or royalty payments from abroad). Yet, in several instances we found that GCEs did not abide by such directives: GCEs have established routines by which they operate on an international scale; to modifty these routines is often an arduous task, therefore, a government policy calling for a change in a GCE's *modus operandi* encounters several difficulties.

These government policies tend to require quick implementation to be effective. For instance, in the case of a monetary crisis in which the national currency is under downward strain, the finance ministry may want companies to defer payments to foreign creditors and use their best efforts to try and obtain quick payments from their foreign debtors. To help the national currency situation, companies must act fast. The more a policy's success is dependent on fast change in corporate behaviour, the more uncertain this success is precisely because – in an Italian executive's words – 'you can't expect to change a large company's habits overnight'.

Further, these policies are most relevant in the context of large GCEs with extensive MN operations: the greater the scope of a company's international operations, the greater its potential contribution to the implementation of a policy. Yet, extensive MN operations mean that MN operating routines are all the more difficult to amend: the longer and the more widespread their MN experience, the more do GCEs have established and hard-to-change processes. This too hinders the effective implementation of governmental policies.

And government policies are all the harder to implement when they interfere with a company's vested interests. If a government's aim merely called for an addition to corporate behaviour without touching existing company processes, its adoption would be less arduous. But the kinds of policies with which we are dealing here necessarily call for a change in current processes generally entailing a cost for the company involved or for the suborganizations concerned. Therefore, these policies often encounter resistance on the part of those who are to put them into practice. Thus, when a government advocates that a GCE refrain from hedging against the loss of value of the national currency, the international division reacts adversely; because such behaviour is to the detriment of the division's performance, it tends to resist following it.

Also, given they generally involve several organizational units, these policies tend to be followed – if at all – in an imprecise way. Thus, an executive from one of the major Italian state holding companies reported:

> The government is trying to make companies' foreign subsidiaries repatriate their earnings more and faster than they really want to. On the whole, there is a lot of resistance to such measures. And where there is some positive reaction to government's directives, this happens in a disorderly fashion. Some divisions over-react while others blow their timing . . .

It is conceivable that such difficulties be overcome by a strong force; or, at least, they can be palliated and policies pursued with some degree of effectiveness. Thus, in one case, the finance minister stepped in and personally made sure that a GCE repatriated foreign earnings swiftly. However, we should note that there are limits to the things to which an individual force can attend. If a minister can indeed check on the behaviour of a GCE, he cannot do so for all. And since the success of these policies usually depends on the aggregate behaviour of all or several GCEs, the impact a force can have tends to be, on the whole, rather limited.

b. Vis-à-vis *circumstantial policies* A government's use of GCEs for certain particular purposes can have an impact on policy as well as on strategic decisions. For example, facing a domestic recession with rising unemployment at home, a government may advocate a transfer of production from abroad to national plants. GCEs respond to such policies much in the same way as they do with regard to the policies discussed above: in so far as such policies require a change in the established *modus operandi* of GCEs, they encounter defficulties in terms of implementation – much the same kinds of difficulties as above. Still, one major difference should be noted.

International monetary questions usually regard all MN companies of a country. Circumstantial policies very often concern only a few companies. Thus, they may concern certain types of companies (such as labour intensive industries) or certain sectors. Given that only a limited number of firms is concerned, it is more feasible for a force to monitor the implementation of a policy. For instance, during the 1973 oil crisis, several governments required particular patterns of behaviour from GCEs. Yet, those who were successful in actually bringing about a change in behaviour of GCEs were those where a force actively got involved in monitoring the change. As a government representative said:

> Our government of the time thought it was enough to make its wishes known for [the relevant GCE] to abide by it. Yet, little happened and the company went on with its usual way of doing

things. In France, things went quite differently: the government faced the same problems and had the same tools – GCEs. But there key individuals dug in and made sure the company complied with government decisions.

Thus, we see that transient norms and regulations tend to be adhered to when a force steps in to actively monitor their implementation. Otherwise, GCEs are most often insensitive to such government policies, or at least do not follow them faithfully.

C. Finance

Several of the issues discussed here are not operating policy issues *per se*. Rather, many are really GCEs' characteristics. Still, these do have a bearing on GCEs' MN behaviour. Five main areas are important.

1. *Financing from direct government sources*

This refers to funds provided by government-equity and endowments or loans by the state. When a GCE wishes to increase its equity base, it frequently encounters difficulties to cause the government to approve the increase and subscribe to the new shares. The reason lies in the difficulty to obtain action on the part of the state bureaucracy. To obtain the green light from the government requires the setting into motion of a number of routines: the sponsoring ministry has to take positive action on the proposal, other ministries have to examine it (for example, the finance ministry), specialized commissions (such as the Italian CIPE) have to be consulted, in certain cases the Parliament has to vote on the proposal etc. As an Italian executive said:

> This is generally a cumbersome process and takes a long time indeed. The bureaucracy is very slow and the frequent changes in government don't facilitate things. A government may begin to take action on a proposal and then a new government arrives and you have to start all over again, that is, the proposal has to go through all the steps another time.

The same can be said for endowment funds or loans from the state. As the same interviewee said: 'Obtaining a loan from the government is only marginally easier. Somewhat fewer steps have to be taken and fewer government organizations have to be consulted, but the basic nature of the problem is the same'.

To expedite the bureaucracy, a force is generally necessary. Since the bottlenecks are primarily in government, it is essentially an in-government force which can be most influential. True, a particularly self-assertive high-ranking executive can have a bearing on the workings of the processes. But, on the whole, 'it is people who are within the government that are most amenable to get things moving', as a British executive put it. This suggests that a proposal originating from within the state apparatus has greater chances of going through than if it originates from a GCE. Now, 'since [as a French executive said] a proposal for a major capital appropriation rarely comes alone and normally comes together with a specific plan of action, it follows that it is generally easier for a GCE to do things which originate in the government than things originating from its own management'. In other words, an equity increase or an endowment are often linked to a clear set of moves or undertakings for the company to accomplish; a proposal for such an equity increase or endowment has the greatest chances of going through when the moves to which it is tied have their origin in the government because then a force is most likely mobilized to defend the moves and therefore the financial proposal which comes with them. Thus one executive reported:

> Each time we go to the government for money it takes ages to get it. This year the government asked us to step in – a particular sector – and buy a number of companies out in view of restructuring it and modernizing it. It never was so easy to obtain financing. The Minister for Industry himself was committed to the idea and threw all his weight in to obtain approval for the necessary funds.

2. *Financing requiring governmental involvement*

GCEs use open market financing vehicles (such as capital markets or financial institutions). Some of this financing a GCE can secure on its own without any formal consultation with the government. But other such transactions do call for governmental sanction. In some cases this is but passive – an assent to go ahead with a particular transaction. For example, if a GCE wants to make a bond issue, it is often necessary for it to have the approval of the government. Similarly, in a mixed enterprise, to proceed with an equity increase, the government's assent is necessary even if the government itself has no intention to purchase any of the new shares. This assent generally takes the form of non-opposition, in other words, what is needed from the government is merely that it does not object to the transaction. In other cases, the involvement of the government has to be active – an explicit endorsement of the transaction. For example, if a GCE has to make a bond issue with a state guarantee on the securities, the government has to formally decide to give such a guarantee. Similarly, for the government to give its assistance to the financing of certain foreign investments requires a conscious choice on its part. For instance, for government guarantees for foreign credits or financing arrangements on a government-to-government basis (for example, in the case of investments in Eastern countries), the involvement of the state must clearly be active.[17]

In both these types of cases bureaucratic problems can arise. The fact that the government needs to give its consent means organizational processes have to be set in motion. Several bureaucratic bottlenecks slow this down. For example, a formal state guarantee on a GCE's loan calls for official approval by a number of state bodies: the finance ministry, the ministry of the state budget, relevant state agencies, in some cases Parliament itself. As with direct government financing, each of these bodies is frequently slow to give its endorsement to a proposal, especially when it falls outside of the routines of its normal ongoing activity. Considerable footdragging may occur, key units slowing approval down by just not taking any action on an issue. Further, other state organizations can also play a role: while they do not have a formal direct function in the approval process, they can create problems in an oblique fashion. Thus, certain governmental units can retard a transaction because it indirectly hinders the attainment of their own goals. Thus, in one case a GCE was trying to issue state-guaranteed bonds; a number of state organizations had to give their endorsement – in particular, the cabinet; within the cabinet, a ministry (not the sponsoring ministry) showed considerable reluctance to go along with the decision.

> The reason was [in the words of the government official who reported the case] that the ministry had other GCEs he was sponsoring and was responsible for; it became clear that it was not eager to facilitate this financial transaction because it perceived that this would give an edge to this GCE to the detriment of one of its own GCEs which more or less was in competition with this company. This was really not a conscious reasoning. Rather, it was obvious that this ministry was not motivated to facilitate the transaction's approval and thus slowed things down by letting the bureaucracy drag out.

GCEs therefore, have a harder time raising certain types of capital than one might otherwise expect. In particular, GCEs' real debt capacity is conditioned by organizational processes. Where raising debt does not require disruption of existing routines, their borrowing capacity can indeed be greater than that of a similar private company. But when raising debt involves new procedures or the upsetting of established procedures, this greater debt capacity is more apparent than real. A French executive said:

> This is primarily true for debt, but it is also relevant for other forms of financing calling for government approval. The bureaucratic difficulties which are then involved often reduce or annihilate the advantages GCEs might have thanks to governmental backup. Sometimes these difficulties are such that they end up in GCEs being worse off than they would be with no governmental backup at all.

Again, these bureaucratic problems can be alleviated by a strong force. Here too, such a force has greater impact if it stems from within the government. And usually, an effective force pushing for approval for a financial transaction does so in view of fostering the pursuit of a certain plan of action: the force really fights for certain moves by the GCE involved and it is in connection with this that it also fights for approval of the related financial transaction.

3. *Financing from government-controlled financial institutions*

These include state-owned banks and insurance companies as well as other credit institutions either general in character or special purpose organizations.

In many cases, preferential bonds have developed over time between GCEs and government-owned financial institutions. As an Italian executive said: 'We have grown into the habit of working together'. It is difficult to generalize about how exactly such habits developed. In general, there appears to be what a French executive termed 'an *a priori* common cultural ground', that is, essentially the fact that key individuals in GCEs and state-owned financial institutions often have a common background. The executive continued: 'Many of us share a common belief in civil service and a common experience at the service of the state. Many of us have been "parachuted" into GCEs after having worked for the government'. Indeed, in many cases it appears that a company started to develop close ties with, say, a government-controlled bank because of personal relations of key executives in the two organizations. Several interviewees reported that GCEs and state-owned financial institutions were led to first work together because of individual ties between top managers. Once these initial ties are made, the organizations continue to work together by virtue of organizational momentum – given that they have started co-operating they go on working together unless the co-operation encounters a major performance failure. Such momentum reinforces the habit of co-operation. As another French interviewee said:

> We started to work with [a given government-owned bank] because a key executive of ours and a top executive of the bank were good friends. They had gone to the same school and had both started their careers working for the state. So, they started some business between the two organizations. Now we go on by habit. You need a bank anyway, don't you? So, why not go on with this one since we know each other well after so many years?

Some of these sources of funds may indirectly influence the recipient GCEs. This is especially notable in the case of special purpose institutions. In the words of a French manager: 'Overdependence on a state-owned specialized credit institution results in the company acquiring some of the biases of these funds' source'. While the importance of this phenomenon should not be exaggerated, it is clear that in some cases GCEs' behaviour bears the mark of particular credit institutions. Given that the scope of such institutions tends to be national, the result is what one interviewee referred to as 'a certain transfer of provincialism'.

4. GCEs' first experience with international capital markets

Here we look at means of raising capital outside of the habitual procedures, that is, which call for new routines to come into play. In particular, the first steps a GCE makes in the area of raising capital on international markets. This is often a cumbersome process and GCEs therefore often delay such a decision.

In a way, the first decision to tap foreign sources of capital resembles the first foreign investment decision. First, difficulties arise at the problem-identification level. In particular, when the company has no other foreign operations of any importance, its existing procedures being geared to the domestic environment, the identification of foreign sources of capital is limited. Unless a force steps in and actively promotes consideration of foreign sources, such opportunities are not identified until existing sources clearly prove to be inadequate. Further, search is usually inadequate. Not only does the foreign financing alternative not receive appropriate attention, but the range of actual foreign financing opportunities is also not scrutinized effectively; only a very partial list of possible financing methods is taken into consideration and the first method which satisfies certain minimum standards is followed. Also, given the company's inexperience, the evaluation of a given alternative is frequently lacking.

Moreover, approval is often cumbersome. For their first financing abroad, GCEs not infrequently have to secure the government's agreement. The same sorts of problems arise then as when governmental endorsement is required. Besides, problems arise within the companies themselves: given that a new route is contemplated, existing procedures tend to be ill-fitted to take action on it. Thus, a proposal may be stranded in in-company procedures or, at least, be unduly delayed. Finally, action itself can run into difficulties. Given the lack of precedents, an international financing deal is accomplished primarily via routines developed in a domestic context. Therefore, the actual implementation of a proposed deal can bear the mark of inefficiency. (Still, we should note that at the level of the planning of the specifics and of the implementation of a financial operation, difficulties tend to be alleviated by the assistance of specialized financial institutions – such as, investment bankers).

Consequently, many of the advantages GCEs could otherwise have in terms of raising capital abroad – and particularly debt capital – are tempered or countermanded by problems stemming from organizational processes. Beyond the relative ineffectiveness with which opportunities are pursued, the timing is often suboptimal: given bureaucratic inefficiencies, opportunities for foreign financing tend to be recognized and exploited with undue delay.

5. *Internally generated funds*

GCEs have a greater capacity to retain earnings than private firms. Retained earnings are a relatively easy means of financing because they do not disrupt existing routines. Given the procedural difficulties encountered by most other methods of financing, the relative simplicity – from an organizational stand-point – of retaining earnings makes this form of financing particularly attractive.

Further, organizational processes in the government are such that the government-stockholder exerts little pressure on GCEs to pay dividends. In an Italian executive's words, this is so because 'the government has grown into the habit of not receiving many dividends. And nobody in government really feels concerned by this; so nobody worries about changing this state of affairs'. And another executive added: 'What the government can expect in terms of dividends is too small anyhow for it to worry. In addition, who has any vested interest in this? It is not the sponsoring ministry that is going to worry. It will not keep the money anyway. So, who else?'

The primary implication of this discussion is that the edge GCEs appear to have over private companies from the 'outside' is in fact lesser when the internal workings of these organizations are examined. It follows that GCEs have an even lower advantage in terms of MN activities than one might think.

III. CONCLUSION

In this chapter we focused on the workings of GCEs with MN experience. We analysed the organizational processes by which these companies take MN strategic decisions – primarily how they decide to make further foreign direct investments. And we analysed the processes which govern their *modus operandi* – how major operating policy decisions are made.

From a strategic point of view, foreign investment decisions are clearly made more easily in these companies: given the tendency of organizations towards doing more of what is done already and given that these companies have existing MN operations, there is an inherent disposition to develop and broaden such operations. In particular, MN activities sooner or later engender the birth of new organizational units especially geared to monitoring the firms' interests abroad (a case in point is the creation of an international division). Such units develop in quasi-independence from the rest of the organization. They tend to have a life and aims of their own; and they generate their own routines, tailored to their particular type of activity and relatively unbiased by the processes in force in the rest of the organization. They tend to be imperialistic – inclined to develop incrementally and broaden the scope of their activity. This naturally leads to a propensity for promoting further MN expansion.

Indeed, chances are greater that new opportunities be identified abroad and that a problem in current operations lead to an MN course of action. Also, the investigation of and planning for an MN prospect are more effective and adapted to an international environment. The approval procedures are more apt to take proper and timely decisions concerning MN projects, and the routines by which decisions are to be accomplished better suited to foreign undertakings.

From a policy point of view, GCEs with recent MN experience tend to transpose SOPs from domestic operations with little adaptation to international operations. Inefficiencies are inevitable. Thus, in its early MN activities a GCE's administrative processes will bear close resemblance to the equivalent domestic processes; they will reflect the same kinds of distortions and will not be adapted to the requirements of the foreign environment. And the firm will be responsive to the same types of issues and norms as at home. This may result in excessive attention to certain variables not truly relevant in a foreign context as well as neglect of other variables which are important abroad. As in the case of strategic decisions, a force is necessary to change the *modus operandi* in any dramatic way. Here too, however, a force's real influence is less than what might appear at first: a force can provide the overall direction for a change and a new pattern of behaviour, but this pattern will be pursued in fact via set processes over which the force can have but limited authority.

On the other hand, GCEs with extensive MN activities have developed procedures especially fit for international operations. Efficiency is therefore greater. Over time, units responsible for MN activities break away from biases exported from domestic operations. Unencumbered by other considerations, they tend to pursue their own performance alone. (A good illustration is the foreign-based finance subsidiary of an MN GCE which gradually acquires its own independence and strives for profits via means often prejudicial to the home government's interests.)

This analysis complements the conclusions of Chapter VI. It provides some further answers to the questions raised by the traditional view:

(1) Just as certain GCEs which have clear MN opportunities and seemingly no impediments to pursue them actually do not do so, others which have clear domestic imperatives, in fact, are aggressive in their foreign expansion. The traditional view was unable to account for such anomalies. Here one understands that once an organizational unit is set up for a particular type of activity, it tends to develop with a considerable degree of freedom of its own. Thus, when, say, an international division is created, MN expansion is pursued somewhat regardless of what happens in the domestic side of the enterprise: to a certain extent, foreign investment decisions are made independently from national investment decisions, the international division pursuing growth objectives of its own. Consequently, a GCE with long established MN operations can often pursue foreign projects even when it is under strong pressures to develop nationally. Indeed, the critical determinants of a GCE's aptitude to

expand abroad are less the demands for action at home than the firm's degree of MN experience and the extent to which international activities are embedded in an organizational setting of their own.

(2) The traditional view could not explain why certain GCEs clearly depart from government directives. There were at least two reasons which caused one to expect perfect observance of such directives. First, GCEs' objectives: assuming they behave in a way to maximize returns to their owners (including non-financial returns), going against government directives is irrational; if GCEs and government are seen as directed by one central mind, departure from a rule to enhance the company's own performance is a senseless endeavour. Second, the assumption of unity led one to expect a total ability by the government to oversee and control the doings of GCEs; therefore, it was inconceivable that a company could get away with any infringement of governmental will.

Our present approach suggests a very different perspective: on one hand, GCEs and government are not one organization and they therefore do not have the same aims; quite normally, GCEs pursue their own ends. On the other, the state's control mechanisms are partial and imperfect; a GCE has considerable latitude to conduct its affairs without much interference by the government.

In particular, the process approach enables us to understand why, while certain GCEs appear to stick closely to the letter and spirit of certain MN regulations, others seem to take considerable liberties with such regulations – for example, in terms of transfer pricing manipulation or currency transactions such as speculation – and to pursue their own self-interest as such and function pretty much like private MNCs: in the early days of its MN activities a GCE is unfamiliar with the administrative practices commonly followed by firms on an MN scale (for example, ways of reducing the fiscal burden or of exploiting currency fluctuations); and its internal norms, borrowed from domestic operations, do not permit the ready adoption of such practices. But with experience, a GCE learns and its operating procedures become adapted to the MN environment. As organizational units are set up for international activities *per se*, administrative practices tailored to MN operations are mastered and norms developed sufficiently independently from domestic operations for such practices to become acceptable (this is how it is possible for a GCE to have, say, an offshore company which regularly speculates on international currency markets).

(3) Similarly, this approach is able to account for the operating policies of foreign subsidiaries. The traditional approach argued that a GCE behaves in a way to maximize its own economic performance as soon as demands from the tool goal are relaxed. In particular, it suggested that abroad, where there are little or no such pressures, a GCE behaves as a profit maximizing undertaking and that its operating policies are tailored accordingly, therefore being comparable to those of private MNCs. Yet, we found that while certain GCEs in foreign countries indeed seem to behave like private companies, others exhibit a particular sensitivity to local social issues despite no particular pressure for

them to do so. The reasons are clear: in the beginning of their MN activities GCEs export their operating routines from their home country where they have been accustomed to be sensitive to a variety of macroeconomic and social issues; they therefore pay special attention to such issues in foreign countries as well. It is only over time that foreign subsidiaries develop routines and values of their own; they then realize there is a cost in more-than-necessary social concern and they increasingly learn to behave like private MNCs, showing no more consideration for such issues than is required by local norms and regulations.

(4) The traditional approach left us with certain doubts concerning the appropriateness of certain explanations. Thus, given the independence of GCEs and government units, one is puzzled by the argument that state organizations are prepared to provide preferential assistance to GCEs because of a 'commonality of goals'. And one is not clear as to why really the government is reluctant to subscribe to new equity issues while granting generous long-term loans which are often not paid back in due course, or while permitting GCEs to retain most of their earnings.

The process approach suggests a focus on organizational routines: the fewer new routines a particular action rests upon, the more readily will it be accomplished. Thus, GCEs are able to retain earnings because this generally does not require major decisions at the government level. As a French interviewee said: 'It merely means not paying a dividend; this is mostly an in-company decision'. At the other extreme, a new equity issue or a state endowment means that a host of routines must be set into motion at the government level. An Italian interviewee said: 'It requires the endorsement of a whole variety of government organizations – the relevant ministries, commissions, departments . . . The bureaucracy is infinite'. Indeed, it is the approval procedures involved which are the main culprits for the difficulties encountered by GCEs to actually obtain funds this way. (In fact, several interviewees argued that these bureaucratic difficulties virtually annihilate the advantage GCEs could have otherwise because of their access to special sources of finance such as state endowments.) And debt financing tends to be in between. While state-guaranteed loans do tend to involve serious bureaucratic problems, loans from government-owned financing institutions call for fewer procedures to be set into motion than new shares to be purchased by the state.

Moreover, the process view explains the willingness of government organizations to assist GCEs by the ties which have developed between the organizations and the companies. Thus, one state-bank president said:

> Over the years, certain bonds have developed between the bank and several GCEs due to the habit of actually working together. These bear much more of the responsibility for our preparedness to lend these firms money somewhat more readily than to private firms than the fact that we think they pursue the same kinds of general ends as we do, in view of our common appertaining to the state.

Yet, here too certain questions remain open. They are similar to those discussed at the end of Chapter VI.

It is not clear when, how and why certain forces intervene. In several instances, even in GCEs with extensive MN experience, we found a sudden departure from the 'normal' way of doing things. For example, a company with a history of investments in advanced industrial nations which suddenly became involved in South America. Clearly, forces step in in such cases. But again, how can one predict when this will occur? What determines the point of entry of a force in the decision process and the point where a force's influence stops and standard routines take over? What happens when several conflicting forces intervene simultaneously in the context of an issue? And the same kinds of questions arise for policy decisions: in what circumstances and how do forces step in to modify a firm's *modus operandi* and how is their relative weight determined relative to existing routines and possibly relative to other intervening forces? For example, in one case we found a GCE which for years had been speculating on international currency markets and suddenly appeared to stop doing this; no one force could be held responsible for this; rather, many individuals had been involved in the shift in policy, but who actually had had the authority to cause the decision to be taken, how did the various individuals interact and how did their interplays yield the particular decision?

Further, here too, we found certain anomalies in GCEs' behaviour. Thus, in certain cases, GCEs with extensive MN activities, enjoying clear success in these operations and under no particular pressure (in particular from the government) to stop their international expansion, actually did do so. Existing processes would lead one to expect that such firms would in fact continue growing abroad; and no particular force could be identified which might have caused such retrenchment. In another type of instance, a decision was taken to pursue a new kind of path, apparently thanks to a force. Yet, close analysis of the force revealed that it was strongly inclined to cause a different kind of route to be taken. The fact of the matter is that while the force was indeed instrumental in causing departure from the existing way of doing things, the actual choice of what to do in fact escaped its control. But what happened then? And in still another case, a GCE put a new plant in a particular area where it never had been before; its existing processes and past behaviour should have led it to invest where it had other operations (especially since – as management itself pointed out – there were attractive opportunities in such areas); and neither was the new location chosen because of a particular man; there were indeed several influential persons involved in the decision but none really favoured that location at all (or had any reason to do so). The head planner commented: 'It was more a choice by default; everybody wanted to go different places; the choice of [that location] wasn't favoured at the outset by anybody; it really emerged as a rather neutral solution – an acceptable compromise between all those involved in the decision'. But what light does the process approach shed on the way decisions are taken in this kind of a circumstance?

248

NOTES

1. Yair Aharoni, *The Foreign Investment Decision Process*, Division of Research, Graduate School of Business Administration, Harvard University, Boston, 1966, pp. 174–175.
2. For details see: John Stopford and Louis Wells, *Managing the Multinational Enterprise*, Basic Books, New York, 1972.
3. Yair Aharoni, *The Foreign Investment Decision Process*, p. 184.
4. Yair Aharoni, *The Foreign Investment Decision Process*, pp. 180, 182, 183.
5. Yair Aharoni, *The Foreign Investment Decision Process*, p. 191.
6. Yair Aharoni, *The Foreign Investment Decision Process*, p. 184.
7. Yair Aharoni, *The Foreign Investment Decision Process*, p. 186.
8. Yair Aharoni, *The Foreign Investment Decision Process*, p. 79.
9. Yair Aharoni, *The Foreign Investment Decision Process*, pp. 79–81.
10. Yair Aharoni, *The Foreign Investment Decision Process*, p. 91.
11. Yair Aharoni, *The Foreign Investment Decision Process*, p. 110.
12. Yair Aharoni, *The Foreign Investment Decision Process*, pp. 110–111.
13. Yair Aharoni, *The Foreign Investment Decision Process*, p. 111.
14. Yair Aharoni, *The Foreign Investment Decision Process*, p. 184.
15. Richard Cyert and James March, *A Behavioural Theory of the Firm*, Prentice Hall, Englewood Cliffs, NJ, 1963, p. 122.
16. See: Pierre Dreyfus, *La Liberté de Réussir*, Simoën, Paris, 1977, pp. 200–201.
17. For details on this type of financial arrangement, see Chapter III.

CHAPTER VIII

An Organizational Politics Approach

The process approach makes a considerable contribution to the understanding of organizations' behaviour. Yet, it should not allow to blur a further level of analysis: the dynamics of leadership within the organizational process: 'The "leaders" who sit on top of organizations are not a monolithic group. Rather, each individual in this group is, in his own right, a player in a central, competitive game. The name of the game is politics: bargaining along regularized circuits among players positioned hierarchically within the organization'.[1] The process approach says nothing about this game.

As with most breakthroughs, the process school and Cyert and March in particular, have arisen considerable controversy and criticism. It is these criticisms which lay the grounds for the politics approach.

A first set of critiques note that Cyert and March are vague about the process by which a 'coalition' is formed: 'While pointing out the importance of coalition formation and the desire of any sub-group to generate support for its particular interests, the authors give scant attention to the process involved'.[2] Whereas they argue at a certain point that a coalition is formed around bargaining over side-payments and policy agreements,[3] they later leave the reader on a note of ambiguity when they write 'patently, therefore, the composition of the viable set of coalitions will depend on environmental conditions'.[4]

Another area of concern is that of power. Talking about March and Simon's *Organizations*, Rex notes that this variable is neglected: 'If there is a conflict of ends the behaviour of actors towards one another may not be determined by shared norms but by the success each has in compelling the other to act in accordance with his interests. Power then becomes a crucial variable in the study of social systems'.[5] Cyert and March indicate their awareness of the significance of power when they say that 'any alternative that satisfies the constraints and secures suitable powerful support within the organization is likely to be adoped'.[6] Yet, as noted by Pettigrew, 'critical questions related to the generation of support and how the structure of the organization might limit such a process are ignored. This makes it difficult to explain why a particular alternative is raised at a specific time, by whom, and with what consequences'.[7]

Soelberg criticizes Cyert and March's theory of organizational goals composed of suborganizations' aspiration levels 'which appear to exist entirely separate from the organization members' individual goals'.[8] He also finds that the description of the suborganizations' goal-formation process is left 'to the

249

reader's imagination'.[9] He himself argues that 'desire for power and concern for personal advancement represent goals which are of central concern to an organizational theory of decision-making'.[10]

For our purpose, the main criticism of the process approach can be summarized in the neglect of the role of the individual in decision-making. In this framework 'decisions are not made by individuals or by role occupants, but via processes which are affected by properties of the unit or units in which the decision is to be made'.[11] This emphasis on processes results in particular in a disregard for the key people in an organization; indeed, the process view pays little attention to the character leadership takes in an organization and its impact. Thus Aharoni notes that 'Cyert and March seem to imply that all active members of the coalition have similar power. By so doing, they implicitly deny the possibility of an innovation, leadership or coercive power and depict an organization as a coalition of mediocre people'.[12] In our own process framework we do of course provide for leadership as such. Yet, two problems remain.

First, leadership does not have a role of pre-eminence in the decision process – it is just another element in the process. In the framework, leaders do not really have the authority to *make* decisions. The closest one seems to get to an active role for leadership is in the search process where leaders have the opportunity to play an active part as initiating forces, particularly when they do not just raise a problem but also advocate a solution – when they suggest a new course of action. But here too they are seen as mere proposers of a given route; even if strong leaders can propel a solution they advocate a fairly long way down the road of investigation and thus commitment, the burden for an actual decision about action on the solution rests on the organization.

Now, it is clear that leaders can, through their style, influence the way an organization operates and pursues certain aims more actively than others; also certain moves are indisputably the product of top management acting by itself, that is, certain decisions are taken by leaders without much reliance on organizational procedures either for data generation or actual investigation about, and commitment to, the issue in question.[13] The process approach says little about this.

Second, nothing is said about the process of leadership formation itself. While the influence of leadership is provided for, little attention is paid to how this influence comes into being – why it develops in one form rather than another. Whatever role the process view attributes to leaders, it considers leaders as a black box, the internal dynamics of which it does not attempt to analyse; and whatever ascendancy it attributes to the top management of an organization, it takes it as given, without attempting to uncover the mechanism responsible for top management taking one particular position and not another. But in fact, top management is not a unified group. Instead, it appears that leadership derives from a group of individuals, in other words, a collection of separate people each with his own mind, behaviour and influence. These individuals have to compete with each other – to assert his power, each individual has to negotiate with others. The nature of leadership in an organization is therefore determined, at least in part, by the personality of certain key individuals and their interrelationships. To truly understand the behaviour of an organization, it is necessary to get a grasp on how leadership influences evolve and to understand the mechanisms of the competitive game played by people with leadership influence.

Taking these remarks as a base, one can formulate a third framework – one focusing on the individuals *per se* who have a part in the decision process. This organizational politics approach sees the behaviour of a firm as the result of bargaining games between the key persons or players in the organization. These players are not solely the leaders in a strict sense – that is, chief executives or government leaders – but also the other people who have a bearing on the decision. Players do not all act according to one set of objectives. Rather, each player has his own interpretation of the overall organizational objectives, the objectives of his own suborganization and his own objectives. Decisions are not made as rational choices in view of common aims but by the 'pulling and hauling that is politics'.[14]

Given the qualitative nature of strategy and policy problems and given the subjective and personal character of players' objectives, there is considerable room for disagreement. And given the importance of the issues usually under consideration, each player tends to fight hard to get his view accepted. Players can only resolve their conflicts by arguing and bargaining among themselves. Organizational decisions emerge out of this political process – the give and take among individuals. Players form coalitions which fight against each other to try and impose and defend their respective views.

> In this process, sometimes one group committed to a course of action triumphs over other groups fighting for other alternatives. Equally often, however, different groups pulling in different directions produce a result, or better a resultant – a mixture of conflicting preferences and unequal power of various individuals – distinct from what any person or group intended. In both cases, what moves the chess pieces is not simply the reasons that support a course of action, or the routines of organizations that enact an alternative, but the power and skill of proponents and opponents of the action in question.[15]

Further, organizational behaviour develops gradually over time. The conception that decisions are made by leaders once and for all and then handed over to the operating people for implementation is naive and just plainly wrong. A firm's strategic behaviour is not the product of a mere exercise in logic. In fact, what constitutes strategic behaviour is not decided upon at one point in time; rather, it is a series of actions decided upon and taken in successive steps at different points in time by leaders who, between one step and another, need to worry about other problems. This does not guarantee

252

continuity. Instead, decisions and actions take the form of collages – a composition of diverse elements pasted to a common canvas. Thus Allison notes that organizational behaviour relevant to an issue is constituted by choices by individual players, by resultants of central games (bargaining among central players), by resultants of minor games (decisions about suborganizations' actions by lower-level players) and 'foul-ups' (misunderstandings leading to unintentionally counterproductive decisions, or non-decisions): 'to explain why a particular formal [organizational] decision was made, or why one pattern of organizational behaviour emerged, it is necessary to identify the games and players, to display the coalitions, bargains and compromises and to convey some feel for the confusion'.[16]

In the rest of this chapter we will present a framework for the analysis of strategic and policy decisions based on such an organizational politics conception. We will first explain in what way organizational action is a political resultant. Second, we will discuss players – who they are, why and how they play. Third, we will focus in particular on some special aspects of strategic and policy behaviour viewed through this approach.

This framework has a number of antecedents – a body of literature on organizational politics surveyed in the Appendix to this chapter. Still, as we see in the Appendix, this literature, while providing a helpful base, does in no way offer an effective framework for corporate strategic and policy decisions: most of the work comes from political scientists and thus deals with different types of decisions (Allison in particular and his predecessors focus on crises decisions in a government context); while management students' contributions do not provide more than certain spot – though often quite perceptive – insights.[17]

I. ORGANIZATIONAL ACTION AS POLITICAL RESULTANT

Corporate actions are political resultants.

> *Resultants* in the sense that what happens is not chosen as a solution to a problem but rather results from compromise, conflict and confusion of officials with diverse interests and unequal influence; *political* in the sense that the activity from which decisions and actions emerge is best characterized as bargaining along regularized channels among individual members of the [organizations involved].[18]

The behaviour of GCEs' is the product of various games which take place among various individuals within the companies, government and often also in other outside positions of influence. Each game is played by different individuals and each individual plays one or more different games with different partners. Each player has power to move certain – but rarely all – elements or pieces of the game in which he is involved. Games are simultaneous and overlapping. But they are not played at random and take place along specific channels and rules. Actions within a game and their sequence should be understood as the result of bargaining among various players, each with different amounts of power over different pieces of the game.

To understand the strategy or policy behaviour of a firm it is necessary to analyse all its actions. This behaviour results from formal decisions by key individuals as well as *de facto* agglomerations of individual's actions – a variety of acts made more or less autonomously one from the other. For example, a GCE's strategy of direct investment in an OPEC country may emerge from certain clear decisions and an addition of individual moves: a minister – say the finance minister – may decide that it is desirable to counterbalance and pay for oil imports via a direct involvement by national firms in oil-exporting countries in order to pay for oil, at least partially, with industrial investments and technology. This may require an interministerial commission's approval and backing which calls for the involvement of several individuals who have to give a judgement on the proposal. The relevant firm will have to be consulted – normally at the top management level. Also, there will have to be discussions with the host country's government representatives. Once the strategy is decided upon in principle, a plan must be formulated in some detail. Again, a number of clear decisions have to be made. Top management, but also other key executives, have to dig in at this point; and in many instances, government officials have to be consulted for certain parts of the plan. Then the plan has to be accomplished in practice. This is done by individuals acting in quasi-independence from each other (for example, there is relatively little interface between, say, the finance people concerned with raising the necessary funds and, say, the technical people responsible for the engineering and construction of the facilities). Various persons take steps to perform their job on their own, with their own personality, perceptions, and objectives; yet, since many tasks overlap with each other, individuals' behaviour affects and is affected by other individual's actions. The accomplishment of the plan is therefore a reflection of this agglomeration of these semi-independent individualities.

In the analysis of GCEs' behaviour one can therefore distinguish three categories: (1) formal decisions and actions which result from a combination of inclinations and relative influence of central players in the game; (2) formal decisions and actions that result from a combination of the inclinations and relative influence of other players with a key role in particular subgames; (3) actions which are really aggregations of quasi-autonomous decisions and actions by individual players.

II. WHO ARE THE PLAYERS, WHY DO THEY PLAY, AND HOW?

A. Who are the players?

They are the individuals whose interests and actions have a bearing on the organization's behaviour.

1. *Within GCEs themselves*

There are 'leaders' (or top management), 'aides de camp' (or staff people attached to leaders), and 'lieutenants' (or executives in charge of executing the plans decided by leaders). In certain instances, lower level individuals – 'soldiers' – can have an important influence (for example, a foul-up by an employee jeopardizing the success of a plan).

2. *In government (including the public administration)*

Here there are 'curatory ministers', that is, ministers with a direct formal say over GCEs' behaviour (such as the prime minister or the minister of state holdings); 'government influentials', that is, other government members or elected representatives (such as members of parliament, hereafter MPs) with ascendancy over GCEs (for example, by being part of a committee for industrial planning whose authority extends to certain areas involving GCEs' actions); 'staffers' – the aides de camp of curatory ministers and government influentials; 'sponsoring administrators' – senior civil servants responsible for certain socioeconomic areas which condition GCEs' behaviour. In this list it is noteworthy that we find on the one hand elected politicians (and people whose fate is directly attached to them – staffers who come and go with particular political figures), and on the other, public administrators who are quasi-permanent elements of the state apparatus (that is, the sponsoring administrators and staffers attached not to an individual but to a post – such as higher employees of a ministry).

3. *Outside players*

These include union leaders (with or without formal means of exerting power over GCEs – via co-determination, for example); authoritative government people (such as major political figures) who are not in directly relevant positions (in the sense of not having responsibility of GCEs' actions or of areas involving GCEs' actions), but who nevertheless have an influence on GCEs' behaviour; members of the press, representatives of important interest groups (for example, industry confederations) and public opinion spokesmen.

As will become clear later, the behaviour of a player critically depends on two variables: his position and his personality. The position determines what a player can and must do; it defines what assets and liabilities each individual has to play and what games he can and cannot enter.[19] It also defines his obligations. A position usually calls for an individual to play in several different, though frequently overlapping, games simultaneously. Therefore, there tends to be competition among games and issues for players' attention. Each player is inevitably influenced in his behaviour in one game by the development of other games. A good illustration is the role of the finance minister who often has direct responsibility for GCEs. In looking at the opportunities or problems of

GCEs, the minister cannot avoid being influenced by other issues with which he has to deal and the options he will push will most often present – more or less consciously for him – positive features, also from the point of view of these other issues of concern to him.

But players are human beings with different personalities. Personal traits are the fundamental motors of individuals' behaviour; they constitute the essence of political motivation: 'Any attempt to isolate a decision by means of separating it from the personality of the decision-maker, his values and the environment in which he operates, is unrealistic'.[20] Each individual has his own aspirations, biases, intellectual abilities, and operating style which determine his attitude in a given instance and his influence in a particular situation. Further, each individual has commitments to particular endeavours and established relations with other individuals, which will influence his behaviour. Such relations exist not only with people within the organization but also with outsiders. For example, an executive can have kept close relationships with people in his alma mater and feel a moral obligation to it and be influenced – possibly subconsciously – to favour it over other not-for-profit organizations in his company's donations budget.

> Any organization is a system of individuals grouped in subsystems according to their role-definitions, mutually influencing each other through a continual process of interactions. However, every participant in the organization is not only an involved member of the organization. He is intimately connected with the wider variety of other systems of which he is part, and which he cannot ignore . . . All these influence the way problems are defined, alternatives are perceived and selected, and opinions are formulated.[21]

These two elements – position and personality – are constants in any organizational politics analysis. They colour individuals' perception of issues, the way players see goals, alternatives and solutions, and the relative weight various persons can have in various games.

B. What determines a player's stand?

By stand we mean the attitude or posture an individual takes *vis-a-vis* a particular issue—the opinion or course an individual has or takes regarding a given action or decision. This depends primarily on the issue and how he sees it; and on his stakes in the issue – what he has to gain or lose from it.

1. *Perception of the situation*

The way a player defines an issue and sees the options has a substantial bearing on the attitude he takes *vis-à-vis* the issue. Perception of a situation is critically determined by two elements.

First, the position an individual is in affects what he sees and how he sees it. The task or set of tasks for which each player is responsible encourages him to focus exclusively, or at least primarily, on certain types of problems. Thus, specialized attention on particular problems will cause him to be sensitive only to those issues involving such problems. This responsibility-influenced perception will be enhanced by factors such as selective information available to he who occupies a particular position, group pressures within the suborganization in which the individual occupying the position finds himself, or the organizational rewards and punishments attached to that position. Therefore, propensities are developed by individuals in particular positions which determine to what situations a player will be responsive (that is, in what cases he will see an issue or not), how he will define it (that is, what he will see as critical in the issue), and what options he will advocate (that is, what courses of action he will be inclined to support). Hammond provides an illustration of this when he describes the controversy about B-36 bombers in which Admiral Radford testified that 'the B-36, under any theory of war, is a bad gamble with national security', while Air Force Secretary Symington argued that 'a B-36 with an A-bomb can take off from this continent and destroy distant objectives which might require ground armies years to take and then only at the expense of heavy casualties'.[22]

Second, an individual's own traits – his intellectual abilities and his knowledge (for example, his professional training) will cause him to see problems in one way rather than another. Cultural or social factors are also important in affecting what and how individuals see. Moreover, their role in other games distorts players' perceptions. An individual is influenced not only by other organizational games he is involved in, but also by his role, or better, variety of roles, outside of the organization; the interrelationships an individual has with people outside of the organization invariably colour his perception of organizational issues.

2. Stakes involved

This refers to the potential benefits or losses an individual can expect from the outcome of a situation. Stakes can be classified in three categories. In each category there is a blend of motives determining the behaviour of players. Players can be driven by a 'cause'. 'The cause is an ideal or goal – or set of these – to which the person is dedicated. In public life a cause may be "better housing for blacks"; within a company a cause may be higher-rank jobs for women, increased use of computers, keeping production concentrated in the Toledo plant, or larger market share than the XYZ Company'.[23] Such causes can be organizational in that they are directly associated to an aspect of the life of the organization. But they can also be detached from the organization. For example, an executive can endorse a particular political regime in a given country and thus act in a way within his company to prompt it to support that regime, say, by trying to cause the company to invest in that country. Often individuals pursue selfish motives (for example, the quest for power or the striving for personal empire-building within the organization). And there is a constant potential conflict between various motives. In particular,

> there are always conflicts between the business role requirements and other personal needs and social and cultural variables . . . A man's utility system is the result of his social system, of the cultural traits of the community in which he lives, and of the way this culture molded his personality and values. The rationality of an individual's behavior can be demonstrated only when all these factors are taken into account.[24]

The first category is players' goals and interests directly related to the issue under consideration. This refers to a player's expectations regarding the outcome of an issue for the sake of that outcome *per se* (as opposed to a desired effect an issue's outcome may have in, say, another game in which the player may be involved). Such goals and interests may be quite broad, ranging from macroeconomic or social motives (in the case of government decisions) to personal motives, going through certain suborganizational goals. For example, a government may want to increase national defence. The defence minister may ask for certain investment programmes to be undertaken by particular arms producers. The goal is the expected benefits from such investments, in other words, the contribution such investments will make to national defence. Executives of the relevant firms will develop an operating programme designed to develop and produce the weapons demanded by government. Here too, the aim is to meet the government's requirements. Finally, each player involved in the process will be influenced in his stand regarding the decisions with which he is confronted by his personal motives. These refer to the personal traits or views of players as they relate to the specific issue under consideration (and not other possible effects of an action in which an individual may be interested for reasons other than those relating to the outcome of the action itself). While there is usually (though, even here, not always) a consensus on broad issues (such as, national security), there is generally disagreement about specifics – what concrete steps to take to enhance security, or, even more, how to actually accomplish such steps (say, in terms of what technology to adopt for a particular defence system). In the more specific issues, individualities become increasingly important. Depending on a player's position, he will feel that such and such an action is particularly important. And personality traits also play a part. Depending on an individual's background, training and values, he will conceive of his role differently and take one position rather than another (for example, past experience with similar issues will influence an individual's stand).

The second category is players' goals and interests about an issue as they relate to other organizational games. To repeat, players are normally engaged in many simultaneous and overlapping games. A move in one game often also affects the course of other games and players' posture in them. Therefore, players have to be concerned with the consequences of their stands *vis-à-vis* an issue on other issues. Not infrequently in fact, are such indirect consequences more important to a player than the outcome of the event itself. There can be certain organizational causes. For example, a politician can espouse the cause of a particular government policy in a given sector not so much because he is concerned with the development of that sector *per se* but because he knows that development of that sector will mean investments in a particular region which in turn may meet his concern for employment in that region. And there can be personal motives. For instance, the head of a plant may push for his company to become heavily involved in a new product, not because he believes in that product but because he knows production will be assigned to his plant, which will enhance his personal standing in the organization. Indeed, while, as we will see, power is the basic means of asserting one's stand, intraorganizational power can also be an end for certain players. As noted by Newman and Warren: 'Power is so important to political effectiveness that its acquisition becomes part of the game. The politically motivated person does things he hopes will place him in a powerful position, and once in such a position, he has added capacity . . . to increase his power even more'.[25]

The third category is players' goals and interests as they relate to motives which are not directly connected with the life of the organization in which it arises. Players' life outside of the organization and their interactions with society at large involve the building up of commitments to other organizations (for example, a church, a golf club or the family) as well as to other individuals. In deciding on one's stand *vis-à-vis* an organizational issue, one cannot ignore such commitments where relevant. In this connection, Aharoni has analysed the impact of the social system on individuals' decision-making in organizations. By analysing the attitude of Jewish-American businessmen *vis-à-vis* investments in Israel, he has shown the relevance of the non-business environment as a critical additive element in the investment decision and the importance of the emotional ties to Israel in such decisions.[26] Moreover, aims which are truly only personal and materially egoistic also play an important part. A typical case is the politician arguing for the purchase by the state of particular equipment not because of the quality of the equipment but because of bribes paid to him by the manufacturer.

Beyond perception of an issue and stakes involved, a player's stand can be affected by the time-frame in which he operates. In many circumstances, people are motivated in their stands by short-term pressures. They do not therefore pursue the otherwise best course possible (best in terms of their set of goals which are a blend of organizational and purely personal objectives). Thus, the division head is typically evaluated on a yearly basis and regardless of how well he can argue that what counts is his line's long-term performance, he knows that top management will be sensitive to what contribution to current profits he can make. And the chief executive has to be sensitive to stockholders' immediate expectations. Thus, decisions can be advocated which are not consistent with the best long-term interest of the firm. Further, a politician is constantly confronted with electoral pressures: he has little time to show the results of his action lest he should not be in office any more when long-term results might ensue.

C. What determines each player's power?

Once a players' stand has been established, it remains to be determined what power an individual has to assert and command observance of his views. But what exactly do we mean by power? This concept is central to any treatment of political behaviour and various authors have dealt with it in some detail. Two points of view can broadly be distinguished.

The first conceives of power as the ability an individual has to affect the fate of others. The emphasis is on other *individuals'* position (in the sense of their material, social or emotional standing), or behaviour. Thus Dahl refers to power as the ability of A to get B to do something that B would not do otherwise.[27] Power here is a property of social relationships as contrasted to something a person has as an individual asset. Such a view implies dependency as a part of these social relationships.[28] In this connection Blau writes that 'by supplying services in demand to others, a person establishes power over them. If he regularly renders needed services they cannot readily obtain elsewhere, others become dependent on and obligated to him for these services'.[29] 'Thus the power of one individual over another', note Mumford and Pettigrew, 'is related to the importance and uniqueness of the services provided by the first individual and the alternative means for obtaining these same services open to the second individual'.[30] Newman follows the same stream of thought when he defines power as 'the ability to supply or withhold something another person wants . . . and the ability to inflict penalties . . . [as] the negative form of power'.[31]

The second point of view stresses the relationship of power and the behaviour and position of the *organization*. The power of an individual is defined and measured in terms of the effect he has on the doings of an organization. For example, Allison defines power of somebody in government as his 'effective influence on government decisions and actions'.[32]

While for our purposes we find the second point of view more useful, the two are not incompatible. For us, a player's power is his ability to influence the outcome of the games in which he is involved. Since the overall behaviour of an organization emerges from the aggregation of the various simultaneous and overlapping games played in the organization, a player's power in the context of the total organization can be conceived as his capacity to affect the doings of the total organization: even if power is conceived of as being circumscribed to a player's influence in the particular game he plays, the interdependency of games and their impact on the overall behaviour of the organization ensure the player's influence on the total organization's actions and decisions. Therefore, an individual's power can indeed be thought of as his ability to influence actual overall organizational behaviour. Still, this conception is in fact akin to the view of power as the ability of an individual to influence another: we regard the behaviour of an organization as the resultant of bargaining games among key individuals; therefore, a player's influence over the organization's doings necessarily goes through his influence over other players.

'Power is an elusive blend of at least three elements: bargaining advantages, skill and will in using bargaining advantages, and other players' perception of the first two ingredients'.[33] More specifically, we can identify seven sources of power. First, formal authority and responsibility. This stems from the individual being appointed to a position which, in view of the organization's formal hierarchy (or tradition) gives him the right to command – to make key decisions and see these decisions followed by the organization. Second, an individual has power when he is in a position of reviewing and vetoing others' decisions. For example, MPs often have the right to review the plans proposed by GCEs' management or by ministers. This clearly gives them the opportunity to influence the actions of these firms. Third, direct control of resources necessary to carry out action. For example, there are many instances in an MN company in which the head of a foreign subsidiary acts without much consultation with top management; yet, if a particular decision requires a certain amount of resources which are managed centrally for the whole company, the person at headquarters who is responsible for the allocation of that resource has often considerable discretionary power over the doings of the subsidiary precisely because the accomplishment of the decision of the subsidiary's head is subordinated to the obtainment of that resource. Fourth, control over vital information. This includes information necessary to identify problems or threats, options or alternatives and estimate feasibilities as well as data to devise plans and monitor or control the implementation and the results of these plans.

Fifth, vital expertise for the planning and accomplishment of key actions. Personal indispensability based on the quasi-exclusive mastery of critical knowledge or on another proprietary asset can confer on an individual considerable power. Mumford and Pettigrew have analysed the role of the technical expert in particular in innovative decisions: 'Experts can as a rule maintain a power position over high-ranking persons in an organization as long as the latter are dependent on them for special skills'.[34] Yet, we should note with Crozier the evolutionary nature of power relationships within organizations and the often self-defeating character of expert power.[35] 'So long as the expert is operating in a new area requiring novel and unprogrammed decisions, his knowledge will give him power. But as soon as a new field of knowledge becomes well covered and first intuitions and innovations become translated into rules and programmes, the expert's power disappears'.[36] Sixth is quick, direct access to other players with power plus the ability to modify their behaviour in their games. This ranges from informal influence positions – for example, access to the president's ear because one meets him socially[37] to the person who can affect the decisions of a powerful player by coercion (in the case of bribery, for instance). Seventh, we find sheer personal traits such as charm, charisma or credibility based on such factors as past professional success or academic titles.

D. What are the rules of the game?

Organizational politics do not occur in a disorderly, random and confused way. Rather, they take place in a regularized fashion. Orderliness stems from set codes of principles and methods for the conduct of political activities. First among these are action-channels – 'a regularized means of taking [organizational] action on a specific kind of issue'.[38] An action-channel is a course through which influence may be moved and directed to yield actual organizational behaviour. An action-channel is usually good (that is, effective) for certain particular purposes but not all. A player involved in several games will typically use different channels for the various games. Moreover, action-channels structure the game by determining 'who's got the action' and by 'pre-selecting the major players, determining their usual points of entrance into the game, and distributing particular advantages and disadvantages for each game'.[39]

To illustrate, consider the way a conglomerate goes about acquiring new companies. A number of action-channels can yield a takeover: a recommendation from the head of the division involved in the field of the acquisition candidate; an assessment by a staff member (for example, in the planning department); a decision by a member of top management; from a member of the acquisition candidate itself approaching a conglomerate's member; from an intermediary (a banker, for example). Most often the action-channel in which the opportunity is recognized also determines who is to produce action about (that is, implement) the opportunity. In this connection, it is worth quoting the description of the acquisition procedure of Litton Industries:

> Potential acquisition possibilities could enter the Litton organization from any one of three sources: (1) From the division manager or group vice-president as a part of their opportunity planning;* (2) from the corporate planning staff or some other member of top management; or (3) from outside the company, such as when people came forward with suggestions or requests for Litton to consider a potential candidate. Generally speaking, the responsibility for consummating an acquisition was placed on the source that recommended it. In the case of the group or division managers, negotiations and details were their responsibility after it had been determined with corporate management that such an acquisition was desirable . . . They were expected to be the driving force behind the acquisition . . . Possible acquisitions that came from the other two sources were usually handled by the corporate planning staff . . . The idea was to actually transfer a man from corporate 'planning' to the acquired company for a period of several months

---

*Litton's multilevel planning process in which the company's major strategic options are identified and alternatives defined by an interaction of top management, group management (for example a vice-president in charge of a 'family' of related products) and division management.

where he was responsible for ensuring that the opportunities that gave rise to that particular acquisition, did, in fact, become a reality.[40]

Beyond action-channels, organizational politics follow certain rules determining what should and should not be done. Certain rules are explicit, others implicit; some are stable, others changing, some are clear, others fuzzy.[41] Written rules include articles of the constitution, legal codes, statutes, company bylaws; and government decrees, conventions or policy statements; within a company they include the formal organizational structure and each position's authority as well as formal 'orders' or operating guidelines or procedures (for example, the requirements imposed by the annual budget). Tacit rules include economic and cultural norms both in terms of intercompany and intracompany behaviour. This refers to the dynamics of the economic environment (for example, the law of supply and demand) as well as social norms either in terms of codes of good conduct in society in general or of principles of proper behaviour within the firm *per se* (that is, *de facto* constraints and obligations among members of the same organization).

Rules determine the game.

> First, rules establish the positions, the paths by which men gain access to positions, the power of each position, the action-channels. Second, rules constrict the range of [organizational] decisions and actions that are acceptable . . . Third, rules sanction moves of some kinds – bargaining, coalitions, persuasion, deceit, bluff, and threat – while making other moves illegal, immoral, ungentlemanly, or inappropriate.[42]

In practice, such rules tend to be quite strict. In the case of explicit written rules, transgressions rarely can go unnoticed (for example, the formal organizational structure places limits on the use of power which are normally hard to infringe). Where such rules are in fact transgressed, it is unlikely that this goes unnoticed; given the 'visibility' of such rules, infringements seldom occur because of a failure in the control of the rules' observance. Rather, infringement occurs because of tacit acceptance of infringement; in other words, transgression is in practice permissible. Here then, an implicit rule substitutes itself for an explicit rule. And tacit rules are usually hard to transgress: they tend to be deeply rooted in the social systems they regulate – firmly embedded in people's culture – and thus notably harder to modify than legal articles or official regulations. Tacit rules are often the most amenable to self-discipline; given that they concern the most practical aspects of the course of a game, the various players can readily check each other's behaviour *vis-à-vis* such rules. Thus, as noted by Newman and Warren, a leader with power favouring one person usually deprives another.[43] If this is considered unfair by organizational standards, the

263

injured individual will try to oppose this behaviour. Usually, this will put an end
to the favouritism, the deviant leader being recalled to order by the other
powerful players as well as by the consequences of his behaviour over his own
posture – beyond any sanctions, he will suffer a loss of credibility and thus of
power in his game.

E. What is the game?

How are players' decisions and actions combined to yield organizational
behaviour? Besides its action-channels and rules, the game has a number of
actual traits which characterize the way it is played in practice: the way
individuals move in fact and the way these moves are combined to produce
action by the firm.

1. *How is an issue raised?*

Up to now we have looked at what happens once players are confronted with an
issue. But how does an issue come up in the first place? By issue we mean the
question a player is confronted with when he realizes he has to take a stand. An
issue is thus composed of a problem – a worrying matter, fact or situation
presenting a threat or difficulty – and a set of alternatives geared to the problem. A problem in itself does not call for a stand; what calls for a stand is a set of
alternative solutions to a problem. Therefore, our interest lies in how a problem arises and how various courses of action emerge and are called to players'
attention pressuring them to take sides one way or another.

In decisions in crises situations (which Graham Allison focuses upon) the
problem is generally raised, so-to-speak, automatically or 'passively' in that the
attention of the players is aroused by the crisis itself. This means that virtually
by definition the problem over which the political game will be played is
specified by the very event creating it. Players are therefore not really responsible for the identification of the problem over which they are to bargain. In
strategy decisions things are different. Except precisely in the case of a major
event raising a glaring opportunity or threat, most problems are defined
'actively': the matter of whether to pursue a new course stems from the
conscious questioning of the existing strategic posture (or parts of it). The issue
does not spring to the attention of players on its own; there must be an explicit
intention to bring it up.

An issue arises thanks to an individual or group of individuals. It is one or a
few individuals who propose an idea for action and raise an issue on which
others will take a stand. Individuals may have an idea for a variety of
reasons – from personal to company or outside motives. Consider the foreign
investment decision. An individual may have personal motives leading him to
think about international operations – a desire to travel and have the opportunity to live abroad, emotional ties to one or more countries or the prestige of

being part or head of an MNC. Or motives can be strictly organizational. Still, here too the idea for action comes from an individual.[44]

A player responsible for bringing an issue up is an 'initiator'. An initiator can either be a top member of the company or somebody lower in the hierarchy. For example, a division manager can make a proposal for his division, which has important implications for the overall strategy of the firm; or even he can directly formulate ideas which outright affect the total enterprise. And certain staff members (for example, corporate planners) have the explicit responsibility of focusing on the problems and opportunities confronting the company. Depending on his standing in the organization, an initiator will command attention more or less readily for an issue he raises.

In contrast to initiators are 'adopters': they are the other players who, confronted with an issue, take one attitude or another. An idea is put in front of them and they have to express a judgement on it. And there is in fact no way for an adopter to escape the obligation of taking an attitude. He can at the most ignore the issue, but this is of course also a way of taking a position – a negative-action position.

2. What is the 'mode' of political behaviour?

This regards the way an issue is forwarded once it is raised – not just the acknowledgement of the existence of a problem but also a choice about what side to take as to alternative courses of action geared to the problem. It is here that the political game really starts.

Another distinction needs to be made – between he who promotes a decision and he who merely supports it. 'Promoting' means being the champion of a proposed course of action, being he who fights for the development, advancement or enactment of an idea. The promoter can be – and indeed often is – the same person as the initiator. But this is not necessarily always so. For example, if an idea is initiated by or springs from a relatively junior staff member, a senior member of top management may become the primary advocate of this idea and use his greater standing, experience and exposure to foster its progress. 'Supporting' refers to giving one's endorsement to an idea or proposed action promoted by somebody else. Clearly, this role is close to that of an adopter. Yet, there are important nuances. Adopting refers to the phase in which an issue is raised. The political game *per se* has not started. The question for individuals is merely to make up their minds as to their attitude *vis-à-vis* the issue and not to engage in any controversy to defend a line of action they are forced to espouse. Supporting, on the contrary, involves a player directly engaged in the bargaining game. Even when a player is not actively doing things to foster the pursuit of one course of action rather than another, his support provides voluntary backing which strengthens the political potency of the idea.[45] In fact, while adopters can take a passive attitude *vis-à-vis* an issue (in other words, ignore it), support implies making a conscious choice (as opposed to choosing by default). Thus, while normally supporters were previously adopters, not all adopters become supporters.

A decision or action is usually proposed by one or a few promoters who take that stand for a particular set of reasons. The proposed decision or action then typically attracts others who give it their support. In fact, widespread backing is most often necessary for a novel, complex or controversial idea to make its way in the organization and be pursued. Thus coalitions are formed. These are temporary alliances among individuals from many origins, functions, responsibilities and interests, for the purpose of fostering the adoption or pursuit of particular decisions or actions. In each coalition 'each member contributes his influence – and if necessary uses his power – to bring about the desired results'.[46] While all members of the coalition back the same basic idea, their motives may be quite varied. Generally, the promoters' interests are closest to the issue *per se* – related most directly to the outcome of the issue under consideration. Supporters are more likely to be motivated by the side-effects of the proposed decision or action, that is, the byproducts in terms of the consequences for them in other games or their own personal endeavours. In particular, supporters can join a coalition merely to help other coalition members (and notably the promoters) for the simple purpose of doing them a favour which they hope they will be paid back elsewhere: people support a coalition with no other goal or interest than building up credit with those they back, which they expect to use at a future date by receiving their support in a coalition of their own or by receiving some other form of payment.

In companies, coalitions are most often informal and spontaneous; yet, on major controversial issues, the coalition leaders or promoters may seek support systematically and modify the proposed plan to obtain crucial backing.[47] Neustadt notes that 'The essence of *any* responsible official's task is to persuade other players that his version of what needs to be done is what their own appraisal of their own responsibilities requires them to do in their own interests'.[48]

It is easier to form and hold a coalition together around a 'negative' cause than around a 'positive' one: people can coalesce relatively promptly against an existing state of affairs or course of action because they have a common desire for the same outcome – the halting, neutralization or ousting of a pattern of behaviour or of the current leadership group – which make them fight side by side regardless either of their own respective motives or their ideas about what should be done instead of the *status quo*. Still, when it comes to agreeing on an actual programme for action, coalitions are more vulnerable. Then individuals' interests appear clearly in their diversity. If there was agreement on what to fight against, the variety of people's motives leads them frequently to advocate many different courses of action resulting in widespread divergence about what to do instead of the *status quo*.

3. *What is the structure of the game?*

Power, responsibilities and judgements are shared among several players. This basic fact conditions the overall way decisions are taken. Decisions and actions are neither taken as choices of a unified group nor the product of a formal summary of leaders' preferences. Instead, decisions and actions result from bargaining among players each fighting for his own point of view. And the adoption of a course of action for the organization is not a function of what is the objectively (according to set criteria) most efficient means of reaching an end or the objectively optimal way to solve a problem. Rather, it is a function of political resultants: the result of power plays and settlements (or quasi-settlements) of differences among players. In other words, the final result – in terms of an organization's decisions or actions – stems not from a rational selection of the 'best solution' but from the views, goals and interests of, as well as the interfaces between, the more influential supporters of particular decisions or actions. A particular decision or action of an organization can be the product of one player's (or one group of players') standpoint, that is, the organization behaves following the points of view of one player or group of players. Generally, however, a compromise has to be reached between the points of view of various individuals, and what is finally done often does not correspond to anybody's original idea: ultimate behaviour is normally a composition of the original proposals of a variety of players.

> The sum of behavior of representatives of an [organization]relevant to an issue is rarely intended by any individual or group. Rather, in the typical case, separate individuals with different intentions contribute pieces to a resultant. The details of the action are therefore not chosen by any individual (and are rarely identical with what any of the players would have chosen if he had confronted the issue as a matter of simple, detached choice). Nevertheless, resultants can be roughly consistent with some group's preference in the context of the political game.[49]

4. Implementation

When a decision about an organization's behaviour is reached formally, the larger game is by no means over. For relatively minor or operating issues, decisions by leaders can be ignored altogether. This is rarely the case of strategic issues. Yet, there is considerable room for 'interpretation' in terms of the accomplishment of a decision. The chances of slippage are considerable since many players are involved and opportunities for close control of each far more dicey.[50] Three points are especially critical.

First, the question of how specific the formal decision is. In particular, the most controversial issues require strong backing; promoters need to secure the most widespread support possible. To do so, it is often necessary to leave some ambiguity around the proposed action and its reasons: 'The necessity to build a consensus behind his [the chief promoter] preferred policy, frequently requires fuzziness: different people must agree with slightly different things for quite different reasons; when an [organizational] decision is made, both the character of the choice and the reasons for it must often remain vague'.[51] Clearly, however, the vaguer a decision the more opportunity there is for distortion of what was originally intended. This is particularly serious for decisions taken at the top of an organization and which involve the doings of the entire organization. Top managers or leaders then take the formal decisions but have to delegate not only most of the implementation but also most of the implementation's control. Deciders can thus not even themselves monitor how others put their decisions into practice and have to rely on intermediaries to do so. The task of controlling a decision's accomplishment for one who has not taken it is particularly arduous when the decision's formulation is fuzzy. Even in the best of all cases, when they are genuinely committed to making sure the decision is implemented as intended, intermediaries may fail in their mission simply because of the vagueness of the prescriptions they are to monitor.

Second, the question of who is to accomplish the decision. Some decisions are quite specific in this respect. Others are vague and leave considerable room for argument as to who should carry them out. For example, an OPEC country government which has nationalized the local subsidiaries of foreign oil companies, finds itself with, say, twenty such companies which it does not consolidate. If the decision is reached that there ought to be some diversification outside of the oilfield but if it is not specified which particular concerns ought to be entrusted to do so, considerable room for debate will be left. One can expect a new game to develop once the game leading to the diversification decision is over. There will first of all be the resurgence of the old opponents of diversification who will try to delay action and to foster the wrong kind of action. In so doing, they both hope to delay what they see as an undesirable outcome and to generate enough illwill about the practical aspects of the decision that it may be revoked or abandoned or at least revised. Further, there will be various players fighting to get the action assigned to those individuals or that organization which they see most fit to achieve their expected results. Thus, several leaders of oil companies may have supported the general decision to diversify. Once it comes to settling which company should actually do so, there may be considerable divergence of opinion, various company heads arguing that their own company should be the main vehicle for diversification.

Third, the question of what can be called 'normal foul-ups'. To repeat, organizational action is a blend of formal decisions and agglomerations of quasi-independent actions of players. In the formulation stage of a given pattern of behaviour, formal decisions obviously prevail. Usually, for strategic decisions, relatively few players are involved, and communication between them is relatively effective, thus avoiding too many misunderstandings and blunders. In the implementation stage, however, it is the actions of many individuals which are critical. Over and beyond any attempt by such individuals to manipulate the decision, errors, miscommunications and omissions are inevitable. This again is all the more likely for those decisions whose accomplishment calls for the mobilization of the entire organization. The difficulty of making sure that the doings of the many individuals concerned are consistent is exacerbated by the simultaneousness and interdependence of the host of games involved. The information which has relevance is so vast and comes from so many sides that it can only be partially absorbed; due to the many interlockings of the games, the flow of pertinent communication is so dense that it is by necessity elliptic and thus often ambiguous, and it takes place in such a noisy environment that parts of it inevitably get lost. Indeed, considerable misperception, miscommunication and misinformation are a standard part of any organization's functioning.[52]

We should note in fact that from a political standpoint, a certain confusion is often desirable: particularly at the implementation stage where so many people are involved, it is necessary to have commitment around a strategy or policy, to get many individuals to adhere to it who are usually quite different in their needs and interests; such different people back a strategy or policy for different reasons but also tend to have differing views about the more specific aspects of a course of action; therefore, it is almost necessary to allow some degree of fuzziness in implementation in order to meet the players' particular expectations. This, of course, is germane to the need – at the formulation stage – for certain decisions to remain somewhat vague to avoid the possibility that certain supporters shy away from backing them because they cannot agree with specific details. As noted by Allison: 'Misperception is in a sense the grease that allows co-operation among people whose differences otherwise would hardly allow them to co-exist'.[53]

III. SPECIAL ASPECTS OF STRATEGIC AND POLICY BEHAVIOUR

In this section we examine five main features of corporate behaviour seen through an organizational politics lens.

1. *Decisions*

(a) Decisions bear the mark of key individuals. The particular preferences of players (and especially those of the most powerful ones) have a major bearing on the actions of the firm.

(b) Decisions are generally not made by one person – be it the chief executive; and neither are decisions normally to be regarded as democratic choices of a college, in other words, majority decisions. Rather, decisions are made by a large number of people. Thus, the chief executive of a diversified company will tend not to make a decision about the actions of a division without extensive conference with the division management. And government members, regardless of how much formal power they have, will not make a decision regarding GCE's behaviour without consulting management.

(c) The formal structure of decision-making is of little consequence, in other words, the formal forums in which decisions should be made do not constrain the actual key players – decisions, therefore, are made in *ad hoc* groups by those players who are *de facto* powerful.

(d) Decisions are generally not the product of a rationale shared by all players. Rather, they result from politics among individuals who see different faces of the issue and who disagree about the options they favour. Therefore, 'actions consisting of a number of pieces that have emerged from a number of games (plus foul-ups) rarely reflect a co-ordinated . . . strategy and thus are difficult to read as conscious "signals"'.[54]

2. Solutions

'"Solutions" to strategic problems are not discovered by detached analysts focusing coolly on *the* problem. The problems for players are both narrower and broader than the strategic problem'.[55] They are narrower because a single player does not focus on the total strategic issue but only on those aspects of the issue of concern to him. Even a leader rarely sees all the facets of an issue. To take the case of GCEs, the chief executive cannot be entirely sensitive to the preoccupations of government members; a government member cannot be expected to see all the aspects of the company point of view; and neither one can see all the consequences of one action or another on all the games on which the issue has an impact. Problems are broader for players than the strategic problem because each decision has an impact not only on the strategic problem but also on the player's stakes – his personal costs and benefits over and beyond the game in which the issue is raised directly; a player sees the potential side-effects of an action on a scale which can be as broad as the scope of his own interests in other company games as well as in extraorganizational concerns of his.

3. Winning collective commitment

The interlocking nature of games and the overlapping nature of players' influence require that he who wants to get a particular action decided upon has to secure the backing of others. Given the multiplicity of issues and games as well as their complexity, and the pace at which they are played, promoters have to fight hard to get others to give some thought to the issue and to do so from a not overly parochial standpoint. And action will be delayed until as few opponents remain as possible.

4. Style of play

A player's position affects his expectations which in turn affect his style of play. There are important differences among players' behaviour – between the business or management orientation of in-company players, the political or macro socioeconomic orientation of players in government and the more specialized or narrower focus of certain outsiders. And differences exist also within these three categories. Thus, in GCEs leaders should focus primarily on strategic and major policy decisions although they find themselves worrying too often about the hottest issue *du jour* and aides de camp typically spend most of their time looking for issues – searching for problems and formulating alternative solutions. Among outsiders, players often have parochial views (unionists, for example).

And among government players major differences exist between elected politicians and civil servants. Elected politicians have in principle the leading role in terms of decision-making; yet, they are conditioned by two important types of limitations: their electoral concerns and their tenure. Most often elected politicians have to give first and foremost attention to the consequences of that decision on the reaction of voters. Their behaviour is normally therefore at least partly geared to the aim of winning popular consent. The result is frequently a quest for highly visible results, to the detriment of longer-term, more deeply meaningful achievements. Further, politicians know they are in power for relatively short periods of time. This means they must depend on the bureaucratic careerists – professional civil servants – who have had the time to master the relevant information and know how to make things happen. Besides, their limited tenure pressures politicians to have a short-term orientation. On the other hand, civil servants have less of a visible role but often a major *de facto* influence on decisions. They have technical competence; and they realize this makes politicians dependent on them. Further, they have considerable job stability and are uninhibited by the need to be popular; they are consequently under less pressure for short-term results.

Moreover, the terms of reference of a player have a bearing on his style of play. Individuals find themselves working in an environment calling for certain patterns of behaviour – certain norms and standards about what is considered proper and improper action. (Such standards and norms are imposed by all the relevant players collectively; yet, from the point of view of an individual, this collectivity represents the 'environment' in which he works). Individuals are under pressure to adapt one way or another to the environment in which they work. This consists of the environment imposing certain 'musts' on individuals' behaviour – 'musts' which can be either positive or negative by generally admitted moral standards. (Thus, Acheson writes that the American Secretary of State works 'in an environment where some of the methods would have aroused the envy of the Borgias'.[56]) Some individuals adapt readily and are co-opted by the environment adopting its norms and standards. Others are not able to operate effectively in such situations because their own values do not legitimize behaving in the way called for by the environment. The environment also imposes certain 'must nots' or fails to impose certain 'must nots' which generally admitted moral standards would call for. For example, the environment of an organization may tolerate the use of organizational resources for individual ends. When a certain abandon enters an organization, certain individuals will invariably take advantage of it.

5. *Debilitating effects of political behaviour*[57]

Key individuals making decisions on the basis of their own political self-interest can clearly act in a way which is negative from the point of view of the overall organization. The problem is probably most vivid in the case of elected politicians' behaviour.

Politicians' sensitivity to their electorate's mood and their short tenure result in their making choices which are inevitably threatened to undermine the real long-range interests of GCEs or of the nation itself: 'Politics usually focuses on short-run tradeoffs. In this process long-run programmes tend to be sacrificed because both the measurements and payoffs from long-range programmes occur well into the future'.[58] Therefore, a somewhat paradoxical situation emerges in which the elected politicans who should have the broadest and longest-term national concerns at heart, are in fact frequently most preoccupied by short-term, flashy, albeit superficial, results.

IV. CONCLUSION

The basic hypothesis of an organizational politics approach is that the behaviour of an organization does not presuppose organizational intention. Rather, the strategy and policies of an organization are the resultant of bargaining games among players within the organization. Therefore, explanation does not stem from logical deductions about what is the right thing to do from the point of view of the total enterprise. Rather, explanation is achieved by displaying the intricacies of the bargaining game. This means uncovering the players' identity – their position, their personality and preferences. In particular, 'for large classes of issues – for example, budgets and procurement decisions – the stance of a particular player can be predicted with high reliability from information about his seat'.[59] This means that when one is dealing with *types* of decisions (for example, foreign investment decisions as opposed to one particular investment by a particular company in a particular country at a particular point in time), one can generally say a lot about what stand and what influence an actor in a given position will take and have, and this pretty much over and beyond personal information about the particular individual occupying that position at that point. For more specific types of issues (for example, a particular investment project) one should know more about the player's personal traits. Besides, displaying the game means analysing the rules of the game (for example, the action-channels). And it also means digging into the real pulling and hauling – the political bargains which take place in actual fact. Behaving in a political fashion in an organization has been defined as choosing one's actions 'primarily on the basis of who will be helped and who, if anyone, will be hurt'.[60] The organizational politics approach penetrates into the power-plays, the give and take, the cabals, the collusions and intrigues taking place among players. Further, given the imperfections of the game – such as miscommunications or misperceptions – it tries to account for the confusion and foul-ups which also contribute to the final product of an organization's behaviour.

In the following two chapters we take an organizational politics approach to GCEs' MN behaviour. Under this approach decisions stem from key individuals and their interfaces. The focus is on players' personality and position as well as on the disputes, clashes, compromises and accommodations between actors who inevitably disagree on what action to take on a given corporate issue.

It should be clear that each decision raises different political variables. Different players are concerned each time. In each case a player has different stands determined by his perception of the issue and the stakes involved (the issue for him not being necessarily confined to the corporate problem as such and frequently including issues outside of those directly related to the decision in question). And in each case a player has different power, also because his own power is affected by other players' power in the particular game under consideration.

Having said this, there are a number of archetypes. The key players having a bearing on strategic and policy decisions are on the whole a known quantity; notwithstanding certain exceptions, such decisions are the result of the politics between a group of individuals which is rather stable. This is not to say of course that these decisions are all made by the same players. Rather, the political games of such decisions are staged by actors who are *drawn* from a finite number of people: those who can have a role in strategic and policy decisions tend to constitute a bounded set. Moreover, the basic strategic and policy issues confronted by GCEs lend themselves to a certain categorization: there are a number of cases representing the majority of strategy and policy decisions faced by GCEs. Consequently, while it is not possible to present a general picture describing and explaining the behaviour of GCEs exhaustively, one can make valid generalizations about main categories of decisions and basic patterns of behaviour. In other words, to explain GCEs' behaviour in full detail would require focusing on the politics of each single decision in each single company. Still, it is possible to draw a typology of the basic decisions covering the majority of strategic and policy issues confronted by GCEs in connection with MN activities. And for each type of decision it is possible to explain the kinds of politics normally involved. Of course such treatment leaves out certain specific aspects particular to such and such a decision but, on the whole, it uncovers the basic kinds of politics involved in the majority of cases.

In Chapter IX we present the basic types of key players. We will see where and when they are likely to step in and what their major concerns typically are. We also deal with their influence in various cases (though here it will inevitably be general since a player's influence in a given situation is a function of other players' influence).

In Chapter X we analyse actual cases, that is, the major types of MN strategic and policy decisions confronted by GCEs. These cases will be defined primarily according to company characteristics (for example, the sector in which the firm operates) and issues to be resolved, i.e. the nature of the decision to be made (like a particular operating policy decision). For the various categories of decisions, we see what persons generally come into play, what stands they are likely to take, and analyse their respective power. We focus on how the principal types of games are played in practice – the interactions among key individuals, the machinations, the negotiations, the rules of the game, the confusion, etc. – and explain how particular decisions and actions actually result.

'Information about the details of differences in perceptions and priorities within an [organization] on a particular issue is rarely available. Accurate accounts of the bargaining that yielded a resolution of the issue are rarer still. Thus the source of such information must be participants themselves.[61] Indeed, more than any other in this book, the following chapters rest on interviews with people who have a direct role in GCEs' strategic and policy decisions. Yet, it should be obvious that the kinds of questions this analysis raises tend to be of the most touchy sort. Therefore, here more than elsewhere, we had to guarantee interviewees that their responses would remain unidentified. Further, the collection, analysis and interpretation of the data is often a fuzzy exercise: 'The use of public documents, newspapers, interviews of participants and discussion with close observers of participants to piece together the bits of information available is an art'.[62] Consequently, some of our arguments are by necessity somewhat speculative and tentative. Indeed, it is in a sense *ex hypothesis* that some of the data used by this approach is impressionistic. Hopefully, the high number and diversity of our sources will have enabled us to address the relevant questions from enough angles to make our argument both accurate and credible.

APPENDIX

This appendix surveys the existing literature on organizational politics. At the outset we must recognize the relative underdevelopment of the theory in this area. It is of recent descent, concepts have not had time to mature in a definitive fashion and supporting empirical data tend to be scanty.[63]

Organization theory has taken business enterprises as its favourite ground for both theoretical reflection and empirical investigation. Organizational politics theory – if indeed one can call theory the more or less formalized set of concepts we have in the field – was developed primarily by political scientists around the behaviour of government organizations. Only in the recent past have management students become concerned with this way of thinking.

Attention to an organizational politics type of analysis was really awakened by the 1960 publication of Richard Neustadt's *Presidential Power*.[64] 'Each [government] is a more or less complex arena for internal bargaining among the bureaucratic elements and political personalities who collectively comprise its working apparatus. Its action is the product of their interaction'.[65] For Neustadt, the various individuals in key government positions have various areas of action and responsibility. Thus, power and influence over overall government behaviour is shared. Explicit rules (for example, constitutional prescription) and implicit rules (for example, government tradition and political practice) enhance a certain individualism among participants who each develop needs and interests of their own. Each individual is primarily concerned with fulfilling his own job, and the President cannot expect full and total responsiveness even of his most direct subordinates. In fact, in certain instances, a particular subordinate acquires such a considerable status through his personality or performance in a particularly important area of government action, that he becomes a direct threat to presidential power. While in formal authority the President is the chief; to actually exert his power, he needs to convince key individuals to go along with his policies: 'Presidential power is the power to persuade'.[66] And the President and the other key players do not 'bargain at random but according to the processes conforming to the prerequisites, responsive to the pressures of their own political system'.[67]

Gabriel Almond's *American People and Foreign Policy* presents a framework for analysing foreign policy as a result of pluralistic politics.[68]

> An outer circle of participants is composed of the 'general public', a group normally ignorant of and indifferent to foreign policy matters, unless aroused about some highly visible issue. The 'attentive public' sits one ring closer to the center, is informed and interested in foreign policy problems, and provides the audience for discussion among the elites. Center stage is surrounded by the 'policy and opinion elites' who give structure to the public discussion and open avenues of access to the various groupings. Finally, the 'official policy leadership' are the actors. The elite structure is characterized by a large number of autonomous and competing groups: autonomous since power is widely dispersed among participants and drawn from a variety of independent sources; competing, since participants differ about both ends and means; and groups, since only by coordination can individuals assemble sufficient power to achieve their proposals.[69]

Along similar lines, Charles Lindblom's work has focused on 'the character of bargaining and expounded the virtues of incremental muddling as opposed to comprehensive choice as the mode of policy making'.[70]

Building on the earlier formulations, Warner Schilling uses an organizational politics approach to analyse the process by which the national defence budget is determined and what the relationships are between the process and the content of the budget.[71] The process is characterized by (1) problems that have no right answer: 'There is no determinant answer to the question of how much to spend for defense'; (2) participants whose policy differences stem from both intellectual and institutional differences; (3) processes that distribute power and advantages differently among participants; (4) a 'strain towards agreement' that encourages compromise and consensus; and (5) outcomes that result from conflict, coalition, and bargaining.[72]

In *The Common Defense*[73] Huntington analyses US defence policies and force postures focusing specifically on 'decisions on the overall size of the military effort, force, levels and weapons'.[74] Such decisions are not the product of rational planning but the 'result of controversy, negotiations, and bargaining among officials and groups with different interests and perspectives'.[75]

In *To Move a Nation*, Hilsman conceives (as Almond does) of the policy-making process as a set of concentric circles: the innermost circle – the President and the individuals in government who actually carry out policy; other departments and agencies; the 'attentive public' (for example, Congress or interest groups).[76] While policy is indeed made primarily by the innermost circle, other circles are relevant too; anyhow, at any level, policy-making is politics. As such it has three basic features: (1) 'A diversity of goals and values that must be reconciled before a decision can be reached'.[77] (2) 'The presence of competing clusters of people within the main group, who are identified with each of the alternative goals and policies'.[78] (3) 'The relative power of these different groups of people included is as relevant to the final decision as the appeal of the goals they seek or the cogency and wisdom of their arguments'.[79] We thus see that policy-making is a process of 'conflict and consensus building'. When various influential individuals have conflicting views on policy decisions, competition for support and means of alliance develop – persuasion, accommodation and bargaining'.[80]

Furthermore, several case studies have been developed analysing governmental policy decisions in terms of an organizational politics approach.[81]

Finally, the most elaborate and precise formulation remains Allison's governmental politics' model.[82] Building on several of the above-mentioned pieces, Allison develops a specific framework of analysis of government behaviour in crisis situations, which he applies to the 1962 Cuban missile crisis. Allison's primary source is Neustadt's approach although Neustadt's attention on presidential action is broadened to focus on governmental behaviour as the resultant of bargaining among several individuals, the president being one among other players – though one with considerable influence. Allison also draws heavily on Schilling, on Huntington and particularly on Hilsman and his notion about conflict and consensus-building.

Allison himself has described his framework in the following terms:

> The . . . model focuses on the politics of a government . . . What happens is characterized as a *resultant* of various bargaining games among players in the national government. In confronting the problem posed by Soviet missiles in Cuba, a Model III analyst frames the puzzle: Which results of what kinds of bargaining among which players yielded the critical decisions and actions? He then fixes the unit of analysis: political resultant. Next, he focuses attention on certain concepts: the perceptions, motivations, positions, power, and

manoeuvres of the players. And finally, he invokes certain patterns of inference: if a government performed an action, that action was the resultant of bargaining among players in games. A Model III analyst has 'explained' this event when he has discovered who did what to whom that yielded the action in question. Predictions are generated by identifying the game in which an issue will arise, the relevant players, and their relative power and skill.[83]

Using this framework, Allison looks at the imposition of a blockade around Cuba by the US following the discovery of Russian missiles on the island; here he analyses the politics of the discovery of the missiles and the politics of the reactions. Further, he focuses on the politics which ultimately resulted in the withdrawal of the missiles from Cuba. Besides, he speculates on why the Soviets placed missiles in Cuba in the first place.

There is little question that Allison has made a major contribution to the theory of organizational politics. His is the most articulate formulation available today and the most powerful tool to explain the behaviour of an organization in terms of the games of key individual actors. Yet, for our purposes this framework provides a base but is not directly applicable: Allison focuses on governmental behaviour in crises, while our concern is with corporate strategic and policy behaviour. Strategic and policy decisions deal with the basic whats and hows of an organization; they determine its most fundamental *raison d'être*; there is normally little time-pressure involved. By definition, the contrary is true about crisis decisions. As discussed earlier, the nature of the two types of decisions is different. This difference begins with how the need for a decision is recognized in the first place: an analysis of crises decisions does not really require much treatment of how the problem calling for decision is raised and recognized by deciders; the problem is brought up 'automatically' by the unforeseen event which constitutes the crisis. But for strategic decisions, the 'issue' is by no means self-assertive: if not consciously searched for, strategic problems are often recognized when it is too late to deal with them effectively. Therefore, while *The Essence of Decision* furnishes a strong starting point, strategic and policy decisions require a framework of their own.

Turning to the work of management scholars, one must say their contributions are relatively scant. Long notes that 'people will readily admit that governments are organizations. The converse – that organizations are governments – is equally true but rarely considered'.[84] Long gives two main reasons for this neglect; 'First, a lack of concern with the "political" structure of the organization and a consequent over-attention to the formal structure of power and legitimacy; second, a heavy reliance on a psychological orientation with a lack of emphasis on sociological analysis'.[85] Further, there are some practical difficulties with studying political behaviour: information is hard to collect, the data are messy and politics are perceived as lacking intellectual substance.[86]

Nevertheless, a few studies of political behaviour in business organizations are available. Strauss discusses what he calls 'office politics' and 'bureaucratic gamesmanships'; he describes the 'politics' used by purchasing agents to increase their status in the organization.[87] Dalton deals with the power relationships between production and maintenance people in an organization and line and staff personnel.[88] Focusing on the French 'Administration', Crozier describes how subordinates can have a bearing on their superiors' behaviour because they are responsible for areas in which there is some novelty and uncertainty involved.[89] Dutton and Walton,[90] using what they call 'a tactical instrumental approach to behaviour describe and analyse the conflicts between sales and production departments in two firms'.[91]

Further, there are a few theoretical treatments. The Carnegie School authors do in fact touch upon at least one aspect of politics – conflict. In *Organizations*, March and Simon argue that the interdependent nature of organizational units causes a 'felt need for joint decision-making'.[92] For them, conflict occurs 'if there is a difference in the goals of the various participating groups and if there is a difference in the knowledge and perceptions of these groups, [and since] conflict is an abhorrent and undesirable phenomenon . . . once it is recognized, steps will be taken to resolve it'.[93] In the *Behavioral Theory of the Firm*, Cyert and March carry their thinking further. They see conflicts of interest as normal parts of an organization's life and while they discuss certain mechanisms of conflict resolution, they regard such resolution as imperfect and accept that organizations operate with latent conflict in them.

Still, the March and Simon conception that conflict occurs when suborganizations have different objectives and perceptions is a partial view of how conflict can develop. As noted by Mumford and Pettigrew:

> It can be argued that there may be other reasons for conflict when decisions are being made. For example, one group may see the result of a decision route taking a particular direction as leading to an enhancement of their own organizational power position and the diminution of a rival group's power. This may make them push their own interests and, in turn, will evoke opposition in the rival group. Thus, the decision-making process may be used for the furtherance of conflicts which are a product of long-standing organization rivalries. If this happens, then battles for power become a major source of uncertainty.[94]

On the other hand, Cyert and March's view of coalitions does lead them to recognize the necessity for suborganizations to obtain support for their particular interests and problem-solutions. But, as noted earlier, they do not explain how such support is sought or secured. Further, an important bound of this stream is that the emphasis is not on individuals but on organizational units; this results in a neglect of the role key persons' differences of opinion, and interests play in the decision-making process.

Aharoni gives the individual a greater role.[95] In particular, he recognizes that a key executive can be a major driving force leading to the decision to look abroad for investment opportunities and that he has an important function in the analysis of such opportunities. Yet, he stops short from any explicit treatment of political games as such. A similar argument can be made for Bower's work.[96]

An important contribution is the work by Pettigrew and Mumford.[97] An organization is seen as an open political system composed of subunits with their own interests which result from their particular functions and responsibilities. But while each subunit has its own aims and tasks to perform, it is often interdependent with and has to relate to other subunits: 'Both this specialism and this interdependence affects any decision-making process and as part of this process interest-based demands will be made. In the absence of any agreed set of priorities in these demands, conflict is likely to ensue with subgroups competing for scarce resources in order to promote their own interests'.[98] A particular claim will be prosecuted when it will appear critical for the survival or development of the unit or of key individuals thereof. A claim will be successfully furthered depending on the group's or individuals' capability to generate support for it. In this process, not only group goals are important but also individuals' aspirations and interests. The authors sum this conception up as follows:

> Individuals within an organization are likely to use decision-making situations to pursue what they perceive to be their own interests or the interests of the groups to which they are affiliated. The extent of their ability to pursue these interests will be a product of their power position and this, in turn, will depend on their ability to influence the attitudes and behavior of others through their possession of some scarce resource. This scarce resource, which can be information, skill or knowledge, will be seen by these others as critical to the successful choice of a solution for the decision problem.[99]

Other management scholars have dealt with organizational behaviour in political terms. Mechanic has shown that dependency can be generated by controlling access to key resources.[100] To the extent that these resources can be controlled, 'lower participants make higher ranking participants dependent upon them. Thus, dependence together with the manipulation of the dependency relationship is the key to the power of lower participants'.[101]

Zaleznik sees business organizations as political structures in which competition for power is a salient characteristic.[102] And Burns argues that individuals do not just have organizational commitments but personal aims as well.[103] Among these, power is important since it offers both material and psychological rewards. Individuals strive for power and enter into conflict with others who equally seek power and this engenders political behaviour – coercion, deceit and manipulation.

MacMillan has provided us with 'a practical model for analyzing political behaviour of individuals within an organization and of firms in their economic and social environment'.[104]

In a normative vein, Newman and Warren address the question of how managers can use the concepts of organizational politics theory to perform their roles more effectively.[105] The emphasis is on the individual: 'We will focus on the pursuit of individually held objectives by doing reciprocal favours and by using power to reward or punish'.[106] Four main issues are discussed: distinguishing features of internal politics (a description of what political behaviour involves); 'causes' and coalitions (the motives of 'politicians' and how and why political attitudes by one politician cause other politicians to join him or his political rivals thus engendering coalitions of politicians); the relation of 'politics' to rational bureaucratic decision-making; and ways of channelling political behaviour (how to cause politicians to behave in a way which is beneficial to the organization as a whole).

NOTES

1. Graham Allison, *Essence of Decision*, Little, Brown and Co., Boston, 1971, p. 144.
2. Andrew Pettigrew, *The Politics of Organizational Decision-Making*, Tavistock, London, 1973, p. 9.
3. Richard Cyert and James March, *A Behavioral Theory of the Firm*, Prentice Hall, Englewood Cliffs, NJ, 1963, p. 32.
4. Richard Cyert and James March, *A Behavioral Theory of the Firm*, p. 39.
5. J. Rex, *Key Problems in Sociological Theory*, Routledge and Kegan Paul, London, 1961, p. 112.
6. Richard Cyert and James March, *A Behavioral Theory of the Firm*, p. 79.
7. Andrew Pettigrew, *The Politics of Organizational Decision-Making*, p. 10.
8. P. Soelberg, 'The Structure of Individual Goals: Implications for Organizational Theory', in G. Fisk (ed.), *The Psychology of Management Decision*, John Wiley, New York, 1963, p. 21.
9. P. Soelberg, 'The Structure of Individual Goals: Implications for Organizational Theory', p. 31.
10. P. Soelberg, 'The Structure of Individual Goals: Implications for Organizational Theory' p. 22.
11. Andrew Pettigrew, *The Politics of Organizational Decision-Making*, p. 22.
12. Yair Aharoni, *The Foreign Investment Decision Process*, Division of Research, Graduate School of Business Administration, Harvard University, Boston, 1966, p. 269.
13. See: Philip Selznick, *Leadership in Administration*, Harper and Row, New York, 1957.
14. Graham Allison, *Essence of Decision*, p. 144.
15. Graham Allison, *Essence of Decision*, p. 145.
16. Graham Allison, *Essence of Decision*, p. 146.
17. Even the author of what might be considered the most far-reaching work on organizational politics in the context of strategic decisions – Andrew Pettigrew – notes that his is intended to be a mere addition to existing approaches to decision-making – notably the Cyert and March work – and not a model which itself attempts to explain overall strategic or policy decisions (see: Andrew Pettigrew. *The Politics of Organizational Decision-Making*. p. XVI and pp. 30–31).
18. Graham Allison, *Essence of Decision*, p. 162.
19. See: Graham Allison, *Essence of Decision*, p. 165.
20. Yair Aharoni, *The Foreign Investment Decision Process*, p. 214.
21. Yair Aharoni, *The Foreign Investment Decision Process*, pp. 32–33.

280

22. Paul Hammond, 'Super-Carriers and B-36 Bombers', in H. Stein (ed.), *American Civil–Military Decisions*, Birmingham, Ala., 1963.
23. William Newman, 'Intra-organization Politics', Graduate School of Business, Columbia University, New York, 1975, p. 7.
24. Yair Aharoni, *The Foreign Investment Decision Process*, p. 213.
25. William Newman and E. Kirby Warren, *The Process of Management* (4th edition), Prentice Hall, Englewood Cliffs, NJ, 1977, p. 422.
26. Yair Aharoni, *The Foreign Investment Decision Process*, Chapter VIII.
27. R. A. Dahl, 'The Concept of Power', *Behavioral Science*, 2, 1957, pp. 201–218.
28. See: Enid Mumford and Andrew Pettigrew, *Implementing Strategic Decisions*, Longman, London, 1975, p. 105.
29. P. M. Blau, *Exchange and Power in Social Life*, John Wiley, New York, 1964.
30. Enid Mumford and Andrew Pettigrew, *Implementing Strategic Decisions*, p. 105.
31. William Newman, 'Intra-organization Politics', pp. 4–5.
32. Graham Allison, *Essence of Decision*, p. 168.
33. Graham Allison, *Essence of Decision*, p. 168.
34. Enid Mumford and Andrew Pettigrew, *Implementing Strategic Decisions*, p. 109.
35. Michel Crozier, *The Bureaucratic Phenomenon*, Tavistock, London, 1964.
36. Enid Mumford and Andrew Pettigrew, *Implementing Strategic Decisions*, p. 110.
37. Enid Mumford and Andrew Pettigrew, *Implementing Strategic Decisions*, p. 105.
38. Graham Allison, *Essence of Decision*, p. 169.
39. Graham Allison, *Essence of Decision*, p. 170.
40. Edmund Learned, Roland Christensen, Kenneth Andrews, William Gurth, *Business Policy* (revised edition), Irwin, Homewood, Ill., 1969, pp. 837–838.
41. See: Graham Allison, *Essence of Decision*, p. 170.
42. Graham Allison, *Essence of Decision*, pp. 170–171.
43. William Newman and E. Kirby Warren, *The Process of Management*, p. 423.
44. See: Yair Aharoni, *The Foreign Investment Decision Process*, Chapter III.
45. See: William Newman, 'Intra-organization Politics', p. 8.
46. William Newman and E. Kirby Warren, *The Process of Management*, p. 425.
47. William Newman and E. Kirby Warren, *The Process of Management*, p. 425.
48. Graham Allison, *Essence of Decision*, p. 177.
49. Graham Allison, *Essence of Decision*, p. 175.
50. Graham Allison, *Essence of Decision*, p. 173.
51. Graham Allison, *Essence of Decision*, p. 177.
52. Graham Allison, *Essence of Decision*, pp. 178–179.
53. Graham Allison, *Essence of Decision*, p. 178.
54. Graham Allison, *Essence of Decision*, p. 175.
55. Graham Allison, *Essence of Decision*, p. 175.
56. Dean Acheson, 'The President and the Secretary of State', in D. Price (ed.), *The Secretary of State*, New York, 1960.
57. See: William Newman and E. Kirby Warren, *The Process of Management*, p. 427.
58. William Newman, 'Intra-organization Politics', p. 12.
59. Graham Allison, *Essence of Decision*, p. 176.
60. William Newman and E. Kirby Warren, *The Process of Management*, p. 421.
61. Graham Allison, *Essence of Decision*, p. 181.
62. Graham Allison, *Essence of Decision*, p. 181.
63. This survey of the literature draws on four principal sources: Andrew Pettigrew, *The Politics of Organizational Decision*-Making, Chapter 2; Graham Allison, *Essence of Decision*, pp. 147–162; Enid Mumford and Andrew Pettigrew, *Implementing Strategic Decisions*, Chapter 5; Michael L. Tushman, 'A Political Approach to Organizations: A Review and Rationale', *Academy of Management Review*, April 1977.

64. Richard Neustadt, *Presidential Power*, John Wiley, New York, 1960.
65. Richard Neustadt, Testimony; US, Congress, Senate, Committee on Government Operations, Subcommittee on National Security and International Operations, *Conduct of National Security Policy*, 89th Congress, 1st Session, 29 June 1965, p. 126.
66. Richard Neustadt, *Presidential Power*, p. 10.
67. Richard Neustadt, Testimony, p. 126.
68. Gabriel Almond, *The American People and Foreign Policy*, 1950.
69. Graham Allison, *Essence of Decision*, p. 153.
70. Charles E. Lindblom, 'Bargaining? The Hidden Hand in Government,' RM-1434-RC, Rand Corporation, 22 February 1955; 'The Science of "Muddling Through" ', *Public Administration Review*, Vol. 19, Spring 1959; *The Intelligence of Democracy*, New York, 1965. See also Charles E. Lindblom and D. Braybrooke, *A Strategy of Decision*, Glencoe, Ill., 1963.
71. Warner Schilling, 'The Politics of National Defense: Fiscal 1950', in W. Schilling, P. Hammond, and G. Snyder, *Strategy, Politics, and Defense Budgets*, New York, 1962.
72. Warner Schilling, 'The Politics of National Defense: Fiscal 1950', in W. Schilling *et al.*, *Strategy, Politics and Defense Budgets*, pp. 21–24.
73. Samuel Huntington, *The Common Defense*, New York, 1961.
74. Samuel Huntington, *The Common Defense*, p. IX.
75. Samuel Huntington, *The Common Defense*, p. 146.
76. Roger Hilsman, *To Move a Nation*, New York, 1967.
77. Roger Hilsman, *To Move a Nation*, p. 553.
78. Roger Hilsman, *To Move a Nation*, p. 554.
79. Roger Hilsman, *To Move a Nation*, pp. 554–555.
80. Roger Hilsman, *To Move a Nation*, p. 561.
81. See: Paul Hammond, 'Directives for the Occupation of Germany', in H. Stein (ed.), *American Civil–Military Decisions*; Paul Hammond, 'Super Carriers and B-36 Bombers', in H. Stein (ed.), *American Civil–Military Decisions*; Paul Hammond, 'NSC-68: Prologue to Rearmament', in W. Schilling *et al.*, *Strategy, Politics and Defense Budgets;* Ernest May, *The World War and American Isolation*, Cambridge, Mass., 1966; Samuel Williamson, *The Politics of Grand Strategy*, Cambridge, Mass., 1969.
82. Graham Allison, *Essence of Decision*, Chapter 5.
83. Graham Allison, *Essence of Decision*, pp. 6–7.
84. Norton Long, 'The Administrative Organization as a Political System', in S. Mailick and E. H. van Ness (eds.), *Concepts and Issues in Administrative Behavior*, Prentice Hall, Englewood Cliffs, NJ, 1962, p. 110.
85. Andrew Pettigrew, *The Politics of Organizational Decision-Making*, p. 16.
86. Such points are made by, among others: T. Burns, 'Micropolitics: Mechanisms of Institutional Change', *Administrative Science Quarterly*, 6(3), 1961, pp. 257–281; and Graham Allison, *Essence of Decision*, p. 146.
87. G. Strauss, 'Tactics of Lateral Relationships: The Purchasing Agent', *Administrative Science Quarterly*, 7, 1962, pp. 161–186.
88. M. Dalton, *Men Who Manage*, John Wiley, New York, 1959.
89. Michel Crozier, *The Bureaucratic Phenomenon*.
90. J. M. Dutton and R. E. Walton, 'Interdepartmental Conflict and Cooperation: Two Contrasting Studies', *Human Organization*, 25(3), 1966, pp. 207–220.
91. Andrew Pettigrew, *The Politics of Organizational Decision-Making*, p. 17.
92. James March and Herbert Simon, *Organizations*, John Wiley, New York, 1958, p. 121.
93. Enid Mumford and Andrew Pettigrew, *Implementing Strategic Decisions*, p. 103.

94. Enid Mumford and Andrew Pettigrew, *Implementing Strategic Decisions*, pp. 103–104.
95. Yair Aharoni, *The Foreign Investment Decision Process*.
96. Joseph Bower, *Managing the Resource Allocation Process*, Division of Research, Graduate School of Business Administration, Harvard University, Boston, 1970.
97. See: Andrew Pettigrew, *The Politics of Organizational Decision-Making*; and Enid Mumford and Andrew Pettigrew, *Implementing Strategic Decisions*.
98. Enid Mumford and Andrew Pettigrew, *Implementing Strategic Decisions*, p. 105.
99. Enid Mumford and Andrew Pettigrew, *Implementing Strategic Decisions*, p. 107.
100. D. Mechanic, 'Sources of Power of Lower Participants in Complex Organizations', *Administrative Science Quarterly*, 7, 1962, p. 352.
101. D Mechanic, 'Sources of Power of Lower Participants in Complex Organizations', p. 356.
102. Abraham Zaleznik, 'Power and Politics in Organizational Life', *Harvard Business Review*, May–June 1970.
103. See: Tom Burns, 'On the Plurality of Social Systems', in J. Lawrence (ed.), *Operational Research and Social Sciences*, Tavistock Publications, London, 1965; and Tom Burns and G. M. Stalker, *The Management of Innovation*, Tavistock Publications, London, 1961.
104. William Newman and E. Kirby Warren, *The Process of Management*, p. 433; see Ian MacMillan, 'The Political System in Business', *Journal of General Management*, Autumn 1973; Ian MacMillan, 'Business Strategies for Political Action', in *Journal of General Management*, Autumn 1974; and Ian MacMillan, *Strategy Formulation: Political Concepts*, West Publishing Co., St Paul, Minnesota, 1978.
105. See William Newman, 'Intra-organization Politics'; and William Newman and E. Kirby Warren, *The Process of Management*, Chapter 20.
106. William Newman, 'Intra-organization Politics', p. 2.

CHAPTER IX

The Players

The relevant players can be classified in three types: in-company individuals, in-government persons, outsiders.

I. IN-COMPANY INDIVIDUALS

We can distinguish six sets of key players.

A. Top management members

This includes the chief executive as well as key individuals at the executive vice-president level. For any major strategic and policy decision, such actors will be involved. It is they who generally have the overall long-term microeconomic welfare of the firm most at heart. Yet, relative to their counterparts in the private sector, they tend to have a greater concern for the 'general interest'. A case in point is Enrico Mattei, ENI's president until his death in 1962. For Mattei, ENI's performance was measurable more in terms of its growth than its profitability. But further, he strove for collective welfare – at least as he perceived it. As an Italian leading figure who knew Mattei well recalled:

> He was convinced he was working for the public good. First, for his country. He felt an obligation to supply Italy with cheaper fuel, which he rightly saw as a key to the national industry's competitiveness. He tried hard to exploit domestic energy sources and to provide employment in backward regions. And he did this without anybody telling him to. In fact, he received considerable criticism for acting in this way – envy for his success and the power (including political power) he achieved by doing so much for the people. Similarly, on the international scene, he was obsessed by the monopoly of the 'seven sisters'. He wanted to break their cartel less for the impact this would have on ENI *per se* than for what he regarded as 'right' in principle. Also, he wanted to give a greater share of the pie to the oil-producing countries because he was convinced that Western nations were injustly exploiting them and that this would inevitably lead to an explosive situation one day or another. And he was right!

The price of this greater social concern is a lesser attention to corporate profitability. As a British executive put it: 'GCEs' leaders are less obsessed by return on investment than their private-sector counterparts'. It is difficult to 'prove' this based on the data available to us;[1] nor does it seem feasible to verify this based on GCEs' financial results, since this would necessitate a basis of comparison which does not exist – a set of GCEs and a valid control group (that is, truly comparable private enterprises).[2] Yet, there is such wide agreement among interviewees (private and public sector executives as well as government officials and outside observers) that this argument can be made with confidence. As a French civil servant said: 'It is not that the *dirigéants* (i.e. high-ranking managers) are less committed to the principles of efficiency in what they choose to do; it is rather that they choose to apply their efforts to other things than just financial returns'. Particularly relevant experiences were those of interviewees in companies recently taken over by the state and who would compare the behaviour of newly government-appointed top managers. As an Italian head planner said: 'Without making any value judgement and leaving aside any consideration about how well he performs in relation to what he chooses to pursue, it is clear that the new boss has other things in his mind than just profits'.

Having said this, we should add a qualification. This argument is mostly relevant for chief executives who come from the government (for example, high-ranking civil servants or prominent political figures) as opposed to coming through the corporate hierarchy. This is what the French refer to as *pantoufler* (literally 'to put one's feet up'). As a civil servant put it: 'A government official, usually with high prestige, becomes head of a company a bit as a reward towards the end of his career'.[3] It further happens that such individuals are named chief executive of a GCE as a way of being put on one side. Apart from certain exceptions, from a managerial point of view, such men tend to be less professional – as reported by a German manager: 'When you have spent all your life in government, you have internalized their inefficiency and you think it is a normal way of life . . . You can't expect such a fellow to be as efficient as a man who spent all his life in a competitive corporate environment'.

Other aspects contribute to the lesser attention given to financial returns. A French interviewee thus said: 'The fact that the government is less dividend-thirsty results in there being a lesser urge for profits'. This inevitably has repercussions on top management's attitudes. Further, the bureaucracy influences management – as noted by an Italian executive:

> Especially when a GCE wants to depart from its existing field of activity, often quite laborious procedures are involved and often nothing happens in terms of governmental approval for a long time. This is discouraging. And it kills the spirit of initiative or entrepreneurship of management. In connection with strategic issues, the first ones to suffer from this are top managers.

GCEs' chief executives themselves often recognize that their propensity to innovate in terms of diversification is blunted by administrative requirements.

Moreover, a certain 'provincialism' can hamper MN expansion. A German interviewee argued:

> Since the majority of the social questions which worry GCEs' management are essentially domestic in scope, many chief executives tend to see national questions more readily than international ones. They are conditioned to think about national issues when they think macro, so even when they think about the company's own strategy they tend to think in domestic terms.

The influence of top management depends primarily on two variables. First, the personality of the player. Again, Mattei is a good illustration:

> A fighting company like ENI, commanded by a dominant personality like Signor Mattei does not readily accept any form of outside supervision. Indeed, it seems nowadays that the bosses of great public enterprises often operate with greater personal freedom of decision than the typical head of the big corporation in private industry. Few of them, however, have carried the method of personal rule to such lengths as Signor Mattei did in ENI. He worked on the *condottiere* principle: he had been handed a fief to look after and he saw it as his task to enlarge its power and extent wherever possible – if at the expense of rivals, so much the better.[4]

Indeed, Mattei's influence was extremely high not only in areas falling within the scope of his attributions but also in issues with which he *a priori* had little to do – particularly political questions. Beyond Mattei who is a bit of an extreme case, other chief executives' personality and credentials call for very high respect and power. As the Chairman of Aer Lingus Patrick Lynch pointed out: 'Such individuals sometimes have such experience and personal standing that their opinion carries more weight than that of government officials who formally are to supervise GCEs'.

Second, the issue under consideration: in decisions involving primarily questions concerning the company alone, top management's influence is generally quite high; in decisions involving important questions of collective interest, the influence of others is higher and thus top management's lower. Therefore if an investment decision does not stir the interest of other players – notably in government – management's discretion is high. If the decision is of concern to others, influence has to be shared. This should become clear shortly.

B. Executives immediately below top management

In a functional organization these are functional heads. Executives at this level tend to get involved in most MN decisions since their field of responsibility is relevant for almost any project of strategic importance. Thus, it is not conceivable that a foreign investment be made without, say, the finance or marketing vice-presidents being consulted. As a production vice-president commented: 'In this type of company, things are so interrelated that over and beyond the formal responsibilities of each person, any major decision inevitably calls all functions into play'.

In a divisionalized organization, these players are division managers. Here a strategic decision may well have no relevance for particular divisions: a proposed investment for a given division may well be of no interest for the head of another division. On the other hand, the manager of the division to which the proposal applies is usually a critical element in the decision process.

Relative to top management, such executives tend to have less of a global perception of the strategic and policy problems of the total enterprise. The functional vice-president will inevitably have somewhat of a specialist's view and tend to treat questions falling outside of his field a bit lightly. And the division head will tend to foster the development of his division to the detriment of other parts of the enterprise. Therefore, if his division's activity is such that there are few chances for it to witness an MN development, a manager will often take a negative stance on MN expansion in general. Further, the tendency to have less of a global view of things is also reflected in these managers' frequent lesser concern for macro issues (especially functional heads).

Again, the personality of such managers has a determining role in their influence. In certain instances, say, a division head can accept being almost 'ordered' to accomplish a certain decision. (Yet, these are rare instances – as noted by a Belgian interviewee: 'A man who has made it to this level is usually a strong individual; he will not accept merely carrying out a decision without having participated in the decision-making itself'.) At the other end, certain executives are so strong that they are able to impose their views to top management.

An individual's influence also varies from one strategic decision to the other. If the issue is whether to set up a fully owned sales subsidiary in a given country or not, a production vice-president will clearly have lesser influence than a marketing vice-president. And we saw that a division head is vitally concerned by projects involving his own division.

A special case is the international division.* 'The head of such a division', said a German executive, 'tends to be less provincial; he is less concerned with national macroeconomic and social issues; he is more open to the outside world'. Indeed, his seat shapes his priorities and perceptions: he generally takes a favourable stance *vis-à-vis* MN expansion.

The international vice-president's influence over MN decisions is often considerable. The existence of such a division means that the rest of the organization is primarily geared to domestic operations: were the company's overall operations involved in MN activities, there would normally be a 'global structure' (that is, a structure providing for all organizational units operating on an MN scale).[5] Few GCEs indeed have reached this stage. In a firm where there is

*Such a division can exist either in a functional or in a divisionalized organization.

an international division as such, the international vice-president is the 'expert' for MN issues. He therefore carries considerable weight. This is especially so when other key actors have limited familiarity with MN questions. Thus, if the chief executive has little international experience, the international vice-president may have greater *de facto* power than top management. It follows that his influence is greatest in the early years of the division's life – when the rest of management has had no chance to develop international experience of its own.

C. Board members

Board members[6] are clearly concerned by strategy and policy decisions, though in practice there are considerable variations in their influence. They can be classified in five categories.

1. *Company executives*

These persons take an active stance on issues of concern to them, and their position as board members is the same as the one they take as managers. In certain cases, an individual at odds with management on an issue can swing the majority of the board towards his position and thus force management to alter its plans. Yet, these are rare instances: most often a board member who is also a company executive will have fought for his position before the issue comes before the board; only when he has not been successful will he try again at the board level. What does happen somewhat more commonly is that an executive is instrumental in bringing a hesitant board to take a positive stand on a proposal. While a board usually does not actually turn down a plan presented by management, it can challenge particular aspects. A board member can then try and convince the board to go along with management's original plan.

2. *Government people (for example, high-ranking civil servants)*

Many corporate issues are of little relevance for such individuals and they have limited influence on them in practice. Their main concerns lie in decisions with a bearing on macro issues – particularly those directly relevant to their special field of interest within government. Thus, a person responsible for regional development will become active in decisions concerning, say, new plant investments. In such instances, his influence can be sizeable especially if the rest of the board does not feel strongly one way or the other. Yet, a person does not usually wait until an issue reaches the board level to make his position known. He often can exert more influence as a government official than as a board member.

3. *Executives of other companies – especially other GCEs*

The primary characteristics of such men is their interest in corporate affairs as they relate to their own company's activity. For example, an executive of a steel company sitting on the board of a car manufacturer may be concerned that the company buy from his own firm. Or the president of a shipyard may try to exert influence on an oil company to cause it to order ships from his yard. And one company reported that it decided to locate a plant in a particular country because the enterprise of one of its board members was already there and needed the company's orders to reach a profitable level of sales. But, as our interviewee said: 'The fact that the man was on our board was not really a determining factor. Particularly between GCEs, there are other ways to exert influence from one top management to the other'.

4. *Worker representatives*

In several countries, company employees elect members of the board.[7] They are of course primarily concerned with issues having a bearing on workers' lives – salaries and other forms of compensation, fringe benefits, working conditions, vacations, etc. And they can influence investment decisions. Thus, worker representatives may fight against foreign plants for fear this might reduce the domestic job offerings. A good illustration is the Volkswagen plant in the US: for years, the possibility of building cars in the US was contemplated, the high point of the issue being in the early mid-1970s. When management and stockholders' representatives were most convinced about the desirability of the plant, worker representatives played a key role in opposing the plan. As we will see, however, here also the authority as board members does not come alone, worker representatives having other powerful means of exerting influence.

5. *Other outsiders (for example, prominent academics)*

Such people do not *a priori* have special interests as far as GCEs' strategic and policy behaviour is concerned as a result of their outside position. They therefore tend to be more objective albeit less determined to defend their stances.

Thus, a board member is rarely concerned by all strategy and policy issues confronted by the firm. Except perhaps for outsiders, board members' interests tend to be limited. For any one decision, few, if any, board members usually get involved and even then focus on certain aspects only. Since other board members often do not feel strongly about the issue, an individual member taking a strong stance frequently can convince others to back his position were it only by default – by not opposing his view. Yet, it is worth repeating that in practice the real influence of the board *per se* is usually rather limited, individuals typically exerting power via channels related to their roles beyond that of board members.

D. Key staffers

These are persons attached to high-ranking executives. Their influence is indirect; they have no real formal say in decisions and their power stems from the influence they can exert on other players with authority. Staffers can be classified in two sets.

1. *General staffers*

These take part in the elaboration of an overall strategic and policy plan. The best instance is corporate planners, who are often responsible for specifically framing problems and alternatives and who have the most detailed knowledge of projects or programmes.

General staffers tend to have fewer outside concerns than the executives to whom they report, and their attention is more specifically geared to micro issues. A corporate planner said:

> Top managers in general have a host of outside issues competing for their attention. Whether they like it or not, they can't help being involved in a variety of questions not strictly related to the company's life, which either involve explicit claims for the company's behaviour or are simply distracting and bias top managers' view of corporate problems and distort their perceptions. In a sense, I see planners' role as that of correcting or at least tempering the effect of such distortions. We are not exposed to so many outside claims and we can therefore focus more objectively on questions strictly concerning the company.

By analysing strategic problems and formulating proposals, staffers shape the thinking of top managers. One planner said: 'Even when we are not asked to make an explicit recommendation, the tone of our reports and the relative emphasis it gives to positive and negative arguments has an influence on top management's judgement of an issue'. Having said this, the typical problem of staffers is how to get an issue on an action channel; while they can have influence over top management if top management listens, the difficulty for them is precisely in getting top management's attention. When an issue is first raised by a top manager and then handed over to staffers for analysis, then the position staffers take has a fair chance of being listened to and their influence can be significant. But when they attempt to raise an issue on their own, they have to fight hard for top management's attention.

2. *Specialized staffers*

These are people with narrower fields of responsibility. They include management-oriented people (for example, finance specialists), technical people as well as men such as lawyers. They intervene on a spot basis as their field of competence is required.

These individuals tend to have parochial concerns. A chief executive said:

> These men tend to see their area as the key of a strategy's success. Lawyers in particular have a tendency of seeing everything through the perspective of their own field of interest. They typically exaggerate the importance of the legal aspects of a plan and often force us to

> spend excessive time on such questions. I have a particular case in mind in which a lawyer nearly caused us to miss an attractive joint venture opportunity because the proposed legal format was in his view imperfect. I think the impact of this imperfection was minimal. Yet, he nearly convinced us that the whole deal was bad because of it.

The influence of specialized staffers varies according to their personal indispensability. If a man's competences are such that he can be readily replaced by another individual with equivalent qualifications, his impact on strategic and policy behaviour is likely to be rather limited. If, on the contrary, a decision hinges upon specialized knowledge which top management does not have, then the one who has this knowledge will have sizeable influence.[8] On the whole, there are relatively few strategic and policy decisions in this case.

E. Managers in the field

Operating people can also have an indirect influence over strategic and policy decisions. They can identify and propose opportunities (for example, a manager of a foreign subsidiary proposing the acquisition of a local enterprise).

Such persons' concerns usually revolve around their own sphere of activity. Thus, a manager of a foreign plant will see opportunities in the country in which he works. In consequence, they rarely have a strategic view of issues and the proposals they come up with, while often attractive from an opportunistic point of view, frequently lack 'strategic fit'. Still, the addition of their influences often does have an impact on the firm's strategic posture; indeed, many companies' field of activity is shaped in great part through the agglomeration of the various projects proposed by operating management.[9]

F. Implementers

These include all those whose job is such that if performed in one way and not another, can affect the success or failure of a strategy. By distorting, misinterpreting or omitting an aspect of a plan, say, a line manager can jeopardize the entire success of a plan. Further, key technical people can be critical. For instance, an interviewee reported:

> Five years ago local authorities compelled us to hire local technicians in our [an LDC] plant. Things worked OK for a while because we didn't have to change much in our manufacturing processes. But when we decided to use a new process (which we were already using domestically) for a new product to launch locally, we ran into problems. Specifically, we found out after the fact that our local people had misinterpreted certain specifications and simply ignored others. In particular, they had used certain pipes whose thickness was

not sufficient. As a consequence, we had several breakdowns and we ultimately had to revamp our entire manufacturing process rebuilding an installation virtually from scratch. Beyond the obvious costs this entailed, we suffered from a setback which delayed our launching of the product. This had serious consequences for our market penetration; ultimately, our overall success with the product was threatened.

These players are quite diverse in their position and personality. Their traits, attitudes and aspirations are too different to allow meaningful generalizations. In common they typically have an ill-awareness of the 'spirit' or significance of their task as it related to the 'big picture' which may cause them to act in a way which is inconsistent with the overall plan being followed.

Their actions are not generally in themselves truly strategic. Yet, such 'details' can often have an important bearing on a strategy's success or failure. The players' influence follows this: they have little bearing on the decision making *per se*; still, they can have considerable influence on the company's actual behaviour: by ineptly handling a key – though often small – task, they can significantly transform the strategy from that which was originally planned.

G. In sum

The in-company players we just surveyed are, at least potentially, in conflict with each other. Individuals' parochial perceptions and priorities lead them to fight for their own concerns which are sometimes complementary but often are competing. Such conflict occurs both vertically and horizontally. Horizontally, in a functional organization, say, the marketing vice-president will have a different view on a proposed plan than, say, the production vice-president. In a divisionalized organization, the head of one division will often more or less subconsciously have a negative bias against an expansion plan for one division which he sees as competing with possible expansion programmes for his own division. And at lower echelons, players also fight with each other. Staffers are often in conflict with staffers of other parts of the organization. Vertically, top managers clearly have a different perspective than lower level players. Thus, the chief executive will be primarily concerned with the overall results of the company and will be willing to sacrifice a unit's performance somewhat if this is a necessary cost to significantly improve the performance of the whole. But the person responsible for it will fight as hard as he can to improve the performance of his own unit.

II. IN-GOVERNMENT INDIVIDUALS

These are members of the executive as well as the legislative body of civil servants. There are six categories of players here.

A. The sponsoring minister

For each GCE there is a member of the executive formally responsible for it. His actual influence varies. Sometimes his involvement in company decisions is limited. He can confine himself to recording results and management's decisions and actions, particularly when a GEC is financially autonomous (that is, not dependent on government financial assistance) and when the decisions to be taken are not of much concern to him or other key members of government. Yet, on the whole, his influence is deeper – as noted by a French interviewee: 'It is quite possible that a sponsoring minister remain outside of some very important decisions. But to say that he stays out of strategy completely is generally wrong. A strategy is developed over time and several key decisions are involved. It is inevitable that the minister becomes active at one point or another'. And indeed, in some cases, the sponsoring minister can actually be vitally involved in most strategic and policy decisions.

There are in fact two main types of sponsoring ministries. In some cases, the range of responsibilities is broad and includes a great variety of questions beyond GCEs. Thus in France, most GCEs are accountable to the 'Ministère de l'Economie et des Finances' which is responsible for the entire economic and financial policies of the country.[10] In other cases, the sponsoring minister's scope is much narrower. Thus, in Italy there is a ministry – for state holdings – whose sole responsibility is to monitor GCEs (and, in fact, not even all of them).

The position of the 'limited responsibility' minister makes him more sensitive to GCEs' behaviour. Of course, such a player is involved in a variety of games – both in government *per se* and outside. But his formal responsibilities call on him to focus principally on GCEs. Therefore, he is encouraged to be active in their decisions.

By contrast, the function of a 'broad responsibility' minister leads him to worry principally about problems which are broader in scope than just GCEs. 'For a man responsible for the economic affairs of a nation, it is clear that the behaviour of a GCE is not the number one concern', said a French interviewee. He really intervenes in two kinds of instances only. On the one hand, when a GCE has a problem – either economic or other difficulties. Thus, a French high-ranking civil servant said: 'Take Renault. The sponsoring minister will stay out of company affairs as long as it does OK financially and as long as there is social peace outside of Paris [that is, no labour unrest in Renault's plants which are mostly at the outskirts of Paris].' On the other hand, the minister will step in when he sees the possibility of using a GCE for a particular aim he pursues (for example, if, as part of his economic policy he wants to promote the industrialization of a particular area, he may ask a GCE to invest there; or he may use a GCE for more personal aims).

Vis-à-vis MN expansion the attitude of a 'broad responsibility' minister tends to be relatively negative. Albeit there may be certain questions involving foreign nations, his concerns are primarily national – at least those having relevance for GCEs. Thus, unemployment can push the finance minister to encourage GCEs to increase their job offerings; or inflation can result in pressure for GCEs to delay price increases. Of course, there are exceptions. Thus, a minister may ask a GCE to invest in a particular country 'with which – in a German interviewee's terms – we have particular economic interests'. But these are, on the whole, rare instances. (In fact, what happens more frequently is intervention in MN policy decisions; thus, pressure on the national currency may cause a minister to ask GCEs, say, to delay foreign payments and accelerate repatriation of foreign earnings.) 'The national character of his preoccupations and duties causes the minister to have a negative bias *vis-à-vis* foreign investments by GCEs', said a company president. Still, this negative attitude is often not very significant in fact; because of their multiple other concerns, ministers tend on the whole, to stay out of company decisions – including MN decisions. A good illustration is Germany. Reportedly, especially under the Adenauer and Erhard Administrations, the government and the finance and economics ministers in particular had a *laissez-faire* attitude. As a chief executive recalled: 'In those days at least, there were very few interventions by government. We were doing well, so they had nothing to worry about as far as we were concerned. We were free in our investment decisions, including, where appropriate, foreign investments'.

The 'limited responsibility' minister is in principle less exposed to concerns biasing his views in a national sense. Yet, this is compensated by his *de facto* exposure to other issues diverting his attention from results of GCEs *per se*: while his formal attributions make him responsible for GCEs' results alone (or, at least, mainly so), he in practice is confronted with a host of other pressures. On the one hand, quite explicitly other influential players (for example, other members of the Cabinet) may press for GCEs to pursue certain actions. On the other, the minister tends to be 'co-opted unobtrusively', as an Italian interviewee said, 'i.e. by being part of the government he is exposed to the sociopolitical and economic turmoil; he therefore cannot retain his objectivity, and his behaviour as guardian of GCEs reflects these biases'. By being part of the government, the minister has to espouse the concerns fo the government at large and not merely those pertaining strictly to his post. This is a point of fundamental importance for any minister: 'We are all part of the same boat', said a minister, 'one cannot just worry about what is best from the point of view of your own mission; one has to worry about what is best for the cabinet as a whole, because if the cabinet does poorly you go down the drain with it'. Indeed, each minister has to be sensitive to the problems of his colleagues – their aims and needs. Therefore, a sponsoring minister's attitude *vis-à-vis* GCEs' MN expansion is not as 'neutral' as his formal job description would suggest *prima facie*. If he is subjected to a variety of demands for GCEs' actions by others (which will inevitably be mostly domestic, as we will see below), his own position on MN expansion will tend to be negative.

The power of sponsoring ministers can be high. It stems from their formal authority – it is they who officially represent the 'owner'. Yet, in practice, a number of factors put limits on this. First, ministers are often busy with things other than GCEs competing for their attention. Further, their attention on GCEs tends to be focused on certain issues only (particularly 'broad responsibility' ministers tend to involve themselves in company decisions only when they see this as helping them in the games vitally relevant to them). Moreover, having several GCEs to monitor, they must be selective in the issues in which they involve themselves. Even more importantly, their generally short tenure in their job does not allow ministers to become acquainted in much depth with the relevant 'dossiers', as the French say – the specific problems concerning GCEs. As a result, their power is erratic: on certain classes of decisions of particular concern to them, they actively become involved and thus can exert authority; in others, they take little interest and thus have limited impact.

B. The head of the executive

Formally, this is the highest authority: while GCEs' managements report to the sponsoring minister, he himself is accountable to the chief of the executive. This person can be the prime minister. This is the case in most EEC countries which either have a president with essentially honorary functions (such as Italy or Germany) or no president at all (such as the U.K.). Or the chief of the executive can be the president – where he is elected by popular vote. This is notably the case in France.[11]

The head of the executive intervenes in GCEs' decisions in special cases only – when a GCE has a major problem or when there is a major political, economic or social question involving a GCE. This is similar to the role played by the sponsoring minister. Yet, there is a difference in degree, the head of the executive intervening but in exceptional instances. For example, when the government pursues a particular policy *vis-à-vis* a given foreign country, the head of the executive may welcome GCEs' involvement in that country and he may supplement the pressure the sponsoring minister exerts in this connection. Another case is that of, say, the prime minister intervening to back the claims of a third member of government: if he feels one of his ministers is right in asking for a given action by a GCE, then he may exert authority for that action to occur. For example, in one case, the energy minister felt that a particular GCE should have invested in a given OPEC country because this would have helped relations with that country. The prime minister agreed. He thus stepped in and made sure the company invested in that country.

The power of the head of the executive is comparable to that of sponsoring ministers – especially 'broad responsibility' ministers. The head of the executive has in principle ultimate power. In practice, however, since he rarely exerts his authority, his impact on GCEs' behaviour is more limited. Again, the causes are competing foci of attention and limited time to become sufficiently familiar with the details of the issues confronting GCEs.

C. Other ministers

Formally, other members of the cabinet have no direct authority over GCEs. Yet, indirectly, they can have a bearing on their behaviour.

There are a number of ministers who can have a stake in GCEs – the ministers of finance, economic affairs (when they are not sponsoring ministers), the budget, industry, labour, energy, depressed regions, foreign affairs, trade, etc. Each has special concerns of his own and his interest in GCEs is limited to those questions related to these concerns. Say, for instance the labour minister is interested in GCEs primarily in so far as they can contribute to solve national unemployment problems. Or the economic minister focuses on GCEs' contribution to his policies (for example, sectorial policies of one kind or another). And they can play a role in MN decisions. For example, in one case the finance minister was anxious to improve the country's access to sources of bauxite; he thus endeavoured to develop better ties with Guinea, which resulted in several GCEs becoming involved in that country (or, at least, developing closer trade relationships with it). Further, the minister for foreign affairs is concerned with whether GCEs add to or detract from his policies *vis-à-vis* foreign nations. Thus, he will often oppose investments in certain countries (such as Chile) and be in favour of investments in others (for example, ex-colonies with which the government wants to maintain friendly relations). He can also be concerned by operating policy decisions. For example, one executive reported that some years ago 'the foreign affairs minister had asked the company to act in a way to engender labour problems in a foreign subsidiary with a view to creating difficulties locally so as to contribute to the downfall of the government and facilitate the coming into power of another group of men'. And several ministers are naturally opposed to MN expansion because they see in it a lessening of the chances for them to advance their own cause (e.g. the minister for depressed regions worrying that foriegn expansion will reduce companies' commitment to backward areas).

The power of such ministers cannot be exercised via formal channels. Rather, they have to exert influence via persons who themselves have a direct say in corporate affairs – management or members of the executive (for example, the sponsoring minister). The latter in particular are instrumental because the issues raised by ministers are of concern to these members of the executive as well. For example, if the labour minister argues in favour of investments by GCE to alleviate unemployment problems, the sponsoring minister, if he is, say, the finance minister, will be sensitive to the labour minister's point of view. Further, 'one minister's problem is other ministers' problem too', as an interviewee put it; if a particular minister faces a problem which is serious enough that it might constitute a threat for the entire government (or simply weaken its political standing), the motivations of the sponsoring minister will be high to try and help the minister. Further, it may happen that the minister having the problem cannot convince the sponsoring minister to cause the relevant GCE to help him; the minister may then go to the head of the executive and try and persuade him to intervene in the GCE's decisions and actions.

D. Major political figures

Up to now we have dealt with members of the executive. Such individuals have either direct authority over GCEs or have ready access to and often high ascendancy over actors with such authority. Here we turn to actors who are part of the legislative body, who have often considerable influence by virtue of their political stature, personal credibility and standing. Two major sets of players should be considered.

1. *Players who are part of the parliamentary majority*

These individuals are concerned with issues related to their own electorate. Thus, a congressman will be interested in the development of his constituency. This may lead him to fight for industrial investments in his region. Further, these players may take certain stances *vis-à-vis* certain issues of general interest in view of their convictions or interests (that is socioeconomic beliefs as well as political and personal aims and aspirations).

These players' influence can be exerted in four basic ways.

(1) As MPs they can vote against or in favour of governmental policies. While being on the same side of government generally makes them refrain from actually voting against government policies as a whole, they may propose amendments – often quite relevant ones.

(2) Via parliamentary commissions – when a particular problem arises, a commission may be formed to investigate it. Such commissions can have considerable power in practice. For example, in 1976 questions arose about the fiscal integrity of French aircraft manufacturers and a commission was formed to look into the matter: 'These men are *de facto* quite influential and can cause certain decisions to be taken virtually unilaterally', said an industry executive. Yet, influence channelled via these commissions is by necessity circumscribed to certain very specfic questions.

(3) Certain major political figures are able to put 'their men' at the head of GCEs. The best instances are found in Italy – as reported by one interviewee: 'Over time, certain notables of the major political parties have been successful in causing men of their own choice and devoted to them to occupy key positions in GCEs'. In particular, certain leaders of the Christian Democratic Party such as Amintore Fanfani have placed their 'faithfuls' in the commanding posts of GCEs. As a major Italian political figure said.: 'Such men owe everything to their political "fathers" who put them where they are. While it does happen that the "protégé" acquiring his own power gives signs of wanting to fly with his own wings, on the whole, he remains faithful to his godfather and complies as far as possible with his wishes'.

(4) Through bargaining with influential individuals – a politician may cause a GCE to take certain actions by exerting pressure over players with power – management, in-government players with authority over GCEs or other major political figures who themselves have ways of influencing GCEs. A politician may convince such a player, say, by promising him support in a game of his own. Thus, he may agree to an exchange of favours: in return for causing a GCE to undertake a certain action, he can promise that he will provoke certain events

in an area in which he has power and in which his interlocutor has little or none. Or he may agree to share the benefits he expects to reap from a given action by a GCE with the one who caused the action. This is most relevant in the context of actions expected to yield returns of a rather 'personal' kind. Again, the best instances are Italian. For example, a politician fights for a GCE to build a plant on a given piece of land. Before the acquisition of the land by the company, he buys the land himself or causes it to be bought by some 'friendly and faithful' investors. He then causes the land to be resold to the company at a healthy premium. To convince management to go along with this, he may promise to share the profits with it.

2. *Players who are part of the opposition*

They too can be concerned with issues directly tied to their electorate as well as with more general interest issues. The latter are especially noteworthy: beyond personal convictions and interests, an opposition member may criticize the action of government systematically, that is, detraction of government's actions for the very sake of criticism in view of political ends.

The concerns of opposition members depend on whether they are conservatives or leftists. Conservatives have typically been opposed to the development of the public sector. When in opposition, they usually try and stop nationalization projects or the creation of new GCEs (see for example, the Tories' attitude since they left power in 1974). When the Left is in the opposition, typically it is critical of the government for allegedly trying to hinder the growth and development of GCEs. Thus, in the UK under the Heath Administration, members of the Labour Party accused the government of limiting the opportunities of certain GCEs. A case in point is air transport: the government was accused of favouring the development of privately owned airlines to the detriment of British Airways (or its predecessors BEA or BOAC). Similarly in France, the Left accuses the government of allowing GCEs to serve the interests of 'private monopolies'. Leftists feel that GCEs accept unreasonably high subcontracting proposals from private firms, that they supply goods and services to private firms at unreasonably low prices, that they deliberately leave lucrative markets to private enterprises. Leftists ask that GCEs be used instead to serve collective interests – alleviate unemployment, build needed infrastructures, schools, hospitals, etc.

In terms of GCEs' MN expansion, the conservatives' overall negative attitude about the public sector can have two types of effects. On the one hand, it can be a hindrance: if growth *per se* is opposed, MN growth will also suffer. But often the opposition to growth is in practice limited to domestic expansion. In such instances, MN expansion can even benefit – as argued by David Kennedy, chief executive of Aer Lingus: 'If you can't grow at home, you go abroad. Hindrances to domestic growth result indirectly in stimuli to grow internationally'. Leftists' attitude is usually a hindrance to MN expansion. By calling for specific domestic investments, they limit the expansion possibilities abroad.

The influence of such individuals can also be exerted via parliamentary interventions (although a proposal by an opposition member has fewer chances of obtaining the necessary backing precisely because his party is in the minority and that majority members of parliament are less likely to back it). They can also exert influence via membership in parliamentary commissions (which more often than not include members of the opposition). And members of the opposition can also exert influence via bargaining and their personal standing. Although their not being part of a governing party reduces their bargaining power considerably, opposition members often have sizeable influence of their own. For example, Enrico Berlinguer, Italy's Communist Party leader – without actually sharing power in the government, his party's support in parliament is essential to the Christian Democratic Cabinet.[12] 'Thus, his power is high since the government is dependent on him for its survival', said an Italian interviewee. Further, his credibility is high – as noted by another Italian: 'He benefits from the doubt of he who hasn't officially been in power and hasn't had to face the test of reality – tackling the real problems of the country. Also, not having been in power has kept him somewhat further away from the temptations of corruption. He can claim he has clean hands'. And a GCE chief executive said: 'His influence is truly great. If he really wants us to do something, the *government* makes us do it'.

E. Staffers

These players are attached to the politicians for whom they work. They share their boss's concerns. Yet, their focus is often different. While their boss is usually busy in a multitude of games and spends considerable time actually playing such games (that is, arguing in the political arena about issues, participating in official forums, investing in public relations, etc.), they have both fewer issues to worry about and fewer external obligations and thus more time to spend on analysis of issues. Therefore, their treatment of issues tends to be deeper. At the same time, they are less action-oriented. Their task is to advise politicians and provide them with information, analysis and recommendations on key issues. In fact, they are often responsible for identifying issues. Political staffers in particular are to raise issues which they see as critical for their boss's political game – his electoral standing as well as the partisan or factional intrigues within his party or with other parties. For example, they may raise the issue of nationalizing companies in a given sector because of the requirements they see their boss to have in his political strategy. Then, they will devise specific action plans and produce arguments to show why the nationalizations are indispensable.

Each politician has a particular set of staffers in a variety of areas. There are technical staffers with responsibility in specialized fields (such as military staffers and, more specifically, say, navy or air force staffers). And there are political staffers who focus on their boss's standing *vis-à-vis* his electorate and on his position relative to other politicians – allies or opponents.

Staffers fight against each other. A staffer attached to one politician fights with a staffer attached to another politician. For example, within a cabinet, staffers of the labour minister fight with staffers of the finance or economics ministers: the former may fight for expansionary policies to solve his employment problem, while the latter will emphasize anti-inflationary policies. And staffers attached to the same politician fight with each other. Technical staffers focus on what they see as best in view of the outcome of the issue *per se*, while political staffers tend to use the issue in view of political ends – fight for a given outcome, say, for the electoral dividends it might yield.

Staffers focus and fight on GCEs. They raise technical questions about them and since they are the object of not infrequently heated political debate, they worry about them from a political viewpoint. In general, those who are most concerned with GCEs' economic performance tend to be inclined to see and support the arguments in favour of MN expansion. On the other hand, those attached to a politician concern primarily with general socioeconomic questions are frequently led to take a negative stance on MN expansion: their concern for macro kinds of issues directs them to fight for GCEs committing themselves at home rather than abroad. Thus, the staffers of a minister for economic affairs will commonly fight for a GCE to invest domestically, say, in a depressed region. This is all the more so for political staffers. Given their concern for the electorate, they always tend to be on the watch for potential opportunities for which their boss could publicly fight, which he can argue would benefit the electorate; such opportunities are naturally mostly domestic.

The influence of staffers can be sizeable. Because they are generally responsible for raising issues and for developing analyses and formulating alternatives, they often have a determining effect on the stands their bosses take. Therefore, the influence they have on GCEs is indirect. This is especially so for issues of which their bosses have little understanding, either due to lack of time to study the issue, or due to a lack of training to have a real grasp of the issue. This is typical of economic issues. Many politicians have little understanding of such problems and vitally depend on their advisers. And for GCEs in particular, many politicians know what outcomes are desirable from the point of view of their aims in the political game they play, but – as an Italian interviewee said: 'They have often no idea what implications this has from the economic viewpoint or what it takes from a managerial viewpoint'.

F. Civil servants

Up to this point we have focused on players who position is directly or indirectly attached to the political situation of the moment. This is clear for elected politicians. The same is true for non-elected cabinet members who are dependent on the choice of other politicians who themselves are elected. And staffers are dependent on their boss's fate. Such individuals, therefore occupy their position for an often rather short period of time. Further, they are frequently vulnerable and their fortunes can change quickly and unexpectedly. By contrast, civil servants have much longer tenure and job stability, which determines their attitudes and perceptions.

There is a wide variety of civil servants concerned with GCEs (for example, planning agencies, industrial development agencies, agencies for energy, central banks, etc.). Each has special interests. Thus, industrial planners are particularly interested in GCEs' investment policies. Their primary concern is to formulate development plans by specifying targets for the economy in various sectors and in terms of various parameters (such as economic growth, investment, employment, etc.) and to provide indicative guidelines as to how such targets should be reached. It is clear that GCEs are critical for planners since they can be instrumental for the attainment of planning objectives. Since planners typically overestimate the targets to be reached, they are usually anxious to stimulate incremental economic activity. They are generally eager for GCEs to do more of certain kinds of investments precisely to contribute to their aims. Since most of the plans are domestic, planners normally exert a nationally oriented pressure. Much of the same can be said for other public administrations: their purpose is to foster economic activities of a particular kind or another, or in a particular area; this virtually always involves domestic issues and their representatives therefore exert pressure for national kinds of endeavours.

A particular case can be certain special purpose agencies, say, an agency for energy. Such an organization's purpose may be to promote energy savings and/or develop an energy procurement policy for the country. In this latter instance, the agency's action results, if anything, in an encouragement to invest abroad.

Central bankers' concern for GCEs varies from case to case. Sometimes, their interventions are quite limited. Where the national currency experiences problems such as pressure for a devaluation, a central banker may intervene in the financial policies of GCEs. In other cases, his role can go even further. Particularly in those countries where the government is weak and lacks continuity, the head of the central bank can take upon himself to guide industry in the national interest. Thus, in the Italian case, the governor of the Bank of Italy has traditionally been involved in national planning. In particular, he has been concerned by the investment policies of GCEs. As an Italian interviewee said: 'The governor is omnipresent in our industrial and economic life. Given our cabinets are so short-lived and our administration so inefficient, he personally assumes responsibility for a host of questions which fall outside of his formal attributions'. When he substitutes himself to the executive, he also takes up their concerns towards GCEs' MN expansion: given their concerns tend to be mostly domestic, he tends to foster national growth.

The influence of these players is quite uneven. Some have limited impact on GCEs' strategic and policy decisions, MN decisions in particular. Others have considerable authority. Probably the best example is Italy's former Central Bank governor Guido Carli. Because he enjoyed high credibility based on a reputation of technical competence and personal integrity and because of the lack of individual competition (no other civil servant had his stature and politicians had relatively limited authority in view of their political vulnerability), Carli reached considerable power indeed – as reported by one GCE's president: 'His authority in practice went far beyond his official functions. Carli at one point was in a position to exert influence on a wide variety of GCEs' activities. He was so much listened to that even when he had no formal way of exerting authority, he could often make his weight felt by merely expressing his "opinion" '.

G. In sum

In-government persons clearly have differing stands on a variety of issues and thus are constantly at least potentially in conflict with each other. We should re-emphasize the specific traits of politicians. Given their dependence on the electoral mood and the generally relatively short time they spend in their position (they rarely occupy a function for more than a few years without having to fight for a reconfirmation of their mandate, generally via an electoral consultation), they exhibit three related characteristics in their stands: they impose a high discount rate on expected outcomes, that is, they have a short-term horizon in terms of the results to which they are sensitive; they seek visible results, that is, they give highest priority to results which can be readily pointed to and exploited politically and electorally; and they take an often partisan view of things, in other words, their stands are not as objective as their position would require and they reflect biases stemming from factional struggles. These players' primary concern is most often to act in a way that will help them first to retain their own position. This, in fact, tends to be a necessity: they often cannot take a long-term view, since if they do not show results in the short term, they will not have the opportunity to pursue long-term ends.

A typical case is the cause of employment – creating jobs either on a national level or in a particular region. This is conducive to politicians pressing GCEs to grow domestically. While this may result in the short run in benefits in terms of the unemployment problem and in 'spectacular' effects (that is, tangible and visible results which are therefore politically helpful), over the long term this may be detrimental for the company and as a consequence for the cause of employment *per se*: exaggerated investments in labour-intensive undertakings may strain the company, and insistence on domestic investments and refusal to produce abroad may result in the loss of foreign markets, and this may in turn hurt domestic job opportunities themselves.[13] Yet, labour ministers commonly fight for short-term national expansion without paying much attention to what this might do over the years; ministers for trade often push for higher exports today and for delaying foreign investments to solve their immediate problem of a weakening currency; the finance minister will also have to indulge in short-term actions – for example, he may have to make concessions on the wages front even if this contradicts, say, an anti-inflation policy, lest unrest develops which would undermine this very policy; even a prime minister frequently has to support short-term partisan causes to preserve both his cabinet's internal cohesion and its outside (parliamentary as well as popular) support; and congressmen bargain for investments in their own region with little concern for whether this is reasonable either from the company or the national viewpoint. Probably, the most paradoxical situation is that of the sponsoring minister. He is officially responsible for monitoring GCEs' behaviour in a global, general interest sense; yet, political realities cause him to take an often quite myopic approach to decisions; and the one whose formal position would require an objective perspective is often among the most partisan of players involved in the decision process.

Thus, in-government players tend to hinder MN expansion: their interests and concerns lead them to focus mostly on national questions; and these three characteristics cause them to push for domestic growth.

III. OUTSIDERS

Three types of players should be discussed.

A. Union leaders

Here we focus on unionists outside the formal structure of the company (that is, not part of, say the board of directors).

At the risk of oversimplifying, we can for our purpose, distinguish between two broad classes of unionists: first, 'reformist' unionists who accept the free enterprise system. Their prime concern is less political struggle as true, tangible improvements in workers' conditions – wages, social benefits, holidays, working conditions, etc. Second, 'revolutionary' unionists. These men have the same kinds of preoccupations, but in addition they fight the system. They tend to be of Marxist obedience and they are generally an arm of the Communist Party, the doctrine of which they espouse. Their worries tend to include rather more global issues. In countries such as France or Italy, in particular, they take an active interest in a wide variety of problems: the government's socioeconomic and financial policies, companies' investment policies, macro industrial planning questions among others. While they do so in view of what they see as the interests of the working classes, their attitude always has political overtones.

Unionists tend to have a particularly exacting attitude *vis-à-vis* GCEs: 'They somehow feel they can squeeze more out of these companies', said a prominent civil servant. And a French interviewee said: 'If they want to push a given claim they know they have to get it through the public sector first. Then the rest of industry will follow. If they can't get their way with GCEs, there is little chance they will make it in the private sector'.

On the whole, they oppose GCEs' MN expansion. They see in foreign investments an opportunity cost in terms of domestic employment (foreign production taking the place of production which might be done at home). In so doing they do not see or do not want to see the long-term consequences – the same as discussed above for the company and indirectly for the country and the workers. The reasons for this myopia are a blend of ideological motives and political necessities.

The ideological motives are a conscious choice of working against the system – as one interviewee put it: 'It is a deliberately negative and nihilist attitude to weaken the system, an attitude which is part of an overall communist strategy to bring the present system to a standstill and force a Marxist system to replace it'. Clearly, this attitude is strongest with 'revolutionary' unionists. While this type of hard line has traditionally characterized Marxists – unionists as well as politicians – there have been recent signs of greater pragmatism. Still, leftist unionists have unquestionably used the practice of creating unrest – particularly in the public sector – to weaken the government and the political (and electoral) standing of the ruling parties. Besides, the more radical union leaders often occupy key posts in the Communist Party. Their union action clearly contributes to their advancement in the political game they play.

Hindering GCEs' MN expansion is part of this attitude. Moreover, opposing MN expansion is consistent with many Marxists' nationalistic attitude. The French communists, especially, have stood for 'national independence' – a notion not devoid of autarchic overtones. In this context, they find grounds for fighting foreign investments to give precedence to domestic growth. Often, more than being convinced by the soundness of such an attitude *per se*, its proponents find that the arguments it provides from a propagandistic viewpoint are effect-ive. Thus, one interviewee said: 'Mobilizing the workers' troops on the issue of foreign investment can be done relatively easily because it is rather straightfor-ward to explain the arguments for the battle. And this even if the arguments are ultimately fallacious. What is important for the unionists is to mobilize the workers and to draw benefits from this in the political struggle they lead'.

The political necessities refer to the fact that unionists are often compelled to adopt what in fact amounts to a myopic attitude because of their own standing *vis-à-vis* the bulk of union members; a union leader often cannot afford to co-operate too closely with the government or employers because he runs the risk of losing control of the 'base'. Workers not infrequently embark on fights for claims of their own, beyond union action *per se*. In particular, this is what has happened in recent years in Italy where, in view of the seriousness of the situation, major unions – including Marxist unions – have shown some willing-ness to co-operate with the government and management. As a result, groups of workers have begun to refuse union disciplines and initiated struggles of their own. A unionist thus said: 'We can't be too reasonable, lest we lose our influence in the face of mounting worker radicalism'. Furthermore, 'reformist' unionists in particular often have to fight harder than they would like for certain issues which they would not particularly endorse otherwise, because of the competition of the more radical unions – as one interviewee said: 'If they cooperate too much with the ruling classes, other hard-line unions will claim they protect workers' interests better and thus cause reformist unions to lose part of their audience – some of their members to revolutionary unions'. In consequence, they have to fight for visible, short-term results even if this is seriously counterproductive in the long run.

Again, this is conducive to fighting for domestic and not MN expansion on the grounds of preserving employment opportunities at home. An Italian interviewee commented:

> It is hard to convince workers that exporting production, though entailing an immediate cost in terms of employment, will strengthen the company over time and thus workers' position in the future. Workers are obviously more receptive to the short-term cost argument which they see clearly, than to the long-term advantages argument which they don't perceive tangibly, especially in view of the problems they face daily in this country.

Indeed, even moderate unionists are often compelled to adopt a hard line *vis-à-vis* MN expansion. To retain the trust and backing of their members, they must stand for issues which workers can understand and relate to readily. As an interviewee said:

> It is much less important that the aims which the union leader claims he stands for be sound and truly in the workers' interest than that they be perceived as such on the moment . . . Hindering MN expansion to preserve domestic production and employment is a clear cause, one having a seemingly unquestionable logic and one having obvious relevance for workers. Unionists inevitably endorse it.

The influence of union leaders is generally sizeable.[14] Though perhaps taking an extreme case, an Italian manager said: 'In this country, by having the power to paralyse the economy, union chiefs can appear to be the most powerful men in the nation'. True, this influence can be undermined either by dissentions within a union (certain groups of workers rejecting union discipline) or by a lack of aggressiveness of workers (union leaders being unable to mobilize their members appropriately). Still, unionists can have a considerable weight in company decisions. Given they know key government persons can have direct authority over GCEs, and given their generally high bargaining power *vis-à-vis* government players, their own say is indeed important. One interviewee noted:

> Union leaders directly or indirectly derive their influence over GCEs from the government: they know they have leverage over politicians who are anxious to avoid social problems in the public sector. So unionists can pressure these men to cause certain actions to be taken in GCEs. But in fact, they rarely need to really have recourse to this: without actually using this weapon, the fact of having it is enough to increase their weight and credibility.

B. Influential member of the business community

These include prominent managers of leading companies as well as of banks. The prime instances are managers of other GCEs.

Suppliers of raw materials, equipment, services (e.g. know-how), financial assets, etc. can try and cause a company to buy from their own firm as opposed to another. Managements of competing firms can try and influence a company to focus on certain markets, leaving others for them. And customers may try to have an influence over corporate decisions (for example, in terms of pricing policy or even product decisions – as in the case of airlines and aircraft manufacturers). While this is true for any type of company, GCEs confront this type of phenomenon in a particular way – essentially because of two reasons.

1. *Outsiders' influence via the government*

Managers from other companies can have an impact on a GCE by exerting pressure on powerful government individuals who in turn can have a bearing on the firm's decisions. Thus, we found that bankers may ask a sponsoring minister to exert his authority to cause a GCE to use his bank's services; or that a chief executive may ask the same minister to cause a customer to agree to pay higher prices for his goods (for instance, the head of a shipbuilder asking for higher prices for his ships, say from government-controlled oil companies). The solicitor's leverage usually stems from a mutual exchange of favours: as we saw, a minister often asks GCEs to undertake certain tasks; these tasks frequently take the form of a favour management does to the minister and in return, management may ask reciprocal favours from the minister. Thus, in one case, a minister asked a shipyard's management to refrain from firing certain workers in a period which was particularly delicate for him in view of the proximity of elections. Management agreed without asking anything in return immediately, yet it built up a certain credit in terms of goodwill *vis-à-vis* the minister. Later, management asked the minister to exert pressure on a government-controlled steel company to sell to it steel at lower prices.

In certain instances, the solicitor does not need to go directly through the sponsoring minister: if he has a certain 'credit' with another minister, he can ask him to himself pressure the sponsoring minister; the minister then uses some of his own credit with the sponsoring minister or builds up a certain debt which the sponsoring minister may in turn use to ask the minister in question for a favour at some future date. Because politicians constantly need to exchange favours of a variety of sorts, a soliciting chief executive may ask a favour of a minister who himself has little to do with the agent who will actually take the action constituting the favour, but who has enough leverage over the one who does have influence over the agent; this player will grant the minister the favour because of his own indebtedness to the minister. The actual origin of such mutual IOUs is in fact of little relevance: a player can owe a favour to another because of a favour the latter made him in one game; the repayment may be a favour in a totally different game. For example, in one case one man supported another in an election; once elected, this man paid the first player back by backing the construction of a plant in an area in which the first player had a personal stake in terms of real estate speculation.

This points to why this process involves GCEs in particular. True, certain chief executives of private companies can also be involved, but GCEs' managements are the major actors in this game – as explained by an Italian interviewee:

> There is an osmosis between politicians and GCEs' top managers. The former are often instrumental in appointing the latter; and they are both beholden to each other in that the latter obtain facilities of all sorts for their companies' activities and the former use the companies for a whole range of personal uses which go from asking companies to hire relatives or friends (who in turn will be allies in future games), to obtaining a tuning of corporate behaviour to personal needs, passing through actual monetary payments from companies to the politicians – for party or personal use. In practice, such a process cannot work as smoothly in private companies. First, the base is not as strong: private industry managers are not elected by the government. Second, private-company managers are accountable to stockholders and auditors. They are more profit-conscious and thus don't lend themselves as much to becoming instruments in the hands of politicians. Third, there is a question of culture: they are all part of the same *mafia*. They have an understanding between them that top priority should be given to their own aims and interests. It is a question of mentality which grows upon such individuals: they need each other so much and they are so deeply caught in mutual favouritisms that they can't get out of this vicious circle.

While Italy is an extreme case, this account does capture the basic mood of many GCE/government relations.

2. *Direct influence over GCEs' management*

For much the same reasons as above, the chief executive of a GCE can have a certain weight over the decisions of a chief executive of another GCE. Thus, in one instance, a shipyard's executive bargained with a shipping company's manager for the latter to order ships from his firm though his firm was objectively not able to sell the best ships at the most attractive prices. In such cases, there can be an exchange of favours – say, the top manager of the buying company receives a bribe for his decision. A case in point is the acquisition by EGAM in 1974 of an ailing shipping concern – Villain and Fassio. In January 1975, a scandal broke out in which EGAM's chief executive – Mario Einaudi – was accused of having paid an exaggerated price for Villain and Fassio in exchange for money. He then was forced to resign.

Again, while privately owned companies are not always extraneous to such practices,

> GCEs, managers are the masters in this field – as a high-ranking civil servant said. Because they belong to the same race, they understand each other well. Each one knows that his interlocutor is most likely to have his same values and that they can talk the same language . . . All these distortions originate from the political class. And most GCEs end up being contaminated one way or the other. Given they are under a *de facto* obligation to make favours to politicians, GCEs' executives reason that they might as well grant favours to each other also . . .

These players can have both domestic and MN demands. In one case, for example, a car manufacturer's chief executive active in a given country exerted influence on a government-controlled steel company for it to start extraction and production of steel in that country so that his company might have access to cheaper steel than the one available locally via imports. Yet, the bulk of such demands concerns national issues. The basic reason is that most companies involved are domestic in scope. One interviewee commented: 'There is no *a priori* reason for these demands to be national in character other than the fact that most favours the people involved are interested in pertain to national questions, because their activity itself is national. There are but few cases in which an MN GCE's chief executive asks favours of other GCEs in connection with foreign operations'.

C. *Ad hoc* players

These are individuals whose role in GCEs' decisions is a sporadic one.

First, those called upon by the company's management. The prime instances are consultants. They are typically concerned with strategy as well as with organizational questions. They tend to be more objective than management – as explained by a chief executive whose company had recently been the object of an in-depth study by a major consulting firm:

> These men are not caught in the socio-psychological distortions we have as a result of our daily activity over the years. In particular, they are not as distracted as we are by macro kinds of issues – the biases we acquire by being constantly in contact with government. As a result, they can take a colder, more hard-nosed view of the business – more hard-nosed from a money-making point of view.

Consequently, such individuals are also less tied to domestic issues: as will be recalled, managers' concern for macro questions frequently results in their not being open to MN opportunities; this is less the case with consultants. Moreover, since they generally have been exposed to MN types of situations in their professional careers, their outlook is often particularly international. They are therefore, on the whole, more likely to advocate MN courses of action than management.

Second, players brought in by government. These are primarily individuals who become part of an *ad hoc* work group to make a study of certain activities of GCEs, generally specific aspects of their operations. This can be compared to the role of commissions discussed earlier. The main difference is that these persons are not in-government players. For example, a few years ago members of the Italian cabinet – starting with the minister of state holdings – asked a major US accounting firm to make an independent audit of GCEs in view of obtaining a more objective picture of their financial status. Here too, obtaining an outsider's analysis is often conducive to a more objective appraisal of the problems under consideration and a less partisan set of recommendations for action. Yet, given such persons tend to be charged with the task of focusing on rather specific issues, it is only rarely that they deal with real strategic questions. Therefore, they tend to be less concerned by the go/no-go MN type of decision than outsiders called in by corporate management. Still, they may have a say about MN *modus operandi* questions.

It is difficult to generalize about the real influence of *ad hoc* players on GCEs' behaviour. In some cases, management consultants can be instrumental in uncovering new kinds of opportunities. And certain companies have made their first MN investment as a result of the work of consultants. Yet, quite frequently the work of outsiders is stored away in company files and little action is taken on the basis of their studies. This is so in all companies but it appears especially so in GCEs. As a French executive said: 'GCEs' managers are so caught up in political games that often the recommendations of consultants focusing on profit maximization alone appear to them as futile exercises in pure logic not speaking to their concerns'. This is all the more so with outsiders called in by government members. As an Italian executive said: 'By the time the consultant has completed his job, there has been a change in government and the successor of he who ordered the study more often than not has no interest in it'.

IV. CONCLUSION

The organizational politics approach sees GCEs' decisions and actions as being determined by the attitudes key individuals take on issues concerning corporate behaviour; and by the games – conflicts, bargains and compromises – that these individuals play with each other. This chapter has focused on the first of these two ingredients – who the key players are, what stands they are likely to take, their power, etc. The second ingredient – the actual interplays between key persons – will be taken up in the next chapter. Here, therefore, we can but draw partial conclusions about corporate behaviour – though these preliminary insights do uncover important aspects of GCEs' decisions. Three main points should be stressed.

(1) We have primarily dealt with the traits of players stemming from their position. Beyond the characteristics of an individual deriving from the seat he occupies – in terms of his perceptions, interests, values, influence, etc. – his behaviour is affected by his personality, that is, his psychic and intellectual traits, his experience, his personal aspirations. We have tried to convey the role of some salient personalities but there is clearly more to the impact of individual traits on corporate decisions than we have been able to cover here. Yet, it is difficult to generalize much further: here more than ever each case is *sui generis*. Therefore, to deal with the question of personality with more precision, we should look at specific cases.

(2) A player's stand in one game takes into account his posture in the other games in which he is involved – his attitude *vis-à-vis* an issue is affected by the other problems with which he is confronted. This is true even if we limit our analysis to position-related behaviour: a player's post itself leads him to be involved in interlocking games. Thus, a player is often far from pursuing what, from an outside analyst's viewpoint, would appear objectively as the best long-run behaviour. Rather, a player acts politically, that is, he does what other games he is involved in require him to do. Further, short-term pressures are conducive to players giving top priority to immediate payoffs.

Executives behave this way. For example, a subsidiary manager who is approaching the day in which he will be evaluated for promotion will be anxious to show the best possible results for the current year even at the expense of actions which may have an infavourable impact over the long-term posture of the company: for him, what is important is to look good now; if he succeeds he will be promoted and will not be in the job any more to bear the consequences of the poor decisions he makes today.

And of course in-government individuals behave in this fashion. Thus, say, a minister responsible for regional development will push for investments by GCEs in certain areas but more often than not, not in terms of what is objectively most effective in view of the long-run interest of the collectivity or local population, but in relation, say, to deadlines he himself faces – an election, for example – or, say, in relation to interests of his allies (such as helping a friend-congressman seeking popular support in that region and thus needing to show that he achieves concrete results which benefit the local population – in his case GCEs' investments for which he can claim credit).

It is worth repeating that what is sought are results which are obvious, highly apparent (when not outright flashy) and prompt – albeit frequently illusory. These characteristics clearly take precedence over durability, veracity and in-depth long-run collective desirability. This tends to be inevitable because of the structure of the overall game: everything from explicit rules to tacit understandings encourages a high discount rate. This is the reality of politicians' games. And it becomes that of GCEs' executives: given the rewards attached to playing politicians' games and the punishments of not playing these games (both in terms of opportunity costs for the firm and for the executives themselves), it tends to be ineluctable that in-company players sooner or later also seek to show proximate, fractionally subservient accomplishments. Further, the same can be said for certain outsiders. Thus, union leaders have to fight for short-term, clearly evident causes: not to lose their credibility and ascendency over workers, they must aim for close targets even if they realize this goes against the true long-term interest of the workers themselves.

(3) Related to the above, the majority of players have a domestic orientation. Given their concern for visible and short-term results, this tends to be inevitable: MN investments generally do not yield immediately apparent benefits to workers, the people in general, or even company results.

Given most players' high dependence *vis-à-vis* other games which are domestic, their attention and interests can only be geared towards the national environment. This is firstly the case for politicians. The best illustration is their attention to their standing with regard to the electorate: given their future depends on voters, they must be sensitive to the voters' mood. And their mood is mostly responsive to the issues closest to them and their lives – close in a geographical as well as temporal sense. Moreover, what is critical is less what is beneficial to the electorate – even if only in the short run – than what the electorate *perceives* to be beneficial for it. These are issues which it can relate to readily and see the impact of. GCEs' MN expansion rarely falls in this category: its benefits are intangible for the average voter, and long-term; politicians cannot point to them readily in their campaigns. Since MN investments generally cannot truly help politicians in their main games – political struggles – they are rarely actively supported by them.

Again, management's attitude cannot but follow that of politicians. Given the incentives that exist in practice for management to go along with politicians and given the games in which they are involved beyond the corporate management game, top executives of GCEs end up also being primarily concerned with domestic questions. And needless to say, influential outsiders such as union leaders are often exclusively concerned with national questions. A case in point are 'revolutionary' unionists who openly claim they want to bring the system down anyway. They not infrequently exhibit little concern for microeconomic considerations. This, coupled with their practically exclusive concern for national workers, often renders them totally unconcerned with foreign activities – apart from opposing new ones.

True, there appear to be some exceptions. Certain managers of GCEs genuinely try to pursue an independent course geared to the highest possible corporate results (both micro results and contribution to the solution of macro socioeconomic problems). These are usually men of exceptional personal qualities who are able to transcend the environmental conditions in which they are forced to work. And there are political figures committed to the advancement of what they see as the common good. Yet here, as far as their attitude *vis-à-vis* GCEs is concerned, the reason of state is often invoked more or less consciously to justify what frequently amounts to using GCEs for partisan causes: even the politician genuinely concerned with the welfare of the collectivity is often led to sacrifice not only the performance of GCEs *per se*, but also the effectiveness of its long-term contribution to society, because of more pressing needs in the broader political game. The following case will illustrate this.

A few years ago a government head, whose commitment to his country's service was beyond suspicion, asked a GCE to build a new plant in a given region whereas the company already had excess domestic capacity while patently needing a plant in a particular foreign country in which it had achieved high market penetration via exports, yet was gradually losing its position in view of cheaper local production. Both he and management agreed that investing locally was objectively a poor choice both from the firm's point of view and for the long-term interest of the collectivity. The prime minister nevertheless insisted that the company invest locally 'to avoid that people's minds become over-heated, i.e. to shun social unrest'. Indeed, the region in which the plant might have been built at home was already hard hit by unemployment and unions were pressing hard for more public sector investments. The prime minister chose to cause the plant to be built at home after all, in order to preserve social peace. As a company executive concluded: 'The choice was made to go for relatively ephemeral immediate results though sacrificing clear juicy returns as well as obvious positive by-products for the collectivity in the long term. But I guess this was necessary in view of what social peace meant to the government at the time'.

Still, what is most important is the *structure* of the game: it pushes players to a political attitude *vis-à-vis* GCEs – essentially towards striving for short-term domestic factional results. Indeed, notwithstanding certain exceptions primarily due to especially strong personal traits, the 'system' is conducive to departures from what objectively is the most effective decision.

This analysis then begins to answer the questions raised by the process approach (as well as questions raised by the traditional approach which the process approach was unable to address).

(1) Certain decisions were termed myopic and were not understood: they quite obviously result in misallocation of resources and performance failures over time.

In particular, it was not clear why GCEs which are losing market share abroad and which have recognized opportunities to set up foreign production facilities enabling them to hold on to their markets abroad, are in fact prevented from doing so; and this despite the clear fallacies in the arguments advanced to justify this – defence of national jobs and balance-of-payments considerations (see Chapter IV).

This should be clear now. Key players are concerned with 'their' problem – not the overall company and collective welfare. Government players in particular focus on that share of the collective interest for which they are responsible. This tends to be conducive to favouring domestic as opposed to foreign expansion. Further, they are concerned with short-term and visible results. Therefore, they stand for national investments: it is here where they can best hope to see their own aspirations fulfilled. And the negative long-term impact such a course has either on the enterprise itself or on the country tends to be of little concern to them.

Another instance is governments' resistance to certain high technology transnational linkups: by refusing to join forces with foreign partners, certain industries seem invariably condemned to mediocrity in their results (either to survive thanks to subsidies or to focus on a few minor segments confining them to a peripheral role in the market).

This is explained in terms of organizational politics: GCEs' actions are a function of players' parochial interests and take their needs into account. Therefore, decisions which, from an objective analyst's viewpoint, appear contrary to reason, in fact have a clear logic of their own when viewed in the light of key individuals' aims. Thus, hindrances to cross-frontier linkups become easy to understand: players are primarily concerned with the short run and they need not worry overly with what their attitude will mean for the industry over time. Given their relatively short-term perspective, they tend not to see the threats of isolationism and the advantages of joining forces on a transnational level. Their position-related motives often tend to push them to favour national solutions (for example, responsibility for today's national defence resulting in a desire to preserve the relevant industries' independence, despite the fact that for tomorrow this may be a self-defeating purpose, this policy altogether leading to the downfall of key industries). And so do their personal motives (for example, electoral concerns resulting in the adoption of demagogic nationalistic stands).

(2) Decisions about particular investment locations were not accounted for. On the one hand, certain GCEs appear to depart from official regionalization policy, and on the other one was left with the question of how certain specific sites are chosen within a given area (especially since certain choices appear suboptimal both from a microeconomic and a collective viewpoint).

The organizational politics approach sheds light on this: key players push for those locations which fit *their* interests best. An example is a congressman pushing for investments in his constituency. Or a politician trying to cause a GCE to locate in a site where he sees an opportunity for real estate speculation. It is such interests (and not objective microeconomic or general interest considerations) which are responsible for the selection of particular spots within the broader directives of official policy (that is, the choice of a specific site within an area of the country – for example, the Mezzogiorno which, say, regionalization plans purport to benefit). In fact, such interests can be strong enough to cause departure from official policy: when key players – including those responsible for official policy – see their interests best served via other routes, formal objectives can be transgressed.

(3) The organizational process approach left us with the puzzle of when forces step in in the decision process and why, and when and why they initiate certain particular organizational actions; the process approach in a sense took forces as a black box, recognizing their role but failing to explain their specific functioning.

The organizational politics view opens up this black box. Players step in when they feel an issue is relevant for their aims. These aims can be quite remote from the game in which the issue arises. Players' attitude is dictated by what they think will cause that organizational action most consistent with their interests. Players' attitude is 'political': given that an issue typically causes several players who take different stands to step in and given the interlocking nature of games, players often adopt an attitude on an issue for quite indirect motives (for example, a man joining a coalition favouring a particular outcome, not in view of any relevance such an outcome might have for anyone with his own problems, but merely to support another man from whom he in turn expects support in a totally different game). Departure from the established strategic posture is caused by players seeing their aims having a better chance of being fostered via a different course, fighting with others who favour the *status quo* or other courses.

This will be clarified in the next chapter.

NOTES

1. It would be necessary to do an attitudinal study to test this kind of hypothesis. But since such a study would require quite specific responses from top management (that is, data lending itself to a quantitative analysis) it seems unlikely that the data for such a study could be collected.
2. A study of this type would require that GCEs' performance be compared to privately owned firms' performance 'all other things being equal'. This is not possible. Given the great differences which exist between companies, it would otherwise be necessary to take very large samples indeed. But this too is not feasible since there are not enough cases which can be validly compared to each other, particularly since financial data are difficult to compare from one country to another. Moreover, so many intervening variables which are difficult to compare have a bearing on companies' performance that it is difficult indeed to imagine how any meaningful inference could be made about management's attitudes based on companies' financial results.
3. True, the same can happen for private companies too (which hire such persons primarily for their contacts in government). However, it is relatively rare that such individuals become chief executives in these firms.
4. Andrew Shonfield, *Modern Capitalism*, Oxford University Press, London, 1965, p. 185.
5. See John Stopford and Louis Wells, *Managing the Multinational Enterprise*, Basic Books, New York, 1972.
6. See Bernard Morau, 'An Analysis of the Role of the Board of Directors in Irish Public State Enterprises', PhD thesis, University College, Dublin, 1975.
7. The prime example is Germany where *Mitbestimmung* laws give workers the right to elect as much as half of the *Aufsichtsrat* – the supervisory board.
8. See: Enid Mumford and Andrew Pettigrew, *Implementing Strategic Decisions*, Longman, London, 1975.
9. See: Henry Mintzberg, Duru Raisinghani and André Théorét, 'The Structure of "Unstructured" Decision Processes', *Administrative Science Quarterly*, Vol. 21, June 1976, pp. 246–275.
10. In fact, from 1976 to 1978, this ministry was held by the Prime Minister himself. And in April 1978 it was split up into two separate ministries – a ministry for *l'Economie* and one for *le Budget*.
11. The French president is the highest authority of the state. He nominates a prime minister who is to form a government which, under his leadership, is to conduct the country's affairs – the president being the guardian of the institutions and providing

long-term guidance to the government's policy. In practice, it is clear that the President has the ultimate say in key matters.

12. As of the time of writing, the communists have decided to give their votes to the cabinet in parliament without having any formal post in the executive.

13. See the discussion at the end of Chapter IV.

14. In this connection, one should be reminded of the 1974 confrontation in the UK which ultimately caused the downfall of the Heath government.

CHAPTER X

The Decisions

The focus is on the major types of decisions relevant to GCEs' MN behaviour. Depending on the type of company involved, its sector, its home country, the actual or prospective host country, the socioeconomic and political conjunctural situation at the time of the decision, the type of issue to be resolved, a decision takes one form or another according to what players are involved, what perceptions and stakes lead them to take what stands, and what relative influence each one of them has. We will first look at decisions concerning strategy, then at decisions concerning policy.

I. STRATEGY DECISIONS

The basic issue is the go/no-go question and its connected aspects such as the choice of location, form (for example, 'going it alone' or in partnership), size of project, etc. The attitudes of players *vis-à-vis* such decisions are critically affected by their concerns and interests. Since many of their preoccupations are fundamentally domestic in nature, the analysis of GCEs' MN strategic behaviour inevitably leads us to discussing matters which are national in character. Specifically, we will deal with five basic classes of decisions.

A. Primary sector decisions – limited domestic natural resources

A number of primary sector GCEs deal with raw materials which constitute essential resources for the economy.[1] Some of these raw materials are available at home. This will be considered in Section (B) below. Here we focus on those cases where raw materials have to be secured abroad.

A double distinction is in order. On the one hand, there are situations in which the supply of raw materials appears stable, at least in the short term, and there are situations in which raw materials are scarce and may be curtailed. On the other hand, we have to distinguish between three main phases of corporate activity – raw materials acquisition, processing or conversion of raw materials into usable products, and sales.

1. *Stable supply of raw materials*

a. Raw materials acquisition   Naturally, this implies MN operations. Relatively few politicians are usually involved: when access to natural resources does not appear to be threatened in the near future, this phase does not 'fall in the realm of politicians' interests and is not of much relevance to them', as a British executive said. And given their short-term view of things, they are seldom truly preoccupied with how the resource supply might evolve in the long run. An oil executive said: 'Politicians can't afford to worry about how the long run might look and what they might do about it, if this doesn't entail tangible returns for them now; and when natural resources are not visibly imperilled, it is hard to be credited for foresight because few people actually see the problem'. And commenting on the limited relevance issues in this phase have for politicians in terms of the games they are involved in, an Italian interviewee said: 'Worrying about natural resource procurement when this is not seen as an issue by most people, does not enable politicians to draw many benefits in terms of their electoral standing or their standing within their party or *vis-à-vis* other politicians'.

This was the case prior to the 1973 oil crisis and is still the case in many other primary sector industries. For example, few politicians have really dug into Finsider's supply policy. Of course, there are exceptions. In particular, key political people are often involved in the creation of GCEs in this field. For example, Churchill for the Anglo-Iranian Oil Company – later BP – or Poincaré for CFP. And General de Gaulle himself and some of his close collaborators were instrumental in the creation of ELF-ERAP. Still, once they exist, these companies are the object of relatively few interventions by politicians. And when they do get involved, they rarely do so in view of the supply *per se* but as a means of serving other aims they have. A case in point is that of the minister of foreign affairs who may exert influence on a GCE to tailor its behaviour to his policy.*vis-à-vis* given countries. Thus, a high-ranking official of CFP reported:

> We have three ministers who act as our guardians – who have responsibility for our behaviour: the finance minister, the industry minister and the minister for foreign affairs . . . CFP has played and continues to play a political role in that we have frequently ensured a certain continuity in the relations with certain countries: when France has deteriorating relations with a certain country and possibly interrupts regular diplomatic ties with it, we can entertain *de facto* unobtrusive relations with local authorities, which are precious for the Foreign Office which can thus continue having contacts with locals. A case in point is Iraq. For years France's official relations with this country were at a virtual standstill because of differences between the two governments. Yet, the minister for foreign affairs could continue its dialogue with Iraqi authorities via our local agents in Baghdad. Thus, in a way, we replaced the French Embassy there.

Of course, such use of GCEs cannot normally interfere excessively in the actual strategy of the company. The same CFP interviewee added:

> The minister of foriegn affairs really limits himself to exploiting our contacts where we have them and never really forces us to get involved in a country where we don't want to. At the most, he 'encourages' us one way or the other, but we never had any real confrontation with him (contrary to what happened with the finance and industry ministers). He understands that he can usually reach his aims without sacrificing our own economic performance.

Other governmental players are more likely to be concerned by GCEs' activities here. Technical staffers of politicians in particular may raise the issue of the long-term security of supply. But then they tend to run into conflict with political staffers who are clearly more concerned with immediate issues whose political payoff for their boss is higher. And technical staffers frequently have a hard time capturing their boss's attention on such issues precisely because he is more concerned by more urgent matters. This is also why in a conflict between technical and political staffers, the politician who has to arbitrate tends to favour the latter because he speaks to his short-term needs.

Further, certain civil servants can become involved. Given they are less pressed by short-term issues, government planners, for example, may become worried about possible restrictions of raw materials supply. Still, on one hand because their own horizon is in fact less long-term than medium-term (five years, for example) and, on the other, because their attention is rarely attracted to issues which are not hot, they too are not as likely to focus on this type of issue as one might think. Besides, planners know that the product of their work ultimately will be appraised from a political viewpoint in that a plan before being approved has to pass the test of evaluation by political players. (Indeed, while indicative planning started out in France as a purely economic device to monitor industrial growth, it is increasingly becoming a political exercise in that included in it are aims and recommendations with a political motivation – for example, those that provide for growth in a sector which is politically critical for the prime minister and his allies.) Therefore, they tend to include in it what they feel is politically realistic and to give precedence to issues which are likely to be endorsed by politicians. Thus, they too rarely give much weight to GCEs' resource-seeking decisions.

It is to GCEs' management that this phase is most important. Given their company's welfare is vitally dependent on it, top managers as well as staffers are concerned by this phase. One chief executive said: 'It is we who focus on this type of decision most. True, in the past we have made mistakes in appraising what certain evolutions might be and we were caught with our pants down. But this was always because we misforecast trends or events; never because we didn't see the relevancy of the problem in the first place'. And a high-ranking civil servant added: 'This phase tends to be the responsibility of corporate management. Decisions are normally made in the context of a microeconomic logic'.

Thus, this phase rarely lends itself to political struggles between players. In most instances, the firm's behaviour is determined by in-company players. Most government persons tend to stay out of it. Since this phase is a *sine qua non* condition for the company to function, there is little room for argument about whether the enterprise should be MN here or not. And since the questions related to how to go MN (for instance, in what specific country) are of concern to relatively few politicians, this too – as the above CFP interviewee suggested – is an area where conflicts are normally moderate and can be ironed out relatively easily.

b. Raw materials processing Here, the choice of location for investment is a very real one since there are many alternatives as to where to build a plant. The choice of a particular location depends on a variety of variables and involves a host of issues. And so do other decisions. Thus, the choice of the resources to be employed (for example, the technology as well as the human resources) touches upon a broad spectrum of questions. Indeed, their financial magnitude, their potential effect on the rest of a region's industrialization, their often spectacular appearance make these investments important to a wide variety of people with a wide range of interests.

In-company players are vitally concerned. Both position-related and personal motives come into play. Regarding the former, cost or efficiency variables are critical: strategic fit (that is, the extent to which a particular project for a plant – a refinery, for example – is coherent with the overall operations of the firm), technological questions, logistics (for example, the extent to which carriers of raw materials can readily accede to the proposed location), labour questions (the availability of well-trained, efficient, disciplined workers) and proximity of and ease of access to markets. At varying degrees, such questions preoccupy most in-company key players (for example, top management and its staffers will worry primarily about strategic fit while the line manager who may end up being responsible for running the project may be mostly worried by the propensity of workers to strike or not).

And a projected plant's location is of considerable interest to company players on personal grounds. Those who will be directly involved in the construction and/or operation of the facilities will be motivated to see that the plant be located in an area attractive to them (close to home, perhaps). Further, there may be financial interests involving high-ranking managers: thus, top executives of GCEs have speculated on land on which the company was to build a plant (that is, buying it themselves and reselling it to the company at a profit). Besides, locating in a particular site may lead top managers to receive personal 'compensations', say, by local notables who themselves derive high benefits from a GCE investing in their region. Finally, causing their firm to invest in a particular area may result in chief executives getting into the good graces of politicians who themselves are interested in the company investing in the area.

In-government players are also clearly concerned by such decisions. Most often, the location, say, of a refinery or a steel mill are politically sensitive issues. Because of the capital outlays involved and their generally perceived importance to the overall development of the local economy, such investments are often widely publicized and the object of many controversies involving a broad spectrum of interests. These include general kinds of problems (for example, the prime minister worrying about the overall supply of energy) and more specialized points of view – for example, the finance minister arguing that a project be selected which costs the country as little as possible in terms of hard currency and thus being in favour of domestic plants using domestic equipment; the labour minister being concerned that the new plant provide a certain amount of jobs and being against the use of the latest labour-saving technology; and influential congressmen trying to cause the plant to be located in their constituency. Here too, personal interests play a key role. Both political and electoral aims can be furthered and venal ends pursued (for example, bribes received from real-estate developers may cause a GCE to build a plant in a given area subcontracting their firms for its construction).

Outsiders can also have a stake in such decisions. Union leaders in particular tend to get involved not only in questions directly concerning workers but also in broader issues. Thus, it is not uncommon to see unionists interfering with plant location decisions. And other GCEs' executives can also exert a certain influence. Thus, a car manufacturer's top manager may push for a steel mill to be located next to his plant.

Each of these players then has a position of his own on investments in this second phase. Many are in conflict with each other. But others converge and tend to yield common patterns of corporate behaviour.

It is with in-company players that MN investments are most likely to be supported. When a company's 'best interest' is considered, the conclusion is often reached that it is most attractive to locate a plant abroad. Indeed, several of the major oil companies have located their refineries abroad close to the oil wells. As a corporate planner of an oil GCE said: 'If one were to consider only microeconomic variables we would invest more abroad'.

Still, given GCEs' strategy, even from a purely company point of view foreign locations are often not as desirable as one might expect *a priori* – as explained by one executive:

> Our overall activities are nationally oriented. Therefore, were it only in view of seeking consistency with the rest of our activities, we are inclined to invest domestically. And I am thinking of very concrete factors when I refer to 'consistency'. The fact that most of our sales are concentrated domestically is a case in point: when you have your sales scattered all over the place, then it indeed makes sense to refine in a concentrated fashion close to the source of the raw materials you use, lest you end up either having to transport your crude first to your refineries, then again from your refineries to your markets, or having to have many small refineries in all your markets: both are inefficient. But when your sales are mostly concentrated, then you can refine more readily close to your end-markets. In the case of many GCEs,

they sell the greatest majority of their refined products at home. Therefore, it is not unreasonable that they refine domestically.

Personal preferences of executives can in certain cases instigate decisions to invest abroad. Yet, on the whole, the personal inclinations of these persons tend to lead them to have a rather stay-at-home attitude. As we will see, their past career-patterns as well as the ties they develop in their jobs cause GCEs' executives in general to exhibit a preference for working domestically. Still, in the particular companies under consideration here, this is generally counterbalanced, at least partly, by the international scope the company usually has in the first phase of its operations: raw materials procurement often leads the firm to invest abroad (unless it merely buys natural resources on international markets, which fewer and fewer GCEs do); 'This percolates into people's mentalities', said a German executive, 'that is, executives, by being exposed to foreign environments by virtue of their firms' activities in up-stream operations, tend to have less of a provincial mentality than executives in other companies'.

On the other hand, the personal interests of GCEs' executives tend to be domestic in scope: 'Their contacts are primarily domestic and it is at home that they can most readily make their more or less licit underhand schemes', said an interviewee. Such interests often call for investments different from what both purely company rationale and their own inclinations would suggest: the more 'venal' interests of executives tend to speak for projects in developing areas. A case in point is the Mezzogiorno, where politicians can reap considerable electoral dividends from industrial investments and where opportunities for speculation are often quite substantial.

In-government players generally have little reason to favour foreign investments. Of course, there are some exceptions. Thus, the foreign affairs minister may wish an investment to occur in a given country with which he wants to develop closer ties; and, say, the president may want more investment by GCEs in a particular nation in the context of his overall foreign policy. Still, when this is the case, they generally tend to think of other investments than these second phase investments. Although here too there are exceptions: thus, refinery or petrochemical plants have been built in oil-producing countries as a result of pressures exerted by such players.

Other than this, the majority of government persons are normally inclined to push national investments – indeed specific sites. These are frequently different from what would be the most attractive for the firm or most appealing to management – they are, rather, politically rewarding sites. Or sites which have very real monetary benefits attached to them for certain players (for example, payments from local landowners whose property may increase in value as a result of certain industrial investments). As an interviewee said: 'It should be clear that such advantages cannot be reaped as readily abroad . . . Abroad they cannot receive bribes as easily either from subcontractors, equipment manufacturers or real estate "financiers". And politically, an investment abroad does not yield anywhere near to what it yields at home'.

Conflicts are not uncommon among in-government players. First, there may be conflicts among those advocating domestic investments and those favouring MN investments. And among those who favour domestic investments, there is room for considerable argument. As one interviewee said: 'When the stake is a major investment – as in the case of a refinery – the cake is so big that many people become interested. And in terms of location, the cake is rarely divisible. Therefore, various factions develop, each fighting for one location or another'.

A special case is that of members of the opposition. From a purely political point of view, they frequently fight a site advocated by government members simply because 'a decision of the majority should always be fought by the minority, as a matter of principle', said a French interviewee. Indeed, members of the opposition may be encouraged to contradict government leaders for the sake of political argument. Further, personal motives can come into play here also. An Italian interviewee said:

> Opposition members are outside the government for so long and are so tired of seeing the others 'eat' [that is, reap personal benefits from one's position] alone, that they are envious. They would like to have a piece of the pie. But since this is difficult if you are not part of the majority, they decry the corruption which they can't benefit from. The result is that when an investment location is chosen by the cabinet, opposition heads often start fighting against it by claiming that there is vast corruption underlying the project.

Outsiders also normally favour domestic investments. Unionists are concerned with employment at home. Given their short-term perceptions, they are not truly sensitive to positive effects induced by foreign investments if they occur in the rather distant future. While they are not as specific in their preferences as, say, politicians, unionists also often favour investments in certain regions rather than others. Thus, in Italy they fight for investments in the South. A union leader said:

> Fighting for investments in the South even if they don't in themselves result in many new jobs, as in the case of these [second phase] investments is quite beneficial for us because it enhances our credibility. Workers understand and relate to what we are struggling for because such investments are seen as having an *effetto trainante* [a hauling effect] for the rest of the local economy.

Yet, unionists often advocate different sites than either in-company executives or politicians. To repeat, they usually do not push for particular places but for broad areas or types of areas. Further, they frequently systematically oppose sites chosen by government individuals. This is comparable to the attitude of political opposition leaders; especially those union leaders who are Marxist make a point to be at odds with government representatives. This is due to their own position as members of the Communist Party as well as to their role as heads of a 'revolutionary' union systematically opposing the ruling majority. Thus, in the autumn of 1976, the French government headed by Raymond Barre was about to launch a set of conjunctural economic measures when Georges Séguy, the head of the CGT – France's most powerful union, affiliated to the Communist Party – stated publicly that he would call for active fighting against the government's plan (including strikes), and this even before the plan had been announced or finalized. In this context, decisions concerning major investments by GCEs can be opposed on an *a priori* basis.

Unions often oppose the use of the latest technology – as argued by a Belgian executive: 'Given national unemployment problems, unions are against anything which reduces jobs. Technological innovation in the production process is a prime target'. Here they are clearly at odds with corporate management.

Executives from other GCEs are also generally favourable to domestic investments. Prospective users of raw materials are anxious that new plants be located next to their own plants. Suppliers and subcontractors tend to exert pressure for domestic investments because they feel they can more successfully bargain for their services to be used in a national context than abroad where they face competition of foreign companies.

Thus, the various players can have quite different stands. We have stressed conflicts with regard to location since this is the basic focus of this study. But there is also conflict in terms of other variables – as we saw, technology, the choice of resources to be employed, size of investments (management typically being relatively conservative, others such as unionists pushing for larger units in view of their employment concerns). Conflict is resolved in terms of the relative power of each player, those players with greatest influence succeeding in imposing their views; also, middle-of-the-road choices are made to satisfy various points of view, and promises are made by players to others in view of securing their support.

It is difficult to generalise about the relative power of different types of players. Certain political figures have considerable power due to their formal attributions (for example, because they can revoke GCEs' top management). Yet, this influence is *de facto* often undermined by individuals' short tenure in their positions and by their personal standing which is often open to attack. As a German interviewee said: 'A man's authority is jeopardized when he can be attacked on the basis of his integrity'. On the other hand, political players can often increase their influence via certain bargaining advantages. An Italian interviewee said:

> A politician can be very powerful beyond his official responsibilities. People owe him favours and they make him favours in view of his past, present and future power. He can distribute 'payments' (not necessarily in monetary terms) to those who abide by his wishes. For instance, if you are the head of a GCE's division, he can promise to push for your promotion for president when the current president

goes. Or he can promise personal things such as helping find a good job for your son. And he can promise to share the benefits derived from your joining his cause . . . Indeed, a politician's major strength is often that of co-opting people and particularly GCEs' executives.

Thus, men such as Fanfani in Italy have acquired considerable authority over the years by securing control of the *sottogoverno* (the underground government) which is itself in many ways more powerful than the formal executive: the executive comes and goes but the institutions remain; over time their leaders become very influential; by winning these leaders to their cause, these politicians develop a power base often of greater strength than that conferred by formal positions.

GCEs' executives also have more or less influence than their position would lead one to expect. Sometimes, not yielding to politicians' pressure to cause GCEs to serve their interests increases a man's power. Yet, as a French interviewee remarked: 'this attitude is conducive to personal strength but it also *takes* strength'. It is often difficult for the one who is in a system of corruption and overall manipulation of corporate and state resources to get out of it: were he to try to do so, a man is likely to be isolated and *de facto* paralysed in his behaviour by the stumbling blocks other actors would put in his way.

One case is particularly illustrative of such games – that of IRI's fifth 'Centro Siderurgico' of Gioia Tauro in Calabria.[2] The project was decided in the late 1960s, officially to meet the rising demand for steel and consistent with the policy of industrial development of the South. It was to employ the latest technology and provide 7500 jobs.[3] As of today over 400 billion lire have been spent but the project is far from completion and its future is at best highly uncertain.

The project has always been extremely controversial and has provoked several scandals. As noted by a major outside analyst – *Il Giornale*'s chief economist Marco Marcello – the location of Gioia Tauro was from any point of view a poor choice. First, from a microeconomic perspective, it was not at all clear from the outset that market conditions required IRI to have a fifth steel plant: from the early 1970s onwards especially (when the first implementation steps were taken), it became apparent that Italy was headed for overcapacity, both in view of stagnating demand (given the developing national crisis) and increasing international competition (particularly from Japanese producers). Further, Gioia Tauro itself was inappropriate. Distant from sources of raw materials and end-markets, its products would be at a disadvantage because of transportation costs. Basic infrastructures were missing and the electricity and water supply was deficient (requiring in particular the construction of costly dams). But, what is worse, the specific site was highly undesirable; while Calabria has plentiful underdeveloped land (with no industrial or agricultural use and no touristic appeal), the land which was actually selected had relatively high value because of the prosperous agricultural activity which locals had developed on it (olive trees in particular). Indeed, expropriation posed immense problems due to land owners' resistance and was very expensive (30 million lire for each of the 600 hectares which were bought). The official justification was that Gioia Tauro was close to a new harbour where raw materials could be unloaded and from which finished goods could be shipped. But the truth of the matter is that the harbour itself did not exist. It was to be built – over a ten-year period – in view of the plant, and could itself have been located elsewhere (the fact is that the proposed harbour location was also far from ideal in view of geographical and cost considerations).

Moreover, the project promised little from a macro point of view. A steel plant in this area would be a typical 'cathedral in the desert' since it would not have much of a multiplier effect in terms of related industries. The technology to be employed was capital-intensive (as early as 1973, it appeared that each new job created would cost some 77.5 million lire – and since then this has escalated dramatically) whereas local conditions called for low-skill, labour-intensive projects. And the specific site's choice aroused the discontent of the local population who saw with dismay the expropriation of the flourishing agricultural activity as well as the end of any hope of developing tourism in the area. One interviewee added: 'People are furious. They see the expropriations and the wasted resources. And now they see the whole project is dragging its feet (precisely because of its increasingly apparent intrinsic faults) . . . They see no hope for the promises which were made to them to materialize . . . the situation is becoming explosive on the social front'.

How did this happen? The idea of Gioia Tauro first came from and then was forwarded by politicians. The central player was Giacomo Mancini, a prominent figure of the Socialist Party (in fact, at the time of the decision he was the party's Secretary General) having held several Cabinet posts, and the deputy of the Gioia Tauro area. At the time of the decision he was accused of several cases of corruption (the press openly called him 'a thief') and his political standing was in decline both in his electorate and within his party itself. To reassert his position he needed to do 'something big' for his constituency, which would give him back the support of his voters, as well as do something to restore his image among his party fellows. Gioia Tauro was an ideal opportunity; it was highly visible and it lent itself to the *argument* that it would engender the development of the area by induced economic activity and the growth of related industries (in fact, as mentioned above, a fallacious argument). Indeed, it was an ideal political vehicle for Mancini to claim credit for local socioeconomic progress. Further, Mancini and his political friends (such as Mario Battaglini – a local politician) expected considerable financial returns as well; via their connections with local 'financiers' (including members of the Mafia) there were particular real-estate speculation opportunities on the land purchases for the plant and the new port, as well as attractive profits in the form of bribes paid by local industrialists who would receive contracts for the building of infrastructures or the supply of equipment. The proceeds of these deals would then partly be shared among the actors personally and partly be paid to the Socialist Party in terms of 'political contributions'. This would serve Mancini's aim of reasserting his position within the party.

In front of Mancini, several players tried to oppose Gioia Tauro. First, IRI management, whose president, Giuseppe Petrilli, denounced the project asking at least that the government pay the costs of the inefficiencies the Institute would incur. Other politicians also opposed Gioia Tauro both because of the weaknesses they saw in the venture and because they entertained hopes of causing the fifth centre to be located in an area more congenial to their own aims. Yet, Mancini won, and this for two key reasons. First, his political indispensability. In the days the decision was made, the Socialist Party was a cornerstone of the ruling government coalition. The Christian Democrat government's survival was dependent on other smaller parties' support, first among which were the Socialists. Within the Socialist Party, Mancini had a key role. In a sense, precisely because of his weakening personal standing, his party fellows saw the need for him to gain back political prestige. (One interviewee said: 'While many in the Socialist Party might have been glad to see his downfall, the majority of the party members realized that the weakness of Mancini – a pillar of the party – was bad for the entire party'.) Besides, the 'contributions' which were to come from the Gioia Tauro venture were appealing. His party was thus inclined to support him. Consequently, Mancini was able to blackmail Christian Democrat leaders: he threatened to cause his party to withdraw its support lest they backed him in the Gioia Tauro decision.

Second, he was able to co-opt many of his opponents. On one hand, he converted certain men to his cause by showing them they could also reap political dividends from Gioia Tauro. The principal figure here is Emilio Colombo – at that time Prime Minister, later Minister of the Treasury, currently President of the European Parliament, a leader of the Christian Democrat Party and the deputy of Basilicata (also a depressed area of the South). Colombo saw that, in particular, he could derive electoral types of advantages in his constituency similar to those of Mancini in his own constituency; his argument was that Basilicata (considered the poorest area of the *Mezzogiorno*) would gain considerable, albeit indirect, economic benefits from Gioia Tauro. Colombo thus became the key ally of Mancini. On the other hand, Mancini co-opted several persons by promising to share with them the proceeds of the land and other speculations (this was also instrumental in gaining support of local politicians originally opposed to the project). In particular, he was able to gain IRI's sponsoring minister to his cause, who in turn exerted authority on the Institute's management, to go along with the decision (as well as on men in charge of the Cassa del Mezzogiorno which was to be a key element in the financing of Gioia Tauro).

Today the project can be considered as having come to a standstill: 'The land has been purchased and a bit of the port has been built . . . But the 40 000 unemployed of the area still don't see much signs of the jobs they were promised . . . And IRI is still waiting for the state to cover most of the costs it obliged it to undergo', said one interviewee. And another interviewee said: 'What will happen next is a question mark; it may well happen that not much will happen at all'.

This is a case where one player (and his allies) is able to impose his views (as opposed to having to settle with others for a middle-of-the road solution). We should note what was essential for Mancini: on one hand, it was to win at the decision level in order to be able to claim credit for the project with his electorate (the political dividends coming mostly at the point when the decision is being debated and announced publicly) and on the other, the first implementation steps, that is, the real-estate deals and the subcontracting deals when most of the financial benefits could be reaped. Besides these two steps, what happens with the project over time was of relatively lesser importance for the central player – as explained by one interviewee: 'The political benefits were reaped at the time of the announcement and the money was made with the early phases of the actual accomplishment of the project. True, after that Mancini still fought for the venture to go on. But the essential part for him had taken place. Now he is not affected by Gioia Tauro and its failure very much any more'. It is noteworthy that comparatively little has happened beyond these two steps.

c. Sales   This is the marketing of, say, refined oil products or steel, and can involve industrial marketing or retail sales. The latter can call for high capital outlays (for a network of petrol stations, for example).

Relative to the second phase, this phase concerns distinctly fewer players. In-company persons are clearly involved – top management as well as key functional executives (primary sector companies are usually organized functionally). And when the company is involved in direct selling it usually has a marketing vice-president who naturally is vitally interested in this phase.

Executives' concerns are tied to their positions. As such they focus on economic considerations – overall company performance as well as the efficiency of the marketing organization *per se*. Personal motives also pay a role. Thus, an executive can be concerned with the extent to which he can personally benefit – in terms of financial rewards – from such and such an operation (for example, real-estate speculation on land where the company plans to build petrol stations). *Vis-à-vis* MN expansion, economic considerations can result in MN preferences. Yet, if the rest of the company's strategy is domestically oriented, marketing operations generally tend to follow. Personal motives mostly tend to push executives towards domestic expansion for much the same reasons we discussed earlier.

In terms of government players, most decisions taken here tend to be less relevant to them than, say, those of the second phase. This is true in view of these players' positions and the concerns which are attached to them, and in view of these players' other games. As a German interviewee said:

> Here decisions are usually less spectacular than elsewhere in this sector [the oil sector] and politicians cannot exploit them as much on an electoral basis. When a company decides to broaden its marketing operations, lesser amounts of money are typically involved, lesser jobs are involved and the whole thing is implemented in such a gradual fashion that there isn't much for a politician to get excited about and to use in his political struggles.

(Of course, there are exceptions. For example, when AGIP bought the entire Italian network of Shell, several politicians got involved. But indeed, this is – in an executive's words – 'a totally abnormal decision'.)

Vis-à-vis MN expansion, politicians also do not usually get overly involved. A French interviewee said: 'Since the opportunity cost for the country in terms of contribution to issues of collective relevance (such as employment) is rarely very high, people haven't worried too much about GCEs expanding their MN marketing operations'. Only those players responsible for national financial matters can truly be involved. Thus, the finance minister may favour an increase in a GCE's sales abroad, or he may be concerned by a foreign investment causing a major capital outlay.

On the whole, it is safe to say that this third phase is not an area of typically high tensions and conflict among players. Decisions are taken primarily by corporate management. Whatever the interferences of politicians may be, they are rarely conducive to outright confrontation with in-company people. As a German executive concluded: 'This phase tends to follow the overall course of the company . . . If the company's overall orientation is international, management is most likely to think of international investments for marketing as well. In this sector, the most international GCE in terms of distribution is BP, which is also the most international company in its overall operations'.

2. *Scarce (or potentially scarce) raw materials*

How different are the three phases where the supply of natural resources is or may become tight?

a. Raw materials procurement   Naturally, it is the first phase which is mostly affected. The best instance is the oil situation after the crisis of autumn 1973.

The major difference is that government players are generally involved. In particular, the finance and economics ministers, the foreign affairs minister as well as the head of the executive himself. Their concern stems from the view that, should raw materials become unavailable, this would have the gravest consequences for the country *and* for those who are seen as responsible for such issues, in other words, leading political figures. This was explained by a French interviewee:

> One should have few illusions about the motivations of politicians. They are moved only by what will affect them. If an event has, both objectively and in their own view, negative consequences for the nation but is not perceived as such by the people, they will do less about it than if an event is in fact trivial but *seen* as important by the people. Here the issue is such that it is both important and seen as important. Yet, don't be mistaken. They act on it only because of the latter.

Certain civil servants and technical staffers often have a sizeable role. Given the importance of the issue, politicians 'have to listen'. Thus, planners develop detailed programmes looking at the issue from the macro viewpoint: 'It is they who make the most genuine effort to think in terms of the collectivity's best long-term interest', said one interviewee. Staffers have to bear in mind the political constraints of their bosses. Here too, despite the fact that the issue *per se* is important for the politician, the politician has to tackle it from a short-term 'visible' viewpoint. This means that the stances he takes on it have to be clearly understandable by his political audience – his voters – and speak to their interests in an explicit fashion: 'Too bad if this does not coincide with the true long-run interest of the country', said a British interviewee. Thus, a politician may have to propose action which favours certain classes representing his electorate, even if from a collective viewpoint this is clearly suboptimal. Staffers must bear such imperatives in mind. They must propose actions whose payoff is as near in time as possible and as easy to grasp as possible for the public.

Company management is vitally concerned. An oil company chief executive said: 'Now *the* problem is crude. All the other questions come afterwards. If we don't have enough crude oil we go under. Top management's priority task is to find crude at good conditions'. And union leaders as well as opposition members are also often involved. Given their importance, their often 'hot' character, these issues are exploitable politically. Therefore, they cannot leave such players indifferent.

While most of these players do have the safety and efficiency of natural resource acquisition in mind, they in practice generally adopt different stands when confronted with concrete decisions. Managements tend to focus on the problem of supply of raw materials *per se* while government players are inclined to look at it in a broader context of national raw materials procurement or in the context of the policies for which they themselves are responsible (that is, the overall foreign policy of the country). And within these two categories there is usually disagreement between persons. Thus, the executives of the company which actually buys the raw materials have the most specific concerns – the raw materials in adequate quantities and price. If the company belongs to a state holding, the parent company's management will want to co-ordinate the actions of the resource-buying unit with those of the other companies of the group. Similarly, a diversified company's management will have a different approach to the problem than that of a firm which is purely an oil company. For example, the top management of a large chemical company such as Montedison which is a heavy user of oil, is not solely concerned with supply as such. Thus, it is frequently concerned that oil be purchased as far as possible from countries which in turn might be clients either for the company's end-products or its technology.

Political players also often have different opinions. A foreign affairs minister tends to be concerned with not making deals which might jeopardize the overall foreign policy of the country. The finance minister is typically concerned with balance-of-payments implications. The sponsoring minister will want to reconcile the actions of oil-seeking GCEs with the overall behaviour of GCEs *vis-à-vis* oil-producing countries. The labour minister will want to make sure that such a co-ordinated action by GCEs generates jobs for national workers (and that not just technology be sold abroad to be exploited locally). The head of the executive will try and arbitrate all these positions with a view to preserving the cabinet's cohesiveness. What is more, all these positions are inevitably tinted with political overtones, the various political actors do not just pursue their aims in order to foster what they believe to be right in the context of their particular responsibilities, but they also seek positive results in view of the purely political games in which they are involved.

And opposition members also tend to draw political advantages from such issues. A French interviewee said: 'Opposition members tend to take exception with the government systematically . . . Oil procurement is an ideal subject on which to attack the government because there is always room for debate which will generally be widely publicized'.

Thus, conflicts emerge from the fact that various players strive for the same overall aim according to their own parochial perceptions and interests. To resolve such conflicts, compromises have to be reached in which the demands of the greatest number of players possible are, at least partially, satisfied. Thus, it is possible to secure resources from those countries, which will not jeopardize the national foreign policy, while trying to co-ordinate the actions of the public sector in general *vis-à-vis* such countries and making sure that a certain value-added occurs using national labour. Apart from the often extreme positions taken by opposition leaders, most position-related concerns of actors who are part of a government can usually be reconciled 'with a bit of give and take by all those involved and with a bit of mediation by the Chancellor', as a German interviewee said. Still, things are more complex when it comes to players' demands stemming from their personal interests – notably their needs in connection with their political games. A French interviewee said: 'Here people tend to start out with unreasonable demands. In practice, either a man is so powerful politically that he is able to impose his notwithstanding reason, or he must give up at least part of his expectations. . . Generally, friction is inevitable'.

This conflict and negotiation process is doubly inefficient from a managerial point of view. On the one hand, the decisions which end up being taken are frequently not the most desirable ones for the company. Decisions emerging from compromise are often a pot-pourri of various demands, a collage of various partial aims rather than a coherent plan devised by one decider pursuing one set of aims. Thus, several GCEs' chief executives often see a plan they propose badly distorted by various amendments, subtractions and additions, the final plan the company ends up pursuing bearing little resemblance to the original. (One executive said: 'In fact, what we ultimately do often can't be called a plan; it is but a set of vaguely related propositions . . .'.) On the other hand, the need to reconcile originally conflicting views and the need to brush aside other unreconcilable demands inevitably engenders a slowing-down of decision-making. Hesitations, bargaining and foot dragging are unavoidable, especially in view of the personal concerns of governmental players – particularly when it is in the politicians' best interest to let things sit and keep options open. One chief executive complained: 'We have to argue with a whole bunch of people as to what the best strategy is to secure raw materials; this takes ages, particularly when governmental figures are part of the picture. You can't imagine how inefficient this is for us'.

b. Processing In the second phase the major difference lies in the new attractiveness which locating plants abroad involves. In the case of oil in particular, producing countries' authorities tend to be eager to attract new industries. They are especially anxious to see the development of oil-related units among which refineries occupy a prime rôle. In return for the construction of such plants, they are willing to concede more attractive terms for the sale of their crude. Such concessions are attractive and several players are sensitive to them.

First, corporate management. A president said: 'Our costs have risen considerably with the new prices of raw materials. And our prices cannot follow *pari passu* not only because this would mean losing market share but also because of government regulations. Therefore, we have to take every opportunity to get a break that we can'. While management is naturally concerned with the terms of raw materials in view of their impact on the firm, foreign plants help other players with their problem even more. The finance minister is often the one who is most anxious that such projects be pursued. The mounting cost of raw materials has a very serious consequence for him – the drain it constitutes on the national balance of payments. For him, the construction of plants ordered by oil-producing countries means potential currency inflows or being able to pay at least part of the oil bill via such projects, thus somewhat easing the strain on the balance of payments. Therefore, he can be vitally concerned by decisions in this phase. Furthermore, other players can be involved. Thus, managements of other GCEs: to the extent that such new projects mean new business, suppliers of equipment or subcontractors have a stake in their pursuit.

Facing such motives in favour of MN investments, there remain the strong motives for domestic investment discussed above. Conflict, therefore, becomes inevitable. To the divergences about what resources to employ or where to locate domestically, we have to add those related to the domestic/foreign debate. On the whole, while most players generally see the arguments favouring foreign investments – in particular, that of the currency savings for the country – rather few people see that there is much to gain for themselves and their own games in MN projects. Most political players outside, say, the finance minister or the prime minister, can foster their interests more readily via domestic investments. They will therefore be led to push for a national location – the labour minister, for instance, to secure jobs for national workers or members of parliament hoping to attract investments to their constituency. And most politicians' interests in other games than those directly related to their position are also conducive to their favouring national investments. For example, in one case a member of parliament who had no hope of causing a particular investment to be located in his constituency still favoured a domestic solution to support the struggle of one of his colleagues who was fighting for the investment to be put in his own constituency. And a French interviewee said:

> Only in those instances where the issue of raw materials supply is so widely publicized and the arguments in favour of foreign investment so clear in the public's mind do most politicians take a stance in favour of it. Then they can't beg the issue. They have to come out for MN investment. But they often do so reluctanctly and if, in an underhand way, they can defer the decision, they will not hesitate to do so.

Moreover, for the same motives discussed above, union leaders fight for domestic investment.

Therefore, the proponents of foreign investment are generally in a minority position. Their major asset is the weight of their arguments *per se* – especially those speaking to the country's interests. Their major liability is the host of interests other players have, tied to domestic investment. Generally, for their view to prevail, the issue of the advantages of MN investment must be sufficiently dramatized in the public's eye so that those who otherwise would be opponents can but go along with it.

c. Sales In the third phase there is a double impact. On the one hand, the relative importance of marketing is reduced due to the greater importance of what happens in the other phases. One president said: 'Now that procurement poses serious difficulties we think less about the marketing end of the business'. On the other hand, by attracting people's attention to the natural resource problems in general, raw materials scarcity results in more people being concerned by GCEs' activities in this field, including activities in this phase. One interviewee said: 'Politicians start out by becoming interested in the problem of raw materials availability. But soon, they invariably become involved in all parts of the company's activities'.

Less attention to marketing reduces the potential for conflict. But more people worrying about this phase tends to result in a more laborious decision-making process.

The involvement of more people does not result in greater conflict *per se*: the issues raised by this phase are on the whole rarely of direct concern to politicians. Rather, politicians' involvement causes a slowing-down of decisions – as reported by one interviewee:

> It is not that they cause you to take truly different actions than you intended to. But they cause you to lose time. They are so concerned with the problems related to this sector [oil] that they want to look into everything. And this even in areas not germane to their preoccupations. And since they don't always know much about management, they take a lot of time making their minds up about what is appropriate or not.

3. *In sum*

The first phase is MN by necessity and no player really seriously takes exception with this. The second phase is far more controversial. Controversy exists practically always about decisions such as the location of investments or the technology to be employed. When raw materials are abundant, the majority of actors usually tend to opt for domestic investments and GCEs are generally more likely to build plants at home than abroad. Exceptions include those cases in which government players have grown into the habit of not taking much interest in company affairs and when the head of the GCE in question is a particularly powerful individual. Then, micro concerns can be the key to decision-making and MN actions can be pursued. When natural resources are scarce, conflict is typically especially strong. Still, proponents of domestic investment frequently prevail unless the arguments for MN investments are both compelling and widely recognized as such. The third phase is more often not a subject of heated debate. MN expansion is more closely tied to overall corporate strategy. On the whole, the major effect of political actors' involvement is the slowing down of the decision process.

B. Primary sector decisions – domestic natural resources

Here we focus on GCEs operating in fields in which there are raw materials at home, sufficient to give the country its autonomy in the sector (or at least potentially so). This includes principally coal or steel (and recently, for certain countries, oil). Here MN operations are not truly necessary since natural resources are available domestically. Yet, a company can still go MN to seek additional or more attractive resources, or to produce more efficiently, or simply to broaden its market.

A variety of players are involved in these companies' strategic decisions. First, management for both position-related and personal motives. These companies are often confronted with mature markets, which means they frequently face declining sales and profit problems. Management is consequently interested in contracting existing operations and in diversification. One interviewee said: 'Our problem is much less what new investments to make as what and how to divest. Only if we can do other things than our traditional basic activity, is it possible to envisage to make new investments'. Another interviewee said: 'Of course, certain companies still make sizeable capital outlays, but generally these are more geared to revamping the equipment and production facilities in view of making them more efficient than to actually expand capacity'. Moreover, as we will see, the degree of political involvement tends to be high. As a result, management has important personal stakes involved in strategic decisions tied to politicians' interests and aims.

For a variety of reasons, in-government players are often quite concerned by GCEs' behaviour here. First, since these companies frequently have cash problems, they need to be either explicitly subsidized or to receive financing from the state at preferential terms.[4] This makes them prone to governmental surveillance and to certain government representatives in particular; such as the finance minister, and other ministers too: 'Since they eat up state funds, they have to be monitored especially closely and one has to make sure they operate in the collective interest', said a French interviewee. Indeed, these companies are supported for specific motives and several political figures are concerned that these motives be satisfied.

First, many of these sectors are regarded as vital for the country:[5] 'A country must do its best to reduce its dependence on foreign producers in these sectors', said a French executive 'not only because of the safety of its supply of these goods but also to be able to control the prices of these commodities which, if suddenly unreasonably increased, threaten the competitiveness of the whole economy'. This causes a number of politicians to worry about these sectors – the sponsoring minister of course, the ministers for finance and economics, for energy as well as sometimes the head of the executive himself; and certain civil servants are also concerned (such as planners).

Further, these companies are relevant as heavy generators of investment and employment. Certain regions are vitally dependent on them. As a result, certain ministers (the labour minister, for example) as well as members of parliament (such as representatives of these regions) are involved. And so are certain civil servants (the DATAR persons are a case in point).

Personal motives are important too. Many decisions lend themselves to being exploited from an electoral viewpoint. Thus, we found several instances of members of parliament convinced that objectively, from a micro as well as from a national viewpoint, the best thing to do for particular GCEs was to close down their plants in their constituencies. Yet, in view of their electoral aims, they could not afford to take such a stand; on the contrary, they fought for more government subsidies for the companies to go on with their activity in those areas. And venal interests often play a central role; for example, one interviewee reported: '[A particular GCE] recently made a major investment to revamp its equipment in one of its mines which was patently unprofitable and in which extraction would be uneconomical whatever machinery was used. Yet, it did so because a major political figure exerted pressure on it to act in this fashion in return for money from the manufacturer of the equipment'.

Members of the opposition are frequently concerned with such decisions. When the opposition is of a conservative bend, the common stand is one of criticism against subsidies. Typical of such an attitude, one of these men said: 'We are going towards a true welfare state. They subsidize anything and especially hopelessly losing propositions'. When the opposition is leftist, the position is the opposite one: criticisms are voiced each time the government indicates it might let down a GCE which is threatening to close down a plant and lay workers off. One interviewee said: 'It is their general philosophy as well as consistent with their marketing strategy to claim they fight for workers' interests and especially for the defence of their jobs. They do this indiscriminately without trying to find out which situations are worthy of government help and which are not . . . It is in their political interest to act this way'.

Union leaders tend to take an active interest in these companies. Again, their stands reflect less a concern for workers' 'true' long-term interest as a concern to appeal to workers via arguments to which they feel they will be receptive. This causes them to fight against layoffs where the only reasonable decision is to shut plants down. And this not merely from a microeconomic standpoint but also from a general interest standpoint; what the collectivity gets out of subsidizing such operations is clearly less than what it puts in and what it could receive were the resources put to better uses. And this is often counterproductive from the long-run viewpoint of workers themselves: by artificially keeping them in jobs which are non-productive, one puts off doing something one will be bound to do later in even more dramatic conditions. A French interviewee said: 'They are kept in a job which they will have to give up anyway at one point or another; were they to do it now, they would be re-cycled and be used in more profitable tasks, which of course, in time, is better for them too'.

The stand of certain unionists, particularly 'revolutionary' ones, as well as of some leftist opposition members – notably communists – is quite dogmatic: 'They fight for certain things because their doctrine tells them to, but there is often little pragmatic foundation underlying their struggles', said a British interviewee. Thus, they fight for job preservation in certain plants when the government and employers propose alternative jobs for the workers who would be laid off, as a matter of principle – 'for the sake of opposition *per se*', as a German interviewee said.

A case in point is the stand taken in the autumn of 1976 by the head of the French CGT, Georges Séguy, favouring the nationalization of the steel sector – as reported by an interviewee:

> One fails to understand why one would take this position. Nationalization in this sector would not resolve anything in the industry's present crisis. The only explanation is that Mr. Séguy is trapped in his political game: he, as well as his communist friends have to advocate nationalizations to preserve their credibility *vis-à-vis* their followers. Otherwise, they would lose their reputation as communists.

And the proof of the pudding of this attitude's purely dogmatic foundation is the fact that some of the most prominent economists of their allies – the Socialist Party – privately acknowledge that the nationalization programme of the Left is for the most part superfluous to any real economic or social change they advocate and is justified only by the concessions the socialists had to make to the communists, who themselves had to push for at least some nationalizations to live up to their image.

The stand of certain unionists' – particularly 'revolutionary' ones, as well as of decisions. When left on its own, management often decides to diversify into more lucrative areas. And this may be conducive to MN expansion. The best illustration is probably the Dutch DSM which diversified from its original activity of mining coal in the south of the country into a variety of other areas (primarily in the chemical industry). This led it to go MN (including a major operation in Georgia, USA). As a company interviewee noted:

We were able to do this because our top management was not encumbered with political considerations. In passing, note that this was beneficial for everybody, including workers: practically all of them were able to find new jobs in our new activities; had we been forced to stick with mining, workers would have inevitably lost over time – despite subsidies, we couldn't have kept them endlessly in losing activities.

This, however, is an exception. Typically, in-government players push for domestic operations. When a sector is considered vital to the economy and looked upon as critical to the country's independence, politicians naturally propend for its development in autarchy. Further, several of these players can solve at least part of 'their problem' via domestic activities. This is the case of the labour minister or the congressmen of the regions involved, who can take short-term credit for keeping certain concerns going. And so can certain civil servants who are *de facto* more rewarded for their immediate results than for the deep impact they have on the country's long-run development.

Even those politicians who are not in a position to have much to gain or lose directly from such domestic operations end up favouring them in view of the political environment in which they are forced to play. A staffer said:

> The prime minister as well as other key 'technical' men in the cabinet such as the finance minister, see that it would be desirable for GCEs to diversify from declining activities – both product and area diversification . . . Thus, even in the case of vital goods which the country can produce locally, it might be desirable to discontinue domestic production and go and seek the raw materials abroad where they may be cheaper. However, these men cannot always encourage this diversification for political reasons.

The reason is primarily that if he does not fight for the preservation of domestic activities, a politician exposes himself to the criticisms of his political adversaries. Thus, if a conservative or centrist government head comes out in favour of the closing down of a domestic operation and of a foreign investment, leftist politicians and union leaders will exploit the situation and attack him. The problem is that their arguments, while usually at best debatable from an objective viewpoint, have considerable impact on the political scene. For the Left, as well as the more radical unionists, often claim – be it for doctrinaire or purely political reasons or both – that such GCEs are to devote their efforts to domestic investments, thus fostering the interests of workers. As a French interviewee said: 'Even if in reality these arguments have little foundation, they work with the public and thus help their proponents in their electoral struggle'. These arguments compel politicians who would otherwise favour diversification to stand for GCEs to continue with their existing range of activities.

In sum, these GCEs therefore tend to have relatively limited MN activities. Political players and union leaders favour domestic operations, and management both puts up with their pressures and tends to be co-opted by politicians' interests. Exceptions are cases of GCEs in which politicians take little interest and where management is free to set strategy on its own.

C. Secondary sector decisions

While some of these companies do not readily lend themselves to MN expansion (shipyards, for example – though it is not inconceivable that shipyards of different countries link up either temporarily or on a permanent basis), most of them are quite amenable to MN activities. Such activities range from wholly owned sales subsidiaries (which we consider MN activities provided they constitute a sizeable share of the value-added[6]) to fully fledged manufacturing concerns.

1. *Wholly owned sales subsidiary*

The question of setting up a subsidiary abroad is typically raised within the company concerned itself. Rarely does it happen that an outsider bring up such an issue – either a government player or, say, a union leader. A company president said: 'Government people only have ideas about corporate action when a problem of theirs is at stake. Otherwise, their mentality and their foci of attention are such that they take little interest in what a company can or cannot do. And the creation of foreign sales subsidiaries rarely can promise much to such actors in terms of their own problems'.

There are certain exceptions. Thus, an executive reported that his company first invested abroad via a sales outfit first proposed, then strongly encouraged, by the minister for foreign trade: 'The country's balance-of-payments situation was so bad that the government wanted to do everything it could to increase our exports. Thus, the minister came up with this idea. And we finally went ahead with it because of his insistence and that of our sponsoring minister whom he had convinced'.

Most ideas for such investments indeed come from in-company actors. First, top managers: their primary concern is to broaden the firm's market scope. (It can also happen that they be motivated by a desire to 'please', say, a minister: in the context of an effort by the government to spur exports, management can decide to set up foreign sales operations.) Marketing men obviously can have similar motivations, and so can staffers. Furthermore, middle managers can be at the origin of such investments because, being in contact with the field, they are often best fit to see market opportunities. And they may hope to foster personal motives; by advocating the creation of a new subsidiary, such an individual may entertain hopes of personal empire building in that he may end up in charge of the subsidiary.

Once the issue is raised, it is still in-company actors who are usually mostly concerned. Those who propose these investments in the first place are normally in favour of them. Yet, others may disagree. Thus, the chief executive may have a personal aversion to foreign operations, or the marketing vice-president may wish to avoid additional headaches. As we saw earlier, ethnocentric attitudes are not infrequent in GCEs and the concept of foreign subsidiaries may be resisted among management. Still, it is within the company that such ideas are most likely to encounter most support.

In-government players (as well as unionists) often take little interest in such decisions. For much the same reasons for which they rarely come up with such an idea to start with, and because of the usually relatively modest proportions of the investments involved, they often feel indifferent. Certain players may favour such a decision. Thus, say, the finance minister may encourage it because of the balance-of-payments advantages he sees in increased exports. Other players may oppose it. There can be a systematic opposition such as that of radical opposition members. Yet, given the general low-key nature of such decisions, they are not favourite targets; these issues are rarely exploitable politically and therefore are generally not used in purely political games. Further, certain people can oppose these decisions because they feel they constitute a first step towards other MN commitments and notably direct investments in manufacturing operations: as we will see, several players oppose anything they see as a step in this direction.

On the whole, these decisions do not run into major difficulties in terms of conflicts between company and outside players. The greatest debates, in fact, occur within GCEs themselves and tend to regard primarily microeconomic questions.

2. Manufacturing operations

Again, most ideas for such investments originally arise among in-company persons. They most often spring from their position-related concerns. The motivation is typically to seek production efficiencies (lower cost locations). There can also be logistics reasons (for example, be closer to end markets) or, say, the aim of avoiding customs barriers. Besides, management may want to transfer production to where there are fewer labour problems (particularly Italian executives confronted with continuous unrest at home). And there may be personal reasons (such as, the desire of empire building).

While it is rather rare here also that in-government players come up with the idea of foreign production, there are instances where they do – when they can use foreign investments for purposes of their own. This is mostly the case in matters concerning foriegn policy. A case in point is Renault's plant in Canada, built at a time when General de Gaulle was pursuing his policy of encouraging Quebec's autonomy and its *rapprochement* with France; the original idea of Renault's investment apparently came from the General himself in view of establishing tangible ties between the two countries. Also, in the context of Willy Brandt's

Ostpolitik, certain ideas for foreign investments by GCEs in Eastern countries reportedly came from government officials.

Whereas many players are indifferent to the national/foreign production question when it is not posed, they do get involved once it becomes an issue. These include in-government actors and first of all politicians. A number of them have an interest in hindering an internationalization of manufacturing. Once more, the primary position-related motives pertain to employment questions. Thus, the labour minister tends to see in any attempt to transfer a share of production abroad an opportunity cost in terms of his problem – the employment situation at home. Given the short-term pressures he is under, he cannot rely too much on the long-term benefits MN production may yield, or on the argument that in due course MN production will induce exports of related products and therefore have positive effects in terms of employment. As one interviewee said: 'Their problem is here and now. They are already too dependent on promises they make in general to the electorate. They must constantly try hard to show immediate results'.

Other ministers share this type of problem – for instance, the ministers for finance, economics, industry, etc.; and the prime minister himself, given the importance of the problem and people's sensitivity to it, is vitally concerned with the employment question. Moreover, even if a particular minister is not by his position formally responsible for anything related to national employment, he is often forced to be concerned with the problem, since the life of the cabinet, and therefore that of his own position, are frequently vitally affected by this question. Thus, a French interviewee said:

> Each time a GCE thinks of setting up a plant abroad, people in government become all excited. They see this as a threat to their efforts to solve key national problems – unemployment in particular. And beyond a threat to the socioeconomic problem *per se*, they see a political risk: they are even more afraid of the reaction the electorate will have as well as of the attacks they may expose themselves to by political adversaries.

Beyond employment as such, other concerns cause a member of government to oppose MN expansion. Regional development is a case in point. Again, political deadlines impose on politicians a need to go for immediate and visible achievements even though they themselves may realize this is bad for the company's health as well as suboptimal for the long-run interest of the collectivity. Further, in certain cases a member of the government can be led to advocate domestic as opposed to MN investments because he sees such investments as being a motor for the rest of industry. Car manufacturers represent a typical instance. Certain government players can be against foreign production on the grounds that domestic investments instead do not only themselves spur the economy but are also generators of important byproducts (for example, increase the volume of subcontractors). Again, while such persons may indeed be convinced that such arguments are valid in and of themselves, what has much more weight are the political aspects related to them. As a French interviewee said:

> While some of this type of reasoning is valid, on the whole the proponents of these arguments themselves know they are, partially at least, fallacious. For instance, over time, keeping production at home *par force* weakens the company and thus is bad for the economy as well. But politically they have to fight as if they believed what they said because the people are convinced these arguments are the ones which are correct, i.e. they only see the immediate effects of either domestic or international investments. And what people believe is all that counts for a politician.

Moreover, as was the case above, domestic investments lend themselves to more private types of interests. Again, we find politicians speculating on land on which a new plant might be built or receiving bribes for causing a GCE to invest in one region or another. An Italian interviewee said:

> Why would you want a member of government to push for a foreign investment? What does he have to gain from it? He knows he probably is in his job for a few months only. During this time he can't really do much for the country. And, anyhow, he rarely cares. So he tries to do as much as he can for himself. With this objective in mind, his best bet, as far as GCEs are concerned, is in the context of domestic activities. It is here that he can sell the favours he can render most readily. Thus, he can sell his influence for a GCE to go in a particular direction; at home he will always find customers because so many people have so much to gain or lose from GCEs going one way or another.

Other politicians are also concerned by these decisions, congressmen, for example. One interviewee reported that a given member of parliament had exerted pressure on his company to build a plant in his region in view of fostering its industrial development and alleviating its unemployment problem. Yet,

> the particular plant we needed was not labour-intensive (though our overall activity is). We told the congressman that the plant we might build would not do much for employment. His answer was that it didn't really matter too much, since the psychological effect our project would have on the people would be important enough. He didn't say what for. But he clearly was thinking of the next elections which were a few months off. In fact, he would have been content with the *announcement* of our project. What would happen thereafter was of much lesser consequence for him.

Further, venal motives can intervene here too. For instance, we learned from several sources that a particular investment by a food company had occurred in a given area because of bribes paid by local agricultural products producers and real-estate developers to the congressman of that region for him to exert pressure for the investment to be located there. In other cases, congressmen can have direct stakes of their own tied to particular GCEs investments. It is clear that this stands in the way of MN expansion.

Members of the opposition usually favour domestic projects. In France and Italy especially we found such players have been quite influential in hindering MN growth. Their motives can be genuine and concrete; they may sincerely see socioeconomic reasons for opposing foreign investment. Yet, their stand is most often primarily motivated by political considerations. As a French top executive said:

> Foreign investments by GCEs lend themselves to being exploited electorally via arguments such as 'companies belonging to the collectivity join the capitalistic carousel of multinational finance' or 'public companies use public money to pursue imperialistic ends rather than serving the interests of the national working classes'. Whether justified or not, such arguments can have a non-negligible impact on the public. And GCEs' behaviour must avoid giving the opposition grounds for voicing them.

(In this connection, it is worth noting in passing the problems raised by the denationalization of certain GCEs. While this has occurred, at least partially, in certain countries such as Germany, in others where the Left is most doctrinaire and influential, this has not been possible. While its arguments appear most often tenuous from an objective standpoint, they are quite powerful politically. A case in point is Renault, which the government, notably in the late 1960s, had thought to, at least indirectly, denationalize in part via the transfer of some of the equity to employees; while a few steps were taken in this direction, on the whole the plan miscarried because of political reasons.)

Political staffers have their boss's political ends in mind. As such, they are motivated to seek arguments in favour of domestic growth since this is what yields the highest political dividends. And they must often find reasons for their bosses to oppose MN expansion when this opposition is in fact primarily grounded in personal motives. As one of these men said: 'Our job is also to find plausible rationalizations which can be made public of what politicians do for completely different reasons'.

Many civil servants also tend to oppose MN expansion. For much the same reasons as in the case of primary sector decisions, they oppose foreign investments when they see this may entail an opportunity cost in terms of their particular area of responsibility.

Non-government players also not infrequently take a negative stance on MN investments. Union leaders in particular, for whom foreign expansion holds little promise in terms of the games in which they are involved – as acknowledged by one of them: 'In these secondary sector cases in particular, workers feel they have a lot to lose from foreign production in terms of national job opportunities. We must satisfy their expectations and stand for the protection of employment. True, this leads us sometimes to take certain positions which may not be the most reasonable ones in the long run . . .'. Further, radical unionists in particular can use government decisions for GCEs to go MN to raise trouble in view of political ends – as explained by a French interviewee: 'Given their often close ties with leftist opposition members, they frequently look for excuses to create unrest in view of the government's policy. Foreign investment projects lend themselves to this because the "base" relates to such issues clearly'. Thus, an Italian high-ranking civil servant reported that a few years ago union leaders started a strike to protest against a project of a GCE to locate a new plant in the north. Reportedly the proposed location was the only logical one: locating in the Mezzogiorno would have been grossly inefficient and would not have done much for local industrial development and employment: 'The unions' attitude was not motivated by a real concern for the benefits locating in the South would entail, but primarily by political reasons. This was part of the overall strategy of the Left to create social and economic chaos and to attempt to discredit the government'.

Finally, certain in-company players can oppose a foreign investment project either because of microeconomic reasons (a manager may personally feel that the project is unattractive either for the firm as a whole or for that part of the enterprise – for example, a division – for which he is responsible) or for personal motives. Among these, one of the strongest motives is that of serving the interests of key political figures.

Facing such negative stands, several players are generally inclined to support MN expansion.

It is among corporate management that MN expansion finds its most numerous advocates. MN expansion generally presents its greatest attractiveness in terms of microeconomic variables and those responsible for such aspects are naturally sensitive to this. In particular, the most frequent argument in favour of MN expansion here is that if production is not transferred abroad closer to end markets, such markets, previously served by exports, will be lost to developing local competition.[7] Here also, if decisions are left to management, chances are that MN opportunities will be pursued. A German chief executive said:

> In this company we have been fortunate enough to be able to function with relatively little interference by politicians. Therefore, our aims are tied to the company's performance *per se* and we are relatively uninhibited by other types of considerations. We seek to exploit every opportunity to improve our results, be it at home or abroad. But I believe we are an exception among European GCEs.

Corporate staff people are frequently among the strongest advocates of MN expansion. A chief executive said: 'They can take a more objective look at the

342

situation and at the possibilities of action we have – including avenues for MN growth which we at top management often fail to see because we are too much caught up in operating issues as well as with questions pertaining to the sociopolitical environment we operate in'.

And in-company players often have personal motivations to push for MN expansion. Beyond the personal aspiration, many managers have – in private as well as in public firms – to develop their organization's scope to MN dimensions,[8] GCEs' managers often have special reasons. In the words of a French executive:

> The interference of government people is a considerable nuisance for us. Many executives resent the fact that so many people interfere in their jobs. Yet, this interference is primarily geared to domestic operations; in MN activities there is much less of it. Therefore, several managers have a desire to go MN in order to have at least a share of their business in which they have some freedom.

In-government players may also take a favourable stance on MN expansion. When an MN investment promises to yield certain benefits for a specific problem a player faces, he will of course tend to support it. Thus, ministers for foreign affairs often back certain projects which can help them solve their problem with certain countries. Secondary sector investments lend themselves especially well to this kind of purpose because of their multiplier effect as well as for their visibility. Furthermore, there are cases where MN expansion is so obviously advantageous for the company as well as for the collectivity that it is hard to oppose it: 'In such cases, even when personal motives are strong for them to fight for a GCE to stay home, politicians are forced not to stand in the way of foreign growth', said a German interviewee.

Moreover, technical staff people of certain politicians may advocate a positive stand on MN expansion. In particular, the staffers of the sponsoring minister tend to take a micro view and see the advantages of MN expansion. They then, in turn, can convince their boss. (But if, on the other hand, he has compelling reasons to favour a stay-home policy, chances are that staffers' impact will be rather limited.)

Thus, we see there is considerable potential conflict among players. A player has different degrees of influence in different circumstances as a function of his formal position, his bargaining power *vis-à-vis* other relevant players, and his and their willingness to fight to have their way. It often happens that an individual with high power chooses not to make use of it, thus allowing another player with less power to have his way in return for his support in another issue.

For instance, in one case a member of parliament, for whom a particular new plant investment by a GCE meant a lot, ended up by succeeding in causing the investment to occur in his region despite the initial resistance of all other players concerned: management wanted to build a plant abroad, the parent holding to whom the company belonged wanted the investment to be located in the industrialized area of the country, the sponsoring minister favoured a location where another GCE had just invested in large facilities producing raw materials the new plant needed and which as yet had an insufficient local market, and other government members opted for other locations – the prime minister in particular wanting the investment in a completely different area. The congressman in question got his way despite his *a priori* more powerful opponents by a combination of forces: first, he was a key representative of a party which was part of the ruling coalition; this party, though the smallest of the coalition, was essential for the coalition to have a majority in parliament; he could thus blackmail key ministers – threaten to withdraw his support (and possibly that of all of his party) from the cabinet if he did not obtain satisfaction. Second, he negotiated with his most important opponents that if they let him have his way in this issue, he would not interfere in other important issues which had to be decided upon in the near future and, indeed, that he would support them in these other battles; for one of these issues he promised he would do his best to convince other members of his party to support them as well (a particularly important argument in view of the fact that these men had otherwise clearly stated they would not support them); and for another one of these issues he promised he would use his best efforts to discourage one of his party's members from embarking in a fight destined to defeat one of his present opponents in a key political struggle. Finally, he promised certain remaining opponents financial compensation for their support: he would cause a group of 'friends' to buy some land in his constituency at a relatively cheap price; he would then arrange that the company would buy that land back for the construction of the new plant at a substantial premium above the price he and his friends would have paid for it; he would then use the proceeds to 'convince' the company's management to go along with his view; and he offered substantial payments to two of the most vocal and influential of his political opponents if they stopped fighting him.

These forces in themselves are not necessarily compelling. It is probable that this player's party would not have withdrawn its support from the cabinet merely for this issue. Also, for the most part, his opponents in fact did not feel that his support (or non-opposition) in the other issues was truly determining for them. And they might have obtained the same or even higher personal returns had the issue received a solution other than the one he advocated. Yet, in the context of the *overall political games*, they figured here that they had more to gain by letting him have his way in this issue than they had to lose by exerting all their power and insisting on another outcome. They figured they had to grant members of the smaller party certain favours anyway; given that the present investment decision meant so much to one of them, they figured that this would be a relatively good bet – as explained by one of the players: 'They saw they could please one of the key representatives of this party at a relatively moderate cost for them – the opportunity cost for them not to have their own way being smaller than the perceived benefits this favour would yield to them. This especially in view of the expected benefits the support of [that congressman] would yield. . .'. While none of the arguments taken separately would have been sufficient to convince his opponents to give in, taken together and considered in the context of the overall political scene, they did prove successful for the congressman to gain appropriate support for his 'cause'.

Moreover, one further element was determining: the dissentions among the congressman's opponents themselves. Indeed, the other players did not agree on any alternative location. And the congressman in fact carefully entertained such divisions; while arguing with others in favour of his position, he deliberately emphasized the risk that the only real alternative was not that advocated by his interlocutor, but that of another player (who often happened to be a political adversary of the interlocutor himself); and he thereby stressed the faults of such a solution, especially from the point of view of the aims pursued by the interlocutor. For example, he showed the sponsoring minister that if his location was not chosen, what would really happen is that management would be able to prove the economic advantages of a foreign location 'and everybody would then lose'. As a direct witness of this case put it : 'He followed the principle of *divide et impera*. Had his opponents been united to push for another location, he wouldn't have had a chance. But they were divided and he did all he could to keep them this way, indeed sometimes to further arouse them against each other. This was the real key to his success'.

In sum, it should be clear that there are more players in favour of domestic investments than of MN expansion. Outside of certain particular instances, the majority of key people tend to oppose foreign investments because such investments do not promise much to them in terms of the particular problems and interests they have. In most cases, for a GCE to become MN, management must have a free hand to set strategy as it sees fit and/or there must be truly resolute support by one or several key persons in this direction. A French interviewee said:

> Of course for a public enterprise to become an MNC takes a great personality – a man of undiscussed capabilities and integrity as well as of superior willpower, since it is necessary to overcome the apathy of government people as well as the outright opposition of many. But this happens. Take Pierre Dreyfus, Renault's president for twenty years. He has been strong enough to get his way and indeed under him Renault became the most dynamic MNC of France.

D. Secondary sector decisions – high technology industries

Industries de pointe deserve a separate treatment. The most typical companies here are computer and aircraft manufacturers. While in the case of the latter, foreign direct investments are hard to conceive given production is normally concentrated in one site, computer manufacturers can have major operations abroad, with marketing, production and R & D activities taking place beyond national frontiers. Besides, both these industries offer the best instances of a special kind of MN activity – international co-operation agreements.

1. *Foreign direct investment*

Many of the players are the same as those involved in other secondary sector industries; and their stands on MN expansion are similar. Yet, their motivations are often different.

It is management which is most likely to come up with a foreign investment idea and to support it most actively. This again stems from its micro orientation: the desirability of MN expansion is strongest in terms of micro considerations; because of its position, it is management that is most sensitive to them. Specifically, here more than anywhere else, size is a critical success factor (were it only in view of the R & D requirements, a company below a certain size has few chances of being profitable). Domestic markets cannot support enough sales to permit the attainment of the desirable volume. And it is rarely possible to be competitive abroad via exports alone; the economics of the industry tend to favour local production, foreign buyers frequently prefer those companies which have at least some local value-added (they are encouraged in this by local authorities who also insist there be some R & D in their country), and given the nature of the products, the customer service is critical and requires a strong local organization. Therefore, foreign investment is often a must – and one most clearly apparent to those within the firm itself.

Within management there are nuances. Top management tends to take a more global view and to be concerned with strategic fit – the match between new opportunities and the current course of the firm. Yet, given its frequent concern for macro issues, it can be distracted from this. Therefore, certain staffers are often most clearly aware of the potential rewards of MN expansion. And certain functional heads can also be sensitive to certain MN opportunities (for example, the marketing vice-president will be most attentive to the possibilities of foreign sales subsidiaries).

It can happen that in-government players push for MN expansion on micro grounds. Thus, certain staffers of the sponsoring minister may identify opportunities abroad which speak to the financial performance of the firm. Yet, this is rare on the whole. Normally, when in-government players argue for a foreign investment it is for political reasons.

Compared to other secondary sector investments, GCEs in these industries are more seldom 'used' for general political purposes: if key government players want to cause certain investments to occur in a certain country for foreign policy reasons, they usually will not go to high technology firms but to more traditional types of industries. Government players attempting to influence high technology GCEs usually have more specific motives in mind. Thus, in one case a minister for foreign affairs wanted to activate a policy of technical or scientific assistance to a country and he thus reverted to one of these companies for it to set up facilities in that nation.

Decisions here tend to be highly visible and can therefore be readily exploited politically. Because of the amount of capital involved and the perceived importance of these industries for national security and independence as well as the prestige attached to national high technology achievements, these issues are frequently watched closely by the public. This makes politicians especially concerned with them. Not infrequently will a key political figure take a strong public stand in favour of the development of such an area with a view to building up an image of banner-bearer of national technical progress and defender of national independence. In so doing, a person pushes for expansion of the industry involved, which naturally leads to MN expansion too. Thus, a French interviewee said: 'A few years ago a Gaullist minister wanted to foster the national data processing industry. He pressed for the rapid development of the sector which, as a consequence, resulted in certain international projects also'.

On the other hand, a number of players oppose foreign investments. Again, the most articulate are in-government persons. Employment is a major consideration, particularly since high technology industries tend to induce employment in other related industries (such as suppliers or subcontractors). Further, these companies' activity is seen as critical for national independence, as explained by an industry executive: 'They are determining for the state of scientific and technological development of the nation, they have a major bearing on national security and defence, in view of the proprietary nature of the know-how involved, from them depends in great part the state's ability to negotiate at a par with other states'. Many feel such activities should be kept domestic – as explained by a French interviewee: 'If a country has advanced research and development in these areas, it is less dependent on other nations. But, for this to be true, these activities have to employ national resources and take place at home. Otherwise, they are not really yours – you can't truly count on them'. Moreover, these industries are generally heavily dependent on government financing. Many politicians take the position that this money should be spent at home; the argument is that public money is spent not only to achieve certain technological results but also to stimulate certain research and scientific activities at home and thus give national technicians and scientists a chance to develop their studies.

Such arguments are made by a variety of players. First, several ministers are involved for issues related to employment, industrial development and financial questions. The attributions of other members of the executive cause them to worry about special issues – scientific development, defence, national equipment, etc. The head of the executive is also often concerned by these decisions. And so are members of parliament who often get on special committees involving these GCEs (for example, a commission responsible for military procurement). Finally, staffers and certain civil servants are involved (such as industrial planners).

Personal motives are essential also. The visibility of such issues works against them as well as for them. Because of this visibility, many players are encouraged to take a stand on them. And these stands are motivated less by sound detached analysis as by emotional, electorally oriented reactions. Many of the arguments pertaining to GCEs' contribution to national independence and to the state's freedom are objectively fallacious or at least questionable: on the one hand, MN growth is often the only way to effectively reach a critical volume capable of ensuring the attainment of the aimed-for technological and scientific degree of development; and on the other, it is not at all clear that if part of the activity occurs beyond national frontiers, its benefits cease to accrue to the country. And their proponents are often aware of this. But this is of little importance. What counts is the way the public perceives these arguments and their soundness. As a French interviewee said: 'When a politician argues against MN expansion in view of preserving the national autonomy, the argument "sounds right" and people give him credit for it. That over time the facts are such that the firm will not be able to survive in autarchy except for massive government backup, people don't see this'.

Thus, politicians oppose MN expansion clearly beyond what they themselves, in view of their position-related responsibilities, would otherwise opt for – let alone what an objective detached analyst would see as reasonable. By leading people to think he fights for the nation's grandeur, the politician flatters people's nationalistic pride. Little does it matter if these are demagogic arguments which mislead people, letting them believe that the country can be self-sustained beyond what it really can. What counts are the political dividends which accrue to the player: standing for a strong national industry in certain hot sectors helps a politician build an image of dedication to national strength and independence. Members of the opposition denounce government-backed projects for MN expansion. And so do many of the more radical union leaders. But members of the ruling majority, because they cannot politically afford to let members of the opposition have the monopoly of patriotism, equally argue for national growth.

Furthermore, venal interests can come into play here too. Given the capital-intensiveness of these sectors and given the often very high sums of government money behind certain projects, 'there are generally the greatest opportunities for corruption here', as a British interviewee said. Particularly since, at least domestically, prime customers of these companies are government-related organizations, in-government players indeed have manifold occasions to receive 'commissions' for causing such and such a purchase to materialize or not. As an Italian interviewee said:

> As long as such deals happen within national frontiers, you are in the 'family' and your exposure to risks is minimal. But internationally things are different. Look at the problems people have with Lockheed. The Americans bring everything out into the open; they don't respect the tacit agreements underlying such 'payments'. The same thing would be true if you allow a national company to go MN. On one hand, there would be less chances of bribery for national politicians. Secondly, the risks of scandal would be higher: management would go on with the practice of corruption overseas; it would invariably be caught at one point or another, creating considerable embarrassment for everybody. Really, nobody sees what there is to gain from multinationalizing certain GCEs.

2. *International joint ventures*

These industries also provide some of the more spectacular cases of international co-operation agreements.[9] Such agreements are characteristic by their scope – the magnitude of the work partners execute jointly and the length of the projects. A case in point is Concorde on which efforts between British Aerospace (then BAC) and Aerospatiale (then Sud Aviation) and between SNECMA and Rolls-Royce (then British Siddeley as far as the engines of Concorde were concerned) started as early as 1961. And the development costs in the 1962–74 period were 2.7 billion US dollars,[10] while the 1971 sales (in US dollars) of the four main companies involved were 663 million for Aerospatiale, 650 million for Rolls-Royce, 382 million for BAC and 248 million for SNECMA.[11] When the extent of the co-operation is so vast and when so many resources are exchanged across national frontiers, it is clear that a transnational joint venture falls into the realm of MN strategic decisions or actions.[12]

The primary motives in favour of international co-operation agreements are microeconomic in nature; given the financial resources required and the risks involved, a company is rarely able and well advised to undertake the typical projects on its own. As a high-ranking executive of such a company said: 'Certain projects in this field are so large in scale, the funds required to be competitive so great, and the uncertainties so high, that European companies can rarely "go it alone". Even with government back-up and financial assistance, we have to undertake these projects in conjunction with other companies'. Frequently, there are very few firms per country in these fields; indeed, there is often but one. A co-operative agreement then means selecting a partner which is abroad. Besides, even when there is more than one company nationally, since these projects are government-sponsored, it is the governments themselves which call for co-operation with a foreign partner: it usually makes less sense to split government support between two companies than to give all the support to one and have it work with a foreign firm which itself will benefit from support from its own government.

Once again, given their position, it is corporate executives who should in the first place be sensitive to these arguments and the microeconomic realities facing the company. Yet, given the personality and background of the men heading some of these companies, this is not always true. Indeed, especially in the aeronautics field, the individuals named at the head of GCEs often come from civil service or even the army. Such men are generally put in such positions, on the one hand because of their presumed technical expertise acquired 'in the field', for their presumed knowledge of the actual needs of the market (or parts thereof) and for their contacts both with the users of the products and with the key individuals in government, who are critical to secure state financing, as well as for anyone of the many bureaucratic procedures which GCEs have to go through in these fields (for example approval by a specialized commission of the technical specifications of new aircraft). On the other hand, these positions may represent what the French refer to as a *voie de garage*: a man who has been in a high-ranking military or public administrative position and who is replaced in this position, is named chief executive of a GCE 'in order to keep him busy in a relatively prestigious and relatively lucrative post', as a French interviewee said.

For example, the head of an aircraft manufacturer may be an ex-general of the air force. This man may have been removed from this post either because judged not competent any more or because he may have become 'disturbing' politically. Given his personal prestige, however, and given the real services he rendered to the nation, it would not have been possible to let him go without any further consideration. A 'golden handshake' would then have been in order and his nomination as the head of a GCE an appropriate solution. Besides, his familiarity with both the aircraft field and government makes him look a natural to head a company in this sector.

A case in point is represented by Sud Aviation which later was to become part of Aerospatiale. In 1962, airforce general André Puget 'who had been France's top military man'[13] became the head of the company. As noted by Hochmuth:

> Although Puget was an airforce officer, he was not a technical man nor did he have any industrial management experience. His dowry to the Sud organization was the eminence of having held the highest military position in France and the corresponding contacts, access, esteem, and influence. In addition, he had the advantage of being an anglophile, with many ties in Britain.[14]

This latter characteristic was especially important in view of Sud's co-operation agreement with BAC on Concorde: 'Throughout his administration, Puget fought hard for Sud. As the costs of the programme continued to mount, Puget had used his great prestige to get quick government approval, much to the envy of the BAC management'.[15] As two other observers noted: 'Whenever a problem arose, he merely picked up the ivory-handled telephone and sent for another lorry-load of francs'.[16] Equally revealing is the story of Puget's replacement: 'Even a reputation such as Puget's had limits to its effectiveness, and in December 1966 he was precipitously named ambassador to Sweden. [He was replaced] by Maurice Papon, prefect of the Paris police'.[17] The present president of Aerospatiale is Jacques Mitterrand (the brother of François, the leader of the Socialist Party), an airforce general.

No matter what their human or intellectual qualities are, such men often lack a professional management training and orientation. As an interviewee put it: 'They are great PR fellows but they have no basis for managing a commercial undertaking. As a consequence, they often don't see all the economic imperatives confronted by the enterprise . . . In particular, they are often blind to those factors which make international agreements with other firms desirable'.

The micro arguments of the kind which make co-operative ventures attractive tend to be recognized more readily by other players – notably staffers. Yet, their problem is to capture their boss's attention: given that a top manager is often concerned by other kinds of issues, the staff man not infrequently has a hard time

350

getting him interested in micro problems. This tends to demotivate the staffer, as testified by one of them: 'The president shows little interest in any analysis of the firm's economic or strategic situation. He is interested in other outside matters and he often doesn't have the training to really grasp the meaning of such analysis. Therefore, we often work for nothing. After a while, we get tired of this and we just stop working as hard'.

It is probably in these industries where we found the greatest sensitivity to micro variables by in-government players. Those ministers who are responsible for GCEs in these sectors may push for international co-operative agreements in view of the company's long-run results. Similarly, those ministers who are responsible for a particular area involving the production of GCEs; for example, the defence minister, may worry about the ability of a GCE to produce certain kinds of military equipment. And other politicians may have a special interest in military or high technology matters, which may lead them to worry about GCEs' performance as it relates to these areas. Still, here also, politicians often have too much of a short-term view of things to be truly concerned by such decisions whose real payoff is inevitably distant in the future. It is then civil servants who are most sensitive to these decisions (members of military procurement organizations, for example).

Politicians can also pursue aims other than economic ones in pushing for international co-operative agreements, foreign policy aims in particular. A typical case is that of a player standing for European integration and feeling that such integration should be led by industry – a position held by many in the 1960s – and by high technology firms in particular.[18] A government player wanting to encourage such agreements naturally tends to think of GCEs, since it is on these firms that his influence is usually the greatest.

Yet, again we must not be overly deluded by the actual motivations of those advocating such arguments. Politicians live in an environment in which the highest priority is on short-term results. They rarely truly take long-term questions more seriously than their needs and deadlines in the near future. Indeed, other motives are typically more critical.

First, international joint ventures can help politicians solve 'their problem'. Contrary to foreign direct investment, such agreements frequently appear as having positive effects on employment. The choice here is often between doing a given agreement in conjunction with a foreign partner or not at all (or at least not in economically viable conditions). As one interviewee said: 'Far from taking anything away from the point of view of employment, such agreements in fact add to the number of jobs available at home'. The positive effects are especially sizeable if one thinks of all the induced work such projects create in terms of orders placed with suppliers and contractors. Therefore, all those concerned with employment tend to favour such agreements – individuals such as the minister of labour, economic affairs, the prime minister himself, etc. And since those areas where GCEs are located are particularly affected by such co-operative agreements, the elected representatives of these areas are also vitally concerned by such decisions. For example, between October 1974 and January

1975, the Concorde joint venture underwent a crisis during which the entire project seemed threatened; at that time 'a socialist deputy from Toulouse, Eugène Montel, was dispatched to London to sway his ideological cousins [members of the governing Labour party]. On his return, he assured the press that French and English workers and engineers would continue to build Concorde'.[19] As a French interviewee said: 'One cannot overstress the importance of the macroeconomic arguments in such decisions. These projects typically have a remarkable multiplier effect on the country's economy and on employment in particular. Anybody in government who is held accountable for such macroeconomic questions typically is interested in seeing the successful accomplishment of such agreements'.

In fact, international co-operative agreements are often seen as beneficial for employment by union leaders themselves who most often favour them. Thus, in the above-cited Concorde crisis instance, 'all three French labour unions rose to the defence of the Concorde'.[20]

Further, fighting for such agreements is often helpful for an individual's image. A German interviewee said: 'In view of their high scientific content and their international character, they confer an aureola of progressiveness to he who supports them. And when they occur at a European level, their effect is even greater'.

On the other hand, a number of arguments can be made against international co-operative agreements.

First, a number of politicians are vigorously in favour of 'national independence'. Doctrinaire Gaullists are a case in point. They argue for the country to be independent from outsiders for any question of vital collective interest. Such individuals may oppose international co-operative agreements on the grounds that projects of essential importance for the nation should be developed and controlled by the country on its own. And, as a French interviewee said: 'They can even go so far as to argue that if a project can't be undertaken without a joint venture, it shouldn't be undertaken at all: since it doesn't add much to national independence, the resources committed to it should instead be devoted to another project which can be developed in autarchy'.

Second, certain players can be concerned by the financial costs involved. Such projects often involve enormous sums of money and, what is worse, they have a history of costing far more than what was originally forecast. A case in point is Concorde, whose 1962 cost estimates gave a figure between $420 million and $480 million and which ended up costing $2.7 billion US dollars.[21] Due to the difficulties encountered in organizing certain government-sponsored joint ventures, several people have developed a certain scepticism as to the efficiency of such agreements. Indeed, many in-government players feel – in the words of a German interviewee – 'that the problems of transnational projects are due to certain intrinsic characteristics of the international joint venture formula *per se*'.

Third, and probably usually most important, are personal motives. Given the visibility of these projects, taking a public stand on them frequently has rather far-reaching political effects. An often-cited instance is when certain politicians are forcefully critical of the high expenditure involved in such projects, claiming there could be more useful things which could be done with such funds, and who in fact have other ends in mind: the controversial character of such positions and their often demagogical nature suggest that their contrivers are moved by electoral motives.

Those who are most likely to take such a position are members of the opposition. A French interviewee said:

> These issues are often ideal terrains to attack the government. There are always things which can be criticized in such agreements and in the way they are pursued. And one can always say something about what could be done with the money otherwise. So opposition members don't miss the opportunity offered by the projects to loudly voice criticisms against those who are actually in power.

For instance, in the autumn 1964 British election campaign, members of the Labour Party, which then was in the opposition, advocated a number of belt-tightening economic measures. High in the list was Concorde, labelled a 'Tory prestige project'.[22] We favour a policy which will give the British people prosperity on the ground . . . not at 60 000 feet in the air,' stated Roy Jenkins (later Minister of Aviation).[23] The Labour Party won the election and, yet, once in power, continued with Concorde.

On the whole, international joint ventures are still easier to decide than many other forms of MN expansion (of course not necessarily easy to accomplish effectively). They encounter less opposition in that key players have less to lose and more to gain from them. The negative arguments we discussed tend to refer to rather sporadic motives and are found in certain cases only. All in all, conflicts about such agreements are less vivid than for other forms of MN operations and active proponents of such agreements are generally more likely to ultimately get their way. In fact, the major stumbling-block of such agreements is not the difficulties posed by players opposing them, as the fact that those who should recognize their desirability (that is, key executives) do not do so.

E. Tertiary sector decisions

Most MN strategy decisions here do not present major particularities. Banks, however, constitute a special case.

1. *Banks*

Their management is responsible for micro performance. It is therefore sensitive to those factors which call for MN expansion on this basis. These are pretty much the same as those which apply to private banking institutions. They include the quest for size to achieve certain operating economies, the need to follow clients in their own MN expansion, the need to live up to competition's expansion or simply the desire to exploit foreign opportunities in general.

Yet, management does not focus on such factors as closely as one might think it would. First, the background of executives has an influence. Many of them are ex-high-ranking civil servants. Thus, the presidents of banks such as Société Générale, BNP or Crédit Lyonnais are all *Inspecteurs des Finances* having spent their life at the service of the state (for example, as members of the central bank, the planning 'commissariat', the internal revenue, the ministry of armed forces). 'This entails that their orientation is often more directed to macro issues and less to a drive to achieve the highest possible efficiency and results for the bank', said a French interviewee. And they are frequently distracted by outside problems upon which they are forced to focus. Dr Jahn, a Commerzbank *Vorstandsmitglied*, said:

> I know government-controlled banks' top managers well. At least as far as Crédit Lyonnais and Banco di Roma are concerned, since we have a close co-operation agreement with them. These banks are led by men who, regardless of their personal value, have a past in government, which is far from preparing them for management positions generally. They have never had to worry about profits and rarely about efficiency. Also, they have been used to a heavy bureaucracy obliging them to work slowly and inefficiently. And this is the way they continue to operate when they are in GCEs. Besides, the conditions in which they work when they are in the bank magnify this. They are often so tied down by bureaucratic requirements that their freedom of movement is hampered. They can't act as quickly as a private bank management and they can't pursue opportunites as aggressively. This affects their motivation. They have so many things they are expected to do which divert their attention from making money and seeking growth! A case in point is the number of their employees. These banks are typically overstaffed. For the same volume of business, they usually employ at least 50 per cent more people than we would. They have to: the state forces them to. Therefore, how can you expect management to really think about profit and expansion opportunities? . . . Further, their past training and experience as well as their current concerns causes them to be primarily interested in national kinds of questions . . . they just don't see the opportunities for an international development of the bank.

Often players who are beneath top management have a greater awareness of micro types of MN opportunities – staffers are a case in point. And executives right under top management also – as explained by a French interviewee: 'While the top men are often from the public administration, those who are one level below tend to be professionals who have spent most of their career in management. It is they who really make the business go and who are able to see most clearly new avenues for expansion'.

A somewhat special case is that of the management of a state holding company to whom a bank belongs. A case in point are IRI banks – principally Banca

Commerciale, Banco di Roma, Banco di Santo Spirito, and Credito Italiano. IRI management not infrequently exerts pressure for a bank to undertake one move rather than another. Notwithstanding official allegations to the contrary, it is clear that such moves are typically geared to assisting group companies. An Italian interviewee said: 'When an IRI company engages in a major investment programme, group banks back it, often giving it special and privileged treatment if group management so decides'. This is particularly so when a GCE is called upon to undertake ventures which are not attractive from an economic stand-point and which are the result of outside pressures triggered by political or personal motives. One executive said:

> The expected returns are then often not high enough to warrant the necessary financing under normal free-market conditions. To secure the necessary backup from the banks, there has to be a particular pressure – here intervention by group management . . . A typical instance is GCEs already operating in the red, which continue to keep certain losing activities alive and to retain excess labour; an unbiased banker would refuse to extend further loans to the firm. Yet, IRI banks frequently do.

Such special ventures are typically domestic in character. Therefore, IRI banks are not infrequently under considerable pressure by group management to operate domestically: 'In a way, this is a process similar to that followed by private banks: it is the principle that a bank should follow its clients. Our clients operating essentially at home – at least our government-controlled clients – we also stay home', said an IRI banker.

In fact, with public banks not belonging to a state holding, a similar process can still take place via the indirect influence of outside managements. This is the case of, say, Banca Nazionale del Lavoro or the French nationalized banks. When a GCE is pursuing a task of particular concern to an influential in-government player, its management can relatively easily exert pressure on such banks via this player. Further, as argued by an Italian interviewee: 'The chief executive of a large GCE can obtain a lot from bankers even if they are not part of the same group. A chief executive has many ways of returning favours to a benevolent banker. The simplest is a promise to share with him the returns of a particular deal made with the bank's collaboration . . .'

In-government players intervene in strategic decisions for two main kinds of reasons.

First, to cause certain actions to occur for the sake of these actions *per se*. Certain players can endeavour to stop a bank from opening up in a given country for political reasons. On the other hand, banks may be urged to pursue certain MN actions for foreign policy motives. Thus, Dr Jahn said: 'Our co-operation agreement between Commerzbank, Crédit Lyonnais and Banco di Roma was initiated by the French bank which in turn acted under the instigation of the government. At least, they were "encouraged" by the French government to do a *European* agreement in the context of a pro-European policy'. Moreover, personal motives can play a role, as noted by a French interviewee: 'Banks can render many services ranging from offering jobs to politicians' protégés to backing a variety of financial deals'. Several in-government players hinder banks' MN expansion because they feel they cannot 'use' a bank as readily if it is MN.

Still, on the whole, these are relatively rare instances. Most of these players cannot 'use' banks to achieve their main position-related ends (such as alleviate unemployment or regionalization problems). And personal interests are often not best served by banks either – as argued by one high-ranking civil servant: 'Opportunities for politicians to draw personal profits from investments by banks are more limited than, say, with manufacturing companies . . . The main problem is that banks are more readily controllable'.

Second, these players intervene to cause certain actions to occur as a means of achieving other ends via other GCEs. Banks are often influenced by government players who are anxious that a certain investment by a GCE occur, which rests upon certain financial conditions. For example, in one case the foreign affairs minister asked a GCE to build a plant in a particular country, which entailed an opportunity cost for the company. To make the deal acceptable, it was necessary for the firm to enjoy special financial terms. The minister then leaned on a state bank's management to grant the GCE such terms. Notwithstanding this case, it is clear that most of these motivations call for banks to operate domestically; given the concerns of politicians related to GCEs' actions are primarily national in nature, they are naturally led to pressure banks to assist these companies in domestic types of ventures.

Conflict among players can produce two main kinds of results in terms of actual patterns of behaviour by banks. On one hand, management is frequently co-opted by the aims of government players. Such individuals often can exert considerable influence over management by a process of mutual favours. Then a certain immobilism ensues *vis-à-vis* MN expansion. Top management becomes further demotivated. And subordinates become disenchanted by the increasing difficulties they encounter in trying to capture their boss's attention for issues related to such expansion.

On the other hand, a bank growing abroad is not necessarily precluded from assisting the pursuit of position-related as well as personal aims at home. Thus, an Italian banker said:

> The real problem for the expansion of our MN activities is that people – particularly in government – believe that if we grow internationally, we will serve their interests at home less well. They think that our top management will be less inclined to comply with their needs – especially for their personal *combinazioni*. This is not so. We can continue to be as 'co-operative' as before at home and still develop abroad . . . If people in government can be persuaded that things will indeed go this way, management is in fact usually freer in banks than in other GCEs to grow abroad.

2. *Other tertiary sector GCEs*

Their decisions are on the whole the object of lesser conflicts.

Government actors tend to be less concerned by these decisions because the issues involved are often but marginally related to their main preoccupations. These companies' activities are usually only marginally relevant for their position-related aims. And contrary to banks, these companies do not have a vital role as means for other companies to undertake certain ventures which government actors value. A French interviewee said:

> Take an advertising agency. Its role is not essential in the overall strategic success of a company or, at least, there is little in terms of preferential treatment a company can receive from an advertising agency which will be key to its overall results. So there are few 'special' favours which can be asked of a state-controlled advertising agency.

An exception can be airlines. Some of their flights are 'political' – motivated by considerations other than microeconomic factors. Here, those players responsible for the country's foreign policy do have an active role. Further, these enterprises being important employers, those concerned with employment questions are also involved. But here their concern does not lead them to take a negative stance on MN expansion; given that even with international development, the majority of their personnel are home-country nationals, MN expansion in this sector tends to contribute to alleviating unemployment problems.

In terms of government players' personal motives, these companies are not particularly helpful either. As an Italian interviewee said: 'They don't lend themselves well to electoral ends; because their activities tend not to be spectacular, they don't yield the kinds of results a politician can readily build on to conquer the sympathies of voters'. Further, more private interests are also not served well here. Certain politicians have used them as placement vehicles for their protégés – to find jobs for individuals to whom they owe something. But such uses clearly have a marginal impact on strategic decisions.

Thus, the only persons in government who have a continued interest in such companies are those who are responsible for them (for example the sponsoring minister or certain civil servants). Yet, if these men have no other reason to be concerned by them, their interest will be limited to their micro performance. When this is the case, their involvement in decisions tends to be scant. Therefore, they too tend to have a limited impact on strategic behaviour.

Union leaders are really the only outsiders with an active interest in these companies. This is focused mostly on airlines. Their concern for employment leads them to push for growth; given the nature of these firms' activitiy, this mostly means MN growth. An example is the early 1977 Air France strike against – in particular – the projected closing down of several international routes, among which the Tokyo–Papeete–Lima route referred to as the 'around-the-world route'.[24]

Therefore, albeit certain regulatory constraints (on which certain civil servants can have a major influence), management is on the whole relatively free in its decisions. And its stands are typically most determined by position-related motives. An airline chief executive said:

> In manufacturing companies, a particular strategic choice can make a difference for the chief executive himself. Therefore, he is often motivated by personal considerations. For instance, if a car manufacturer puts a plant in one place rather than another, the president himself has plenty of opportunities to make gains himself. And not necessarily in terms of financial returns. Given the high value politicians put in plants being located in certain areas, by indeed putting a plant in one of these sites, he can please them and thus build up a certain 'goodwill' which he might use in some other circumstance by asking them some kind of favour. But in our field, this is not so. A president has little to gain or lose personally, say, if we concentrate our efforts on developing certain routes rather than others. So our decisions are essentially based on company-related economic factors.

This primary emphasis on such variables results in less conflict among managers than when other variables come into play: while people's personal motives can make them disagree substantially, focusing on micro motives results – in the words of a British executive – 'in people at least being interested in the same thing – company performance . . . Still, the fact remains that management's background and personality, as well as the bureaucratic requirements it must put up with, often stand in the way of international opportunities being exploited aggressively'.

II. POLICY DECISIONS

> Once a GCE is MN, few outside people have much interest in how it operates. In general, outsiders – including government men – have an interest in the amount of MN activities a company has: thus, they are indeed concerned in issues involving either expansion or contraction of corporate MN operations. But *how* a company goes about conducting its MN affairs – given a certain constant level of MN activity – is generally of little concern to people outside of management.

As suggested by this Italian interviewee, most policy decisions tend to be the doing of in-company players. Of course such and such a government player can step in to exert pressure for a certain pattern of behaviour to be followed (for example, the foreign affairs minister arguing for a particular kind of attitude in a particular country); but these are both relatively rare instances and do not fundamentally affect a company's *modus operandi*. Still, there are two exceptions – purchasing decisions and finance decisions.

A. Purchasing decisions

Several MN GCEs have to make sizeable capital outlays for equipment purchases for their international operations (such as aircraft, ships, computers, machine tools as well as subcontracting jobs). The choice of suppliers is critical and several individuals play a major role in such decisions – in-company as in-government players – and outsiders.

Management is concerned with micro questions: cost considerations, the expected efficiency of equipment (reliability, durability, flexibility . . .), financing considerations (credit terms or the trading-in value a supplier is willing to give to old equipment). An airline president said: 'The choice of our equipment may well be the most important decision we have to make. A decision which affects us for a long period of time. It affects our financial standing, our marketing, the safety of our service as well as more elusive things such as our labour relations – say, the degree of satisfaction of our employees'. And an oil company executive said:

> The choice of our ship builders is critical not only because of the size of the capital outlays and the length of time we are stuck with the ships, but also because of the length of time over which the contracts extend. For example, consider the foreign exchange question; the currency fluctuations can screw up a deal completely; given the amount of money involved, a parity change of 20 per cent (which is common over a contract's lifetime) changes the conditions of a deal completely. In fact, the time factor is important beyond the single order of an individual ship. In this business you build up a relationship with your suppliers. The same is true with aircraft or computers. The choice of a plane or a ship often really involves the choice of a supplier for a long period of time – at least a tacit commitment to stick to a supplier which it may be costly to get out of.

In many instances, foreign suppliers are more attractive than national ones (that is, those from the company's home country). This is particularly so for foreign subsidiaries; were it only in view of transportation costs and customs barriers, local producers frequently offer more attractive equipment. And even for equipment to be used across national frontiers (aircraft, for instance), foreign suppliers are often more competitive.

Beyond overall micro considerations, various in-company players have a number of concerns related either to their position or to their personal interests. As will be clear below, such decisions can have an important role in outside games. Management can take a given stance in view of such games (such as favouring a national supplier to help the manager of that company or to contribute to solving a politician's problem – for instance the finance minister's struggle with the balance of payments deficit). Further, given the other concerns GCEs' managers often have, they may be inclined to make a particular choice to advance their interests elsewhere. For example, in one case we found that a president caused his company to buy equipment from a particular company because he was soon to change jobs and become president of the supplying company. Venal motives can also be powerful – in more than one instance it was clear that a particular choice had been made because a particular potential supplier had paid bribes to company top management.

Moreover, certain individuals can have other reasons of their own to prefer one kind of equipment or the other. Thus, an airline interviewee reported the case of an aircraft purchase decision: 'The finance men propended for one manufacturer because of the attractive terms he offered, the marketing people preferred another one because they felt that, from the passenger viewpoint, his planes were more attractive, and most technically oriented men were in favour of still another firm whose engineering sophistication appealed to them'.

In-government players also have position-related and personal motives. The decision to purchase one type of equipment or another has macroeconomic and social as well as political repercussions. Of course, the sponsoring minister is involved. When the choice is between national and foreign equipment, those concerned with balance of payments questions (such as the finance minister) are included in the decision process. This is often especially so for equipment to be used in foreign subsidiaries: using nationally produced equipment helps the balance of payments. Similarly, those concerned with employment are anxious that orders go to national suppliers. The sponsoring minister of potential domestic suppliers (when he is not the same person as the one responsible for the buying GCE) exerts pressure for orders to go to 'his' GCEs. And the minister for foreign affairs is often involved when foreign suppliers are considered (for example, he may exert pressure to cause the purchase of European equipment in view of fostering his EEC policy aims).

Such position-related stands tend, however, to be distorted by a number of factors. First, players' time horizons – contrasted to the long-term scope of many contracts, many politicians have by virtue of their own precarious position, a short-term view. One executive said:

> Even in terms of the responsibilities deriving from their position, they are interested in the short-term impact of certain choices which they can be held accountable for; what happens in ten years is of little concern to them ... For instance, the sponsoring minister is in practice only moderately concerned with the long-term impact of the choice of equipment on the company's welfare.

Further, politicians have other concerns. For example, the finance minister can be responsible for the buying GCE as well as for a potential supplier. He may then cause the former to buy from the latter, not because this is in his view the best choice from a micro standpoint, but because this will enable the seller, say, to maintain his employment level – a key consideration in view of the minister's main responsibility as guardian of the national economy.

Besides, the individuals tend to be first of all politicians. As such they have important stakes in electoral games as well as in games with other politicians (either allies of opponents). Decisions about a company's supply policy often have high 'visibility' in view of the amounts of money involved, the jobs which can be at stake, and their frequently spectacular nature. Therefore, these players are careful to play their cards subtly to try and reap the highest benefits from a political standpoint. Thus, say, the finance minister may be led to take a particular stand which appears, in the eyes of the electorate and particularly in those of workers, as the most attractive one, say, because of its (real or apparent) effects on the job market: 'That this may entail negative effects over time is often relatively trivial; what counts are the immediate dividends in terms of one's electoral standing', said one interviewee.

Personal motives are important as well. The ties between government players and the chief executives of GCEs can play a role. Thus, to make a favour to a given potential supplier's president, a sponsoring minister can exert influence on a GCE to buy from that firm. And venal interests are also often critical.

Members of the opposition are often involved. Again, given the visibility of these decisions, they try to build on them to attack the government. For example, if a GCE ends up buying foreign equipment, they will accuse the government of not safeguarding the interests of national workers in the sector. If on the contrary, the government pressures a GCE to buy from a national producer despite an opportunity cost for the GCE, the criticism will be that normal market forces are distorted by ruling politicians in view of personal aims they are accused of pursuing.

Among outsiders, the most concerned individuals are managers from firms which are potential suppliers. The most weighty are those from other GCEs. There are then frequently personal ties between executives and there often is a process of mutual influence.

Moreover, union leaders frequently play a role – when a purchase involves labour-intensive goods, they naturally fight for GCEs to buy national.

There is clearly room for conflict among these various players. For our purposes, the most important issue concerns the question of buying national or buying foreign equipment. On the whole, the latter tends to find its strongest advocates among in-company people. Not that this results from any *a priori* preference. Rather, in-company people tend to opt for the most attractive product available, considering product characteristics alone. And this happens often to be a foreign product. On the other hand, government actors, as well as union leaders are more resolutely in favour of national equipment. And naturally, so are executives from potential domestic suppliers.

Once more, it is hard to say in general how such conflicts are resolved. For example, in the mid 1970s, a big debate developed around the decision for Air France to buy new short/medium-haul aircraft. Management opted for Boeing

727s, while the Finance Minister, Jean-Pierre Fourcade, exerted pressure for the company to buy Dassault's Mercure. Management's reasons were cost consider- ations as well as Boeing's willingness to take in old aeroplanes at a more attractive price. Fourcade's reasons were balance-of-payments and employ- ment considerations as well as the general desire to give a boost to the French aircraft industry. Nothing actually happened until the next government came into office. With Raymond Barre the issue came up again. This time, the government representatives wanted Air France to delay the acquisition of the new aircraft until a new version of the Airbus became available in the early 1980s. Management, again, argued this would hurt its results unduly. A com- promise was finally reached: the new Airbus would be bought when available but, in the meantime, Boeings would be leased. But then, in early 1978, the unions blocked this solution. As yet, no way out has been found.

In other cases, the bias in favour of national equipment is weaker. First, when the expected benefits from forcing purchase of national equipment are modest, there may not be much of an issue for lack of strong defenders of domestic suppliers. Also, the opportunity costs for choosing national equipment are so high that the task of the proponents of national suppliers is truly very arduous. Finally, in certain cases, the best equipment may be bought even if foreign, simply because of the stubborn position of key executives. As an interviewee said:

> With our previous president we ended up in most cases with what was best for the company. His personality was such that he never would give in to more or less 'orthodox bargains' with politicians. And they knew it. And they didn't try in most cases for fear a scandal might break out. But this is an exception. In most cases, managers are too weak and invariably end up being co-opted by politicians. I have to say that in a way this is what happened in this company once our former president had left.

B. Finance decisions

Two main classes of decisions should be distinguished: those involving the government directly and those involving state banks and other state financial institutions.

1. *Decisions involving the government* per se

These include new equity issues the government is to underwrite, state loans or state endowments as well as financing requiring the state's involvement (for example in the case of state-guaranteed debentures).[25] Both in-company and government players are critical.

Within the GCE concerned, top management, specialized functional man- agement and staffers come into play. These persons are first concerned by the efficiency with which capital is raised – obtaining the appropriate amounts, at the best possible terms at the right time. The attitude of top management in particular can also reflect other interests. For instance, an Italian interviewee reported that his president had given up fighting for a state loan 'which we were, objectively, absolutely entitled to given the "services" we had rendered and were planning to render to the government (notably, investments in the Mezzogiorno)'. His motivation apparently was that the minister of the treasury who had primary responsibility to decide upon the loan, had already overextended himself in terms of expenditures for that period – especially in connection with 'contributions' to state organizations – and was confronted with severe criticisms by his political adversaries. Further, a reshuffling of the cabinet was expected in the near future, in which the minister would probably be assigned to another post. Given that the minister was a close friend of the president who owed him a lot in terms of past career promotions, the president decided not to press the minister for the financing question, delaying it until the new cabinet was in place.

A special case is that of state holding companies. Here the management of the parent company can be at odds with the management of the company in quest for capital. The parent company's management may feel that another group company has a more pressing need for the funds. (A case in point is when the group has companies which are unable to effectively raise money otherwise while the operating company in question is in a position to raise money on the free market; in such instances, group management often prefers to allocate the state funds it is able to secure to the more needy companies which have limited alternatives for raising money.) Given that state funds as well as state-guaranteed funds are mostly attributed to the parent holding and not to operating companies, the parent's management has considerable discretionary power as to the allocation of such funds.

Within government, a number of players are also concerned. The sponsoring minister usually fights for funds for his GCEs. The ministers responsible for administering state funds (the finance minister, the minister for the budget, the minister of the treasury, the chancellor of the exchequer, etc.) are generally torn between various demands for funds by various people. Their problem is generally to limit state expenditures, and therefore they are often reluctant to grant government money to GCEs. Besides, certain civil servants are important. Thus, planners often try and exert influence for a GCE in a given sector to receive financing to enable it to develop so that their sectorial aims may be attained.

Further, when decisions about financing are involved, which are tied to particular investment plans, those players who are concerned by these plans also become important. Thus, a minister for depressed regions may play an active role in the decision to allocate funds to a GCE which would use them in backward areas. Similarly, a member of parliament representing a given constituency will have a part in the financing decision of a major project to be developed in his region. And certain civil servants can also be concerned (for example, DATAR officials).

Political and private motives are important too. Politicians can influence certain financing decisions to foster their aims in terms of GCEs' projects; thus, if an individual wants to hinder a project but cannot act upon the decision about the project itself, he can interfere in the financing decision. Besides, certain financing decisions *per se* lend themselves to purely electoral types of games. Members of the opposition not infrequently use such decisions to attack the government, for instance, accusing it of being cavalier with public money by allocating it too liberally to GCEs, suggesting clearly, though often not explicitly, that personal venal interests of ministers lie behind such allocations. And indeed, such venal interests exist too. There is little question that, in many instances, key government players receive personal compensations for backing certain financing proposals for GCEs.

Conflict between such players can be sizeable. It is clearly those players officially responsible for administering state funds who have the greatest formal power (though in certain cases, the head of the executive can step in and himself exert influence). Yet, they cannot ignore the context in which they play. They have to be receptive to the demands of their fellow cabinet members. Were it only to preserve a certain coherence within the executive, they have to listen. Also, certain demands of other ministers are justified politically: they are necessary to safeguard the credibility in the cabinet's action; should they refuse to respond to them completely, the entire cabinet would be threatened and they with it. Besides, they owe other ministers favours in other games. Therefore, the weight of these other ministers can be quite strong, particularly when they have strong bargaining advantages: the possibility of offering reciprocal help, personal indispensability (for example, when one is an influential member of a party essential for the survival of the ruling coalition), the possibility of offering high personal rewards, etc. Certain members of parliament can also be in this kind of situation – particularly when they are prominent political figures.

Company management's influence varies considerably. On paper, its influence is rather limited since it has no formal way to exert power on the resource allocation decision process. Yet, in practice, things are often different. First, management can simply take the position that if it does not receive the funds it requires, it will not be able to accomplish what is expected from it – the kind of behaviour government players want the company to pursue. Also, it can threaten to close down some of its operations and lay off workers massively, thus causing, among other things, social unrest. This kind of argument is usually powerful indeed. Of course, government people can always use the weapon of replacing a GCE's executive who takes such a stand. But if he is an influential figure with high public standing of his own, this may be embarrasing for the government.

In fact, such extreme arguments usually need not be invoked. A GCE's top manager can usually exert influence on key government players more subtly; if not directly over the player who is formally empowered to allocate state funds, he can influence other members of the government who in turn can pressure this player.

There is room for considerable bargaining. When all those concerned happen to agree, decisions can be quick. For instance, when the sponsoring minister is the finance minister, if he wants a GCE to undertake a project on which management has previously agreed and for which there is no major opposition, things are relatively easy at the finance decision level. But when there are differences in opinion, decisions are cumbersome. As a French interviewee said: 'When politicians start disagreeing, we have learned that this is a sign that funds will be slow to come. Indeed, the first result of disagreement is no action. And this is especially so when the disagreement involves other than economic questions – political or personal questions'.

2. *Decisions involving state-controlled banks and other financial institutions*

These decisions concern short, medium and long-term debt capital. They involve players from the prospective borrowing company and from the prospective lending institution as well as government persons.

The management of the borrowing company is again concerned with efficiency. But personal motives are also important (for example, personal ties between the finance vice-president and a key manager of the prospective lending institution).

The management of the lending institution also has micro variables in mind. Yet, given the personality, background and interests of high-ranking managers of such organizations, they frequently have other considerations in mind as well. Thus, in view of their macro concerns, they tend to have a bias in favour of GCEs which pursue what they consider socially desirable ends. And more private considerations are equally relevant. Thus, several bankers reported that their organization had preferential ties with certain companies because of friendships between members of the bank and of the companies. Further, bankers often make certain choices in view of favouring such and such a government member. For example, we found that one bank's president was a close friend of a member of parliament representing a given region; it appeared clear, at least in one case, that a loan had been extended to a GCE because it was going to develop a project in that region which was particularly important to the politician in question.

Here also, a special case is represented by banks belonging to a state holding company. The parent company's management can intervene and amend the decisions taken by the bank's management. When group management wants one of its companies to undertake a given action requiring bank financing, it may exert pressure to cause one of its banks to extend a loan, thus perhaps going against the inclination of the bank's management. Thus, we found that in several cases, a GCE obtains particularly favourable terms from a group bank because of personal ties between the GCE's top management and one or several key members of the parent's top management.

Among in-government players, sponsoring ministers try and exert influence for the GCEs they are responsible for to obtain the best possible terms. And here too, when a bank loan is related to a particular project, those players who are directly concerned by the project actively fight for the loan to be granted. As these persons often do not have much direct formal power over the bank's decisions, they channel their influence through others who do – say, the sponsoring minister or the bank's management itself.

Conflicts can be intense and complex. Players' power varies from one decision to the next. Thus, in several cases company management is in a position to impose its conditions to the bank thanks to its contacts with those who have influence on the bank's management – either group management in the case of a bank belonging to a state holding company, or influential government players. And government players with no formal say in such decisions can in fact have their way because they have strong means of exerting pressure on those who do have such say. Here too, the process of reciprocal exchange of favours is typically far more relevant in terms of who actually has power than the official attributions of each player.

Beyond these two main classes of decision, there are of course other means of financing available to GCEs: free market financial tools, (that is, regular capital markets), private financial institutions as well as internally generated funds. Games between various actors exist for such decisions also. Thus, the finance minister may try to delay or anticipate a GCE's major bond issue in view of certain conjunctural requirements. Similarly, certain civil servants (the head of the central bank, for example) can intervene in this fashion. Yet, on the whole, such decisions tend to be less political. Technically, government players do not need to get involved and personal motives are rarely relevant – as explained by a German interviewee: 'If a given project is dependent on, say, a bond issue, a politician to whom the project is important cannot do much to influence the issue; if the project itself has been approved and if management is decided to go ahead with the issue, there remains only to go to the market; there is little bargaining to do for anything'. Consequently, games tend to be relatively straightforward, decisions actually being mostly taken by management.

3. Implications

Regarding equity, a GCE can raise funds more or less easily depending on the stand taken by key players, which in turn is affected not only by their stakes in and perceptions of the financing decision *per se*, but also by their perception of and stakes in the prospective use of these funds by the company. When funds are tied to the accomplishment of a project which is important to key players, these individuals will stand for positive action on the decision; and if there is no strong opposition, a favourable decision may be reached relatively quickly. Otherwise, if influential actors take a negative stand, the decision-making will be slow due to the inevitable bargaining between players.

Many of the more influential players tend to take positive stands *vis-à-vis* financial decisions related to domestic projects: most players outside a company, as well as many insiders, have interests attached to national investments; it follows that they often take a positive stand on the financing decisions related to these kinds of investments.

In MN projects, many of the key players have little to gain. Financing decisions attached to foreign ventures, therefore, most often encounter distinctly less support. As a French interviewee said: 'Certain decisions require support and not mere abstention or non-opposition. Given many of these decisions don't concern many of those whose support is needed, delays occur due to the time necessary to convince these men to grant their support. The problem, then, is one of motivating them to actually "make it happen" '.

The same type of reasoning can be made for state loans or endowments as well as for certain state-guaranteed debentures. Players will support a decision if it meets their interests. And again, it should be clear that for most of them – particularly those outside the company – this occurs mostly for financing decisions tied to a proposed set of domestic actions. And the argument is probably even more pertinent in the case of debt from government-controlled banks or other financial institutions: here the use of the funds can be traced more readily than with other forms of financing (it is not always easy to relate, say, a bond issue with a particular project); a player can tell relatively clearly for what purpose, say, a bank loan will be raised; therefore, he readily knows what he is fighting for – he knows to which financing decision a pet project of his is tied and, accordingly, fights for positive action on this decision. As a result, players' support for domestic undertakings can be focused quite specifically.

III. CONCLUSION

In this chapter we have looked at GCEs' behaviour as a resultant of inter-actions between players. We have analysed these interactions for the various types of GCEs in the context of strategic and policy behaviour. For each class of decision, we have asked which players are involved, what their interests and influence are, and we have sought to have a grasp of the actual bargains among players from which action results.

There are particular conclusions for each class of decision. These were drawn in each section. Here we add a few more general points. In many ways these corroborate directly our conclusions at the end of Chapter IX.

(1) Far from being tools for the advancement of collective ends, GCEs are often really instruments at the service of major individuals. Decisions reflect individuals' subjective, biased and incomplete perceptions and their parochial and personal aims. When a GCE's actions are of concern to government players, what they do serves (a) macro-type ends, though partial, prejudiced and partisan ends: it reflects influential players' particular position-related responsibilities and problems; and (b) personal ends – particular political (for example, elect-oral) as well as private pursuits of key players. In such cases management itself tends to be less concerned with aggressively exploiting economically appealing opportunities. It is only when government players stay out of the decision-making process that micro ends can be pursued effectively.

(2) Because players are caught in many overlapping games at a time, their stand in the game in which the issue under consideration arises – here GCEs' MN behaviour – is inevitably affected by their stakes in other games. Two major consequences ensue: a strong preference for highly visible results and a short-term view of problems. Given the deadlines they must meet in other games,

politicians in particular push for immediate results with a *clear* appeal to the people. Further, rarely do actual decisions appear to be the product of a systematic reflection about what is objectively the best course of action – either from the company point of view or the point of view of the general interest. Rather, decisions are the product of bargaining among individuals, few of whom have the heart to promote the pursuit of that course of action which would be most rewarding for the firm or for the collectivity, and many of whom even do not have the ability – given their imperfect perceptions – to see what such action would be. Each individual pushes for a given course of action because of his own limited view of things and of what he himself has to gain or lose. And the outcome of the game is not a rational summary (or weighted average) of the various players' aims. Rather, shared power but differing aims means that pulling and hauling among individuals with discretionary influence is the mechanism of choice. Sometimes what is done is what one player or coalition advocates (though typically he or it must make certain side-payments or promises for reciprocal favours to his or its opponents). In other cases – indeed, most frequently – what is done is a compromise between various players' views. And in certain instances, what is done bears little resemblance to the initial stands of individual players – the only solution on which players are able to agree as being a neutral one.

(3) On the whole, given the traits of key players, GCEs are unlikely to develop abroad as extensively or aggressively as their private counterparts.

This is true given the overall attitude of in-company players. While their position should cause them to focus on the micro performance of the firm which generally offers the most compelling arguments for MN expansion, managers' attitude is often distorted by what they know is behaviour which gets rewards and which is not. Actions which promise to yield positive results for the company in the long run tend not to 'pay' for the one who takes them. What does 'pay' is action which yields both immediate and most useful results – useful primarily for key political players. MN expansion usually promises to yield neither one.

Besides, given their background, personality and experience, many of those who head GCEs have interests other than the pursuit of the firm's growth and profitability – especially beyond national frontiers. And the bureaucracy with which they must live jeopardizes their entrepreneurship. In addition, more private motives also push them towards domestic options.

Of course, there are exceptions. These are GCEs in which management is most professional, is the most free from interventions from non-company players and is not involved in outside games. Decisions are then taken more on the basis of micro considerations. And MN opportunities tend to be exploited more systematically. This is the case in particular of several German GCEs.[26]

And the overall attitude of government players limits the MN expansion capacity of GCEs. Their position generally makes them responsible for one or few aspects of the collective interest only (except for the head of the executive – who himself, however, is forced to be selective about what he devotes his attention to). And they more or less explicitly tend to use every opportunity for advancing their own aims. Thus, they exert influence on GCEs to cause them to act not in a way which is most advantageous in view of the *overall* collective interest but in a way which is most advantageous in view of that share of the collective interest for which *they* are responsible. It is of little concern to players that this is not conducive to the best possible use of GCEs' resources. What is important is that this helps them with their individual ends. These are mostly domestic in scope.

Besides, to repeat, they tend to push for short-term and highly visible results. This reinforces their propensity to support domestic actions. This is especially relevant for those politicians responsible for the overall collective interest (for example, the president). While their position should lead them to be concerned with the general long-term best interest of the collectivity, the realities of the political games they are forced to play push them to focus on what yields the highest political returns. Therefore, their attitude *vis-à-vis* GCEs tends to favour national undertakings. And sponsoring ministers are in a similar position: while they should be concerned with firms' long-run performance, they are first of all politicians, and as such they are led to manipulate GCEs for political purposes. Once more, this produces a domestic bias.

Moreover, players' personal motives tend to push them to stand for GCEs' national development as well.

On the other hand, there are instances in which a government player stands for MN growth. This occurs when the arguments in favour of MN expansion are so obvious – including to the public – that it is not possible to oppose it. This can also occur when a leader is committed genuinely enough to long-term progress and development, when he has a sufficiently clear understanding of what this means in terms of industrial action, and when he is strong enough politically to bear the attacks and costs standing for this entails.

Finally, most outsiders' attitudes too generally hinder MN expansion.

We should stress that this discussion applies to the majority of players in the majority of cases. Yet, there *are* players who stand for MN expansion. Indeed, in most GCEs there have been persons at one point or another, who proposed and fought for developments beyond national frontiers. But the point is that usually such individuals fight from a position of weakness. While they may objectively be right in their stand – and intimately seen as such by many of their adversaries – they generally face massive and determined opposition: the other players either cannot afford the costs MN expansion entails for them personally (in view of their interests and their stakes in other games) or do not want to incur the opportunity costs involved. And given who they are and their usual numerical superiority, they are normally stronger. And if they see a risk of losing, they can break the coalition favouring MN expansion by luring away certain coalition members and winning them over to their cause, via side-payments – payments they are able to make precisely because pursuing their self-interest above all gives them power and resources to distribute rewards to their followers. Therefore, not only do most player's attitudes hinder MN expansion, but also so do the actual bargaining games between players – standing for MN expansion tends to mean playing with losing cards.

Having said this, we should repeat that there are GCEs which do develop multinationally. On the whole, this occurs in one of three cases. First, when politicians in particular stay out of company affairs and when management is motivated and left free to pursue microeconomic ends. Second, when the arguments in favour of MN expansion are so strong that hardly anyone can dispute them with any cogency. Third, when there is a strong enough leader committed to exploiting the most attractive opportunities wherever they might be, who is able to overcome opponents of MN development.

This analysis completes the conclusions of Chapter IX and further clarifies the puzzles of our previous accounts.

(1) The process view left us with questions concerning the way certain changes in strategy come about. Thus, changes were identified without there being any particular force which could be held accountable for the shift. In several cases, a force was found instrumental in causing departure from the current strategy but was clearly not a determining factor in the setting of a new course; since no other force was either, we were left with the double question of what happened to the force itself and how the new course was selected.

The organizational politics approach suggests focusing on the players involved and the games taking place among them. This uncovers the fact that in many of these cases, an individual was indeed instrumental as an initiator – to cause the existing strategic posture to be called into question. But then, once the issue was on the table, other players' attention was aroused. Several individuals with partial views and interests became involved in the decision process, each standing for different actions. The initiator then just becomes one other player. If others have greater power, he stands little chance of imposing his views. In other cases, the very way the issue comes up is not the product of one individual's intervention but is itself the resultant of bargaining games between several individuals, some of whom are in favour of the *status quo*, others arguing for strategic change.

(2) We were left with several anomalies concerning GCEs' behaviour. Thus, a GCE had long operations in particular parts of the world. While looking at past experience (as the process approach suggests) leads one to expect new MN investments to occur in such countries (unless a force intervenes), at one point the firm stopped investing there and began operations in totally different types of countries. The process view was unable to offer any satisfactory explanation. We also found GCEs with a history of abiding by government policies, which suddenly depart from this without any identifiable reason.

This should be understood now. Decisions result from the pulling and hauling between leaders. Departures from habitual courses are not necessarily caused by the active intervention of one individual, but can be the product of bargaining games in which several persons are involved and in which no one player overshadows the others, indeed in which no individual or coalition is able to impose his or its views. Thus, a company suddenly abandoning its traditional respect for government policies can be the product of conflict, compromise and confusion among players, who all stand for the firm to give more attention to particular parts of government policies (each player fighting for more attention to that share of the collective interest for which he is responsible), with the result that ultimately the company does less of what it was doing up to then in terms of macro ends, without doing much more in terms of new such ends. As one interviewee from a company in this situation said:

> Up to last year we were doing our share with regard to the general interest. Over time, we had grown into the habit of making certain decisions in a way which took into account government planning (e.g. invest each year a bit more in high unemployment areas). Then a debate broke out among politicians as to what we should do *vis-à-vis* collective goals. This broke the equilibrium up. So many people began asking for so many different things! No consensus could apparently be reached in government and we received no clear directives as to what was expected from us. So we just stopped worrying about the general interest and ended up focusing on little else than our own company goals.

Similarly, a company shifting its investment focus to new areas can do so as a product of interactions between several individuals arguing about the current focus and proposing a variety of new foci. The actual new focus can then emerge with nobody really having stood for it, as a resultant of quasi-settlements between players as well as a succession of essentially unco-ordinated actions.

(3) Related to this, we saw that certain investment locations are chosen which are outside of the scope of the existing routines and while the key persons involved are all in favour of alternative locations. The process view was unable to account for this.

Here we see that often what is finally done is something which no player advocated at the outset but which is the only compromise acceptable to all. Thus, one interviewee reported:

> The story of the choice of the site for our new plant is typical. . . At the beginning all those involved – in our company itself, in the parent company, in government and among union leaders – advocated different sites . . . People fought *against* others' sites as much as *for* their own. We finally settled for a neutral solution – one which was nobody's pet idea and which therefore satisfied the key requirement that nobody win over anybody else . . .

(4) This account further clarifies the way forces function. As argued at the end of Chapter IX, we now understand when and why a force intervenes and how. And we see what determines the point where forces cease to exert influence and standard procedures take over; players stop either when they feel they have

reached their goal or when they see they are unable to do so. When an individual realizes that his struggle has resulted in the action he wanted, he withdraws from the game and lets things follow their course. And when he understands that he cannot expect any further benefits from the situation because he has reached the limits of his authority in the game, he also stops. The Gioia Tauro case we discussed is a good illustration; once Mancini and his allies had reached their basic aims – the public announcement of the location and the early implementation steps – and once they realized the weakness of the project had become so glaring that their position had practically become untenable, they felt much less urge to remain in the game.

Moreover, this approach explains what happens when there are several conflicting forces. As we saw, for each kind of MN strategic and policy decision, various players are involved with diverse interests and unequal influence. Action emerges from the bitter fights, cabals and accommodations between such individuals.

(5) The organizational politics view also sheds new light on certain aspects of GCEs' MN *modus operandi*. Thus, the process approach suggested that GCEs frequently have a hard time in raising capital when a formal involvement of the government is required: because of set procedures, such decisions are typically slow and cumbersome to be made. This was the case with equity financing, state loans or endowments as well as for state-guaranteed debentures. Our present view has suggested that this may or may not be the case. The decision process may indeed be cumbersome when many players are involved with conflicting views on the issue; if, for whatever reason, certain key individuals choose to oppose a particular financing operation, a struggle will develop with those favouring the operation, and the decision may drag out considerably. On the other hand, if all the critical persons happen to feel – even if for different motives – that the operation is a highly desirable one, the decision may be taken relatively swiftly. Similarly, for financing from state-owned financial institutions such as banks. We argued earlier that GCEs had an advantage here over private firms, though this advantage was often tempered by a bureaucratic sluggishness. Here we see in fact that the sluggishness with which decisions are made is a function of the pulling and hauling which takes place: decisions will be slow if there is disagreement between players; but they can be rather straightforward if all those concerned support them. Thus, GCEs' comparative edge in these areas really varies from case to case; they do have an advantage over private firms in those instances (rarely those related to MN activities) where the key players are motivated to cause a positive decision to occur – but when they are not, this advantage tends to vanish.

NOTES

1. See Chapter IV.
2. See: Antonio Spinosa, 'Gioia Tauro: Acciaieria o Rivoluzione', *Il Giornale*, 10 October 1976, p. 5.

3. See: Avison Wormald, 'Growth Promotion: The Creation of a Modern Steel Industry', in Stuart Holland (ed.), *The State as Entrepreneur*, Weidenfeld and Nicolson, London, 1972.
4. See Chapter III.
5. See Chapter IV.
6. See Chapter I.
7. See: Robert Stobaugh, 'U.S. Multinational Enterprises and the U.S. Economy', Graduate School of Business Administration, Harvard University, Boston, 1972.
8. See: Yair Aharoni, *The Foreign Investment Decision Process*, Division of Research, Graduate School of Business Administration, Harvard University, Boston, 1966, p. 59.
9. See: Milton Hochmuth, *Organizing the Transnational*, A. W. Sijthoff, Leiden, 1974.
10. *Aviation Week and Space Technology*, 6 August 1973, p. 28.
11. Annexes I and II of 'Les Actions de Politique Industrielle et Technologique de la Communauté à entreprendre dans le secteur aéronautique', EEC Commission, document III/2457/72F, Brussels, 21 December 1973.
12. See Chapter I.
13. Milton Hochmuth, *Organizing the Transnational*, p. 134.
14. Milton Hochmuth, *Organizing the Transnational*, p. 144.
15. Milton Hochmuth, *Organizing the Transnational*, p. 147.
16. John Costello and Terry Hughes, *The Battle for Concorde*, Compton Press, Salisbury, Wiltshire, 1971, p. 34.
17. Milton Hochmuth, *Organizing the Transnational*, pp. 147–148.
18. See: Renato Mazzolini, *European Transnational Concentrations*, McGraw-Hill, London, 1974, p. 5.
19. Milton Hochmuth, *Organizing the Transnational*, p. 142.
20. Milton Hochmuth, *Organizing the Transnational*, p. 142.
21. Special Report, and First, Second and Third Report from the Committee of Public Accountants, Session 1964–1965, H.M. Stationary Office, London, p. XXIII.
22. See: Milton Hochmuth, *Organizing the Transnational*, p. 141.
23. Jean Fusil, *Concorde*, Editions France-Empire, Paris, 1968, p. 62.
24. See: *Le Figaro*, 6 January 1977, p. 5.
25. See Chapter III.
26. See: Badouin Bollaert, 'F.R.A.: à l'école du Liberalisme', *Le Figaro*, 15 January 1977, p. 6.

CHAPTER XI

Conclusion

After so many pages, this chapter is intentionally as concise as possible. We will first briefly pull together our three theoretical approaches. Then we will make a few concluding remarks on GCEs. And finally we will say a word about possible future research.

A. The theory

Our three conceptual approaches yield different, indeed often contradictory accounts. The obvious question arises at this point: is there a 'right' view? We can but begin to answer this here.

First, a certain incongruity appears among the three approaches.

The traditional approach looks at corporate strategy and policy as a set of choices. In analysing the foreign expansion of a GCE, the analyst produces an argument for an objective (or a vector of objectives) which makes that behaviour plausible. Location in a particular country is understood as a value-maximizing choice and so is the pursuit of a specific project. And the MN *modus operandi* of a company is viewed as the product of an effort to select the most appropriate ground-rules for the functioning of the organization. This conception implies coincidence of perceptions, control over the selection of actual moves, and total co-ordination within the firm seen as a unitary actor.

The organizational process and politics approaches take exception with such a view. They recognize the fragmentary nature of organizations. Routines critically affect decision and action and corporate behaviour flows more from processes than from central choice. Further, the key players perceive 'the problem' quite differently, evaluate the various possible outcomes quite differently and are influenced in the stands they take by differing interests.

In the process approach a GCE's foreign investment is seen as the output of organizational procedures: the type of investment, its location, the way it is accomplished are the product of standardized packages and programmes of action; these determine the formulation of a project, the feasibility study, the actual implementation. The consequence is that a GCE's MN behaviour does not reflect value maximization (that is, it does not exploit the most attractive opportunities in an optimal fashion). Rather, it reflects the particular processes which came to bear on the decisions affecting that behaviour.

In the organizational politics approach a GCE's foreign investment is seen as the resultant of political games. The company's behaviour is determined by the particular inclinations of certain individuals and their impact. A GCE invests abroad or not according to the aims and relative power of those men 'that count'. And their MN policies also reflect such individuals' preferences and relative influence. Thus, a GCE will undertake certain actions and not others, primarily as a function of who is in a position to affect corporate decisions.

Indeed, the three approaches produce different interpretations. But a closer look suggests that what really happens is that the three approaches look at different phenomena.

The traditional view looks at strategy as an aggregate behaviour. The formal decision and their implementation are seen as constituting a rational, coherent whole based on a logical, comprehensive analysis of the environmental and corporate context. The two other views split a strategy up in various pieces. The process view looks at parts such as how was the need for a new strategy perceived, how was a route conceived, how was it investigated, how was it actually approved and what were the details of its execution. The politics view focuses on the emergence of the strategy among key individuals – the pulling and hauling, conflict and accommodation between those individuals who have a say in the game of strategy determination.

To explain corporate behaviour, the first approach examines the corporate strategic calculus: the problem faced by the firm, its criteria for action, its possibilities for action and its competences or capabilities. Explaining means placing the strategy in a pattern of purposive response to a problem. Given our concern for GCEs' MN behaviour, this view leads us to ask: What are the objectives? What are the companies' resources? What are the competitive threats and market opportunities? What are the alternatives (given micro and macro objectives)? What are the costs and benefits of each . . .?

In the second approach, the 'solution' emerges as a product of set routines. It emphasizes organizational constraint in choice and organizational procedures in implementation.[1] This view leads us to ask: what are the relevant organizational units and how do they traditionally act? What are the routines to gather relevant information and the process by which this information is treated and taken into account or disregarded? What repertoires exist for generating alternative solutions and what are the programmes to investigate alternatives? What mechanisms exist for the approval of proposals and what types of alternatives are likely to be acted upon favourably and which not? And what routines are there for implementing alternative courses of action?

The third approach looks at the conduct of those players who have an impact on strategy and policy decisions. It analyses players' traits which cause them to behave in a particular way and thus exert a given kind of influence on corporate action. And it analyses the effects of their interplays. This view leads us to ask: Which players in what positions are involved? What aims are they inclined to have given their position-related concerns, the other organizational games they have a stake in, and their personal interests? What power does each player have, given the attitude of others? How can players (either as individuals or by forming coalitions) actually cause certain actions to occur or not to occur? Where are foul-ups likely?

The three approaches thus raise different issues. The question then becomes: are they compatible and can they be reconciled? We can attempt to begin to answer this here.

As suggested especially by the concluding remarks of Chapters IX and X, the process and politics approaches are really complementary: as we saw, at a given point in a decision process, leaders cease to play the key role and routines take over; it is usually clear that the impact of players tends to be limited to triggering one routine rather than another. The politics approach says little about such routines. Moreover, our 'process' chapters underlined the fact that for strategic and policy change to take place, a force has to intervene. Yet, little was said about the way forces evolve in fact. Therefore, one can conceive of the politics view stopping where the process view begins: decisions are first the product of leaders. Here the emphasis of the politics view on the internal dynamics of leadership is critical. But leaders cannot be responsible for all the elements of decision and action. At that stage the burden of making things happen is transferred to procedures which are by necessity standardized. To understand what happens then, the process view is needed.

Given that corporate behaviour *is* affected by leaders, their doings must be analysed. The politics approach does this. It focuses on those individuals who actually have the decision-making power. It looks at the pressures their jobs exert on them, at their personalities, as well as at the attitudes they have taken in the past. It also asks what the existing action channels are and what the relative weight of each individual is. And it uncovers the struggles and bargains between players.

Yet, players are constrained by the bureaucratic context in which they operate. This is the focus of the process approach. It looks at the relevant suborganizations and the pre-established programmes and rules by which they operate. It analyses what procedures players must rely upon to secure data on the performance level of the organization, on facts and trends in the environment and on the potential of given resource allocation proposals. It analyses the procedures by which projects are evaluated and accepted or rejected. And it analyses the organization's repertoires – what it knows how to do – which will govern the accomplishment of decisions. Such analysis determines the limits of organizational action. It is within these limits that leaders have to play.

How about the traditional approach? The politics and the process view appear to be essentially complementary. On the other hand, as we saw in Chapter V, certain assumptions and conceptions of the traditional approach are plainly misleading. Thus, certain conclusions it leads to are erroneous. Still, the traditional approach does produce insights which in many ways are useful. And its ease of use often makes it particularly attractive. Therefore, while the results it yields cannot be taken indiscriminately, we should determine the conditions and bounds of its applicability and function.

The traditional approach is helpful to understand certain basic motivations of central players in the politics approach. It asks what the predicament is, what the options and parameters for choice are. It does this from an 'objective', total enterprise viewpoint, thus determining what would be best for the firm given its purpose. Now, it is clear that leaders will at least partly follow this type of reasoning at one point or another; though their stands are heavily influenced by parochial priorities and personal motives, they must have some concern for their stand's effect on the outcome of the issue under consideration and the impact of this on the performance of the organization *per se*. True, each player's perceptions are biased and what one player sees as right may not be the same as what another player (or an outside analyst) will see as right. But the point is that individuals go through this kind of analysis and they do so starting from similar premises. Thus, the traditional approach identifies basic motives which will be brought to bear on corporate behaviour; the factors it deals with have an influence on players' assumptions and attitudes. At least, this is so for certain players – those responsible for the firm's welfare. Thus, top managers will have to give a minimum amount of attention to economic results. Sponsoring ministers or heads of the executive will also have to give some thought to this aspect, even if their political concerns distort their views. (And other players can also be seen as influenced by this type of reasoning: other in-company players, while having more limited responsibilities, should be at least somewhat sensitive to the total company's point of view; whereas other government players as well as relevant outsiders should be aware of certain basic micro considerations, even if their own ends bear little direct relationship to corporate performace as such.)

Of course, the organizational politics approach takes such motives into account anyway: by focusing on players' position-related interests and perceptions these factors rise to the surface. Yet, the traditional approach retains a principal merit: it clearly traces the contours within which organizational action must take place. By analysing corporate performace *per se*, it emphasizes fundamental factors which more or less consciously tend to be common to leaders; its focus on formal objectives uncovers the values central players more or less explicitly share. Key individuals have to agree on a minimum around such factors and values, which puts limits on what must and must not be done. Therefore, the traditional view defines the broad context in which the game is played and it fixes the larger patterns of corporate behaviour. In this sense it can also serve as a quick summary of fundamental tendencies in companies'

strategies and policies, all the more convenient in light of its relatively parsi-
monious use of data.

The above is clearly a tentative and preliminary conception. The last section
will acknowledge some of the unresolved problems and suggest where solutions
might be sought.

B. GCEs' MN behaviour

Each substantive chapter of this book concluded with a summary of the aspects
of GCEs' decisions and actions that it had uncovered. Further, we encountered
problems and anomalies in the perspectives and explanations of each account.
These were taken up in the context of subsequent accounts. As we moved along
with our successive lenses, we identified new aspects of corporate behaviour and
found solutions to and reasons for the puzzles and seemingly inexplicable
phenomena of earlier views. This too was synthesized at the end of each chapter.
It is therefore superfluous to try and summarize our findings here. Yet, it is useful
to briefly pull together the highlights of our analyses of GCEs' MN strategic and
policy behaviour. At the risk of oversimplifying, the following is a synopsis of the
answers to the three basic questions this study set out to address.

1. *Why do GCEs have or not have MN activities?*

Government control of companies generally reduces the chances of these
companies going MN. All three accounts bear this out. The traditional view
defined the broad patterns of behaviour of GCEs. It concluded that their special
characteristics do not significantly affect the attractiveness for them of MN
expansion from a profit goal viewpoint; but from a tool goal viewpoint GCEs
have more reasons to stay home than to go abroad. This conclusion flows even
more clearly from our two other views. Companies' internal bureaucratic
mechanisms as well as relevant government procedures are geared to domestic
activities. And key persons' perceptions and interests lead them to worry primarily about questions calling for national answers. Thus, political games between
players yield for the most part decisions to stay home.

Only in companies which are MNCs – with extensive MN experience and
existing activities abroad – is this surmounted. Continued exposure to foreign
undertakings and environments has then reduced company leaders' provincialism. Also, MN operations have developed an organizational life of their own;
processes therefore exist which permit a sounder consideration of foreign
opportunities; and management has acquired a certain autonomy from government which enables it to take action on foreign projects more freely. Relatively
few GCEs are in this situation.

For GCEs with no MN experience, to make their first investment abroad
requires a force to intervene. This means that leadership must actively be exerted
to break the tendency to preserve the *status quo*. Given players' own propensity

towards a national outlook, this does not occur easily. When it does happen that key individuals fight for MN expansion, they are usually confronted with a majority of players who oppose it. To overcome this, particularly determined and powerful leaders are required.

2. What are the distinctive features of GCEs' MN strategic behaviour?

a. Where   From a general point of view, GCEs may be under government policy pressure to become involved in certain places and not others. Moreover, in their first foreign investments, GCEs tend to go where they have *points de chute*. Multinational GCEs have a propensity to do more of the same – to invest incrementally in those areas where they are already active. Departures from this pattern occur when a force intervenes. In most cases, this is when one or a few players seek to solve their problem via a particular action. Therefore, this reflects partisan ends and partial perceptions.

b. When   For those GCEs with limited foreign activities in particular, there are important inefficiencies in the timing of MN moves. Generally, opportunities are slow to be recognized, and formulation and implementation of plans are cumbersome. In particular, data are slow to be collected and processed, there are frequent delays in the approval of proposals and action is plagued by many hesitations. Besides, political games are a cause of further lateness; players' struggles and bargains unduly retard decisions. With experience, companies learn and inefficiencies are reduced.

c. How   On a broad level, GCEs often appear less fit for certain forms of MN expansion than others (for example, their image may be a deterrent for joint ventures with private firms). And government policy may push them to particular types of MN actions (for example, co-ordinate their undertakings with other GCEs). Yet, organizational processes condition the way GCEs react to such characteristics or pressures. Thus, the behaviour of a company with limited MN activities is but a rough approximation of what a rational pursuit of efficiency would command. Patterns of planning and action tend to emulate those followed in domestic activities. Consequently they are inadequate. Studies and analyses for projects tend to omit consideration of critical variables. And implementation itself tends to be maladjusted to local conditions. Here too, forces can at least partially palliate such inefficiencies. But here especially their reach tends to be limited. In fact, individuals' interventions often end up compounding these problems; given the frequent multiplicity and diversity of players' aims, actual behaviour reflects compromise between various inconsistent demands which are partially satisfied, and collages of often incongruous actions. Again, inefficiencies are usually alleviated only in companies with extensive MN activities.

It is worth stressing that while individuals can consciously endeavour to do something about such and such an aspect, they cannot deal with all the elements which make up corporate behaviour. Moreover, players step in only for those aspects which lie close to their own hearts. Thus, if say, a key government person wants a particular project in view of a given end he pursues, he will give his attention to those aspects of the project which are important in light of that end. For the rest, things will follow the course dictated by the existing bureaucracy.

3. *What are the distinctive features of GCEs' MN policy behaviour?*

In terms of the larger patterns, there are pressures on GCEs to follow certain norms. Thus, GCEs should not speculate against the national currency or distort transfer prices to reduce their tax liability to their home country. And they are expected to show particular sensitivity to social issues. On the other hand, in their foreign operations, when no particular government policy stands in the way of this, GCEs are to strive for the best possible microeconomic results.

Yet, more than such objective pressures, GCEs' *modus operandi* is determined by the existing organizational processes. In its early MN steps, a company functions essentially via routines borrowed from domestic operations. Inefficiencies are therefore inevitable. Abroad, care is taken to do certain things or to avoid others – at a real cost or opportunity cost – in pursuance of certain principles, but principles which are imported from the home country and which enjoy little credit locally, with the result that the efforts made are essentially useless if not plainly counterproductive. And the techniques to draw the most out of operating in an international context have not been mastered. Companies learn with experience. Foreign subsidiaries' routines are better adapted to local conditions, and the firm as a whole is able to exploit opportunities operating on an international level offer. Thus, government-controlled MNCs do make use of techniques such as leads and lags in their international cash management, intracompany payments manipulation or the utilization of tax havens.

Forces can intervene and modify certain aspects of companies' *modus operandi*. While there are limits to their influence (details of action always tend to remain the province of set procedures), they can have a determining role in causing a given type of behaviour to be adopted as well as in unblocking bureaucratic bottlenecks. To understand when and how forces are exerted, one must look inside the game of leadership – politics among players struggling for different outcomes for different reasons and with different degrees of power.

C. Current problems and future solutions

In this section we hint about some limitations of this work and we briefly suggest what directions future research might usefully take.

1. *The conceptual side*

Our overall framework as well as our three approaches cannot be considered definitive formulations. Thus, the traditional approach is the object of continued refinements by business policy students. Closer to the particular subject of this book, we argued that this approach permits the understanding of what is the appropriate thing to do from a rational objective viewpoint, and that players must at least partially take this reasoning into account. But several questions can be raised: are the distortions of bounded rationality taken into consideration? Can the limits of information be incorporated? Is bias in perceptions accounted for? Further, we argued that this approach fixes the broad context in which behaviour must take place. But how different are the bounding lines of this context depending on the nature of the decisions and the respective role of various types of players? We said that this approach defines shared values of key individuals. Yet, one may wonder the extent to which such values are truly common to all those who have influence on corporate behaviour for all types of decisions. While this may be the case for broad issues in which the basic health of the organization is not at stake, in other more specific instances this is still certainly so for general managers as well as others who are accountable for overall corporate performance; but then others may have more restricted and parochial views (especially non-company players). Can it be determined precisely for what types of issues this approach is relevant? And can this approach be expanded to take into account such diversity in rationality?

The process and politics approaches also need clarification and refinement. For instance, in the former, radical departures in strategy and policy are explained by the intervention of forces. But what are the details of the functioning of such forces? When are they actually likely to cause these departures? What precise direction are such departures likely to take? True, the politics approach at least partly answers such questions. But should not this be tied in more explicitly with the concepts of the process view? Besides, there is room for improvement in the politics approach as well.[2] Thus, players' motivations are not totally clear: What are the specific causes of their attitudes? How do information flows affect their perceptions? Are individual cognitive processes properly understood? For apparently the same type of issue in the same type of context, games and outcomes are often different without our being able to fully understand why: certain individuals seem to participate or not depending on the moment, their expectations, needs and obligations in other games, the behaviour of other players; individuals' stands and relative influence vary according to what they see at that point, their interests, and as a function of what other players do. Such independent variables do not always seem to be truly and completely accounted for. And neither are all the determinants of all actual resultants.

Moreover, more work is needed around the overall framework. The three approaches need to be integrated more clearly. Remaining points of friction need to be smoothed: angles of vision yielding contradictory accounts of corporate behaviour must be identified and dealt with more precisely, accurate and pertinent conceptions distinguished from false and misleading ones. The applicability of each view must be further clarified. We need to learn how to use the three lenses more systematically and coherently – exactly how to utilize each lens and for what: each view is not equally applicable to any situation; a clearer typology of decisions and elements of decisions, some of which are more amenable to analysis in terms of one approach and some to another, should be developed.

Focusing on such questions and problems should result in further progress towards the understanding and prediction of corporate behaviour. Refinement of our approaches and a full grasp of how to combine them and use them in conjunction with each other should ultimately enable us to generate a true model of strategic and policy decisions and actions, and to formulate specific hypotheses to be tested empirically. At that point, it might be possible to shift to a normative mode.

We submit it is this line of inquiry which promises the most significant advances in the field of business policy.

2. *The substantive side*

The objective of this book was not to develop a neat theory of how GCEs behave and then verify it in terms of actual hypothesis-testing. We did not know enough to do this. As with the development of all anthropological theory, the starting point had to be observation of what goes on in practice – lest propositions we might formulate might bear little relevance with respect to reality. But such observation had to be as systematic as possible. Thus, our aim was to look at how GCEs function from logical angles. We hoped our three vantage points would uncover previously hidden or underemphasized aspects of and causes of corporate behaviour.

We are satisfied that we have reached this objective. While specifics of what happens in a GCE and why remain unsettled, we now have a reasonable understanding of aggregate patterns of behaviour. Of course, there are limitations to this account. These stem first from the complexity of that which is to be explained: as argued by Mintzberg, this is typical of business policy-type research which inevitably leads one 'to use less rigorous, more exploratory approaches, that can encompass more variables . . . This applies especially to phenomena that involve the close interrelationships of many variables, most of which are difficult to measure'.[3] Besides, a lot of our data are impressionistic. This is inevitable in view of the intricateness of the phenomena to be studied and the intrinsically soft character of many variables, compounded by the touchiness of several issues. Moreover, given our aim and given the evasiveness of key questions, we had to have a broad data base to develop a valid general conception of GCEs' typical patterns of action. Yet, this was clearly purchased at the cost of internal rigour. Consequently, certain aspects of this study lack precision and certain accounts are but approximations of reality (thus, certain nuances may be misrepresented; especially when several elements come to bear on organizational behaviour, some of our accounts may have somewhat distorted the

382

relative importance of individual elements). And since we have dealt with aggregates, our abstractions are surely not totally devoid of a certain naïveté: given the specificity of each decision, we have necessarily oversimplified in more than one instance.

The next steps should aim at correcting these weaknesses. We are now ready for tighter research. This study affords a source of propositions about the causes of various outcomes. These need to be made explicit and verified empirically. As mentioned above, the theory must be refined and formalized. Precise hypotheses will ensue which will have to be tested.

A promising route is the case study. One or a few decisions should be identified in one or a few companies and analysed systematically (for example, a given pattern of strategic behaviour such as a GCE's multinationalization). While such a clinical approach constitutes a threat to the external validity of research, it provides precision and rigour. In fact, given the *sui generis* character of many occurrences, this is the only way to specifically account for certain decisions. By enabling one to see the theory at work more closely, this route should also yield advances on the conceptual front. Mintzberg notes: 'Researchers must rely largely on the field study. A significant share of the research efforts should be devoted to intensive probes into single organizations. Small sample research will bring order to the array of soft variables in question'.[4]

NOTES

1. See: Graham Allison, *Essence of Decision*, Little, Brown and Co., Boston, 1971, p. 250.
2. See, for instance, a recent formulation of a colleague of mine at Columbia: Ian MacMillan, *Strategy Formulation: Political Concepts*, West Publishing Co., St Paul, Minnesota, 1978.
3. Henry Mintzberg, 'Policy as a Field of Management Theory', *The Academy of Management Review*, Vol. 2, No. 1, January 1977, p. 94.
4. Henry Mintzberg, 'Policy as a Field of Management Theory', p. 94.

BIBLIOGRAPHY

BOOKS

Acheson, Dean, 'The President and the Sectetary of State', D. Price (ed.), *The Sectetary of State*, New York: 1960.

Aharoni, Yair, *The Foreign Investment Decision Process*, Boston, Mass.: Division of Research, Graduate School of Business Administration,'Harvard University, 1966.

Allison, Graham T., *Essence of Decision – Explaining the Cuban Missile Crisis*, Boston: Little, Brown and Company, 1971.

Almond, Gabriel, *The American People and Foreign Policy*, New York, 1950.

Anshen, Melvin (ed.), *Managing the Socially Responsible Corporation*, New York: MacMillan, 1974.

Ansoff, H. Igor, *Corporate Strategy*, New York: McGraw-Hill Book Company, 1965.

Archibald, K. (ed.), *Strategic Interaction and Conflict*, Berkeley, 1966.

Auby, J. M. and Ducos-Ader, R., *Grands services publics et entreprises nationales*. Paris: PUF, 1969.

Barnard, Chester I., *The Functions of the Executive*, Cambridge, Mass.: Harvard University Press, 1938.

Bauchet, Pierre, *La planification française*, Paris: Editions du Seuil, 1962.

Baumol, W. J., *Business Behaviour, Value and Growth*, New York: MacMillan, 1959.

Berthomieu, C., *La gestion des entreprises nationalisés*. Paris: Presses Universitaires de France, 1970.

Blau, P. M., *Exchange and Power in Social Life*, New York: John Wiley, 1964.

Bower, Joseph L., *Managing the Resource Allocation Process: A Study of Corporate Planning and Investment*, Boston: Division of Research, Graduate School of Business Administration, Harvard University, 1970.

Brachet, P., *L'État patron*, Paris: Editions Syros, 1973.

Braybrooke, David and Lindblom, Charles E., *A Strategy of Decision*, Glencoe, Ill., 1963.

Brink, Victor Z., *Computers and Management*, Englewood Cliffs, NJ: Prentice Hall, 1971.

Burns, Tom and Stalker, G. M., *The Management of Innovation*, London: Tavistock Publications, Second Edition, 1966.

Cannon, Thomas J., *Strategy and Policy*, New York: Harcourt Brace and World, 1968.

Caroll, T. H., (ed.), *Business Education for Competence and Responsibility*. Chapel Hill, NC: University of North Carolina Press, 1954.

Chamberlain, Neil W., *Private and Public Planning*, New York: McGraw-Hill Book Company, 1965.

Chandler, Alfred D. Jr., *Strategy and Structure*, Cambridge, Mass.: The MIT Press, 1962.

Chenot, Bernard, *Les entreprises nationalisées*, Paris: Presses Universitaires de France, 1963.

Christensen, C. Roland, Andrews, Kenneth and Bower, Joseph, *Business Policy Text and Cases*, Homewood, Ill.: Irwin 1978.

Cohen, M. and March, J., *Leadership and Ambiguity*, New York: McGraw-Hill, 1974.

Coombes, David, *State Enterprise. Business or Politics?* London: George Allen and Unwin Ltd., 1971.

Costello, John and Hughes, Terry, *The Battle for Concorde*, Salisbury, Wiltshire: Compton Press, 1971.

384

Crozier, Michel, *Le phénomène bureaucratique*, Paris: Editions du Seuil, 1963.
Crozier, Michel, *La société bloquée*, Paris: Editions du Seuil, 1971.
Crozier, Michel and Friedberg, Erhard, *L'acteur et le système*, Paris: Editions du Seuil, 1977.
Crozier, Michel, Friedberg, Erhard, Grémion, Catherine, Grémion, Pierre, Thoenig, Jean-Claude, and Worms, Jean-Pierre, *Où va l'administration française?* Paris: Les Editions d'Organisation, 1974.
Cyert, Richard and March, James G., *A Behavioral Theory of the Firm*, Englewood Cliffs, NJ.: Prentice Hall Inc., 1963.
Dalton, M., *Men who Manage*, New York: John Wiley, 1959.
Deaglio, Mario, *Private Enterprise and Public Emulation*, London: The Institute of Economic Affairs, 1966.
Denning, Basil W. (ed.), *Corporate Planning Selected Concepts*, London: McGraw-Hill, 1971.
Dewey, John, *How We Think*, Boston: D.C. Heath, 1933.
Dreyfus, Pierre, *La liberté de réussir*, Paris: Jean-Claude Simoën, 1977.
Dufau, P., *Les entreprises publiques*, Paris: Editions de l'Actualité Juridique, 1973.
Dunning, J. H., *The Role of American Investment in the British Economy*, PEP Broadsheet, 1969.
Eccles, M. S., *Beckoning Frontiers*, New York, 1951.
Etzioni, A., *The Active Society*. Collier-MacMillan, 1968.
Fayerweather, John, *International Business Management: A Conceptual Framework*, New York: McGraw-Hill Book Company, 1969.
Fisk, G. (ed.), *The Psychology of Management Decision*, New York: John Wiley, 1963.
Fusil, Jean, *Concorde*, Paris: Editions France-Empire, 1968.
Galbraith, J. K., *The New Industrial State*, Boston: Houghton Mifflin, 1967.
Giscard D'Estaing, V., *Démocratie française*, Paris: Fayard, 1976.
Gordon, Robert A., *Business Leadership in the Large Corporation*, Berkeley: University of California Press, 1961.
Haley, B. F. (ed.), *A Survey of Contemporary Economics*, Homewood, Ill.: Irwin, 1952.
Harris, Seymour, *International and Interregional Economics*, New York: McGraw-Hill, 1957.
Hilsman, Roger, *To Move a Nation*, New York, 1967.
Hochmuth, Milton S., *Organizing the Transnational*, Leiden: A. W. Sijthoff, 1974.
Holland, Stuart (ed.), *The State as Entrepreneur*, London: Weidenfeld and Nicholson, 1972.
Holland, Stuart, *The Socialist Challenge*, London: Quartet Books, 1975.
Huntington, Samuel, *The Common Defense*, New York, 1961.
Jewkes, John, *Public and Private Enterprise*, Chicago: University of Chicago Press, 1965.
Kahn, Robert L. and Boulding, Elise, *Power and Conflict in Organization*, New York: Basic Books, 1964.
Kapoor, A. and Grub, Phillip D. (eds.), *The Multinational Enterprise in Transition*, Princeton, NJ.: The Darwin Press, 1972.
Katona, George, *Psychological Analysis of Economic Behavior*, New York: McGraw-Hill, 1951.
Katz, Robert L., *Cases and Concepts in Corporate Strategy*, Englewood Cliffs, NJ.: Prentice Hall, 1970.
Katz D. and Kahn, R., *The Social Psychology of Organizations*, New York: John Wiley, 1966.
Kenen, Peter, *International Economics*, Englewood Cliffs, NJ.: Prentice Hall, 1967.
Kindleberger, Charles P., *International Economics*, Homewood, Ill.: Irwin, 1963.
Kindleberger, Charles P., *The International Corporation*, Cambridge, Mass.: The MIT Press, 1970.

La Palombara, Joseph, *Italy: The Politics of Planning*, Syracuse, NY.: Syracuse University Press, 1966.

Layton, Christopher, *European Advanced Technology – A Programme for Integration*, London: George Allen and Unwin PEP, 1969.

Lawrence, Paul R. and Lorsch, Jay W., *Organization and Environment: Managing Differentiation and Integration*, Cambridge, Mass.: Harvard University Press, 1967.

Learned, Edmund, Christensen, Roland, Andrews, Kenneth, and Gurth, William, *Business Policy* (revised edition), Homewood, Ill.: Irwin, 1969.

Lindblom, Charles E., *The Policy-Making Process*, Englewood Cliffs, NJ.: Prentice Hall, 1968.

Lindblom, Charles E., *The Intelligence of Democracy*, New York: 1965.

Lindblom, Charles E., and Braybrooke, D., *A Strategy of Decision*. Glencoe, Ill.: Spring 1963.

Lutz, Vera, *Italy: A Study in Economic Development*, London: Royal Institute of International Affairs, 1962.

MacMillan, Ian, *Strategy Formulation: Political Concepts*, St Paul, Minn.: West Publishing Co., 1978.

March, James, *Handbook of Organizations*, Chicago: Rand McNally, 1965.

March, James G. and Simon, Herbert A., *Organizations*, New York: John Wiley, 1958.

May, Ernest, *The World War and American Isolation*, Cambridge, Mass.: 1966.

Mazzolini, Renato, *European Transnational Concentrations*, London: McGraw-Hill, 1974.

McArthur, John H. and Scott, Bruce R., *Industrial Planning in France*, Boston: Division of Research, Graduate School of Business Administration, Harvard University, 1969.

Merton, Robert K., *Social Theory and Social Structure* (enlarged edition), New York: 1968.

Mintzberg, Henry, *The Nature of Managerial Work*, New York: Harper and Row, 1973.

Mumford, Enid and Pettigrew, Andrew, *Implementing Strategic Decisions*, London: Longman Group Limited, 1975.

Musolf, Lloyd D., *Mixed Enterprise*, Lexington, Mass.: Lexington Books, D.C. Heath and Company, 1972.

Naville, Bardou, Brachet, and Levy, *L'État entrepreneur, le cas de la Régie Renault*, Paris: Editions Anthropos, 1971.

Neustadt, Richard E., *Presidental Power*, New York: John Wiley, 1976.

Newman, William H. and Logan, James P., *Strategy, Policy, and Central Management* (7th edition), Cincinnati, Ohio: South-Western Publishing Co., 1976.

Newman, William H. and Warren, E. Kirby, *The Process of Management. Concepts, Behavior and Practice* (4th edition), Englewood Cliffs, NJ.: Prentice Hall, Inc., 1977.

Pescatore, Gabriele, *Interventi straordinari nel Mezzogiorno d'Italia*, Milano: A. Giuffrè, 1962.

Pettigrew, Andrew M., *The Politics of Organizational Decision-Making*, London: Tavistock Publications Limited, 1973.

Pfiffner, John M. and Sherwood, Frank P., *Administrative Organization*, Englewood Cliffs, NJ.: Prentice Hall, 1960.

Posner, M. V. and Woolf, S. J., *Italian Public Enterprise*, London: Gerald Duckworth and Co. Ltd., 1967.

Pryke, Richard, *Public Enterprise in Practice*, London: McGibbon and Kee, 1971.

Reid, Graham L. and Allen, Kevin, *Nationalized Industries*, Baltimore: Penguin Modern Economics.

Rex, J., *Key Problems in Sociological Theory*, London: Routledge and Kegan Paul, 1961.

Robock, Stefan H., Simmonds, Kenneth, and Zwick, Jack, *International Business and Multinational Enterprises*, Homewood, Ill.: Richard D. Irwin, 1977.

386

Saraceno, Pasquale, *La programmazione negli anni '70*, Milano: Etas Kompass, 1970.

Saraceno, Pasquale, *Il finanziamento delle imprese pubbliche*, Milano: A. Confalonieri, 1963.

Sayles, Leonard R., *Managerial Behavior: Administration in Complex Organizations*, New York: McGraw-Hill, 1964.

Scalfari, Eugenio and Turani, Giuseppe, *Razza padrona. Storia della borghesia di stato*, Milano: Giangiacomo Feltrinelli Editore, 1975.

Schelling, Thomas C., *The Strategy of Conflict*, Cambridge, Mass.: Harvard University Press, 1960.

Schilling, W., Hammond, P., and Snyder, G., *Strategy, Politics, and Defense Budgets*, New York, 1962.

Selznick, Philip, *Leadership in Administration*, New York: Harper and Row, 1957.

Shonfield, Andrew, *Modern Capitalism. The Changing Balance of Public and Private Power*, London: Oxford University Press, 1965.

Simon, Herbert A., *Administrative Behavior*, New York: The Macmillan Company, 2d edition, 1975.

Simon, Herbert A. *The Shape of Automation for Men and Management*, New York: Harper and Row, 1965.

Simon, Herbert A., *Models of Men*. New York: John Wiley, 1957.

Simonnot Philippe, *Le Complot pétrolier*, Paris: Editions Alain Moreau, 1976.

Stein, H. (ed.), *American Civil-Military Decisions*, Birmingham, Ala.: 1963.

Stein, H. (ed.), *Public Administration and Policy Development*, New York: 1952.

Steiner, George A. and Cannon, Warren M., *Multinational Corporate Planning*, New York: Macmillan, 1966.

Stoffaes, Christian and Victorri, Jacques, *Nationalisations*, Paris: Flammarion, 1977.

Stoleru, L., *L'impératif industriel*, Paris: Seuil, 1969.

Stopford, John and Wells, Louis, *Managing the Multinational Enterprise*, New York: Basic Books, 1972.

Thoenig, J. C., *L'ère des technocrates*, Paris: Editions d'Organisation, 1973.

Tivey, Leonard (ed.), *The Nationalized Industries since 1960. A Book of Readings*, Toronto: University of Toronto Press, 1973.

Turani, Giuseppe, *Montedison. Il grande saccheggio*, Milano: Arnoldo Mondadori, 1977.

Turvey, R., *Public Enterprises – Selected Readings*, Middlesex, England: Penguin Books, 1968.

Uyterhoeven, Hugo, Ackerman, Robert, and Rosenblum, John, *Strategy and Organization*, Homewood, Ill.: Irwin, 1963.

Vernon, Raymond (ed.), *Big Business and the State*, Cambridge, Mass.: Harvard University Press, 1974.

Vernon, Raymond, *Sovereignty at Bay: The Multinational Spread of U.S. Enterprises*, New York: Basic Books, 1971.

Vöchting, Friedrich, *La questione meridionale*, Napoli: Istituto Editoriale per il Mezzogiorno, 1955.

von Neumann, J. and Morgenstern, O., *Theory of Games and Economic Behavior*. Princeton, NJ.: Princeton University Press, 1953.

Wells, Louis T. Jr., *The Product Life Cycle and International Trade*, Boston: Harvard Business School, Division of Research, 1972.

Williamson, Samuel, *The Politics of Grand Strategy*, Cambridge, Mass.: 1969.

JOURNAL ARTICLES – TITLED

Anshen, Melvin and Guth, William D., 'Strategies for research in policy formulation', *The Journal of Business of the University of Chicago*, Vol. 46, No. 4, pp. 499–511, October 1973.

Becker, Howard S., 'Notes on the concept of commitment', *American Journal of Sociology*, Vol. LXVI, No. 1, July 1960, pp. 32–40.

Berg, Norman A., 'Strategic planning in conglomerate companies', *Harvard Business Review*, May–June 1965.

Burns, Tom, 'Micropolitics: Mechanisms of institutional change', *Administrative Science Quarterly*, 6 (3), 1961, pp. 257–281.

Carter, E. Eugene, 'The behavioral theory of the firm and top-level corporate decisions', *Administrative Science Quarterly*, 1971, pp. 413–428.

Charnes, A. and Cooper, W. W., 'The theory of search : optimum distribution of search effort', *Management Science*, 5, 1958.

Child, John, 'Organization structure, environment, and performance', *Sociology*, Vol. 6, 1972, pp. 1–22.

Cohen, A., Robinson, E., and Edwards, J., 'Experiments in organizational embedded-ness', *Administrative Science Quarterly*, Vol. 14, 1969, pp. 208–221.

Cyert, Richard M., Dill, William R., and March, James G. 'The role of expectations in business decision-making', *Administrative Science Quarterly*, Vol. 3, No. 3, December 1958.

Cyert, Richard M. and March, James G., 'Organizational structure and pricing behavior in an oligopolistic market', *American Economic Review*, 1955, pp. 129–139.

Cyert, Richard and March, James G., 'Organizational factors in the theory of oligopoly', *Quarterly Journal of Economics*, Vol. 70, 1956, pp. 44–64.

Dahl, R. A. 'The concept of power', *Behavioral Science*, 2, 1957, pp. 201–218.

De Alessi, Louis, 'An economic analysis of government ownership and regulation: Theory and the evidence from the electric power industry', *Public Choice*, Vol. XIX, Fall 1974.

De Alessi, Louis, 'Managerial tenure under private and government ownership in the electric power industry', *Journal of Political Economy*, Vol. 82, No. 3, May–June 1974.

Drucker, Peter, 'Business objectives and survival needs: Notes on a discipline of business enterprise', *The Journal of Business*, Vol. 31, No. 2, April 1958, pp. 81–90.

Dutton, J. M. and Walton, R. E. 'Interdepartmental conflict and cooperation: two contrasting studies', *Human Organization*, Vol. 25, No. 3, 1966.

Gordon, R., Short-period price determination', *American Economic Review*, Vol. 38, 1948.

Guth, William D., 'Formulating organizational objectives and strategy: A systematic approach', *Journal of Business Policy*, Fall 1971.

Guth, William D., 'Toward a social system theory of corporate strategy', *The Journal of Business*, Vol. 49, No. 3, July 1976, pp. 374–389.

Hall, William K., 'Strategic planning models: Are top managers really finding them useful?' *Journal of Business Policy*, 1973, pp. 33–42.

Hickson, D., Hinings, C., Lee, R., Schneck, R., and Pennings, J., 'A strategic contingencies theory of intra-organizational power', *Administrative Science Quarterly*, Vol. 16, 1971, pp. 216–229.

Hinings, C. R., Hickson, D., Pennings, J., and Schneck, R., 'Structural conditions of intraorganizational power', *Administrative Science Quarterly*, Vol. 19, March 1974.

Lamont, Douglas F., 'Joining forces with foreign state enterprises'. *Harvard Business Review*, July–August 1973, pp. 68–79.

Lindblom, Charles E., 'The science of muddling through', *Public Administration Review*, 19, No. 2, Spring 1959, pp. 78–88.

Luraghi, Giuseppe, 'Alfasud – Mezzogiorno di fuoco', *Espansione (Documento)*, No. 64, 1975, pp. II–XXXII.

MacMillan, Ian C., 'Business strategies for political action', *Journal of General Management*, Autumn, 1974, pp. 51–63.

MacMillan, Ian C., 'Organizational politics: A prerequisite perspective for general management', *Business Management*, Vol. 6, No. 4, 1975, pp. 11–20.

MacMillan, Ian C., 'Politics and business decisions', *Systems*, Vol. 4, No. 2, Johannesburg, South Africa, 1975.

MacMillan, Ian C., 'The political system in business', *Journal of General Management*, Vol. I, No. 1, Autumn 1973.

March, James, 'Business firm as a political coalition', *Journal of Politics*, Vol. 24, 1962, pp. 662–678.

Marchal, André, 'Nécessité économique des fusions et concentrations intracommunautaires', *Revue du Marché Commun.*, No. 109, January–February 1968.

Mazzolini, Renato, 'European corporate strategies', *Columbia Journal of World Business*, Spring 1975.

Mazzolini, Renato, 'Our European mergers? . . . They are being ambushed by governments', *European Business*, No. 38, Summer 1973.

Mechanic, D., 'Sources of power of lower participants in complex organizations', *Administrative Science Quarterly* 7, 1962, pp. 349–64.

Mergolis, I., 'The analysis of the firm, rationalism, conventionalism, and behaviorism', *Journal of Business*, Vol. 31, 1958.

Mintzberg, Henry, 'The manager's job: folklore and fact', *Harvard Business Review*, Vol. 53, No. 4, July–August 1975.

Mintzberg, Henry, 'Policy as a field of management theory', *The Academy of Management Review*, Vol. 2, No. 1, January 1977.

Mintzberg, Henry, 'Strategy-making in three modes', *California Management Review*, Vol. XVI, No. 2, Winter 1973.

Mintzberg, Henry, Raisinghani, Duru, and Théorêt, Andreé, 'The structure of "unstructured" decision processes', *Administrative Science Quarterly*, Vol. 21, June 1976, pp. 246–275

Pettigrew, Andrew M., 'Information control as a power resource', *Sociology*, Vol. 6, 1972, pp. 187–204.

Pettigrew, Andrew M., 'Towards a political theory of organizational intervention', *Human Relations*, Vol. 28, 1975.

Pfeffer, J. and Salanick, G. R. 'The bases and uses of power in organizational decision-making: The case of a university', *Administrative Science Quarterly*, December 1974.

Pfeffer, J. and Salanick, G. R., 'Organizational decision making as a political process: The case of the university budget', *Administrative Science Quarterly*, June 1974.

Pounds, William F., 'The process of problem finding', *Industrial Management Review*, Fall 1969, pp. 1–19.

Prahalad, Coimbatore K., 'Strategic choices in diversified MNCs', *Harvard Business Review*, July–August 1976.

Quinn, James Brian, 'Strategic goals: process and politics', *Sloan Management Review*, Vol. 19, No. 1, Fall 1977.

Riboud, Antoine, 'The time for the corporate "social" plan', *European Business*, No. 36, Winter 1973, p. 47.

Robock, Stefan H., 'The case for home country controls over multinational firms', *Columbia Journal of World Business*, Summer 1974, pp. 75–79.

Rothschild, K., 'Price theory and oligopoly', *Economic Journal*, Vol. LVII, No. 227, September 1947.

Simon, Herbert A., 'A behavioral model of rational choice'. *Quarterly Journal of Economics*, 69 (1), 1955.

Simon, Herbert A., 'On the concept of organizational goals', *Administrative Science Quarterly*, Vol. 9, No. 1, June 1964, pp. 1–22.

Simon, Herbert A., 'Theories of decision making in economics and behavioral science', *American Economic Review*, Vol. XLIX, No. 3, June 1959, pp. 253–283.

Spinelli, Altiero, 'Pour une stratégie communautaire en matière d'informatique', (statement before the European Parliament), *Bulletin des Communautés européennes*,Vol. 2, 1972.

Stobaugh, Robert B., 'How investment abroad creates jobs at home', *Harvard Business Review*, September–October 1972, pp. 118–126.

Stobaugh, Robert B., 'The multinational corporation: measuring the consequences', *Columbia Journal of World Business*, January–February 1971, pp. 59–64.

Strauss, G., 'Tactics of lateral relationships: the purchasing agent', *Administrative Science Quarterly*, 7, 1962.

Tichy, N., 'An analysis of clique formation and structure in organizations', *Administrative Science Quarterly*, Vol. 18, 1973, pp. 194–208.

Tinbergen, J., 'Economic planning: Western Europe', *International Encyclopedia of the Social Sciences*, XII, New York: Macmillan Co., 1968.

Tushman, Michael L., 'A political approach to organizations: A review and rationale', *Academy of Management Review*, April 1977.

Vernon, Raymond, 'International investment and international trade in the product cycle', *Quarterly Journal of Economics*, May 1966.

Wrapp, Edward H., 'Good managers don't make policy decisions', *Harvard Business Review*, 45, September–October 1967, pp. 91–99.

Zaleznik, Abraham, 'Power and politics in organizational life', *Harvard Business Review*, May–June 1970, pp. 13–26.

MISCELLANEOUS – TITLED

Anastassopoulous, Jean-Pierre, 'The strategic autonomy of government-controlled enterprises operating in a competitive economy', PhD dissertation, Graduate School of Business, Columbia University, New York, 1973.

Bodinat, Henri de, 'Influence in the multinational enterprise', doctoral dissertation, Harvard Business School, Boston, Mass., 1975.

Bonnefous, Edouard, 'Entreprises publiques – rapport d'information' No. 421, Paris, Sénat – Session extraordinaire de 1975–1976.

Bower, Joseph L. and Doz, Yves, 'Strategy formulation: a social and political process', working paper, Graduate School of Business Administration, Harvard University, Boston, 1977.

Carter, Eugene, 'A behavioral theory approach to firm investment and acquisition decisions', doctoral dissertation, Graduate School of Industrial Administration, Carnegie Mellon University, 1970.

Channon, Derek F., 'Strategy as an analytical process', Paper delivered at the International Conference in Strategic Management, Aix-en-Provence, May 1976.

Child, John and Francis, Arthur, 'Strategy formulation as a structured process', discussion paper given to the European conference on business strategy, Aix-en-Provence, May 1976.

Dahl, R. A., 'The politics of planning – decisions and decision makers in the modern state', Paris: UNESCO, 1967.

Doz, Yves L., 'National policies and multinational management', DBA dissertation, Harvard University, Boston, 1976.

Edwards, John P., 'Strategy formulation as a stylist process', April, 1976.

Faucheux, Claude, 'La formulation strategique comme processus culturel', Paper delivered at the 'Strategy Formulation: Different Perspectives' Conference, Aix-en-Provence, May, 1976.

Fligler, Carlos, *Multinational Public Enterprise*, International Bank for Reconstruction and Development, 1967.

Forrester, Jay W., 'The structure underlying management processes' in *Evolving Concepts in Management*, Academy of Management, New York, 1964.

Friesen, Peter, Miller, Danny, and Mintzberg, Henry, 'Patterns in strategy formation', working paper, McGill University, Montreal.

Garner, M. R., 'Background paper 2: Relationships of government and public enterprises in France, West Germany and Sweden', National Economic Development Office, London, 1971.

Gill, Stanley, in 'Letter to the Editor', *New Scientist*, 24 August, 1972.

Goldberg, Paul, M., 'The evolution of transnational companies in Europe', PhD dissertation, Massachusetts Institute of Technology, Sloan School of Management, 1971.

Hedberg, Bo and Jönsson, Sten, 'Strategy formulation as a discontinous process' invited paper to the CEROG Conference on 'Strategy Formulation: Different Perspectives', Aix-en-Provence, France, 20—22 May 1976.

Hession, Enda and Moran, Bernard, 'Policy and objective formulation for strategic planning in state enterprise', paper delivered at joint INSEAD–EIASM Analytical Approaches to Strategy Workshop, INSEAD–Fontainebleau, December 6–8, 1976.

Hochmuth, Milton Samuel, 'The effect of structure on strategy: the government sponsored multinational joint venture', DBA dissertation, Graduate School of Business Administration, Harvard University, Cambridge, Mass., 1972.

Holland, Stuart, 'Regional under-development in a developed economy: the Italian case', Vol. V, *Regional Studies*, London, 1971.

Hymer, Stephen, 'The international operations of foreign firms – A study of direct foreign investment'; PhD dissertation, Massachusetts Institute of Technology, 1960.

Krapels, Edward N., 'Controlling oil: British Oil policy and the British National Oil Corporation', 95th Congress, 1st Session, Publication No. 95–59, US Government Printing Office, Washington 1977.

Lindblom, Charles E., 'Bargaining? The hidden hand in government', RM-1434-RC, Rand Corporation, February 22, 1955.

Mintzberg, Henry, 'The making of strategic decisions', working paper, McGill University, Montreal, 1973.

Mintzberg, Henry, 'Strategy formulation as an evolutional process', paper presented at the Conference on 'Strategy Formulation: Different Perspectives', Aix-en-Provence, France 20–22 May, 1976.

Moran, Bernard, 'An analysis of the role of the Board of Directors in Irish Public state enterprises', PhD thesis, University College, Dublin, 1975.

Neustadt, Richard, Testimony; US Congress, Senate, Committee on government operations, Subcommittee on national security and international operations, 'Conduct of national security policy', 89th Congress, 1st Session, 29 June, 1965.

Newman, William, 'Intra-organization politics', Graduate School of Business, Columbia University, New York, 1975.

Pavan, Robert David John, 'The strategy and structure of Italian enterprise', DBA dissertation, Graduate School of Business Administration, Harvard University, Cambridge, Mass., 1972.

Pettigrew, Andrew M., 'Strategy formulation as a political process', paper presented at the conference on 'Strategy Formulation: Different Perspectives' in Aix-en-Provence France, 20–22 May, 1976.

Pipe, Russell, 'Towards central government computer policies', mimeograph OECD, 1972.

Steinbrunner, J., 'The mind and milieu of policy makers: a case study of the MLF', doctoral dissertation, MIT, Cambridge, Mass., February 1968.

Stobaugh, Robert B., 'US multinational enterprises and the US economy', Graduate School of Business Administration, Harvard University, Boston, Mass., January, 1972.

Zwick, Jack, 'Aspects of the foreign capital rationing procedures of certain American

Manufacturing corporations', DBA dissertation, Graduate School of Business Administration, Harvard University, August 1964.

MISCELLANEOUS – UNTITLED

American Management Association Seminar, 'Going abroad: the profit opportunities of international business for the smaller company', New York, Washington, Government Printing Office, 1961.

Annuario del Gruppo IRI, Edindustria, Rome, 1977.

The Boston Consulting Group, 'Perspectives on experience', Boston, 1971.

The Boston Consulting Group, 'Experience curves as a planning tool', Boston, 1970.

Les Cahiers français, *Les Entreprises publiques*, documentation française, Paris, October 1971.

CEEP, *L'entreprise publique dans la Communauté Economique Européenne*, Bruxelles, 1978.

CEEP, *Les Problèmes Actuels posés aux Entreprises publiques dans les Communautés Européennes*. Bruxelles, 1975.

CEEP, *L'Impact Economique Actuel des Entreprises Publiques dans la Communauté Européenne*, Brussels, 1975.

CEEP, *The Evolution of the Public Enterprises in the Community of the Nine*, Brussels, 1973.

Economie et Politique (Revue Marxiste d'Economie), 'L'internationalisation des entreprises publiques', Collective authorship, October 1975.

The 'Economist Intelligence Unit', *Motor Business*, London, No. 53, January 1968.

EEC Commission, 'Les actions de la politique industrielle et technologique de la Communauté à entreprendre dans le secteur aéronautique', Document III/2457/72F, Brussels, 21 December, 1973.

First Report from the Select Committee on Nationalized Industries, Session 1972–1973, British Steel Corporation, London: Her Majesty's Stationery Office, 1973.

French National Assembly, Finance Committee, 'Le contrôle des entreprises publiques', June 1972.

Groupe de Travail du Comité Interministériel des Entreprises Publiques, 'Rapport sur les entreprises publiques', La Documentation française, Paris, 1967.

The Labour Party, 'Individual choice in democracy', Leith, 1973.

The Labour Party, 'Labour's programme: Campaign document 1974', London, 1974.

The Labour Party, 'The national enterprise board', Opposition Green Paper, London, 1973.

Mediobanca, *La finanza delle assicurazioni sociali in Italia*, Milano, 1964.

Ministero del Bilancio, 'Progetto di programma di sviluppo economico per il quinquennio 1965–1969, Rome, 1965.

Programme de Gouvernement du Parti Socialiste et Programme Commun de la Gauche, Flammarion, Paris, 1972.

Sistema industriale e sviluppo economico in Italia, Il Mulino, Bologna, 1973.

Special Report, and First, Second and Third Report from the Committee of Public Accountants, Session 1964–1965, HMSO, London.

Trades Union Congress, *Industrial Democracy*, London, 1975.

Index

394